ADIEUX

SIMONE
DE BEAUVOIR

TRANSLATED BY
PATRICK O'BRIAN

PANTHEON BOOKS, NEW YORK

ADIEUX

A FAREWELL TO SARTRE

ALSO BY THE AUTHOR

NONFICTION

The Second Sex
A Very Easy Death
Memoirs of a Dutiful Daughter
The Prime of Life
Force of Circumstance
The Coming of Age

FICTION

She Came to Stay
The Blood of Others
All Men Are Mortal
The Mandarins
The Woman Destroyed
Les Belles Images
When Things of the Spirit Come First

Library of Congress Cataloging in Publication Data
Beauvoir, Simone de, 1908–
   Adieux: a farewell to Sartre.

   Translation of La Cérémonie des adieux.
   Includes index.
   1. Sartre, Jean Paul, 1905– —Biography. 2. Sartre, Jean Paul,
1905– —Interviews. 3. Beauvoir, Simone de, 1908– —Biography.
4. Authors, French—20th century—Biography. I. Sartre, Jean Paul,
1905– . II. Title.
PQ2637.A82Z56413 1984   848'.91409 [B]   83-19327
ISBN 0-394-53035-7
    0-394-72898-X (pbk.)

Book design by Gina Davis

Manufactured in the United States of America

First Pantheon Paperback Edition

To those who loved Sartre
who do love him
who will love him

CONTENTS

A FAREWELL TO SARTRE

THE FAREWELL CEREMONY

This is the first of my books—the only one no doubt—that you will not have read before it is printed. It is wholly and entirely devoted to you; and you are not affected by it.

When we were young and one of us gained a brilliant victory over the other in an impassioned argument, the winner used to say, "There you are in your little box!" You are in your little box; you will not come out of it and I shall not join you there. Even if I am buried next to you there will be no communication between your ashes and mine.

When I say *you*, it is only a pretense, a rhetorical device. No one hears it. I am speaking to no one. In reality it is Sartre's friends that I am talking to—those who would like to know more about his last years. I have described them as I lived through them. I have spoken about myself a little, because the witness is part of his evidence, but I have done so as seldom as possible. In the first place because that is not what this book is about, and then because, as I replied to a friend who asked me how I was taking it, "These things cannot be told; they cannot be put into writing; they cannot be formed in one's mind. They are experienced and that is all."

This narrative is chiefly based on the diary I kept during those ten years, and on the many testimonies I have gathered. My thanks to all those whose written or spoken words have helped me to recount Sartre's last days.

1970

Throughout his life Sartre never ceased calling himself into question; he did not underestimate what he called his "ideological interests," but he did not wish to be wholly taken over by them. He often thought it right to "think against himself," trying hard to "break bones inside his head." The political upheavals of 1968, in which he was involved and which affected him deeply, led him to reflect upon the intellectual's role and to modify his conception of it.

He often explained his views on this point. Up until that time Sartre had seen the intellectual as someone who was tormented by the contradiction between the universality of practical knowledge and the exclusiveness of the ruling class which had produced him—he was thus the incarnation of the guilty conscience as Hegel defines it, and soothing his conscience by his very awareness of its guilt, he felt that it allowed him to be on the side of the proletariat. Sartre now thought it was necessary to go beyond that stage. Against the *classic intellectual* he set up the *new intellectual* who endeavors to become integrated with the masses so as to bring about the triumph of true universality.

Sartre tried to follow this line of conduct even before he had distinctly formulated it. In the fall of 1968 he undertook the editing of *Interluttes*, a bulletin that circulated among the political activists. He had met Geismar several times and was keenly interested in his idea of publishing a paper in which the masses could speak. It came into existence however when Geismar joined the *Gauche prolétarienne* (G.P.) and he and the Maoists brought out *La Cause du peuple*. It had no owner, was written directly or indirectly by the workers, and was sold on the streets by the militants. Its aim was to give an idea of the struggles carried on by the working class in France from 1970 onward. It was often hostile to the intellectuals and, where Roland Castro's trial was concerned, to Sartre himself.*

After certain articles in *La Cause du peuple* violently attacked the government, its first two editors, were arrested. Geismar and other militants suggested that Sartre should take their place. He agreed without hesitation, because he thought that the weight of his name might be useful to the Maoists. "I cynically tipped the scales with the fact that I was well known," he said later during a lecture in Brussels.

---

* Roland Castro, a militant member of *Vive la Révolution* (V.L.R.) had, together with Clavel, Leiris, Genet, and a few others, occupied the offices of the C.N.P.F. (The French employers' organization [trans.]) to protest against the death of five immigrant workers who had been asphyxiated by gas. The C.R.S. (a special branch of the police, often used for dealing with riots [trans.]) had knocked them about, arrested them, and then let them go, all except Castro, who jumped out of the police van at a red light and tried to run away. The police caught him and charged him with having assaulted them. He was found guilty, because the judge would not conduct the trial on a political basis, the only one that made any sense. Sartre bore witness in Castro's favor and *La Cause du peuple* made hostile, ill-natured remarks about his evidence.

From that point on the Maoists were persuaded to revise their opinion of the intellectuals and their tactics toward them.

The first issue of *La Cause du peuple* edited by Sartre came out on May 1, 1970. The authorities did not attack him, but the minister of the interior ordered the seizure of each number at the printing plant. Fortunately, the printer managed to get most of the copies out and away before they were taken. The government then went after the vendors of the paper, who were brought before a special court and charged with reconstituting an organization that had been banned. However Sartre and I and several friends sold the paper in the heart of Paris without being seriously disturbed. One day the authorities grew tired of the pointless struggle and it began to be sold in the kiosks. An association of "Friends of *La Cause du peuple*" was formed, with Michel Leiris and myself at the head of it. Associations have to be declared, and an official receipt is delivered. This was at first refused to us and we had to appeal to the administrative court to get it.

In June 1970 Sartre helped to found the *Secours rouge,* an organization whose aim was to struggle against repression. The national steering committee, in a declaration largely written by Sartre, stated among other things:

> *Secours rouge* will be a democratic, legally declared and independent association, its essential aim will be to ensure the political and legal defense of the victims of repression and to provide them and their families with material and moral support, no one being barred . . .
> . . . justice and freedom cannot be defended without organizing solidarity among the people. *Secours rouge,* which arises from the people, will help them in their struggle.

The organization included the main leftist groups, *Témoignage chrétien,* and a number of well-known people. Its chief purpose was to resist the wave of arrests initiated by Marcellin after the dissolution of the G.P. A great many militants were in prison. What had to be done was to collect information on their cases and decide what action to take. Several thousand people belonged to *Secours rouge,* and primary committees were set up in various districts in Paris and in the provinces. The Lyons committee was the most active of those in the departments. In Paris the organization was particularly concerned with the difficulties of the immigrant workers. Although generally speaking the committees were politically eclectic, it was the Maoists who were the most active and who more or less took them over.

Although Sartre zealously carried out his tasks as a militant, he still spent the greater part of his time on his literary work. He was finishing the third volume of his great book on Flaubert. In 1954 Roger Garaudy had said to him, "Let us both work on one and the same character, with me explaining him according to Marxist and you according to existentialist methods." Sartre chose Flaubert, whom he had treated very harshly in *What Is Literature?* but who had quite won him over when he read his correspondence. What he found most attractive in Flaubert was his exaltation of the imaginary above all other factors. At that time Sartre filled about ten large notebooks; then he wrote a thousand-page essay which he abandoned in 1955. He went back to work, completely recasting the book between 1968 and 1970. He called it *The Family Idiot* and he wrote it both eagerly and easily. "It was a question of showing a method and at the same time of showing a man."

He explained his aims on several occasions. It was not a scientific work that he was concerned with, since he did not make use of concepts but rather of notions, a notion being a thought that includes the factor of time—the notion of passivity, for example. With regard to Flaubert he adopted an attitude of empathy. "To prove that any man is perfectly knowable so long as one uses the right method and possesses the necessary documents—that is my goal." He also said, "When I point out how Flaubert does not know himself and how at the same time he understands himself very well indeed, I am showing what I call the experienced, the lived-through, aspect: that is, life lived in understanding with oneself, without any knowledge, any positively stated awareness being evident."

His Maoist friends were more or less opposed to this undertaking. They would have preferred Sartre to write some militant treatise or a great novel designed for the people. But on this point he had no intention of yielding to any pressure whatsoever. He understood his comrades' point of view, but he did not share it. "If I look at the subject matter," he said, speaking of *The Family Idiot*, "I have the impression of an escape. If, on the other hand, I look at the method, I have a feeling of being here, in the immediate present."

Later he returned to the question in a lecture he gave in Brussels. "For seventeen years I have been harnessed to a work on Flaubert, a book that could not interest the workers because it is written in a complicated and certainly bourgeois style. . . . I am bound to it. That is, I am sixty-seven, I have been working on it since I was fifty, and I used to dream about it before that. . . . Insofar as I am writing about Flaubert I am an *enfant terrible* belonging to the bourgeoisie, a subject for reclamation."

His basic idea was that at no matter what point in history and whatever the social and political context, it was still essential to understand people and that his study of Flaubert might be of use to that end.

Sartre was therefore quite satisfied with his various commitments when we returned to Paris in September 1970 after a happy stay in Rome. He lived in an austere little apartment on the tenth floor of a building in the Boulevard Raspail, opposite the Montparnasse grave-yard and quite close to my place. He liked it there. He led a fairly even life that varied little from day to day. He regularly saw long-established women friends—Wanda K., Michèle Vian, and his adopted daughter, Arlette Elkaïm, at whose home he slept two nights a week. The other evenings he spent with me. We talked, and we listened to music. I had built up a large collection of records and I added to it every month. Sartre was much interested in the Viennese school, particularly Berg and Webern, and in some modern compos-ers: Stockhausen, Xenakis, Berio, and Penderecki as well as many others. But he was always happy to go back to the great classics. He loved Monteverdi, Gesualdo, Mozart's operas—above all, *Così fan tutte* —and Verdi's. During these home concerts we would eat a hard-boiled egg or a slice of ham and drink a little Scotch. I live in what real estate agents call "an artist's studio with loggia." I spend my days in a big, high-ceilinged room; an inside staircase leads to a bedroom, which is connected to the bathroom by a kind of balcony. Sartre slept upstairs and came down in the morning to have tea with me. Some-times, one of his friends, Liliane Siegel, would come and take him out for coffee at a little place near his building. He frequently saw Bost at my apartment in the evening, and quite often Lanzmann, with whom he had many ties in spite of certain disagreements about the Israeli-Palestinian question. He was particularly fond of Saturday evenings, which Sylvie* spent with us, and of lunchtime on Sunday, when we all three met at La Coupole. At long intervals we also met other friends.

In the afternoons I worked at Sartre's place. I was waiting for *Old Age* to come out and thinking about one last volume of my memoirs.

---

* Sylvie's friendship has played an important part in my life.

He was revising and correcting his portrait of Dr. Flaubert in *The Family Idiot*. It was a splendid autumn, blue and gold. The opening year promised very well.*

In September Sartre took part in a great meeting organized by *Secours rouge* to denounce King Hussein of Jordan's massacre of Palestinians. Six thousand people were present, including Jean Genet, whom Sartre had not seen for a long while. Genet was connected with the Black Panthers and had written an article about them in *Le Nouvel Observateur*. He was getting ready to leave for Jordan, where he wanted to stay in a Palestinian camp.

Sartre's health no longer worried me, and had not for a great while now. Although he smoked two packs of Boyards a day his arteritis had not grown worse. It was suddenly, toward the end of September, that I began to be frightened.

One Saturday evening we had dinner with Sylvie at Dominique's, and Sartre drank a great deal of vodka. Back at my studio he first dozed and then fell fast asleep, dropping his cigarette. We helped him up to his bedroom. The next morning he seemed to be perfectly well and went back to his own apartment. But when at two o'clock Sylvie and I went to fetch him for lunch, he bumped into the furniture at every step. When we left La Coupole he was staggering, although he had drunk very little. We took him to Wanda's place in the Rue du Dragon in a taxi, and as he got out he nearly fell.

He had had fits of giddiness before this. When we were in Rome in 1968 his legs gave way when he stepped out of the car in the Piazza Santa Maria dei Trastevere to such an extent that Sylvie and I had to support him. I did not think it of much consequence, but I was surprised, since he had drunk nothing! Yet these disturbances had never been so marked as they were now, and I had a suspicion of their gravity. In my diary I wrote, "This little apartment, so cheerful since I came back, has changed its color. The pretty velvet-piled carpet brings mourning to mind. That is how life will have to be: with happiness and moments of delight when all goes well, but with the threat hanging there—life set between parentheses."

As I copy out these lines I am filled with astonishment: how did I come to have that dark foreboding? I think that in spite of my apparent calmness, for more than twenty years I had never really stopped being on the watch. The first alarm was the attack of high blood

* We had kept the habit of reckoning by school years.

pressure that had taken Sartre to the hospital just after his journey to the USSR in the summer of 1954. Then in the fall of 1958 I was extremely anxious.* Sartre only just escaped a stroke. Since that time the threat was always there; the doctors had told me that his arteries and arterioles were too narrow. Every morning when I went to wake him I was impatient to make sure that he was breathing. I was not really worried; it was more an effect of the imagination, but it was one that meant something. These fresh disturbances compelled me to become fully and tragically aware of a frailty that in fact I had been conscious of all the time.

The next day Sartre had pretty well recovered his balance, and he went to see his usual physician, Dr. Zaidmann. He said that tests would be necessary, and he advised Sartre not to tire himself before he saw a specialist on the following Sunday. The specialist, Dr. Lebeau, would not be categorical. The lack of balance might be caused by trouble in the inner ear or in the brain. He called for an encephalogram, but it showed nothing abnormal.

Sartre was out of sorts. He had an abscess in his mouth and he felt the beginnings of flu. But it was with joy and delight that he delivered the huge manuscript of Flaubert to Gallimard on October 8.

The Maoists had organized a journey that would take him to Fos-sur-Mer and other industrial centers so he could study the workers' living conditions and the nature of their employment. On October 15 the doctors forbade him to go. In addition to Zaidmann he had seen specialists who had examined his eyes, ears, skull, and brain—no less than eleven consultations. They had detected grave disturbances in the circulation in the left hemisphere of his brain (the hemisphere that has to do with speech) and a narrowing of the blood vessels. He was to smoke less and to undergo a series of drastic injections. In two months they would take another encephalogram. By that time he would no doubt be cured. But he was not to overdo things, above all, physically. In fact, now that the Flaubert was finished, there was no reason Sartre should tire himself. He read manuscripts and detective stories, and he dreamed vaguely of writing a play. In the course of that October he also wrote a preface for the catalog of Rebeyrolle's exhibit, a show that Rebeyrolle called *Coexistences*. We were very fond of his painting. He had come to spend two days with us in Rome and we had the greatest liking for him. When we met his wife, a lively,

* See *The Force of Circumstance.*

amusing little Armenian, we had the same feeling for her. We saw them quite often in the years that followed. They were friends of Franqui, the journalist who had invited us to Cuba in 1960 and who had later gone into exile because he was opposed to Castro's pro-Soviet policy.

In spite of the trouble with his health, Sartre carried on his political activities. It was at this juncture that the police raided the plant of Simon Blumenthal, the printer of *La Cause du peuple*.

On October 21 Geismar was tried. At the rally to protest the arrest of the editors, Le Dantec and Le Bris, five thousand people had shouted "All out into the street on the twenty-seventh!" Several speakers had addressed the crowd, but only Geismar had been arrested, obviously because he belonged to the G.P. Furthermore, the demonstration of the twenty-seventh caused no bloodshed—the C.R.S. had used tear gas and the demonstrators had thrown a few bolts but no one had been hurt. Yet for all that a severe sentence was expected. Sartre had been summoned to give evidence. But rather than play the conventional part before a court of bourgeois justice, he preferred to go and talk to the workers at Billancourt. Management would not allow him into the works, and the Communist party had had a tract handed out at eight in the morning to warn the Renault workers against him. Perched on a barrel and using a megaphone he spoke outside, addressing a rather limited audience. "It is for you to say whether Geismar's action is right or wrong," he said. "What I want to do is to bear witness in the street because I am an intellectual and because I think the connection between the people and the intellectuals that existed in the nineteenth century—it didn't always exist but when it did it got very good results—should be revived today. For fifty years the people and the intellectuals have been separated. Now they must be reunited—now they must make one single body."

Sartre's opponents did their best to make fun of his intervention. The Communists retorted that the connection between the people and the intellectuals was ensured because a great many intellectuals were members of the party. Meanwhile, Geismar was sentenced to eighteen months imprisonment.

Sartre shared in the setting up of a new paper, *J'accuse,* whose first number came out on November 1. The team who ran it—Linhart, Glucksmann, Michèle Manceaux, Fromanger and Godard among them—were all friends of his. The paper was not written by militants, but by intellectuals. Sartre wrote a few articles for it. Only two more numbers came out after the first: one appeared on January 15, 1971, the other on March 15. Liliane Siegel, under her maiden name of Sendyk, was the editor legally responsible for the publication. She kept the position when *J'accuse* merged and became *La Cause du peuple —J'accuse.* Since the government did not wish to arrest Sartre, it was she who twice appeared in the dock, with Sartre giving evidence in her favor.

Yet his health continued to worry me. When he was bored—and he forced himself to do a good many wearisome tasks—he drank too much. In the evening and even during the day he was often drowsy. Dr. Lebeau, whom he consulted on November 5, said that this sleepiness was caused by the medicines prescribed for his dizziness and he reduced the doses. On November 22 another encephalogram was taken and it was entirely satisfactory; shortly afterward Dr. Lebeau assured him that he was completely cured and that he was no more threatened with vertigo than anyone else. This pleased him very much, but one other anxiety still remained—his teeth. He was going to have to have a plate made and he dreaded it for obvious symbolic reasons and because he was afraid he would no longer be able to speak in public. As things turned out, however, the dentist did an excellent job, and Sartre's mind was set at ease.

He was pleased with the publication of Contat's and Rybalko's book *The Writings of Jean-Paul Sartre.* He corrected the proofs of *The Family Idiot.* He was on the top of his form in December, when he presided over the coal mines trial.

I described this trial in *All Said and Done,* but since Sartre attached a great deal of importance to it, I should like to return to the subject here. In February 1970 sixteen miners were killed and many others wounded by a firedamp explosion at Hénin-Liétard. Since the Houillères, the state-owned coal mines, were obviously responsible, some unidentified young men threw Molotov cocktails into the offices of the management in retaliation, causing a fire. Without the slightest hint of proof the police arrested four Maoists and two former convicts. They were to be tried on Monday, December 14, and *Secours rouge* summoned a people's court for Saturday, the twelfth, in the town hall of Lens.

The people's court exposed the Houillères' responsibility with the most startling clarity. Sartre summed up the proceedings in a powerful indictment that ended with these words: "I therefore put the following decision to you: the State-proprietor is guilty of the murder of February 4, 1970. The management and the engineers responsible for Pit 6 are those who carry out its orders. Therefore they are equally guilty of deliberate homicide. They deliberately preferred output to safety; that is, they set the production of material objects above the men's lives." On the following Monday the six alleged incendiaries were tried and acquitted.

A little before this Sartre had agreed to edit two other leftist papers in addition to *La Cause du peuple: Tout,* which was the mouthpiece of V.L.R., and *La Parole du peuple.*

1971

At the beginning of January there were two trials that attracted a great deal of attention, the one in the USSR, at Leningrad, and the other in Spain, at Burgos. On December 16, 1970, eleven Soviet citizens—one Ukrainian, one Russian, nine Jews—appeared before the Leningrad court. They had planned to hijack a plane in order to get out of their country, but there were leaks, and during the night of June 15–16, before they had begun to carry anything into effect, they were arrested in various cities. Two of them were sentenced to death—Kuznetsov, who had worked out the plot, and Dymschitz, the airline pilot who was to take over the controls once the crew had been tied up and put out of the plane. Seven of the accused were given ten to fourteen years of hard labor, and two others four and eight years.* On January 14, 1971, there was a great meeting in Paris to support them, and Sartre took part in it; Laurent Schwartz was also there, as well as Madaule and our Israeli friend, Eli Ben Gal. They all denounced the Soviet Union's anti-Semitism.

At Burgos the trial was of Basques, members of the E.T.A. who were accused by Franco of plotting against the state. Gisèle Halimi was present as an observer, and she gave an account of the trial in a

---

* Dymschitz and Kuznetsov were not put to death, thanks no doubt to the pressure brought to bear by the French president. In 1973 the manuscript of Kuznetsov's *Journal d'un condamné à mort* reached Paris—it was published in French and it excited the greatest interest. In April 1979 Kuznetsov, Dymschitz, and three other members of the conspiracy were exchanged for two Soviet spies arrested in the USA.

book published by Gallimard. She asked Sartre for a preface, and he readily agreed to write one. He gave an exact description of the Basques' problem and an account of their struggle, referring especially to the history of the E.T.A. He spoke indignantly of the Franco government's repression in general, and in particular of the way in which the Burgos trial had been conducted. Since he had a perfect example at hand, he took this occasion of amplifying an idea that was near to his heart: the conflict between an abstract universal—that upon which governments base themselves—and the particular, concrete universal as it is embodied by flesh-and-blood human beings. It was the second, he asserted, that was being supported by the rebellions of colored peoples, whether they were colonized from without or within; and it was the second that was truly valid, because it recognized men as they existed in their human condition, their culture, and their way of expressing themselves, and not as empty concepts.

In opposition to a centralizing, abstract socialism, Sartre asserted the value of "another socialism, decentralizing and concrete: such is the Basques' particular universal, the one that the E.T.A. rightly set against the abstract centralization of the oppressors." What should be done, he said, was to bring "socialist man" into being "on the basis of his land, his language, and even his old ways and customs restored. It is from that basis only that man will gradually cease to be the production of his own product and at last become the son of man."

It was from the same point of view that two years later Sartre devoted an issue of *Les Temps modernes* (August–September 1973) to the claims of the Bretons, the Languedocians, and all the national minorities oppressed by centralism.

Geismar was imprisoned at the Santé. Although his was a comparatively favored form of confinement, he made common cause with the other political prisoners, who had begun a hunger strike to enforce their demand for more bearable conditions of imprisonment for the common-law convicts and for themselves. A few leftists decided to go on a hunger strike too, in order to support their claims. A priest with advanced views sheltered them in Saint Bernard's Chapel in the Montparnasse railway station. Michèle Vian was one of the strikers, and Sartre visited them quite often. He went with them when, after twenty-one days, they broke off their fast and tried to have an interview with Pleven. Since they were too weak to go far, they were driven to the Place de l'Opéra and from there they walked to the Place Vendôme. They called at the ministry of justice, but Pleven refused to see them. Later he gave in, granting the prisoners who had taken part in the strike a special status and promising to improve the common-law convicts' lot—a promise that was scarcely kept at all.

On February 13 Sartre let his Maoist comrades persuade him to take part in a rather foolish venture—the occupation of the Sacré Coeur. During a *Secours rouge* demonstration a V.L.R. militant named Richard Deshayes had been disfigured by a tear-gas grenade. In order to arouse public opinion the G.P. decided to occupy the basilica. They counted on Msgr. Charles's consent. Accompanied by Jean-Claude Vernier, Gilbert Castro, and Liliane Siegel, Sartre went into the church—there were some worshippers present—and asked to see Msgr. Charles. The priest he spoke to said that he would pass on his request. A quarter of an hour went by and the priest did not come back. Then all the doors but one were closed and the demonstrators —a considerable number by now—saw that they were trapped. As the C.R.S. came in by the one door remaining open, hitting everyone without distinction, Castro and Vernier grasped Sartre and Liliane and hid them in a corner. Then they managed to get them out, made them get into Vernier's car, and set them down at a café. When they came back a little later they said that the clash had been very violent. One young man had had his thigh pierced through by a railing spike. Sartre thought the whole thing lamentable—it could not but discourage the militants, who had already been severely knocked about at the end of a demonstration a few days earlier. On February 15 he and Jean-Luc Godard gave a press conference about the affair, and the papers devoted a great deal of space to it. On February 18 he withdrew from *Secours rouge,* in which he thought that the Maoists had become too powerful.*

A few days later the Guiot affair erupted. Guiot was a boy at a state secondary school, a lycée, who was falsely accused of hitting a policeman and who was arrested, allegedly in flagrante delicto. The other lycéens protested in force, and thousands of them sat on the sidewalk in the Latin Quarter, where a great number of police vans were drawn up. In the end Guiot was acquitted, but the atmosphere in the streets of Paris remained very tense. On all the walls there were huge photographs of the disfigured Deshayes. In the middle of March the leftists and *Ordre nouveau* came into extraordinarily violent conflict and many policemen were wounded.

---

* He withdrew from the directing committee, but he still took part in many of the actions organized by *Secours rouge.*

Sartre followed all this turbulence and unrest closely. His health seemed very good. He went on correcting the proofs of *The Family Idiot;* he attended all the *Temps modernes* meetings, which took place in my apartment.

At the beginning of April we left for Saint-Paul-de-Vence. Sartre went by train with Arlette, and I drove down with Sylvie. The hotel where we stayed was at the entrance to the little town—a town crowded with tourists during the day but quiet in the mornings and evenings, when it was exactly like our cherished memory of it. Arlette and Sartre were in an annex, Sylvie and I in a little house at the bottom of a garden filled with orange trees. It had a big bedroom opening onto a very small terrace and an immense living room with white, roughcast walls and exposed beams; on the walls there were beautiful, vividly colored pictures by Calder. The room had a long wooden table, a couch, and a sideboard, and it gave on to the garden. It was there that I spent most of my evenings with Sartre, drinking Scotch and talking. We dined on a piece of dried sausage or a slab of chocolate, but for lunch I took him to the good restaurants in the neighborhood. Sometimes all four of us went together.

The first evening we were astonished by the huge illuminations on the hillside facing Saint-Paul: it was the greenhouses, brilliantly lit at night by electricity.

In the afternoon we often read on our own, or we went for walks, going back to the places we had liked. Among others we were happy to see Cagnes again and the charming hotel where we had had a delightful stay many years before. One afternoon we went to the Fondation Macght, with which we were already familiar. They were having a Char exhibition, and the pictures grouped around his manuscripts and books were very beautiful—pictures by Klee, Vieira da Silva, Giacometti, and many by Miró, whose work became richer and richer the older he grew.

On the last day Sartre ordered aioli, and since there was no sun we ate it in the "chauffoir," a pleasant, spacious room with an immense fireplace and many books. He left by train that evening with Arlette, and Sylvie and I drove off the next morning. Sartre had truly enjoyed this vacation.

He was very happy, too, to be back in Paris, where he received a huge case from Gallimard, full of copies of *The Family Idiot*—two thousand printed pages. He told me that it gave him as much pleasure as the publication of *Nausea*. It was most warmly and appreciatively reviewed at once.

At the beginning of May Pouillon told us of the death of the friend I called Pagniez in my memoirs. According to him, when Pagniez retired he was so bored that he let himself die. He had hepatitis, and it degenerated into cirrhosis of the liver. As Mme Lemaire had died a few years earlier, Pagniez's death meant that the whole of one happy period of our past had finally vanished. But for a great while Pagniez had been a complete stranger to us, and we heard the news unmoved.

It was also at the beginning of May that Goytisolo telephoned Sartre and in a voice trembling with emotion asked him to sign an exceedingly violent letter of protest addressed to Fidel Castro on the subject of the Padilla affair. This affair had had various stages: (1) the arrest of Padilla, a poet very well known in Cuba, on the charge of sodomy; (2) a polite letter of protest signed by Goytisolo, Franqui, Sartre, myself, and some others; (3) Padilla was released and wrote an insane self-criticism in which he accused Dumont and Karol of being agents of the C.I.A. His wife also produced a self-criticism, stating that the police had treated her "tenderly." These declarations aroused a great many protests. In *Le Monde*, Arcocha, our former Cuban interpreter, who had also chosen exile, said that Padilla and his wife must have been tortured to produce confessions of such a kind. In the background of all this loomed the sinister figure of Lyssendro Otero. In 1960 he had been with us during almost the whole of our journey; now he seemed to have culture in its entirety under his thumb. Goytisolo was of the opinion that Cuba was under the control of a veritable gang, all belonging to the police. We learned that Castro now looked upon Sartre as an enemy, and as being under the baleful influence of Franqui. In a speech he made at this period Castro attacked most of the French intellectuals: Sartre was unmoved, since he had no longer had any illusions about Cuba.

As well as everyday contacts and his leftist comrades, Sartre and I also saw various friends when the holidays were over and everyone was back in Paris. Tito Gerassi told us about the American underground. Rossana Rossanda described the ups and downs of her paper, *Manifesto*, which was to change from a weekly to a daily. Robert Gallimard let us know what was happening behind the scenes in the publishing world. We had lunch with Ali, the Egyptian journalist who had escorted us during our tour of his country in 1967. At the beginning of May we met our Japanese friend Tomiko again, and she told us about the long journey she had just made in Asia.

On May 12 Sartre took part in a meeting held before the Ivry town hall. Behar Behala, a somewhat feeble-minded immigrant, had stolen a pot of yogurt from a van; the police fired and wounded him seriously. After an investigation *Secours rouge* organized a demonstration against the police.

At this point Sartre was staying much of the time with me, because his elevator was out of order, and he found it very tiring to walk up ten flights of stairs. On Tuesday, May 18, as on all other Tuesdays, Sartre arrived at my place in the evening; he had spent the previous evening and night with Arlette. "How are you?" I asked in the ordinary, rather casual way. "Well, not so good." And indeed his legs were giving way under him, he spoke indistinctly, and his mouth was a little twisted. I had not noticed that he was ailing the day before, because we had been listening to music and had hardly talked at all. But that evening he had reached Arlette's in a bad way, and he had awakened this morning in the state in which I saw him now; obviously he had had a slight stroke during the night. I had dreaded an occurrence of this kind for a long while, and I had vowed I would keep my head. I forced myself to remember the case of friends who had gone through the same sort of trial and who had recovered perfectly. In any event Sartre was to see his doctor the next day, and that calmed me a little, but only a little. I had to make a great effort not to let my panic show. Sartre insisted upon drinking his usual dose of whiskey, so that by midnight he could not pronounce his words at all and found it very difficult to drag himself as far as his bed. All night long I struggled against anguish.

The next morning Liliane Siegel went with him to Dr. Zaidmann's. He telephoned to tell me that all was well; he had a blood pressure reading of 180, which was normal for him, and he was going to start on a serious course of treatment right away. A little later Liliane, also speaking on the telephone, was less sanguine. According to Zaidmann the crisis was worse than that of October, and it was worrying that the anomalies should have come back so quickly. No doubt one of the reasons was that since March he had no longer been taking his medicines, and it had also been very bad for him to walk up ten flights of stairs every now and then. But the essence of the matter was that the blood had great difficulty in circulating in a certain area on the left side of his brain.

I went to see Sartre in the afternoon and I found him neither better nor worse. Zaidmann had strictly forbidden him to walk. Fortunately, his elevator had been repaired. That evening Sylvie drove us to my apartment and she stayed with us a while. Sartre drank nothing but fruit juice. She was horrified at his appearance. I imagine that although he may not have realized it, the stroke must have been a terrible shock; he looked quite prostrated. His cigarette kept dropping from his lips. Sylvie would pick it up and hand it to him; he would take it and it would slip out of his grasp. I do not know how many times the process was repeated during the course of that ghastly evening. Since there was no question of conversation, I put on records, among others Verdi's *Requiem,* which Sartre was very fond of. "It's most appropriate," he murmured, chilling Sylvie and me through and through. She left shortly after this and presently Sartre went to bed. When he woke up it seemed to him that his right arm was so heavy and numb that he could scarcely move it. When Liliane came to fetch him for breakfast, she whispered, "I think he looks worse than yesterday." As soon as they were gone I telephoned Dr. Lebeau at the hospital. He could not come himself, but he would send another specialist. I joined Sartre at his apartment and at half past eleven Dr. Mahoudeau arrived. He examined Sartre for an hour and he reassured me; the underlying perception was unaffected, the mind was unharmed, and the slight stammer came from the twist to his mouth. The right hand was weak. Sartre still found it difficult to hold a cigarette. His blood pressure was 140; this was a disturbing fall and it was caused by the medicines he was taking. Mahoudeau wrote a new prescription and advised the utmost care for the next forty-eight hours. Sartre was to rest a great deal and never be alone. If he did this, he would recover entirely in ten to twenty days.

Sartre had meekly submitted to all the examinations, but he refused to stay in his room. It was Ascension Day, and Sylvie did not have to go to her lycée. She drove us to La Coupole, where we all three had lunch. Sartre was distinctly better. Yet his mouth was still twisted. The next day, when he was lunching in the same place with Arlette, François Périer saw him, and coming to my table he said, "It's odious, what's happened to him, with that mouth all pulled sideways—it's very serious." Fortunately, I knew that *this time* it was *not* very serious. During the following days things went well, and on Monday morning Zaidmann said that presently Sartre would be able to stop the treatment, but he added that the subsequent return to normal life would take a long time, and he even told Arlette that perhaps Sartre would never be entirely cured.

Yet by Wednesday, May 26, when we spent the evening with Bost,

Sartre had completely recovered the power of walking and speaking, and his good humor had come back. Laughing, I told Bost in front of him that I should certainly be compelled to wrangle with Sartre to keep him from drinking too much alcohol, tea, coffee, and stimulants. Sartre went upstairs to bed, and from the balcony that overhangs my living room he quietly sang, "I don't want to grieve my Castor even to the slightest degree . . ."* It touched me deeply. And I was touched, too, when we were having lunch at La Coupole and he pointed out a dark-haired girl with blue eyes and a rather round face, asking, "Do you know who she makes me think of? You, when you were her age."

His right hand was still weak. It was hard for him to play the piano, which he liked doing at Arlette's, and it was hard for him to write. But for the moment that was of no great importance. Until he should start work again, he was correcting the proofs of *Situations VIII* and *IX*, and that kept him busy enough.

In June he and Maurice Clavel set up the Libération press agency. They both signed a paper in which they set out the aims of the agency, which reckoned on being able to publish a news bulletin every day:

> We all wish to create a new instrument for the defense of truth to-gether. . . . It is not enough merely to know the truth; one must also make it heard. The Libération press agency means to be a new platform where journalists who want to say everything may speak to the people who want to know everything. It will give the people the right to speak.

At the end of June Sartre began to suffer cruelly from his tongue. He could neither eat nor speak without pain. I said to him, "Really, this is a horrible year; you have troubles all the time." "Oh, it doesn't matter," he replied. "When you're old it no longer has any importance." "How do you mean?" "You know it won't last long." "You mean because one's going to die?" "Yes. It's natural to come to pieces, little by little. When you're young, it's different." The tone in which he said this overwhelmed me; he already seemed to be on the far side of life. What is more, everybody noticed this detachment. A great many things seemed to leave him indifferent, no doubt because he was losing interest in his own fate. He was often if not sad then at least remote. I never saw him really cheerful except during our evenings

* Castor, "Beaver," a play on Beauvoir, was Sartre's nickname for her. (trans.)

with Sylvie. We celebrated Sartre's sixty-sixth birthday in June at her place, and he was radiant.

He went back to his dentist and his pain stopped. At once the progress that he had made since May became apparent. Zaidmann acknowledged that he had entirely recovered. And several times Sartre told me that he was very pleased with his year.

Still, I felt very anxious leaving him. He was going to spend three weeks with Arlette and two with Wanda while I traveled with Sylvie. I liked these journeys, but parting from Sartre was always something of a wrench for me. This time we had lunch together at La Coupole, where Sylvie was to come for me at four o'clock. I stood up three minutes before the hour. He gave me an indefinable smile and said, "So this is the farewell ceremony!" I touched his shoulder without replying. The smile and the words stayed with me for a great while. I gave the word farewell the ultimate meaning it was to have some years later; but when that happened I was the only one to say it.

I left for Italy with Sylvie, and the next night we stayed at Bologna. In the morning we took the highway that led to the east coast. The landscape was drowned in a warm fog, and never in my life have I known such a feeling of absurdity and forsakenness. What was I doing here? Why had I come? My love for Italy soon seized me again, but every night before going to sleep I wept for a long while.

Meanwhile, Sartre was in Switzerland; from time to time a telegram told me that he was well. But when I reached Rome, where he was to join me, I found a letter from Arlette. On July 15 Sartre had had a relapse. On waking he realized what had happened, as he had the first time. His mouth was even more twisted than it had been in May, pronunciation was difficult, and his arm insensitive to heat and cold. Arlette took him to a doctor in Berne, and Sartre utterly forbade her to let me know. Three days later the crisis was over, but she had telephoned Zaidmann, who said, "His arteries must be very worn, for him to have spasms like that."

I went to fetch him at the Termini Station. Before I caught sight of him he hailed me. He was wearing a light-colored suit and he had a cap on his head. His face was swollen—one of his teeth was abscessed —but he seemed in good health. We settled in our little apartment on the sixth floor of the hotel. It had a terrace which gave us a boundless view out over the Quirinal, the roof of the Pantheon, Saint Peter's and the Capitol, whose lights we saw go out every night at twelve. That year, part of the terrace had been turned into a drawing room, separated from the open-air section by a glass screen, and we could sit there at any time. Sartre's abscess went down, and he had no other trouble. He no longer seemed remote, and he was full of life and merriment. He stayed up until one in the morning and rose about half past seven. When I came out of my room toward nine I would find him sitting on the terrace, gazing at the beauty of Rome or reading. He slept for two hours in the afternoon, but he no longer had fits of drowsiness. In Naples with Wanda he had gone for long walks; among other things he had revisited Pompeii. In Rome we scarcely felt any desire to walk; without having to stir we were everywhere.

About two o'clock we would eat a sandwich near the hotel; in the evening we walked along to dine in the Piazza Navona or in a nearby restaurant. Sometimes Sylvie drove us to Trastevere or the Via Appia Antica. Sartre prudently put on his hat when he crossed a sunny stretch. He took his medicines regularly, drank a single glass of white wine at lunch, beer at dinner, and then two glasses of whiskey on the terrace. No coffee, and tea only for breakfast (in other years he had drunk an exceedingly powerful brew at five o'clock). He corrected the third volume of *The Family Idiot* and amused himself by reading *gialli,* Italian detective stories. From time to time we saw Rossana Rossanda, and one afternoon our Yugoslav friend Dedijer called on us.

Looking at Sartre as he was during this Roman vacation one would have given him twenty years of life to come. What is more, he reckoned on it himself. One day, when I complained that we always chanced on the same *gialli,* he said, "It's natural. There's only a finite number of them. You can't hope to read new ones all through the twenty years to come."

Sartre was still very well when he was back in Paris—his blood-pressure was 170 and his reflexes were good. He went to bed at about midnight and got up at half past eight, no longer sleeping during the day. His mouth was still very slightly paralyzed and this made it hard for him to chew and sometimes he lisped. Nor was he in complete control of his handwriting. But these things did not worry him. Once again he was paying the closest attention to people and events. He very much appreciated the cordial reception that the first two volumes of *The Family Idiot* had met with; he delivered the third to Gallimard and set about the fourth, in which he intended to study *Madame Bovary*. He read and carefully criticized the manuscript of my next book, *All Said and Done,* and gave me very good advice. In mid-

November I wrote, "Sartre is so well that I have almost entirely stopped worrying."

At the end of November, together with Foucault and Genet, he took part in a demonstration in the Goutte d'Or district to protest against the murder of Djelalli, a fifteen-year-old-Algerian. The concierge of his building had shot him down with a rifle on October 27; the boy made too much noise, he said. Then, not caring whether he contradicted himself or not, he stated that he had taken him for a thief.

Sartre walked along the Rue Poissonnière in front of Foucault and Claude Mauriac, who carried a banderole on which could be read an appeal to the workers of the district. The cops recognized Sartre and did not intervene. He made a speech, using a megaphone and announcing the setting up of the Djelalli Committee's office. It would be available from the next day onward in the parish hall of the Goutte d'Or until another place could be found for it. The procession went on as far as the Boulevard de la Chapelle, Foucault speaking on several occasions. Sartre wanted to take his turn at the committee's office, but when he and Genet had lunch together some days later, Genet advised against it, not considering him fit enough.

I do not know whether Sartre was aware of this unfitness, but suddenly, during the evening of December 1, he said to me, "I've used up my store of health. I won't live beyond seventy." I protested. He went on, "You told me yourself that people find it hard to recover from a third stroke." I could no longer remember having said that; no doubt it had been a warning against possible overindulgences. "The ones you've had were very slight," I said. He continued, "I'm afraid I shan't finish the Flaubert." "Does that grieve you?" "Yes, it does." And he spoke to me about his funeral. He wanted a very simple ceremony, and he wanted to be cremated. Above all, he did not wish to be buried in the Père Lachaise graveyard between his mother and stepfather. He hoped that a great number of Maoists would follow his coffin. It was not often that he thought about it, he told me, but think about it he did.

On this subject, fortunately, his mood was changeable. On January 12, 1972, he said to me, with a happy look, "Perhaps we'll live a great while yet." Now and then he would make a laughing allusion to his "miniplegia," but he did not think that he was in any danger.

1972

As Pleven's promises about changing the prison system had not been kept, Sartre decided to give a press conference at the Ministry of Justice. On January 18, 1972, he and Michèle Vian went to the Continental Hotel to meet members of *Secours rouge* and some of their friends—Deleuze, Foucault, and Claude Mauriac. Two radio cars, from Radio Luxembourg and Europe 1, were there. The delegation moved off to the Place Vendôme and made their way into the Ministry of Justice. Foucault spoke and read the report sent by the prisoners at Melun. There were cries of "Pleven resign. Pleven to the black hole. Pleven murderer." The C.R.S. dispersed the meeting. They arrested Jaubert, a journalist who tried to intervene when an immigrant was being clubbed and who was so savagely beaten up that he had to be taken to a hospital.*

Sartre and Foucault stepped in to have him released. From the ministry the demonstrators went on to the Libération press agency; here there were about thirty militants and journalists who had not been at the Place Vendôme, and among them was Alain Geismar, who had just come out of prison. Sartre sat at a table next to Jean-Pierre Faye. He gave an amusing account of what had happened: "The C.R.S. were not particularly brutal," he said, "but they were not particularly gentle either: their usual selves." When he had finished, the meeting broke up and he went home.

One undertaking that he agreed to with a great deal of amusement was the film that Cantat and Astruc made of him. He was surrounded by his *Temps modernes* colleagues,† and in reply to their questions he talked and recounted his life. The filming usually took place in his apartment, sometimes in mine. It was perhaps a little monotonous, seeing him always engaged with the same questioners, but it was because he was so used to them that he expressed himself so freely and naturally. He was full of life and merriment—at his best. He had not written a sequel to *The Words* for fear of hurting Mme Mancy and

---

* All the journalists in Paris combined to protest: they organized a great demonstration in front of the Ministry of the Interior.
† Except for Lanzmann, who was then in Israel.

because he had been taken up with other work: in that book he had spoken of his mother's remarriage, his inner break with her, his relationship with his stepfather, his life at La Rochelle, where, classed as a Parisian and more or less cold-shouldered by the other schoolboys, he had learned about loneliness and violence. When he was eleven he had all at once realized that he no longer believed in God; and at about fifteen, earthly immortality had taken the place of everlasting afterlife for him. It was then that he had been seized by what he called "the writing neurosis"; and under the influence of the books he read he began to dream of fame, which at that time he associated with phantasms of death.

He described his friendship with Nizan and their rivalry, and his discovery of Proust and Valéry. It was at this period, near the age of eighteen, that he began to write down his ideas, alphabetically in a notebook he had found in the métro, put out by the manufacturers of the Midy suppositories. The main idea was already that of freedom. Then he gave a short account of his happy years at the Ecole Normale, and he told how he and his friends had mildly persecuted conservative, pious youths. He had come to philosophy through a reading of Bergson, and since then it had remained essential for him: "What binds everything I do together is philosophy."

He spoke of his stay in Berlin and Husserl's influence on him; of his calling as a teacher, his intense dislike of growing up, the neurosis caused both by this dislike and by his experiments with mescaline, which were connected with his researches into the imaginary. He also explained what *Nausea* and the tale "The Wall" meant to him.

The conversation then moved on to his time in Stalag XII D, the production of *Bariona,* his return to Paris, and *The Flies.* Then to the vogue of existentialism, the attacks directed against him at the end of the forties, the meaning of literary commitment, and his political attitudes—his joining the R.D.R.,* his breaking with it, his decision to move closer to the Communists in 1952 because of the sinister wave of anti-Communism that was sweeping France, and especially because of the case of Duclos and the carrier pigeons. He mentioned de Gaulle, "a baneful figure in History," and he cried out against the abject nature of present-day society.

He spoke of the way in which he had always been concerned with ethics and of his pleasure in finding these same preoccupations, in another form, among his Maoist friends, who linked ethics and poli-

* *Rassemblement Démocratique Revolutionnaire.*

tics. He defined his moral views at length: "Fundamentally the problem for me was to know whether to choose politics or ethics or whether politics and ethics were one and the same thing. Now I have come back, perhaps somewhat richer, to my original position—setting myself at the level of the masses' action. At present there is a moral question almost everywhere, a moral question that is none other than the political question; and it is on this plane that I find myself wholly in agreement, for example, with the Maoists. . . . Fundamentally I have written two ethics, one between 1945 and 1946, completely misled . . . and then some notes round about 1965 on another system of ethics, with the problem of realism and that of morals."

In the end he went back to a subject which he thought of the very first importance—the antithesis between the classical intellectual and the new intellectual that he had now elected to be.

The film was not yet finished when, on February 24, a Belgian friend, a lawyer named Lallemant,* had Sartre invited by the young barristers of Brussels to give a lecture on repression. We left about one o'clock in the afternoon, taking the autoroute. Sylvie drove. It was a fine sunny day and we stopped in a rest area to eat the croissants and ham that she had prepared. We reached Brussels at half past five and straight away we found the hotel, where rooms had been reserved for us. When we had settled in we went to have a drink at the bar, where Lallemant and Verstraeten joined us.† Verstraeten still had his fine blue eyes, but he was so thin that he looked like Conrad Veidt. We had dinner with them and some other friends at Le Cygne, on the Grand Place, a square that we admired all over again. We strolled for a while in the little streets nearby and then we set off for the Palais des Congrès.

At once we saw that the audience was entirely middle-class—it was obvious that the elaborately dressed women had just had their hair done. Sartre had given up ties and regular suits since 1968, and that evening he was wearing a black pullover, which was looked upon with disapproval. In fact he had nothing in common with these people, and we could not quite understand why Lallemant had invited him.

Without much animation Sartre read his piece on Class Justice and

---

* Lallemant had taken part in the struggle for the F.L.N. He and some friends had helped Algerians cross the frontier. He had arranged for Sartre to give an important lecture on the Algerian war in Brussels.
† Verstraeten was a Sartrian professor of philosophy. He had written a book on Sartre, and together with Sartre he ran the philosophical series published by Gallimard under the title of *Bibliothèque de philosophie*—a series that had been started by Sartre and Merleau-Ponty.

People's Justice. In France, he said, "there exist two kinds of justice: the one, which is bureaucratic, is used for binding the proletariat to their proletarian state; the other, which is untamed, is the deep thrust by which the proletariat and the plebs just assert their freedom against proletarization. . . . The source of all justice is the people. . . . I have chosen the People's Justice as the deepest and the only true form." He went on, "If an intellectual chooses the people, he must know that the time of signing manifestoes, of placid protest meetings, or of articles published in reformist papers is over. His duty is not so much to speak as to try, by the means that are at his disposal, to give the people the right of speaking." With this he explained the nature of *La Cause du peuple* and of the part he himself played on the journal.

To demonstrate the false direction of bourgeois laws he quoted the cases of Geismar and Roland Castro and the affair of the Friends of *La Cause du peuple*. He described the prison system—a system that had continually worsened during the past ten years, and he denounced the heavy pressure that was brought to bear on the judges.

All this floated over the heads of his listeners. There were a few relevant questions asked by leftists, and a great many foolish ones that Sartre answered in an offhand way. The only cheerful thing in this meeting was the sight of Astruc, creeping along the ground with his camera to film Sartre as he talked; his trousers drooped and his bare bottom appeared. The front row of the audience found it very hard to keep their faces straight.

As everybody was leaving, a woman looked at Sartre and said angrily, "It wasn't worth dressing up," and another, "When you speak in public you make an effort; you put on proper clothes." At Erasmus's charming, well-furnished house, where the young barristers were giving a cocktail party, the theme was taken up again by another member of the audience. This one attacked Sartre directly. She had *raised* herself from the working to the middle class, she said, and the first thing workers did who had risen like this was to wear a tie.

The next day Sartre went back by train with Arlette, who had arrived shortly before dinner; and I by car with Sylvie.

In Paris we learned of the murder of Overney. It was the tragic end of a long story. There had been arbitrary dismissals at the Renault works, dismissals that had in fact a political motive, and two of the workers who had lost their jobs, the Tunisian Sadok and the Portuguese José, began a hunger strike; the Frenchman Christian Riss joined them. They found refuge in a church in the Rue du Dôme at Boulogne. Late in the afternoon of February 14 Sartre went to the Renault workshops on the Ile Seguin in order to talk with the workers. He got in secretly by means of a van, together with the singer, Colette Magny, some members of the Gacem Ali committee* and a few journalists. They handed out tracts protesting the dismissal of militant Maoists, particularly those who were on the hunger strike, but they were brutally expelled by the security men. Sartre spoke about the event at a press conference: "We went to Renault's to talk to the workers. Since Renault has been nationalized one should be able to walk about there freely. We were unable to speak to the workers. That proves that Renault equals fascism. When the security men saw that there were no longer any workers to defend us, they grew violent. Several people were savagely struck and a woman was thrown downstairs."

Every day since the end of January, Maoist militants at the Emile Zola gate of the Billancourt works had been distributing the tracts of the *Comité de lutte Renault*. On February 25 they called for a demonstration against the dismissals, and against unemployment and racism, that evening at Charonne. Among them was Pierre Overney, who had been dismissed by Renault a year earlier and who now drove the delivery van for a laundry. The eight uniformed security men guarding the entrance were on edge, for it was the time when the workers were beginning to come out and the gate was open. There was an argument between Maoists and guards and then a scuffle. A man in civilian clothes was watching the scene from a sentry box. As the Maoists moved forward a few steps into the works he shouted, "Get the hell out of here or I'll fire." Overney, who was six feet from him, fell back. Tramoni pulled the trigger; the shot misfired. He pulled it again, killing Overney. Then he fled into the factory.

After this murder there were demonstrations and outbreaks of violence on the part of the workers, and fresh dismissals on the part of the management. Sartre went to carry out an inquiry in front of the Renault works. "You feel you have to make an inquiry yourself?" asked a journalist. "You don't have confidence in official justice?" "No, none at all." "And what do you think about the Communist party's attitude?" "It's absurd. They tell you 'The fact that they † kill

---

* A committee that was set up at Boulogne to denounce any racist or repressive action directed against the immigrants.

† By "they" the Communist party meant the leftists and the bourgeoisie.

one another is a proof that they're accomplices.' That seems to me a pretty unsound argument. It is rather the Communists who are in league with the government against the Maoists.''

On February 28 Michèle Manceaux drove Sartre and me over to join in a great demonstration organized to protest against Overney's murder. There was an enormous crowd. We did not stay long because Sartre had difficulty in walking. I was not able to go to the funeral with him because of a meeting of *Choisir.* We went with Michèle Vian. His legs did not allow him to follow the coffin all the way, but he was deeply impressed by the huge gathering. Never since May 1968 had the new revolutionary left wing brought so many people into the streets of Paris. According to the papers there were at least two hundred thousand, and they all spoke of a revival of leftism and emphasized its importance.

Yet Sartre did not approve of the kidnapping of Nogrette, the man in charge of dismissals at Renault: the *Nouvelle Résistance populaire* (N.R.P) had abducted him by way of retaliation a few days after the murder. With considerable uneasiness he wondered what kind of a statement he would make if he were ever asked for one. The kidnappers were uneasy too. They quickly released Nogrette, without having made any claim.

The N.R.P was the militant side of the *Gauche prolétarienne,* and it had survived it by going underground. After the kidnapping of Nogrette it was at the parting of the ways: either it must launch itself wholeheartedly into terrorism or it must cease to exist. It revolted against terrorism and chose the second solution. A little later, this brought about the disappearance of *Secours rouge;* the organization had in fact come under the control of the Maoists, and once they had decided to disperse they lost all interest in it.†

It was at this period that Sartre wrote a preface for Michèle Manceaux's *Les Maos en France,* a book that contained her interviews with some of their leaders. In this preface he explained how he looked upon the Maoists and the reasons for his agreement with them. ''The Maoists' regard for spontaneity,'' he said, ''means that revolutionary thought arises from the people and that the people alone carry it into its full growth and extent by means of action. The people do not yet exist in France, but wherever the masses move on to praxis they are

---

* A feminist group of which I was one of the leaders. My presence was essential that day.
† It nevertheless carried on for some little time.

already the people. . . ." He particularly stressed the ethical dimension in the Maoist attitude. "Revolutionary violence is immediately *ethical* because the workers become the subjects of their own history." According to the Maoists, said Sartre, what the masses wanted was freedom, and it was this desire that turned their actions into festivities —the sequestration of the employers in factories, for example. The workers were trying to build up an ethical society, that is, "one in which man, set free from his alienation, may discover himself in his true relation with the group."

Violence, spontaneity, morality: these were the three immediate characteristics of Maoist revolutionary action. Their struggles were less and less symbolic and circumstantial and more and more realistic. "With their antiauthoritarian praxis the Maoists show themselves as the only revolutionary force capable of adapting itself to the new forms of the class war in the period of organized capitalism."

Meanwhile, although he rejected the role of the classical intellectual, Sartre had not given up signing manifestoes when he was asked to do so. At the beginning of March he and Foucault, Clavel, Claude Mauriac, and Deleuze launched an appeal in favor of the Congo.

It was spring—a sudden and magnificent spring. From one day to the next the sun became the sun of summer; buds opened, the trees turned green, flowers bloomed in the squares, and birds burst into song; there was the smell of fresh grass in the streets.

In general, we continued with the same agreeable routine as that of the year before; we saw the same friends and sometimes people we liked but knew less well. We lunched with Tito Gerassi, back from America, and he gave us a long account of the rivalry between the two leaders of the Black Panthers, Cleaver and Huey. In spite of his liking for Cleaver—more intelligent, livelier—he had a higher opinion of Huey's sense of responsibility. He would have liked Sartre to support him, but realizing that he did not know enough about it, Sartre would not take sides.

We also lunched with Todd, who, after a long search, had found his father again. It appeared that for him this was very important. Since he had left his wife, Nizan's daughter, whom we were very fond of, we had seen scarcely anything of him. As he was perpetually looking for a father, Sartre, whose deep benevolence often took the form of easy kindness, dedicated a book to him—"For my rebel son." But in fact Sartre had never had the least notion of having a son. He said to Contat in "Self-Portrait at Seventy," "I have never wanted to have a son, never; and in my contacts with men younger than myself I am not looking for a substitute for the paternal relationship."*

At Saint-Paul-de-Vence, with Sylvie and Arlette, we led much the same life as we had the year before. We read, we went for walks under a magnificent blue sky, and we listened to France-Musique on our transistor. We revisited Cagnes and the Maeght gallery. Sartre seemed very happy.

Back in Paris he immediately returned to his militant activities. At that time there were 165,000 unoccupied dwellings in greater Paris. The people who lived in the Goutte d'Or quarter were almost all immigrants from North Africa. Some of them had occupied one of these houses on the Boulevard de la Chapelle. They stayed there only two days before the police surrounded the building. The besieged squatters retreated to the top floor. The cops brought a long ladder and broke every window in the place, compelling all the squatters to leave. The men were taken to an unknown destination, the women and children to an official center.

By way of protest *Secours rouge* organized a press conference directed by Roland Castro. Claude Mauriac, Faye, and Jaubert were there, and Sartre also took part. He summed up all the actions carried out since the Djelalli affair and brought out their political significance. He denounced "what in this case must be called the enemy," that is, the forces of order against whom these actions had been directed. In the first place, he said, these dwellings are uninhabitable; one really had to be quite homeless to put up with them. Second, expelling the unfortunate occupants was evidence of a high degree of racism—the Djelalli family, for example, had not found a decent apartment. And that was why poor people without a roof over their heads had taken refuge in that wretched hovel. It had been bought by a company that intended to raze it one day in order to put up an apartment building —an inhuman undertaking that the local population reacted against spontaneously. Once again we were in the region of class warfare. It was capitalism that we were up against. "And you will observe," he added, "that when the police clear the squatters out, they destroy houses that can still be used."

Sartre was interested in concerns that varied widely, but that were, in his opinion, all interconnected. In April he provided a preface, in the form of a letter, to a work on mental illness written by the

* Sartre was all the less eager to have Todd for his son since he did not like him at all and had only a very superficial relationship with him, which is the contrary of what Todd tries to insinuate in his book.

members of the Heidelberg society of patients. He congratulated them on having carried into practice "the only possible radicalization of antipsychiatry" on the basis of the idea that "illness is capitalism's only possible form of life," since alienation, in the Marxist sense, finds its truest expression in mental alienation and the repression that sanctions it.

As usual the way we best liked spending our free time was seeing friends. That spring we had lunch with the Cathalas.* They told us that in the USSR the intellectuals' situation was worse than ever. Four years earlier, Cathala had published an article in *Le Monde* on the latest novel by Chakovsky, the editor of the most important literary weekly in Moscow. Cathala had translated it himself, and he stated that the book was not only extremely bad but that it was Stalinist too. No more translations were offered him in Moscow. He lived by translating one of Alexis Tolstoy's books for a French publisher. His wife, Lucia, had been refused a visa for France unless she would declare that she did not share her husband's views. That was why they had not been to France for the last four years. In the end she had lost her job, and now she was unemployed, but thanks to the French embassy, she had obtained a passport. They intended to come back to Paris for good in a year's time. Solzhenitsyn was in worse odor than ever because of his latest book, which was to appear in France but not in the USSR.

Once again Sartre had trouble with his teeth. The dentist told him that in October he would have to fit him with a real plate, and that it would make speaking in public difficult. Sartre was deeply concerned. If he could no longer speak at big meetings or even in gatherings of a fair number of people, then he would be forced to retire from political life. He also complained of losing his memory, which was true for some little things. But the fear of death did not touch him at all. Bost, whose elder brother Pierre was dying, asked him whether he ever felt it. "Yes, sometimes," said Sartre. "On Saturday afternoons, when I am going to see the Castor and Sylvie in the evening, I tell myself that it would be stupid to have an accident." By accident he meant a stroke. The next day I asked him "Why Saturday?" He replied that the only two times it had happened to him he had not thought of death but only of being deprived of his evening.

He gave Goytisolo an interview for *Libre*, a Spanish-language maga-

---

* We had seen them during each of our stays in Moscow. "Cathala, a former schoolfellow of Sartre's at the Ecole Normale, had been a Gaullist during the war and he had become a Communist in 1945. He worked at translating Russian books into French. . . . His wife was Russian . . . and worked on a magazine." (*All Said and Done*)

zine published in Paris, in which he analyzed the political problems that arose in 1972 and returned to the question that was so important to him, the role of the intellectuals. In May, writing in *La Cause du peuple,* he dealt with views on people's justice at greater length.

La Cause du peuple was not doing well at all; it even suspended publication. Every morning Sartre attended the meetings at which those in charge of the paper discussed ways of saving it. He woke very early and he grew very tired. In the evening, listening to music, he would drop off to sleep. Once, after no more than a single glass of whiskey, he began to talk nonsense and staggered as he went up to bed. The next day he got up by himself at half past eight and he seemed perfectly normal. Still, in the plane that was taking me to Grenoble to give a lecture for *Choisir,* I felt anxious; when I came back to Paris the next day I expected bad news. And indeed, at half past eleven Arlette telephoned me. She, too, had been away from Paris late on Thursday, and Sartre had spent the evening alone in her apartment to watch television (he had no set at home). When Puig came to her place a little before midnight he found Sartre lying on the floor, drunk. It had taken Puig half an hour to get him to stand up. Then he walked back with him. Sartre lived not far away, but he fell and bloodied his nose. In the morning he telephoned Arlette and his mind seemed clear. I went to see him at about two. He had scraped his nose and his lips were rather swollen, but his wits were in order. At my urging, he promised to go and see Zaidmann on Monday. We had lunch at La Coupole, where Michèle joined him for coffee. I went back to his apartment, and from there I telephoned Zaidmann. He said that Sartre should not wait until Monday but come immediately. I went back to the restaurant. After a little grumbling, Sartre went off to see the doctor with Michèle and came back about six. His reflexes were good; there was nothing wrong except for his blood pressure— 210. But that was the result of his drunken night. Zaidmann had prescribed the same medicine as before and had given him an appointment for the following Wednesday.

Saturday evening with Sylvie was delightful. Sartre did not begin to feel very drowsy until midnight, then he slept until half past nine without a break and woke up feeling well and in good spirits. June ended very well. *La Cause du peuple* came out again, and the first new issue was a success.

At the beginning of July Sartre went off with Arlette for a brief stay in Austria. I traveled in Belgium, Holland, and Switzerland with

Sylvie. Sartre sent me telegrams, we telephoned one another, and his health seemed excellent. In Rome, on August 12, I went to fetch him at the station, but I missed him. I went back to the hotel and shortly after he arrived in a taxi. His speech was blurred but he said at once, "It'll be all right in a minute." He had taken advantage of being alone to drink two half-bottles of wine in the restaurant car. He got over it quickly, but I did wonder why he was like this—why he drank too much whenever he could. "It's pleasant," he said, but the answer did not satisfy me. I supposed that the reason he escaped from himself in this way was that he was not pleased with his work. In the fourth volume of *The Family Idiot* he intended to study *Madame Bovary;* and since he was always anxious to extend his range he wished to use structuralist methods. But he did not like structuralism. He gave his reasons: "The specialists in linguistics try to treat language from without, and the structuralists, who base themselves on linguistics, also deal with a whole from outside; for them it is a matter of carrying concepts to their utmost limit. But I cannot do that because I set myself not on a scientific but a philosophic plane, and that is why I do not need to exteriorize what is entire." So to a certain extent his plan was distasteful to him. And perhaps he also realized that in themselves the first three volumes of *The Family Idiot* contained the implicit explanation of *Madame Bovary,* and that by now, trying to work back from the book to its author, he ran the risk of repeating himself. He thought about it; he made notes; but he did not possess a general, comprehensive idea of what he was going to do. And he did not work much: he lacked enthusiasm. In 1975 he said to Michel Contat, "I found this fourth volume both the hardest and, for me, the least interesting."

Yet for all that we had a pleasant vacation, first with Sylvie and then by ourselves. During June, Sartre had sometimes been rather absent-minded, rather remote; in Rome, not at all. We still had that terraced apartment that delighted us so. And as we always did, we talked, we read, we listened to music. I do not know why, but that year we took to playing draughts and quickly we became passionately fond of it.

When we came back at the end of September Sartre was in great form. "I like being back here," he said to me. Returning to my apartment pleased him. "As far as the rest is concerned, I don't care. But I'm glad to be in this place again." We spent some happy evenings there, and again I almost stopped worrying.

But not for long. In the middle of October I once more became aware of the irreversible deterioration of old age. In Rome I had noticed that when we went after lunch to eat Giolitti's wonderful ices, Sartre would hurry to the lavatory. One afternoon, when we were going along by the Pantheon, back toward the hotel, and he was walking very quickly ahead of us, he stopped and said, "Cats have just pissed on me. I went close to the balustrade and I was wet on." Sylvie believed him and laughed about it. For my part I knew what was the matter, but I said nothing. In Paris, at the beginning of October, Sartre got up to go to the bathroom—he was in my apartment—and there was a mark on his chair. The next day I told Sylvie that he had spilled some tea. "You would say that a child had had an accident," she observed. The next evening, in the same circumstances, there was another mark. So I spoke to Sartre about it. "You are incontinent. You ought to tell the doctor." To my utter astonishment he replied in a perfectly natural voice, "I have told him. It has been going on for a long while now. It's those cells that I lost." Sartre had always been extremely puritanical; he never referred to his natural functions, and he carried them out with the utmost discretion. That was why I asked him the next morning whether he did not find this lack of control exceedingly embarrassing. He answered with a smile, "When you're old you can't expect too much, your claims have to be modest." I was touched by his simplicity and by this moderation, so new in him; and at the same time his lack of aggressiveness and his resignation wounded me.

In fact his chief worry at that particular time was his teeth. He often had abscesses and they gave him much pain. He ate only soft things, and he could no longer avoid having a plate. The day before the dentist was to finish taking out all the teeth of his upper jaw he said, "I've had a sad day. I was depressed. There was this odious weather. And then my teeth. . . ." I did not put on any records that evening; I was afraid he would brood. We looked at my day's letters and played draughts. By noon the next day all his upper teeth had vanished. He came to my place, and he was ashamed of being seen in the street. In fact with his mouth shut he was much less disfigured than when he had an abscess. For lunch I gave him mashed potatoes, brandade, and stewed apples. The next afternoon the dentist fitted his plate, telling him that for a week he would no doubt find it somewhat uncomfortable, but that he would be free of all those infections that had tormented him before. Sartre was relieved to know that the process was underway and was distinctly less gloomy than he had been the evening before.

Two days later he came home at about half past five in high spirits. His new teeth did not bother him at all—no difficulty in speaking and he chewed better than before. Later, when he came to my apartment about midnight, I asked him how the evening had gone—an evening that he had expected to be boring. "It was deadly dull," he said. "But I thought about nothing but my teeth and I was so pleased!"

At once he was gayer and more full of life than ever. On November 26 we watched the showing of the film about him, and just as he appeared on the screen so he was in life; there were moments when he seemed to me to be overflowing with youth. (What was so extraordinary about Sartre and so disconcerting for those around him was that he could emerge, cheerful and intact, from the bottom of abysses that seemed to have swallowed him forever. I had wept over him for a whole summer, and yet he had returned entirely to his former state, wholly himself again, as though "the wing of weakness" had never brushed him. These resurrections, this returning from limbo, explain the fact that later on I could say from one page to another, "He was very ill. He was very well." He possessed a fund of physical and mental health that resisted all attacks until his last hours.)

He was still busy with *La Cause du peuple.* In October, he and his friends who worked on the paper wrote a piece, "We accuse the President of the Republic," which was distributed in the form of posters and reproduced in the supplement to the twenty-ninth issue of the paper. In December, together with a hundred and thirty-six other intellectuals, he signed an appeal called "The New Racism" that was published in *La Cause du peuple* and in the *Nouvel Observateur.* It was also *La Cause du peuple,* on December 22, that printed his interview with Aranda. Aranda, a technical counselor to the minister of equipment, had published documents in *Le Canard enchaîné* proving fraud and corrupt use of influence on the part of certain important people belonging to the government. He handed the relevant files over to the legal authorities and he was the only person charged. His character intrigued Sartre, who said he would like to have a conversation with him. Aranda agreed; and Sartre tried to persuade him that by denouncing the misdeeds of the administration he was attacking the state, and that in order to prevent malpractice a "government supported and supervised by a people capable of refusing any such unjust acts" should be set up. Aranda was deeply wounded because Pompidou was trying to stifle the affair, but even so he recoiled from calling the state into question and spoke of the weakness of human nature. Sartre maintained that whether he liked it or not, in his way Aranda was "an agent of direct democracy."

In November he embarked upon an undertaking that attracted him very much—a series of conversations with two leftist friends, Pierre Victor and Philippe Gavi. In these he would take stock of his political progress and would attempt to define leftist thought as it had developed since 1968. The whole would be published under the title *On a raison de se revolter* (To Rebel Is Justified).

Geismar had introduced his interlocutors to him two years before. Pierre Victor—Benni Lévi was his real name—was a young Egyptian Jew who had studied philosophy and who had been to the Ecole Normale. He had been one of the leaders of the Marxist-Leninist movement; then, with Geismar, he had led the G.P. until it was dissolved. He had already had many conversations with Sartre, who had a very high opinion of him and who was charmed by his youth and his militantism. He spoke about this in 1977, in a dialogue with Victor that was published in *Libération:*

SARTRE: I lunched with you one day in the spring of 1970.

VICTOR: What kind of person did you think you were going to meet?

SARTRE: An odd character whom I thought of as being something of a Milord l'Arsouille. . . . After what I had been told, I was quite curious to see you that morning. . . . A mysterious character.

VICTOR: Now you see me as I am . . .

SARTRE: I see you; and what pleased me at once was that you seemed to me much more intelligent than most of the politicians I had met up until then, especially the Communists, and much freer. I insist on the point: you didn't refuse to talk about subjects less wholly political. In a word, you had that way of conversing outside the main subject which I like in women—talking about what's happening, which one rarely does with men.

VICTOR: You didn't see me wholly as a leader nor just as a guy.

SARTRE: Yet you were just a guy; but a guy who had some feminine qualities. I liked you from that point of view.

VICTOR: When did you become interested in a theoretical, fundamental discussion between the two of us?

SARTRE: That came about little by little. . . . I had a relation with you that gradually changed its nature. . . . There was real freedom between us—the freedom of endangering one's position.

Gavi was a young journalist who had written some interesting articles for *Les Temps modernes.* He belonged to V.L.R. (Vive La Révolution)—a less dogmatic, more anarchist movement than Maoism—whose paper, *Tout,* Sartre had edited for a while. Sartre was very fond of him as well. And he was pleased with the idea of giving his relations with the Maoists concrete form in a book, since it was because of them that he had renewed his political thought. With a happy look he told Bost and me one evening that his friendship with them had made him feel young again. He was only sorry that he was somewhat too old for it to be entirely profitable. He said in the course of one of his first conversations with Victor, in December 1972:

"Nineteen sixty-eight came rather late for me. If it had happened when I was fifty it would have been better. . . . For a well-known intellectual to carry out all that can be required of him, carry it through to the end, he has to be between forty-five and fifty. I can't last to the end of a demonstration, for example, because I have a leg that no longer works. At Overney's funeral, for instance, I could only go part of the way. . . .

"I have stated the objective reasons why I am with you and I shall state them again. One of the subjective reasons is that the Maoists' demands make me feel young again. . . . The only trouble is, if you go on mixing with politically active people after you're seventy, you are taken there in a car with a folding chair. You are a nuisance to everybody and age turns you into a mere image. . . . I say this without sadness; I've had a well-filled life and I'm satisfied. . . .

"And I'm satisfied with your relations with me. Of course I exist for you only insofar as I am useful to you. I fully approve of that. But when it's a question of carrying out an action together friendship comes into it, that is, a relation that goes beyond the action undertaken, a relation of reciprocity. . . . That's the underlying significance of my relations with you. It seems to me that if you call me into question and I argue with myself in order to be on your side, then, as far as my abilities go, I am helping to create a society in which there will still be philosophers, men of a new kind, worker-intellectuals; but men who will ask themselves the question 'What is man?' "

The only inconvenience about these meetings was that in order to carry on until two o'clock in the afternoon, Victor and Gavi ate sandwiches and drank red wine; Sartre, who lunched later, drank some too, but without eating. No doubt that was why he was often out of form and drowsy in the evening. In January Liliane Siegel, who was a friend of theirs, asked Victor and Gavi to see that Sartre drank less, though without his noticing it. This they did, and in January Sartre stopped being drowsy.

Victor and Gavi were extremely excited by a plan that also interested Sartre to the highest degree—the launching of a paper that was to be called *Libération*. On December 6, at the new offices of the *Agence de presse Libération,* 14 Rue de Bretagne, there was a preparatory meeting which Sartre attended. Gavi set out the program of the paper, which was to appear in February. Sartre spoke of the part he intended to play: "Whenever I am asked for articles, I shall write them." He also blamed *La Cause du peuple* for the headline in its last issue "The Guillotine, but for Touvier."* Of course it was unthinkable that Touvier should have been let out. But he had been sentenced to imprisonment, not to death, and there was no reason to demand that he should be guillotined.

1973

There was another preparatory meeting on January 4. And on February 7, 1973, Sartre agreed to be interviewed by Jacques Chancel in the television series *Radioscopie* in order to present *Libération*. Chancel tried to make him talk about his life and his books, which would have suited the nature of the program. Sartre eluded him and brought the conversation back to the only subject that interested him—*Libération*. A little later, and still to make the paper known, he went to a rally in Lyons, coming back quite pleased with the results. I went with him to another meeting at Lille. It was held in an immense hall giving on to the main square. A considerable crowd was present, most of them young. Sartre and two other speakers explained what *Libération* in-

---

* Touvier was a former member of the *Milice* (an armed body of collaborators during the German occupation of France responsible for the murder of resisters and Jews or an accomplice in these killings [trans.]). He was condemned to death in 1945 and 1947, and then twice to five years imprisonment and ten years local banishment for theft in 1949. He had just been pardoned by Pompidou. For war crimes there was negative prescription, but not for common-law offenses. His death could not therefore be called for, but only prison and the local banishment.

tended to be. The audience eagerly took part in the discussion and pointed out various scandals, demanding that *Libération* denounce them.

At the beginning of February *Libération* was launched at its offices near the Porte de Pantin. Sartre had sent out eighty invitations and a copious buffet had been provided, but—and we never understood why—almost nobody came. The only people there were those who worked on the paper. Toward seven o'clock Cuny, Blain, and Mouloudji put in an appearance.

Sartre had a great many other activities. In January 1973, referring to prisons, he put out a message that was published in *Le Monde* on "this régime that keeps us all in a concentration-camp world." He gave the Belgian magazine, *Pro Justitia,* an interview in which he spoke of the Aranda case, of the Bruay-en-Artois affair, of Michel Foucault's positions, and of justice in China. He wrote a preface for Olivier Todd's book, *Les Paumés,** which was a reprinting of *Une demi-campagne,* published by Julliard in 1957.

He gave M.-A. Burnier an interview that appeared in *Actuel* in February 1973—"Sartre on the Maoists." He analyzed his political action since May 1968, particularly his commitment to *La Cause du peuple:* "I believe in illegality" he said. He still paid great attention to *Les Temps modernes,* in whose January issue he published an article "Elections, a trap for fools." In this he refused the system of indirect democracy that deliberately reduced us to powerlessness—it was a system that atomized the electors, reducing them to mere ciphers. All the articles in this number had the same general drift and they were evidence of the team's political unity. The issue was a great success with the readers and Sartre was thoroughly satisfied. He returned to his analysis of French politics in an interview he gave to *Der Spiegel* in February.

In that same month he and the *Libération* journalists went to investigate the great housing complexes of Villeneuve-la-Garenne. He did not think the expedition very profitable. It was the occasion for a discussion that *Libération* published in June, a discussion in which a number of young people spoke but in which Sartre, who was present, remained silent.

At the end of February he had bronchitis. He soon recovered, but

* This was an example of his kindness: he never refused a favor even if he had little liking for the person who asked it.

it left him rather fatigued. On Sunday, March 4, the first round of the parliamentary elections was held. *Libération* had asked him for an article on the subject and that evening Michèle Vian and I went to the editorial office with him. A great many people were there and everyone followed the results amid the noise of the radio and the arguments. Sitting at the corner of a table Sartre wrote an excellent article for the first number. He was proud of having written it so fast and efficiently in spite of the din. For my part I was worried. The evening had been very trying for him. The next day he lunched at La Coupole with Michèle, who always made him drink too much, and he went back to *Libération* with her for an interview. There were traffic jams: three-quarters of an hour in a taxi going and the same coming back. I had a glimpse of him that evening and he told me that it had been extremely wearing. At about eight he went to Arlette's to watch a film on television, and afterward she told me that when he arrived he seemed out of sorts. She telephoned me the next day at about noon. "Sartre is not well." The evening before, toward ten o'clock, he had had a stroke. His face had twisted, his cigarette had fallen from his fingers, and sitting there in front of the television he asked, "Where's the telly?" He looked like a dotard of ninety. Three times his arm had been paralyzed. Zaidmann, alerted, gave orders for injections of Pervincamine to begin at once. Sartre had already had the first. The use of his arm had come back and his face was no longer distorted, but his brain was not too good. I telephoned Dr. Lebeau at the Salpêtrière and he told me he would see Sartre in two days time.

That evening Bost came to see us. Sartre arrived before him. I talked to him about his stroke; he remembered almost nothing. With Bost we discussed the elections. Sartre made a point of drinking two glasses of Scotch, and toward eleven he fell to pieces. I packed him off to bed. Bost left at about midnight and I lay down on my divan fully dressed.

At about nine in the morning Sartre appeared on the balcony above my living room. "How are you?" I asked. He touched his mouth. "Better," he said. "My toothache has gone." "But you didn't have a toothache . . ." "I certainly did, as you know very well. All through the evening with Aron." He vanished into the bathroom. When he came down to drink his fruit juice, I said, "It wasn't Aron who was here last night. It was Bost." "Oh yes. That was what I meant." "You remember. The evening began very pleasantly. And then when you had drunk a Scotch you felt unwell." "It wasn't because of the Scotch, it was because I had forgotten to take my ear plugs out."

I was panic-stricken. Liliane came to fetch him for coffee, and toward ten she telephoned me. Things were going badly. Sartre had said to her, "I spent an excellent evening with Georges Michel.* I'm glad to be reconciled with him. It was stupid, being on bad terms. They were very kind, and let me go to bed at eleven." (Sartre was not on bad terms at all with Georges Michel.) He had gone on wandering in his speech.

I telephoned Dr. Lebeau, asking him to see Sartre that day. He said that this was not really his province and he would arrange an appointment for me with a neurologist, Dr. B. The appointment was fixed for six in the evening.

At half past five Sylvie and I went to fetch Sartre at Arlette's. He seemed normal, and I took him in a taxi to see Dr. B., to whom I explained the facts. He examined Sartre and gave him a prescription and the address of a woman doctor to whom he was to go directly for an encephalogram. Sylvie had been waiting for us in a café and she came too. We left Sartre in the hall of a large modern building and went to sit in a ghastly café lit up in red where a bird perpetually whistled and called out *"Bonjour, Napoléon!"* After an hour we went up to the doctor's and waited in a quiet, comfortable reception room. Sartre joined us at about eight. The electroencephalogram did not show any serious anomaly. We took a taxi back to my apartment, dropping Sylvie on the way. Sartre said the doctor had been very kind; she had taken him onto the balcony to show him the view and had offered him a glass of whiskey. This was obviously untrue. Dr. B. had prescribed medicines, had urged Sartre to drink very little, and had forbidden him to smoke. But Sartre had decided to take no notice. We spent the evening playing draughts and went to bed early.

The next day Sartre seemed well. But at eleven Liliane told me on the telephone that while he was having breakfast with her he had grown strange. He did not recognize her—sometimes he took her for Arlette, sometimes for me. She said she was Liliane Siegel. "I know Liliane Siegel," he replied. "She lives next door and she teaches yoga." That was true; but he would not identify Liliane with this teacher of yoga. He also asked, "Who was that girl who came yesterday with the Castor and me?" "No doubt it was Sylvie." "No. Not Sylvie. It was you."

I had lunch with him. He told me again about the glass of whiskey

* An author and dramatist whose plays Sartre liked very much. He was a great friend of Liliane's.

that the doctor had offered him. I told him that it was certainly a false memory. He admitted it. I spent the afternoon at his place. He read. So did I.

The next morning he had an appointment at half past eight with Dr. B. at the Salpêtrière. When I reached his door at eight, I found Arlette, who was to come with us, ringing without getting any reply. I opened the door with my key. Sartre was fast asleep. He dressed quickly and a taxi rushed us to the hospital, where a male nurse took charge of him. While Arlette and I were trying to find a taxi, she suggested that Sartre should spend a few days with her at Junas, to recover. I proposed that afterward he should join me in Avignon. But would he agree? She pointed out that his no often meant yes, and that when his hand was forced he was not displeased. At noon I saw Dr. B. at the Salpêtrière. He told me that Sartre had had an attack of anoxia, that is, asphyxia of the brain, caused partly by tobacco but above all by the state of his arteries and arterioles. He approved of the plan of a stay in the country, and Sartre agreed to it without debate. B. asked him to write his name and address, and Sartre did so with ease, whereupon B. said confidently, "We shall cure you."

I saw Sartre again in the afternoon and he spent the evening at Wanda's, where Liliane Siegel's son picked him up to drive him to my apartment. Later she told me that he had been wandering, telling her at length about a negress who sat on his knee . . .

On the next day, Saturday, our evening with Sylvie was not a success. Sartre obstinately drank and smoked and we were horrified. We reproached him at lunch the next day, which put him out of countenance. Once again his elevator was not working, but he insisted on climbing the ten flights of stairs to go back and work in his room. By working, at that juncture, he meant preparing an article he had been asked for on the Greek resistance: he read and reread an excellent book, *Les Kapetanios,* but I do not think he retained anything. In the evening we played draughts at my flat. He was markedly better, but his memory was still clouded.

On Monday evening, having spent the whole day reading *Les Kapetanios* again, he left for Junas. Arlette called me on Tuesday. The weather was fine; Sartre was glad to be in the South again; he was reading detective stories. But his mind was still troubled. He had asked "Just why am I here? Ah, it was because I was unwell. And then we are expecting Hercule Poirot." She thought the detective stories incited him to fabulate and she took him out for walks as often as possible. On Friday she told me that he was in an excellent mood, and that he had amused himself by climbing the rocks in the quarries that were to be found in the *garrigue,* the wild countryside. But when Puig, his secretary, came to spend two days with them, Sartre cautiously asked Arlette after he had left, "Did Dedijer come?" (Dedijer had not the slightest resemblance to Puig, but he too was a close friend of Arlette's.) On Saturday she confirmed that he was well, but there was one odd thing—on Thursday and Friday he had forgotten to ask for his usual whiskey before going to bed. Later I heard that he had also forgotten it on Saturday. When I reminded Sartre about the whiskey he said in a vexed tone, "It's because I'm senile."

In the train that was carrying me to Avignon on Sunday morning I felt extremely anxious. I did not know what kind of Sartre I should find. When I saw the trees in blossom and after Valence the cypresses, it seemed to me that the world was lurching, swinging over into death, and forever.

Sartre got out of a taxi in front of the Hôtel de l'Europe, where I was waiting for him. He was unshaven, his hair was too long and he seemed to have grown much older. I took him to his room and I gave him some books (a life of Raymond Roussel and Joyce's letters). We talked for a little while and then I left him to rest.

We went out at dusk and walked toward the nearby Place de l'Horloge. "We must turn to the left," he told me, and he was right. And showing me a hotel, he added, "I waited for you in front of that hotel this morning while you went into a shop." I replied that we had not yet been for a walk in Avignon. "Then it was Arlette." But Arlette had not got out of the taxi. Sartre could not manage to pin this false recollection, but he clung to it. We had an excellent dinner, with which we drank châteauneuf-du-pape. In his room I gave him a glass of Scotch with plenty of ice and we played draughts, but he found it hard to focus his attention.

He was in fine form the next morning when we had breakfast in his room. A taxi took us to Villeneuve-lès-Avignon. Some years before I had spent three weeks at the hotel where we had lunch, and the young proprietress recognized me. She told Sartre that her son, who was seven, would have been delighted to see him, because he was learning some of his poems at school. This surprised us. When we got up to go she handed Sartre the visitors' book. "Your signature, please, Monsieur Prévert." "But I am not Monsieur Prévert," said Sartre, leaving her open-mouthed. We visited the Fort Saint André once more. There was a great wind blowing and it tousled Sartre's hair. How vulnerable he looked to me! We sat on the grass for a little while and then on a bench by the gate of the fort with Avignon and the Rhône laid out before us: it was a magnificent spring—masses of trees in blossom. The weather was mild and gentle; it was quite like happiness.

From the square in Villeneuve a taxi took us back to the hotel. The concierge went with us to the nuns who were to give Sartre an injection every day. It was only twenty yards from the hotel and I left him there. He came back by himself without any difficulty. After dinner in the Place de l'Horloge, we played draughts and Sartre was in full possession of his wits.

The next morning we hired a chauffeur-driven car to go and revisit Les Baux. The first view was quite superb—a desert of rocks under a perfect sky. Sartre smiled with pleasure and in a happy voice he said, "When we travel, the two of us, this summer . . ." I took him up, "You mean when we are in Rome?" "Yes," he said. But several times he repeated, "When we travel, the two of us . . ." We had a drink in the sun at l'Oustau de Baumanière, where we lunched. We walked about the dead town. We came back by way of Saint-Rémy through a lovely countryside all gay with flowers. Sartre looked at his watch. Smiling I asked, "Have you an appointment?" "Yes, of course, with that woman we met this morning in a café." I said we had not been in a café. "Oh yes we were—by the side of the road, as we left Avignon." He hesitated. "Or perhaps it was yesterday." I persuaded him that we had no appointment at all. Later he told me that it had been a floating impression, no more, and that even if he had been left to himself he would have gone straight back to the hotel. After that we stayed in his room, reading side by side. He read very slowly. It took him two days to get through *Le Nouvel Observateur*. Yet he was perfectly aware of what was going on. In the evening he said to me, "But you really must get back to work, you know." "So I shall," I said, "once you are quite well again."

The next day, March 21, the weather was still dazzlingly beautiful. "It's spring!" said Sartre gaily. We went by car to see the Pont du Gard again. As we were drinking a glass of whiskey on the sunlit terrace of the Auberge du Vieux Moulin he asked me, "Is that a nineteenth-century bridge?" With pain in my heart I set him straight. After the meal we walked a little way along the paths that run behind the bridge. Sartre sat down on every bench. It was the food that made him feel heavy, he said. And when he kept looking at his watch again on the way back to Avignon, I said, "We have no appointment, you know." "Oh, yes we have," he replied, "with that girl . . ." But he did not dwell upon it. The day before, when he was going for his injection, he had met a pair of secondary-school teachers who belonged to a *Libération* committee; as he came back the young woman was waiting for him at the corner and he had talked to her. The idea of a rendezvous was linked to that incident. In the evening I made Sartre recapitulate his day and he remembered it very well. We played draughts and talked.

The next morning he woke at ten, just as our breakfast was arriving. "We had a pleasant evening yesterday," I said. He hesitated. "Yes. But yesterday evening I thought I was invisible." "You didn't tell me about it." "It's since I came here. I felt I was *in danger* with regard to other people. So I thought I was invisible." When I pressed him, he told me that he was not afraid of anyone in particular but that he had the feeling of being an object, without any relation to others. "But you *have* relations with them." "If I cause them to exist." He also asserted that it was always I who ordered the meals, apart from the wine, which was untrue. From all this I concluded that he was completely confused and that he did not understand what was happening to him. He made light of the gaps in his memory and his slight wandering, yet he did say that he was "out of sorts," if not ill. Twice during this stay he repeated, with a look of extreme dejection, "I am going to be sixty-eight!" Once, in Paris, shortly before his stroke, he had said to me, "In the end they'll cut my legs off." And when I protested, he went on, "Oh, as for my legs—I could do without them." Obviously, he was suffering from a generalized anxiety related to his body, to his age, and to death.

That day we went to Arles. After lunch at the Jules César we looked at Saint Trophime's, the theater and the amphitheater once again. Sartre seemed very-low spirited. In the amphitheater he asked me, "Has that thing that was lost been found?" "What thing?" "The thing we needed to see the amphitheater. This morning it was lost." He became confused and repeated it several times. At Saint Trophime's we had taken a ticket valid for the church only, then at the theater a ticket that covered everything: was it that he was dreaming about? In any event, he was quite bewildered. We went back by way of Tarascon, where we visited the castle again. When we reached Avignon, Sartre said to the chauffeur, "So it's agreed that you will be paid tomorrow." "Oh, no," I said, "tomorrow we are leaving. We shall not see one another again." Sartre paid, giving an enormous tip. The nun who gave him his injections had said he could pay for them all together, on the last day. No doubt he had confused the two in his mind.

The next morning he told me that he was delighted with his stay, but that going back to Paris seemed to him "normal." He had not left an address with Michèle Vian and I asked him whether she would not be offended. "Oh, no," he said. "She knows very well that you had to leave without telling anyone your address on account of that man who annoyed you." "Me?" "Yes. Because he wanted notes about my illness." I denied it, and Sartre said, with a look of surprise, "I had always thought so." These imaginary recollections, which went back to the first days of his stroke, did not worry me unduly.

That morning some journalists telephoned, but Sartre would not see them. We had a drink in the sun on the Place de l'Horloge and lunched on the first floor of a restaurant. Sartre amused himself by watching the people who went by in the street. We went for a long walk around the town, and it did not seem to tire him at all. At six we took our places on the train and dined aboard. Liliane Siegel and her son were waiting for us at the station at half past eleven, and they drove us to my apartment.

The next day Sartre had his hair cut, which made him look much younger. He had lunch with Arlette, and told me she was not pleased with him, but he did not tell me why. She let me know by telephone. Sartre had told her that his cigarettes had burned in the gutter, and when she looked at him with a doubting expression, he added, "You think I'm senile, but it's true, for all that." He also claimed to have given an Englishman an interview.

In the afternoon I brought him his suitcase. He went through his mail and looked at the books that had been sent to him. At my place, in the evening, with Sylvie, he could not keep up a conversation, and went to bed at about half past eleven.

When he woke he remembered the day before perfectly. He was happy at the idea of seeing a young Greek woman toward noon; she had written an essay on him and he was fond of her. He seemed perfectly aware of everything, but I wondered when he would be capable of going back to work.

That evening he did not notice that Sylvie had put water in the bottle of whiskey. I very much disliked this little betrayal, but I could think of no other way of diminishing his ration of spirits. In the course of the evening he repeated, "I'm going to be sixty-eight!" I asked him why that should strike him so. "Because I thought I was only going to be sixty-seven."

The next day we saw Dr. B. again. I talked to him about Sartre's states of confusion. Sartre was there and he listened unmoved. Then B. took him into the laboratory to examine him. He did not think his condition bad. Sartre's handwriting was considerably better than the time before. B. told him that his greatest enemies were alcohol and tobacco, but of the two he would rather forbid him the alcohol, which might ruin his brain. All he allowed him was one glass of wine at the end of lunch. He prescribed certain medicines. When we went out Sartre was somewhat overwhelmed at the idea of having to give up spirits. "It's sixty years of my life that I'm saying goodbye to." A little later, when he was not there, I telephoned Dr. B. He told me that in the event of another stroke he was not sure that he would be able to put Sartre back on his feet again. "He is in danger?" I asked. "Yes." he said. I had known it; but even so it was a stunning blow. More or less clearly Sartre knew that he was threatened, because that evening he said, "One has to end by coming to an end. After all, I have done what I could. I have done what I had to do."

When he woke in the morning he once again rambled a little. He told me about a preface that he was to write for some Greeks, which was true, but also of another for a young man who had wanted to kill himself because his relatives kept him prisoner. Sartre could no longer remember his name, but it was a friend of Horst and Lanzmann. In fact there had never been any question of this young man at any time. Yet in the evening Sartre seemed to be perfectly all right; he seemed quite resigned to giving up alcohol and he beat me at draughts.

A short respite. Two days later Arlette rang me up in the morning to say that Sartre was giddy: he had fallen. Dr. B., consulted by telephone, had advised reducing the doses of his medicines; but if in spite of that the disturbance continued, Sartre would have to go into the Salpêtrière for observation. When he was with me in the afternoon he staggered as he walked.

His balance was better the next day. But when he was drinking morning coffee with Liliane he wandered again, talking about an appointment he was supposed to have with some workmen. Nevertheless, that day we spent a delightful evening with Sylvie. Cheerfully he said to us, "When I'm seventy I shall drink whiskey again." That comforted me, because it seemed to mean that he would keep off it for two years.

During this early part of April he was fairly well, in spite of a certain weakness in his legs and a few cloudy passages in his mind. He read a little critical book on *The Wall* which interested him. He began to regret not working. He wrote a letter, published in *The New York Review of Books,* calling for an amnesty for those Americans who had deserted during the war in Vietnam.

He spent a few days at Junas with Arlette. Sylvie and I went by car to get them and take them to Saint-Paul-de-Vence. When we reached the house, Sartre came down from the balcony where he had been sitting in the sun. As it happened every time when I saw him after an absence, I did not think he looked well—his face was swollen and there was something numb and awkward about his movements. We set off, all four of us, across the beautiful countryside of the Languedoc —*garrigues* and vineyards, fruit trees in blossom, blue hills in the distance. We drove over the Crau, skirted the Camargue, caught a glimpse of Arles, and stopped for lunch at an agreeable hotel at the entrance to Aix. Sylvie stayed in the car to sleep. We set off again in the direction of Brignoles, going through that Aix landscape I love so much. At one point Sartre said, "But what's happened to that young man we had with us? Has he been forgotten?" He did not dwell on it. Afterward he told me that it was Sylvie's absence during lunch that had muddled him.

He gave no further signs of mental confusion during our stay at Saint-Paul, but he had no energy. The sun shone splendidly; the countryside was brilliant. He liked driving about, seeing Nice, Cagnes, Cannes, Mougins. But in his room he dragged endlessly along with *Les Kapetanios,* and he could scarcely manage to read even detective stories. "He can't go on like this," Arlette said to me, and her voice was frightened. He himself was aware of his state. One morning, as he lit his first cigarette, he said to me, "I can't work any more . . . I'm gaga, as they say. . . ." Yet he retained his pleasure in life. When I was talking about Picasso, who died at the age of ninety-one, I observed "That's a fine age. It would give you another twenty-four years." "Twenty-four years is not much," he replied.

He went back to Paris with Arlette; I with Sylvie. When I lunched with him the day of my return he was lively and affectionate; my account of the journey from Saint-Paul to Paris amused him. At his place, in the afternoon, he took pleasure in opening his letters and leafing through the books that had been sent. But on other days he seemed to me shrunk in upon himself, lackluster, drowsy. This alternate hope and intense anxiety wore me out.

We saw Dr. B. again. While he was testing Sartre's reflexes in another room, I heard him say "Good . . . very good . . ." Everything was all right except the blood pressure: 200/120. When they came back into the consulting room, Sartre complained of his numbness of mind. With a kind of charming simplicity, he said, "I'm not stupid. But I'm empty." B. prescribed a tonic and reduced the whole range of medicines. Then, since Sartre could no longer write serious books, he advised him to try poetry. When we left, Sartre, who was beginning to recover his aggressivity, cried, "He's done nothing for me, that goddamn fool!" When I protested, he replied, "Zaidmann would have done quite as well." In fact, he thought that he would have got better by himself, which was utterly untrue.

He went on having ups and downs. He slept a little in the afternoons, and on waking he often uttered jumbled words. One day, when Arlette was telling him that she had been to see the private screening of Lanzmann's film, *Pourquoi Israël?*, he said, "You weren't the only one. Arlette was there too." "Arlette?" "Yes, it interests her because she's a *pied-noir* Jewess." * Then she asked him, "And what about me? Who am I?" Sartre recovered himself. "Oh, I meant you had taken another girl with you." She told Sartre that there was a bomb scare at the beginning of the show and that the place had been searched. He only told me that the showing had started late. He had forgotten why. Things slipped off him, and as all his friends noticed, he was far away, rather sleepy, almost glum, with a fixed smile of universal kindness on his lips (a smile caused by a slight paralysis of the facial muscles).

Yet I often spent pleasant evenings with him. He drank his fruit juice with pleasure, and the Sunday meals with Sylvie were always lively. Tito Gerassi, who wanted to write a political biography of Sartre, lunched with him and me at La Coupole and then talked to him alone. He thought Sartre was in excellent shape. On May 21 Sartre resumed his conversations with Pierre Victor and Gavi, and they said to Liliane Siegel, "He was extraordinarily intelligent: exactly as he was before." At the end of May he took part in a *Les Temps*

---

* The *pieds-noirs* were the people (mostly European) living in Algeria who had to leave when the country became independent. (trans.)

modernes meeting. Horst and Lanzmann (who had had the most deplorable impression when Sartre came back from the South) thought him as lively and as intelligent as he had ever been. He still hesitated over proper names, and he had a very poor recollection of the various stages of his illness, particularly the fits of dizziness. Sometimes he referred to his "miniplegia," and one day he said to me, "It can't have been much fun for you." "No," I replied, "but even less for you." "Oh, me. I didn't realize what was going on."

Sartre was very glad to have gone back to his conversations with Victor and Gavi. During our evenings with Sylvie he was cheerful and even funny. On June 17 he talked to Francis Jeanson about his adolescence. He defined his relation to violence.

The only dark cloud was his eyes. As he did every year he had been to see an ophthalmologist, who found that he had lost four-tenths of his vision—almost half. And he had only one eye that worked. He was to follow a certain treatment for two weeks and if that gave no result, then a minor operation would have to be considered.

Two weeks later the oculist could not be sure of the nature of the trouble. The fact was that Sartre saw badly. I remember him, leaning over a big magnifying glass that our Japanese friend had given him and anxiously peering at newspaper articles. Even with the magnifying glass he could not manage to read everything. He tried again and again, always without success.

A few days later Arlette telephoned me—Sartre's dizziness had returned, and he had fallen as he was getting out of bed. That same afternoon he saw a well-known specialist. In the evening, when he told me about this consultation, he was dejected; the oculist had discovered a thrombosis in a temporal vein and a triple hemorrhage at the back of the eye. On the other hand, Dr. B., with whom I had made an appointment, was encouraging. The dizziness had stopped and Sartre could walk properly again. The blood pressure was still high—200/120—but from the neurological point of view everything was normal. B. gave me a letter for the ophthalmologist in which he stated that Sartre was suffering from a "cerebral arteriopathy with spells of giddiness," that he had high blood pressure, and that he was prediabetic. At a certain level I had known all this, but seeing it written down overwhelmed me. At the sight of my distress, Lanzmann telephoned a friend of his, a physician named Cournot. Dr. Cournot explained that Sartre would need at least a year for a complete recovery, but once he had recovered he might live till ninety. If another stroke were to occur, there was no telling whether it would be mild or very serious indeed.

When Sartre saw the oculist again the doctor said that two hemorrhages out of the three had been cured and two-tenths of the vision regained. Two or three more weeks would be required for the restoration of the whole. Sartre was still uneasy. At a luncheon with some friends he was fond of—Robert Gallimard and Jeannine, Michel's widow—he did not utter a word. On leaving them he asked me, not without anxiety, "It didn't look odd, did it?" But generally speaking he bore his misfortune patiently. In his conversations with Victor and Gavi he did not speak much, but he followed the arguments attentively and his interventions were all very much to the point. He took part in a discussion with the young workers of Villeneuve-la-Garenne (he had been there for an investigation) that appeared in *Libération* halfway through June. He signed an appeal for the banning of an *Ordre nouveau* meeting; and when, on June 21, the meeting took place, he attacked Marcellin's decision in *Libération*. At the *Les Temps modernes* gathering of June 27 he was thoroughly cheerful and so he remained during the days that followed. Dr. B. was perfectly satisfied with his health, and it seemed to Sartre that his sight was improving.

As usual, he spent three weeks with Arlette. I was traveling in the South with Sylvie, and Arlette gave me news of him. It was good news, though walking soon tired him and he found reading hard. On June 29 we went to Junas to fetch him and take him to Venice, where he was to meet Wanda. Once more, seeing Sartre again was a joy mixed with sadness. Because of his twisted mouth and his bad sight, his face had a set expression; he seemed old and devoid of resilience.

Yet the four days we spent traveling from Junas to Venice were pleasant. Sartre was rather bewildered, rather vacant, but lively. In spite of not seeing well, he could make out the countryside and the motion kept him interested. We went through Nîmes and followed the Durance, avoiding Arles and Aix because of the traffic jams. We lunched, and lunched very well, at the Château de Meyrargues, and Sartre drank a glass of old châteauneuf. I had booked rooms at the Bastide du Tourtour, and we got there by charming little side roads. The view from our balconies was sensational: pine woods and mountains blue in the distance.

The next morning, when I rejoined Sartre on his terrace, giving onto the wonderful Provençal landscape, I found that he had already been sitting there for more than an hour. Had he not been bored? No.

He liked gazing at the world, doing nothing. At Junas he would sit on the balcony for long periods and contemplate the village. I was glad that he did not find idleness wearisome, but it rather wounded my heart that to find pleasure in it he should have to be really "empty," as he had said to the doctor.

Bost had advised us to go to Menton and eat a fish soup with aïoli at Francine's. Sartre was very eager to do so. We had a table on the terrace of the little restaurant; they brought us the soup, and almost immediately he overturned his plate onto his feet. There was no great damage. We mopped his shoes and the waitress brought another plateful. Sartre had always been clumsy, but now, with his bad sight, he seemed quite disoriented. He observed the accident with an abnormal indifference, as though he no longer felt responsible for his actions or concerned by what happened to him.

We reached Genoa by a highway crowded with lorries, and the way into the town was long and difficult, but far from growing impatient, Sartre was in a charming mood. We took rooms in a hotel near the station and had a light dinner at a restaurant in the square.

Once again, at about nine in the morning, I found Sartre at his window; he had risen at half past seven and since then he had been amusing himself by watching the station square and its activities. He had the feeling of being in Italy, and it delighted him. We lunched at Verona, eating a delicious ham baked in pastry, and we checked in at a hotel with very pretty, rather baroque rooms where I had been with Sartre ten years before. While he had a rest I went for a walk with Sylvie. Later we all three had a drink in one of the many cafés on the main square, beside the amphitheater. Sylvie was tired and I dined alone with Sartre in a little restaurant close to the hotel. He walked, taking little steps, but without too much difficulty, and he looked very happy.

In Venice, Sylvie left the car at the enormous garage in the Piazzale Roma and we stepped into a gondola. Having left Sartre at his hotel on the Grand Canal, we went on to the Cavaletto, behind Saint Mark's Square, and settled in. Then we went to find Sartre. We gave him the transistor so that he could listen to music in the morning while Wanda was still asleep in the next room. He took us to the Fenice for lunch, scarcely mistaking the way at all. As a protection from the sun, which was dangerous for him, he wore a straw hat that he loathed. "I'm ashamed of being seen in this hat," he told me later, in Rome. We drank cocktails in Saint Mark's Square and then went back to Sartre's hotel; from there a motorboat took him to the airport to fetch Wanda. Standing in the boat he waved to us, smiling with that kindly, almost too kindly, smile that rarely left his lips. For no clearly defined reason I was afraid for him; he seemed to me so very vulnerable!

Two days later, on August 3, I met him at nine o'clock in the morning at a café in Saint Mark's Square. We met in the same way for the three following days. Sometimes he was there before me. Twice, being unable to see the time on his watch, he had got up at four and dressed. Only then did he realize that it was still dark and go back to bed. Wanda gave him his medicines with meticulous care. He walked about a good deal with her, sometimes for nearly an hour. He loved being in Venice.

Then one morning I left him. I did not want Sylvie to get bored with Venice, which she was beginning to know by heart. And even though these morning encounters pleased Sartre ("I shall miss you," he said), they did put him out a little. I left addresses with Wanda, and I set off for Florence.

I reached Rome on August 15, and on the next afternoon I went with Sylvie to meet Sartre at Fiumicino. Peering through the glass we recognized him at once by his hat, his height, and more than anything else by the way he walked. In one hand he was carrying a little traveling bag and in the other the transistor. He took great pleasure in seeing our terrace at the hotel again. He was well, but even so he was still a little ill-adapted. Sylvie put the transistor down on a table. "Don't you want to keep it for yourself?" he asked. "Why no. It's for you." "Oh, I don't need it." Yet afterward he spent hours listening to music and he admitted that being deprived of it would have been very disagreeable.

During the days that followed, when I got up in the morning at about half past eight, Sartre would already be there on the terrace, often having his breakfast and gazing vaguely at the scene below. His sight was much worse than it had been at the beginning of August, and he could neither read nor write. I got Michèle to telephone his oculist, who said he had no doubt there had been a fresh hemorrhage. He advised that a local specialist should be consulted. The hotel told me of one who was said to be the best in Rome; he had cured Carlo Levi of a detached retina. We arranged an appointment for the next afternoon. The doctor lived in the Prati district, an open, cheerful quarter on the other side of the Tiber. He was young and likeable. He established that there was a hemorrhage in the middle of the eye.

Nothing could be done, apart from waiting. There was also the beginning of glaucoma and the pressure within the eye was too great. He prescribed drops of pilocarpine and diamox. The next time we went to see him the pressure had diminished, but then I had given Sartre his diamox drops that very morning. When he went back again without having taken them, the pressure was higher but it was not excessive. The oculist hoped that the pilocarpine alone would neutralize the glaucoma. At the last consultation he would not let Sartre pay a fee. He asked only for a signed book. Sartre took him three in which he had blindly written a few words. This friendly, encouraging doctor pleased him very much.

We liked the regularity of our days. In the morning I read aloud to Sartre (that year I read him works on Flaubert, an issue of *Les Temps modernes* devoted to Chile, Horst's* and Le Roy Ladurie's latest books, as well as two fat and unusually interesting volumes on Japan, and Mathiez's *La Vie chère sous la Terreur*). Then after a quick lunch he would sleep for a couple of hours. I went for a walk with Sylvie or we read side by side in the covered part of the terrace. It was hot there in spite of the air conditioning, but I liked that warmth, the dimness and the smell of imitation leather. When Sartre woke I read him the French and Italian papers. In the evening we dined with Sylvie.

It was at meals that Sartre worried me most. He was no longer incontinent, and he only drank the allowed quantities of alcohol, coffee and tea. But it grieved me to see him gulp down such quantities of pasta and above all of ices, when he was prediabetic. And then, because of his false teeth, the near-insensibility of his lips, and his half-blindness, he did not eat in a clean fashion; there was food all round his mouth, and I was afraid of vexing him if I told him to wipe it. He struggled with the spaghetti, taking up huge forkfuls and letting them fall. He could hardly be brought to let me cut up his meat.

Intellectually, he was often very lively and his memory was keen. But every now and then he would drift away. Sometimes it irritated me; at others it almost brought tears of compassion to my eyes, for example, when he said to me, "I'm ashamed of myself in this hat," or when he whispered to me as we left a restaurant, "People are looking at me," in a voice that implied, "They think I'm in a very bad way."

---

* Horst wrote under the name of Gorz and he appeared by that name in the editorial committee of *Les Temps modernes*. But I am using his real name throughout this book.

But I was also absolutely astonished by his good humor, his patience, and his care not to seem dreary. He never complained of no longer being able to see properly.

The magazine *Aut Aut* devoted an issue to Sartre, publishing the text of the statement he had made on "Subjectivity and Marxism" at the Gramsci Institute in 1961, as well as articles about him. I read it aloud, translating as I went. Occasionally we met Lelio Basso or Rossana Rossanda. Sylvie left us on September 5, taking the car back to Paris, and the day after that Alice Schwarzer, a German newspaper-woman, whose acquaintance I had made at M.L.F. meetings and for whom I had a liking, shared by Sartre, came to see us. She made a short film of me for German television and she filmed both of us on our terrace in the evening. We had an agreeable dinner with her. Our friends the Bosts also came to see us and spent a few days in Rome.

As we were leaving I felt anxious. "Shall we ever come back?" I wondered, casting a last glance over the city. "So this Roman vacation and its sad sweetness is over," I wrote when I was back in Paris. The fall was splendid, but I was afraid of the fatigues of Paris for Sartre.

He changed his living quarters, his place on the Boulevard Raspail having become too small. Arlette and Liliane had found him a much bigger apartment; it, too, was on the tenth floor, but there were two elevators. The apartment had a big study overlooking the Rue du Départ, with the new Tour Montparnasse highrise in the foreground and the Eiffel Tower in the distance. Sartre would have one of the two bedrooms whose windows opened onto an inner garden, while someone else could sleep in the other, so that he would no longer be alone at night. He visited this new and as yet unfurnished dwelling and liked it.

He was in an excellent frame of mind, and he said he could see a little better. There was no question of reading, but he could play draughts. He spoke of what he called "my illness" with a certain satisfaction. "I'm too fat," he told me. "It's because of my illness." And in the street, when we were going to have lunch, "Don't walk so quickly; I can't keep up with you because of my illness." I said, "But you aren't ill anymore." "What am I then?" he said. "Failing?" The word wrung my heart. "Of course not," I said. "It's only that your legs are a little weak." But I was not really sure what he thought of his condition.

However, a few days later he did feel tired. "I've been seeing too many people. In Rome we saw nobody." How would he bear the stress of the trial that was going to take place on October 8? This was an old story. In May 1971 *Minute* had called for Sartre to be put in prison. In June the minister of justice and the minister of the interior charged him with libel on the basis of articles selected from *La Cause du peuple* and *Tout*. As he was left at liberty, he spent his vacation in Italy. The preliminary judicial investigation began in October and was soon finished. In February 1972 the time of the trial was still not known, but now the date was fixed.

On October 8 Sartre would appear before a Paris court, sued by eight members of *Minute*'s editorial staff, who claimed 800,000 francs by way of damages for libel, insults, and threats of death. It must be confessed that *La Cause du peuple* had not handled them gently. It had called them "a gang of undesirables, ill-purged at the Liberation, half-pay members of the O.A.S.,* and professional inciters to murder." Those legally responsible for *La Cause du peuple* had thrown the writs into the wastepaper basket and Sartre was therefore estopped, precluded from making any denial. In order to counterattack, he was obliged to call witnesses who would state that in all good faith, he had the right to think what his paper had printed. At the end of September we began to work on the *Minute* papers that Sartre's counsel, Gisèle Halimi, had sent us, and we drafted the main lines of the statement he would make to the court.

But he was not well. Once again his elevator was out of order; he walked all the way up to his apartment; he had pains in the back of his neck. He saw Dr. B., who could not say that he was either well or ill and who wanted a general checkup. When Sartre woke the next day he seemed a little bewildered, something that had not happened to him for a long while. I said to him, "Today you're going to see the oculist." "No, it's not the oculist." "Yes it is." "No. I'm going to see the doctor who takes care of me after Dr. B." "That is the oculist." "Oh, really?" He asked whether it was Dr. B. who had prescribed the pilocarpine. He was extremely unwilling to have a consultation about his eyes or even to think about them. Arlette and Liliane went to the oculist's with him, and when he came back he told me he would never get his sight back entirely and for a long while he would not be able to read. He looked upon the prospect with a kind of dejected apathy. I learned from Zaidmann that he had a thrombosis which inevitably produced hemorrhages.

---

* O.A.S. was an armed and violent body opposed to the independence of Algeria. (trans.)

He stayed with me much of the time during his move from one apartment to the other, which was taken in hand by Arlette and Liliane. On September 26 he signed the Union of Writers' appeal against repression in Chile and another against the lack of official news concerning that country. We perfected his statement about *Minute* and he tried to learn it by heart, but he could not manage to memorize more than the beginning, and I wondered how he was going to manage. Our evenings were pleasant, but he went heavily to sleep in the afternoons.

On October 8 Gisèle Halimi and one of her young colleagues arrived in a car to take us to the Place Dauphine for lunch. They were rather nervous, they said; Sartre not at all. He was remote, as he often was these days. We went to court 17 and for an hour we listened to quickly decided minor offenses. At two o'clock Sartre's case was called. None of *Minute*'s people was there. They had briefed Biaggi as well as their usual counsel. First there were arguments about procedure, then the witnesses were told to leave and Sartre addressed the court. He dealt with *Minute* on the lines we had agreed upon, and he did so quite powerfully. But he made the mistake of referring to the abduction of Nogrette, and on this point he got into difficulties with the presiding judge. Then the witnesses were heard. In his altercation with Biaggi, Daniel Mayer was very funny. Biaggi had presumed to say he was attacking Sartre because of his play *The Flies*. Debû-Bridel replied that a good many resisters, including Paulhan, were of the opinion that one might express oneself publicly during the Occupation so long as what was expressed was efficacious, which was the case with *The Flies*. Claude Mauriac let himself be bullied and became rather flustered; he was there out of friendship for Sartre, but he had not liked coming at all. Then there were still more arguments about procedure. *Minute* had abandoned the charges of insults and libel, retaining only that of threats. Their young counsel inflicted a vehement, empty speech on us. The presiding judge sharply told him to stop perpetually banging on the table, because it interfered with the microphones. Then Biaggi poured out a flood of insults; he obviously had not studied his brief, otherwise he would have been able to find a good many unwise passages in *La Cause du peuple* instead of limiting himself to abuse and literary quotations. Gisèle Halimi spoke for more than an hour. She drew up a pitiless indictment of *Minute*—its references to the O.A.S., its incitements to murder, its racism. From time to time the judge reminded her that the question lay elsewhere, but he let her go on. Before bringing the sitting to a close he let it be understood that in order not to condemn *Minute* yet again, the suit would be annulled, since the writ that coupled insults and libel was not admissible.* We left, very happy to be done with it.

That evening Gisèle Halimi telephoned to tell me that she had been accosted by *France-Soir* journalists who asked, with man-eating expressions on their faces, "What's the matter with Sartre? He doesn't look well." "He's convalescing," she replied. And they, without the slightest shame, "If anything happens, you'll let us know, won't you?" The fact is that with his dragging walk, his corpulence, and his remote, vague look, Sartre was a sad spectacle. We had passed Simone Signoret in the Place Dauphine, and she had seemed much struck by the sight of him. He had some suspicion of it. One day as we were walking slowly along the Rue Delambre on the way to have lunch at the Dôme, he said, "I don't look too much like an invalid, do I?" I lied reassuringly.

Late on the afternoon of the day of the trial he went to the oculist's with Arlette. The oculist told him flatly that the retina was affected —partly affected toward the center—and therefore there was no hope of a cure. An optician would provide him with a special apparatus that might allow him to read perhaps an hour a day, using lateral vision. Sartre still looked shattered the next morning. I said, "The trial has worn you out." "No, not the trial. It was going to see the doctor." In itself the consultation had not been tiring, but the oculist had given him a crushing blow. That evening, when Bost came and I told him about the trial, Sartre never said a word and he went to bed as midnight struck.

On October 12 he underwent a complete examination at the Salpêtrière; Arlette took him there and I went to fetch him at noon. Dr. B. told me that he would not be able to work for several months. It was obviously true. He had about three hours of real health a day; then he slept or his mind was far away. When the examinations were over he seemed quite overwhelmed.

On Tuesday, October 16, I went to the optician's with him. The optician left him scarcely any hope either. Perhaps Sartre might be able to read for an hour a day, though in uncomfortable conditions, by means of the special apparatus that we were to order from him. That evening, for the first time, we spoke about his near-blindness,

* As it turned out, Sartre was condemned to pay 1 fr. damages and 400 fr. fine.

and he seemed to mean it when he told me that he did not suffer all that much. (Yet, apart from certain toothaches, he had never admitted that he was suffering, not even when renal calculi were making him writhe with pain.) I saw the results of the Salpêtrière examinations the next day. They were not good. Sartre had diabetes and his encephalogram had changed for the worse. Later Dr. B. told me over the telephone that this change had no doubt been caused by the diabetes. So perhaps it was reversible, I thought hopefully. Slow waves had been detected in his brain, and these might explain his states of drowsiness. (But even now I am still convinced that they were a defense against his anxiety over his eyes.)

The optician had lent us the apparatus he had told us about, but it was useless to Sartre. The words went by so slowly that he preferred hearing them read aloud—so slowly that it was impossible for him to revise and correct his own texts. He was not disappointed because he had never had any illusions on the subject. We sent the apparatus back.

Sartre returned to his conversations with Victor and Gavi. He listened to them, he criticized a little, but he scarcely intervened at all. One Sunday morning the *Temps modernes* team came to his apartment to talk about a lead article on a question that was important to him and that we often discussed, the conflict between Israel and the Arabs. He did not say a word, and the next day he told Arlette that he thought he must have slept. Lanzmann and Pouillon were appalled. He often dropped off while I was reading aloud, even when it was *Libération,* which interested him. He did not realize his condition. He told one of his old friends, Claude Day, "My eyes are no good, but as far as my brain is concerned, everything's fine."

During our evenings with Sylvie he was cheerful and sometimes he even laughed, which was now very unusual for him. But when we had lunch one day with her and our friend Lena, who had just come from Moscow and whom he had looked forward to seeing again, he was silent and lifeless. Lena was low-spirited; I was tired. Only Sylvie provided a little animation, and that not without effort. Fortunately, we had a more relaxed evening with Lena some time after this.

At the end of October Sartre began to rally. He took an interest in our conversations. One morning, when a new tenant was moving into the apartment over mine, there was such a noise that on leaving me he said, "This is certainly the very first time I've ever been glad to go away from your place!"

Our main subject of discussion was the Yom Kippur War, and this time we both had exactly the same attitude. He explained his in one of his conversations with Victor and Gavi. "I am not for Israel in her present form. But I don't accept the idea of her destruction. . . . We must fight so that these three million people are not done away with or reduced to slavery. . . . You can't be pro-Arab without also being somewhat pro-Jew, as Victor is, by the way, and you can't be pro-Jew without being pro-Arab, as I am. So this leads one to a curious kind of attitude. . . ."

On October 26 he gave Eli Ben Gal an interview over the telephone.* At the end of the Yom Kippur War he made a statement in which, among other things, he said, "My hope is that the Israelis will realize that it is the Palestinian problem that provides the driving force behind the Arabs' warlike spirit." He dictated to me a declaration for *Libération* which the paper printed on October 29 although it did not agree with his words at all. "This war cannot but check the Middle East's evolution in the direction of socialism," he said. And he analyzed the responsibilities of the two sides. On November 7 Sartre, Calvel and Debû-Bridel confirmed that they had officially charged some unknown person† with listening to the *Agence de presse Libération*'s telephone and opening its letters. (The charge, of course, led to nothing.)

Since he was now feeling better, Sartre began to find his illness more wearisome. He disliked having injections morning and evening. "Are they going to carry on with this treatment all my life?" he asked me in an irritated voice. I went with him to a specialist in diabetes, whose diagnosis was that he had a slight degree of glycemia; he prescribed some pills and a sugarless diet, and he forbade him the fruit juice that he drank in the evening. Dr. B. thought he was improving and cut out some of his medicines. On leaving, Sartre said, with a dissatisfied look, "He's not interested in me!" And it was true that although B. paid great attention to Sartre's illness, he did not seem interested in him as a writer, since he had suggested that he should turn to poetry.

The following days, with Arlette, with me, Sylvie, and Lena, he was immediately present and full of life. He no longer went to any

---

* Published in *Al Hamishmar* on October 26 and in French on November 5 in the Mapam's *Bulletin*. There were some extracts in *Le Monde* and *Les Cahiers Bernard Lazare*.
† In French this is *porter plainte contre X:* legal terms can only be translated approximately. (trans.)

entertainment at all, but one evening, with Michèle Vian, we did go to the little theater in the Rue Mouffetard to see a very good play based on the Thévenin case, *J'ai confiance en la justice de mon pays.** Sartre applauded it heartily. The next day, at the *Les Temps modernes* meeting, which took place in his apartment, he listened attentively to the reading of Pouillon's lead article on the Israeli-Arab conflict. He discussed it and made comments. And that evening too, when Bost was there, he was full of life.

But the next morning he had a discussion with July, the editor of *Libération,* on the subject of the rape of a Vietnamese student by one of her companions, a black immigrant, and it tired him very much. When I came to see him at five I made him go and rest. He slept the next afternoon as well, while I was reading him the two versions of a chapter in *Madame Bovary* at his request. In the evening, when Sylvie was with us, he was wide awake and he delighted in the fine fur-lined coat we had given her. She prepared cold spiced tea to take the place of the forbidden fruit juice, and he liked it very much. The next morning he took pleasure in seeing his young friend the Greek girl again; she had come to live in Paris for a while to follow the lectures on philosophy at the Sorbonne. But in the afternoon he slept heavily once again.

The morning after that he and July were to reread their conversation about the rape. At half past nine I went to the café where he usually had his breakfast with Liliane. She was there, and so was July, but there was no Sartre. I looked over the text July had brought. It was a disconnected jumble. And still Sartre did not appear. At ten Liliane telephoned him; he had only just awakened. At last he arrived, and when he had drunk a cup of coffee and eaten a little, I took him home with me. In two hours and a half we had drawn up a suitable piece, and it appeared in *Libération* on November 15. In this article Sartre reflected upon the moral and political implications of the Vietnamese girl's rape. In the evening I read him an excellent paper by Oreste Puciani on his—Sartre's—aesthetic thought, a paper in which he was keenly interested.† Then we tried to play draughts, but he could no longer see well enough and we had to give it up. What distressed me

---

* A young prisoner named Thévenin was supposed to have killed himself, whereas it was quite obvious that his "suicide" had been arranged. His relatives tried to throw light on his death, but in vain.

† An American friend whom Lise had introduced to me. At this period he was a professor teaching in a California university, and a specialist on Sartre.

most at that particular time was that he believed—he wanted to believe—that in three months time his eyes would be cured.

The new apartment was ready; they had even installed the telephone. Settling in amused him. From this time on I stayed there in the evening, and five nights a week I slept in the bedroom next to his. The other two nights Arlette slept there.

Sartre went on sleeping heavily in the afternoon; and even after long nights of sound sleep he would sometimes drop off in the morning while I was reading to him. He had undoubtedly become indifferent to many things. One morning, as he was getting up, I wiped a little saliva off his shirt. He said, "Yes, I dribble. For a couple of weeks now I have been dribbling." I had not mentioned it, for fear of embarrassing him, but he attached no importance to it. What did displease him a little was his drowsiness. "It's stupid, sleeping like this." He also told me sadly, "I'm not making any progress." One Saturday evening he and Sylvie and I were invited to eat couscous at Gisèle Halimi's home; he did not utter a word. And he scarcely spoke when we had lunch at a restaurant with Lena, either.

I decided to ask Dr. Lapresle for an appointment: Dr. Cournot had strongly recommended him. We went to see him at the Bicêtre on November 23. He was astonished at the contrast between Sartre's vascular *history* and the results he observed, which were very good. According to him there was nothing pathological about the encephalogram. As for the drowsiness, he could not understand it. He ordered the kind of brain examination called a gamma-encephalogram. He very strongly urged Sartre to stop smoking. Your sight and your intelligence are at stake, he told him.

When we left, Sartre told me that he was going to go on smoking. But nevertheless he smoked less the next day, and Sylvie and I had the surprise of a delightful evening, an evening such as we had not known for a great while. Sartre talked about Flaubert and the problems of passivity; and he said, "In a couple of weeks I shall have given up smoking completely." Later he allowed himself three cigarettes a day; during the days that followed he smoked eight, then seven, then six, and he reached his three. So he liked living and he was prepared to struggle for it.*

And indeed, his pleasure in living seemed to be coming back. He often saw his young Greek friend, and she brought happiness into his

---

* A little later he went back to smoking heavily.

days. One evening he had a very cheerful dinner at the Cloche d'Or with Tomiko, Sylvie, and me. And we had some very agreeable times, just the two of us. I read him a collection of articles of which he was the subject and he thought them very sensible.

He told me that he was taking on Pierre Victor as secretary. Puig would still be his ordinary secretary; Victor would read aloud and work with him. Liliane telephoned me to say that she was delighted with this decision; and Arlette to tell me that she was furious—she was thinking of Schoenmann's relations with Russell and she was afraid that Victor might become Sartre's Schoenmann.* But Sartre was very happy at the idea of working with Victor. And it suited me, no longer having to read aloud every morning. I had a little time to myself once again.

At the beginning of December he was no worse, but he was no better either. He slept. Even in the morning, when Victor was reading to him, he slept. It was a form of escape, I am sure. He could not accept his near-blindness. There were many other signs that showed this refusal. When I asked him, "What did you do this morning?" "I read and I worked." I stressed the point. "Why do you say you *read*?" "Well, I thought about Mme Bovary and Charles again. I remember a great deal. . . ."

One Thursday I went with him to Dr. Ciolek, a young and very likeable ophthalmologist. He left us no hope: the hemorrhage was healing over, but it had left ineradicable scars on the middle of the retina, which was now dead tissue. As we left, Sartre said to me, "So I shall never be able to read again?" He sat huddled in the taxi on the way back and dozed off to sleep. During the days that followed he was no sadder than he had been before. He had heard this verdict before, and although he ran away from the truth, he knew what it was. Now, in spite of his knowledge, he still went on running away. For example, he would say to me, "No, don't take *Libération*. I'll look at it tomorrow morning." One day, when I had moved the lamp away from his chair, he asked me to put it nearer again. "You say the light bothers you." "Yes, but I need it when I'm reading." He checked himself. "Well, when I leaf through a book." In fact, he could no more leaf through a book than he could read it. Yet he always wanted to hold

---

* See *All Said and Done* on the Russell tribunal. Schoenmann was one of the chief secretaries of the Russell Foundation. At the tribunal, of which he was the secretary-general, he claimed to represent Russell and to be the principal authority. When he wanted to have his own way he would say "Lord Russell insists that . . . ."

the new ones I brought him—to hold them in his hands for a moment. Intellectually, he was too numbed to suffer much from his infirmity. Would this state of balance last? And should one hope that it would?

According to his gamma-encephalogram there was nothing wrong with his brain. Yet sometimes he would utter very strange words. One morning, when I was giving him his medicines, he said to me, "You're a good *wife*." At the *Temps modernes* meeting on Wednesday, December 12, he dozed. Still, he did listen closely that evening when I read aloud *Le Monde*'s review of various books on him.

When I went to his apartment on Saturday, December 15, I found him sitting at his worktable, and in a heartbroken voice he said, "I have no ideas." He was to draw up an appeal in favor of *Libération*, which was doing very badly. I advised him to have a short sleep, and afterward we both worked on it together. He found it hard to concentrate, but even so he gave me the essential lines. Gavi came for the paper and he was pleased with it. A little later I read Sartre the end of Geneviève Idt's excellent little book on *The Words*. It filled him with satisfaction. But then once again he pierced my heart. Looking around his study, he said, "It's odd to think that it's mine, this apartment." "It's a very fine one, you know." "I don't like it anymore." "Oh, come. You were very pleased with it." "One gets tired of things." "You tire quickly. I've been in mine eighteen years now and I like it still." "*Yes, but this apartment is the place where I don't work anymore.*" A few days later, when I was reading him a passage from Baudelaire's correspondence, I told him he would have to read a book on Louise Colet. "I'll do so as soon as I'm back in Paris," he replied. Then he corrected himself. "As soon as I've got used to this way of living." This new apartment and this new way of living all meant that he was no longer at ease, no longer in his real place.

He had always wanted to be clear-sighted—to think clearly—but now, as far as his eyes were concerned, he went on denying what was obviously true. When in answer to his question I cautiously replied that he would never wholly recover his sight, he said, "I don't want to think so. In any case, I feel that I am seeing rather better." At lunch one day, Contat asked him how he was taking things, and he answered, "Obviously it's bearable only if you think it's temporary."

Most of the time he contrived to hide this anxiety. He and Sylvie and I saw the new year in very cheerfully indeed at my place. He was better at this period; he dozed less, and now and then he was entirely the Sartre of former days—at the *Temps modernes* meeting of January 2, 1974, for example. At other times he fell back into apathy. When he came home on January 8 at about half past seven his face was so dejected, so set, that Lanzmann, who had come to spend a little time with us, was horror-struck. When he left he kissed Sartre, and Sartre said to him, "I don't know whether you're kissing *a piece of a tomb* or a living man," which froze us through and through. He slept a little and then listened to France-Musique. At the end of the evening I asked him what he had meant. "Oh, nothing. It was a joke." I pressed him. He felt empty, he said; at present he had no desire to work. Then he looked at me with a look of anxiety and almost of shame. "Shall I never get my eyes back?" I said I was afraid he would not. It was so heartrending that I wept all night long.

1974

A few days later Dr. Lepresle told me again over the telephone that Sartre was doing very well, that he did not need to see him again for three months, and that it was normal that he should take refuge in sleep from a truth that was too distressing to confront. I told Sartre that according to Lapresle his health was excellent. "And my eyes? What did he say about my eyes?" There was a poignant mixture of intense anxiety and hope in the question. "Eyes are not his concern," I said. "But everything is connected," said Sartre. And he went to sleep. I was shattered. It is appalling to watch the death agony of a hope.

During the days that followed he went on dropping off to sleep while I read him Baudelaire's letters and then Strindberg's *The Son of a Maidservant*. When we were having lunch with Sylvie he was so silent that I said, "What are you thinking about?" "Nothing. I'm not here." "Where are you?" "Nowhere. I'm empty." This kind of absence often occurred. One morning at the end of January I was working with him, revising one of his conversations with Victor and Gavi. He fell asleep. He was more and more pessimistic as far as his sight was concerned. The fog was thickening, he told me. He also said, when we were lunching together at the Coupole, "I have the impression that my sight will not get better." He went on, "As for the rest, I'm all right." Then with a timid look, "I'm as intelligent as I was before?" I said yes, of course. And I added, "My poor dear, you're not very cheerful." "There's nothing to be cheerful about."

He had almost entirely stopped smoking, and another day I asked him, "Don't you find it burdensome?" "I find it makes me sad." Another time he said to me, "Bost has been talking to his friend Cournot. He said that after what I had had, it would take eighteen months to recover completely." "Really? He told me twelve months." At this, Sartre said rather sharply, "You don't suppose that I shall have got my sight back in two months do you?" * For him, sight and general condition were one.

I made an appointment with Dr. Ciolek. He said that Sartre would not go blind but that he would never recover anything like clear, sharp sight. I begged him not to tell Sartre this fact too bluntly. When we went to see him at the end of January he told Sartre that his sight had not grown worse. But when Sartre asked him whether he would be able to read again, Ciolek was evasive. In the corridor Sartre said "He didn't seem to think that I should be able to read and write again." He paused, as though his own words had shocked him; then he added, "For a long time yet."

The next day we talked about how he might try to work in the meantime. Abruptly, just before going to bed, he said in a harsh voice, "My eyes are done for . . . according to everything everybody tells me." The day after that he picked up a detective story that was lying about in his apartment and put it down under his big lamp. "I want to see the title." He made it out correctly, although quite often he could not read the newspaper headlines. Unfortunately, this did not prove much. He did have a certain margin of vision, but it was very much reduced. The next day I asked him whether he would like us to try working. "No, not yet; not right away." He, who was usually so far from touchy, reacted at once where his eyes were concerned. As we were going along the covered way in the big garden in the inner court of his building, I caught sight of our reflection in a far-off glass door. "Oh, it's us!" I cried, like a fool. "Let me beg of you not to be the all-seeing wonder," he said crossly.

The medicines his doctors stuffed him with had brought back his urinary incontinence and had caused him to lose control of his bowels. Going home one afternoon he fouled his clothes. I helped him deal

* He had had his stroke ten months earlier.

with the catastrophe, but I was afraid that these troubles might get worse and that they might make him suffer. Zaidmann said that it was the normal effect of certain medicines, that Sartre's blood pressure was excellent and his reflexes perfect.

One thing astonished me. He who would never go to see a doctor in the old days now blamed Ciolek and Lapresle for not paying enough attention to him. He wished to see the Roman oculist again, the one who had treated him the year before. He liked him, because he had kept up his hopes.

From the intellectual point of view, he began to improve in February. Since he could not *see* people, when there were many of them present he retired within himself. But at the *Temps modernes* meeting in February he surprised everyone by his lively awareness and his intelligence. He produced good ideas for articles and investigations.

In the middle of this meeting Vidal-Naquet telephoned to protest against two articles in *Libération* which appeared on February 20 and 21 under the title, "A Point of View on the Syrian Prisoners in Israel." They called Sartre and me into question for having signed an appeal "for the liberation of the Israeli prisoners in Syria," published in *Le Monde* and also signed by Frédéric Dupont, Max Lejeune, and Ceccaldi-Raynaud. We at once sent a clarification, denying all solidarity with the other signatories. This made no difference in *Libération*'s attacks. Sartre immediately replied to the authors of the articles, in *Libération* itself, accusing them of bad faith.

At this period he agreed to join Le Dantec and Le Bris (both, like him, former editors of *La Cause du peuple*) in running a series called *La France sauvage,* which was first published by Gallimard and then by Les Presses d'Aujourd'hui. Together they drew up an introductory text.

Wild France. In a way the "real" country as opposed to the "legal" country. Or again, wild, as one speaks of a wildcat strike. Which does not imply either archaism or necessarily violence. Fundamentally, it is a question of a process of effervescence at a given point of the social surface, an effervescence that induces a social group to rise up and, by agitation, to assert itself as a free community outside any institutional framework that might cramp it. . . .

We choose hope. We dare to make a bet on a possible break, a general movement that is conceivable only on the basis of the convergence of the common people's wild, untamed, unregulated activities. . . .

This means that the aim of our collection is both modest and ambitious. Modest, because we mean to base ourselves on facts and perpetually return to them. Ambitious, because it seems to us that it is a path by which a possible philosophy of freedom may be reached.

The first work in the series was one by Le Bris on the Languedoc which I read aloud to Sartre and which we both found exceptionally interesting. The *La France sauvage* series was to include—and eventually did include—the collected conversations of Sartre with Victor and Gavi, the last few of which took place in March. They summed up their discussions. Sartre had profited by them in that he had "relearned" the theory of freedom; he had rediscovered "the possibility of conceiving a political struggle centered on freedom." As he saw it, "from beginning to end the dialogue was directed at the ever more precise, ever more progressive elucidation of the idea of freedom."

Yet Sartre's psychological balance was still unsteady. From time to time he would try to work. This amounted to making illegible marks on paper. At the end of February we had lunch with the Rebeyrolles. In a blind alley opening out of the Rue Falguière they had an immense studio, one part of which was very pleasantly arranged as living space, while Rebeyrolle worked in the other. Before the meal he showed us his latest canvases, and Sartre observed sadly, "I can't see them." And he added, "I hope I shall be able to in a few months." He now knew that this was not so; but he *wanted* to believe that time was on his side.

On March 17 we lunched with Sylvie at L'Esturgeon, a restaurant at Poissy that we had liked when we were young because of its enclosed terrace that overhung the Seine and that had a big tree growing through it. Sartre was delighted to be there. He thought the food was excellent, which was most unusual for him. Yet, as it so often happened, he was far away. That evening he left for Junas with Arlette, who telephoned me on the following days; he was well, and he slept a great deal.

"Now my real vacation is going to begin," he said to me some days later, when we met at Avignon. We were about to leave for Venice with Sylvie. A train took us to Milan, and there as usual we went to the Hotel de la Scala. We had stayed there in 1946, when we so happily rediscovered Italy. Another train took us to Venice, where a gondola carried us to the Hotel Monaco, on the Grand Canal, near Saint Mark's quay, where we had rooms looking onto the canal itself.

In the mornings I had breakfast with Sartre in his room and I read aloud to him. At about one we ate a sandwich, either on the quay in the sun or indoors at Florian's, according to the weather, which was most unsettled, sometimes very fine, sometimes overcast—a thick fog often drowned Saint Mark's Square in the evening. While Sartre slept in the afternoon I went for a walk with Sylvie, and toward five o'clock we would all three go out together. I showed Sartre the former ghetto; we looked at the Rialto quarter again; and we went to the Lido. All the hotels were closed, and with some difficulty we found a little restaurant on the shore, where we ate a meager lunch, enveloped in a warm mist. In the evening we all three had dinner at one of the places we liked and then drank a glass of whiskey in the hotel bar.

Sartre always felt well in Venice, but now from time to time he grew uneasy. One morning, when I was reading to him in his room, it was so fine that we decided to go down to the terrace on the water's edge; I made as if to take the book. "What for?" he asked. Then he added, *"Before,* when I was more intelligent, we didn't read. We talked." I protested that I only read to him because of his eyes; and down there, on the terrace in the sun, we talked. He had in fact retained his intelligence; he made remarks about what we read and discussed the books. But he would let the conversation drop quite soon; he did not ask questions nor did he offer fresh ideas. Not many things interested him on any level. But by way of compensation he grew very set in his ways, making it a rule to keep to given sequences, replacing real pleasure in things by obstinate adherence to a pattern.

A newspaper published a photograph of us, giving the name of our hotel. A few troublesome people tried to get in touch with us, but we also had the pleasure of a telephone call from Mondadori,* who came to have a drink with us at the bar of the hotel. He had a beard, he had aged, and he stammered a great deal. He was separated from his wife, the beautiful Virginia. A friend came with him, a musician who was conducting Donizetti's last opera, *Maria di Rohan,* at the Fenice. The final performance was to take place on Sunday afternoon, the next day. The theater was fully booked but even so they found us three places in the royal box. We were enchanted by the magnificent bel canto and the excellent performers. But for Sartre the stage was no more than a black hole, which saddened him. Generally speaking he

---

* Our publisher's son, with whom we had traveled in Italy in 1946 and whom we had often seen since then. (See *The Force of Circumstance.*)

was worrying more than ever about his eyes, perhaps because more than ever he wanted to *see*. When I asked him, as we were leaving, whether he had had a good stay, he warmly replied "Oh yes!" But he added, "Except for my eyes."

On the evening of Tuesday, April 2, we got into two communicating sleeping-car compartments where we ate croissants with ham and drank merlot. The Italian railwaymen were on strike and we moved off an hour late. In the morning the steward brought us our breakfast and told us of Pompidou's death. Some French travelers were panic-stricken; they saw anarchy breaking out. One deeply disturbed woman wailed, "The stock exchange will utterly collapse!"

In order not to go back to his Paris ways at once, Sartre stayed a few days with me. On Saturday morning I went with him to see Ciolek. The ocular pressure was good; there was no more hemorrhaging. It was natural that at the theater he should have been so dazzled by the lights on the stage that he saw nothing. As he left, Sartre was quite pleased. "All in all, I am well. Everything is in order." He went on, but without apparent dejection, "He seems to think that I shall never entirely recover my sight." "No, you will not recover it all," I said, leaving the amount that would or would not be recovered undefined. However, for the first time Sartre spoke of Ciolek without dislike. I think that in Venice he had been afraid of going completely blind and now he was relieved to know that his sight was stabilized. Yet even so, having seen the diabetes specialist and Dr. Lepresle, who were both satisfied with his health and who reduced their prescriptions, Sartre still said in a very sad voice, "My eyes? I shall not get them back."

In spite of springlike and even summerlike weather, he was rather gloomy. "I have the feeling of perpetually living the same day over again. I see you, I see Arlette, various doctors . . . and then it is all repeated." He added, "Even as far as the elections are concerned . . . people come to fetch me and they get me to speak; but it's very different from the Algerian war." I told him I had much the same impression with the feminists. "It's age," he concluded, not too sadly.

On April 13 and 14 Sartre gave *Libération* an interview on the elections. He wanted Charles Piaget to be a candidate. (Piaget was the man who organized the Lip workers' struggle, and Sartre had followed their adventures with close attention.) He stated that he would not vote for Mitterrand. "In my opinion the Union of the Left is a joke," he said. In a conversation with Gavi and Victor he sided against the classic left wing. "I can't see that left-wing governments could tolerate our way of thinking. I can't see why we should cast our vote in favor of people whose one idea is to knock our heads off." He said that he would willingly vote for Piaget, because he was sure he would never be elected. "I don't know that I should vote for Piaget if Piaget had a chance of getting in," he ended, laughing.

On April 28 he went to Bruay with Gavi and Victor to introduce the hitherto unpublished book, *On a raison de se révolter* (To Rebel is Justified), which they had just finished. There was a *Justice et Liberté* committee at Bruay, and it had invited them. He did see former militants, but the meeting was not very useful. The book came out early in May as part of the *La France sauvage* collection. *Le Monde* at once gave it two very favorable reviews. Sartre discussed it with Victor, Gavi, and Marcuse, whom he now met for the first time. His Greek friend was present at the conversation and she wrote an account of it for *Libération*. On May 24 he sent the paper a message, resigning his post as editor. Because of his health he gave up all the responsibilities that he had taken on in the leftist press.

Since the beginning of 1974 he had signed many protests. One was in *Libération* in January—a text drawn up by the G.I.A. (*Groupe d'informations asiles*) on the subject of Jérôme Duran, a man from the French West Indies wrongfully confined in a lunatic asylum at Amiens. On March 27, in the same paper and in conjunction with Alain Moreau, a communiqué appeared referring to Alexandre Sanguinetti's complaint against Alain Moreau's interview published in *Libération* on January 9.

At the beginning of June Sartre was really well. Indeed, I thought him "transformed." He no longer dropped off to sleep; he wanted to write a book about himself and he was now reflecting on it. We talked as we used to talk in former times. We spent very lively evenings with Sylvie, and on one occasion we had a really cheerful dinner with Alice Schwarzer. One day, I suggested that during the vacation we should tape-record talks concerning literature, philosophy, private life. He agreed. "That will cope with *this*," he said, pointing to his eye with a heartbreaking gesture.

One evening Sylvie took us to the opera to hear *The Sicilian Vespers*. Sartre wore a white shirt and a tie bought for the occasion. For him, this was a sort of fancy dress, and it amused him. He liked the show. The casting was not all that it might have been, but there were some very fine arias and the choruses were splendid. The production, the scenery, and the costumes were outstanding. Unhappily, their beauty more or less escaped Sartre, although he saw better than he had at Venice. But for all that he was very cheerful when we had supper afterward at the Cloche d'Or.

On the evening of the elections Sartre came first to my house and gave Sylvie a recording of the Verdi opera, and then we went to Lanzmann's to follow the results on television. They did not really move us much. It was no great misfortune that Pompidou's disastrous inheritance should fall to Giscard.

During these last days of June Sartre continued to be well. He seemed almost resigned to his half-blindness. With Sylvie we celebrated his sixty-ninth birthday, and he did full justice to the delicious dinner she had cooked. We drank his health with the greatest enthusiasm.

He had only one cause for anxiety. Hs friend the Greek girl seemed not only much overexcited but actually to be going mad in the full sense of the word. She made a public scene in an Auteuil street and she was carried off to Saint Anne's, which she left to go to the hospital for university students. The psychiatrist told us that perhaps it was a question of nothing more than a *bouffée délirante,* a transitory delusional state, but she seemed more deeply affected than that when I went to the Boulevard Hourdain with Sartre on the morning of June 5. I waited in a little room while he went to see her, and they joined me an hour later. She was wearing a long white nightgown, her hair floated free, her face had grown thinner, and she looked the very image of the classic madwoman as movies show her. She greeted me with her usual politeness. Sartre and I called a taxi and went to have lunch at Balzar's. His interview with Melina had quite staggered him. She had been hostile, accusing him of having arranged her confinement and insisting that he should have let her out. He protested. "You certainly had Althusser shut up," she retorted. (At the Sorbonne she had been attending the lectures of Althusser, who had just been taken to the hospital with a nervous breakdown). Her father, summoned to Paris, was to take her back to Greece in a few days time. "I don't think I shall ever see her again," said Sartre regretfully. I felt wretched at leaving him under these conditions. Sylvie came to get us, and we left Sartre at the entrance to the building where Arlette lived; he was to set off with her for Junas that evening. In his hand he held a plastic bag in which I had packed his toilet things. He looked at us through a curtain of rain and his own private mists.

I traveled in Spain with Sylvie, reassured about Sartre's health by telegrams from Junas, Paris, and Florence where he was staying with Wanda. The journey ended badly. At Montpellier, as we were on our way from Spain to Italy, Sylvie heard of her father's death, struck down by a heart attack. Leaving me at Avignon she set off for Brittany and I went on to Florence by train.

When I saw Sartre again in the hall of his hotel, I scarcely recognized him, because of his cap and a thick white moss that hid his chin. He could not manage shaving and nothing on earth would induce him to go to a barber. In the train that was taking us to Rome he dozed. But the next morning, when we were in our terrace apartment once more, I saw with pleasure that he was indeed well. The hotel barber succeeded in winning his confidence; he let the man shave him, and this made him look much younger. After that he shaved himself perfectly well with an electric razor that Sylvie bought him when she joined us again some days later.

She taught me to use a tape recorder, and I began the series of dialogues with Sartre that we had talked about in Paris. He took part in them wholeheartedly, except on some days when he was rather tired and we made little headway. Apart from this innovation, our life had pretty well the same rhythm as in former years—short walks, music, the reading of papers and a few books. Among others I read Sartre Solzhenitsyn's *Gulag Archipelago* and Fest's *Hitler*. In the evenings we had dinner on the terrace of one of our favorite restaurants.

One night, as we were coming back on foot through the narrow, dark streets, a hand came out of a car that was passing us and grabbed my bag. I tried to hold on, but in spite of my efforts it was torn from me and I fell full length on the ground. Sylvie and Sartre helped me back to the hotel, which was quite near. They called a doctor at once and he told me that my left arm was dislocated. He bandaged it, and the next day I had it put in a cast. There were a great many of these attacks that year, and we never went out on foot in the evening again.

Sylvie took the car back to Paris. The Bosts came to see us, staying only a little while. As we were now by ourselves, we recorded several conversations. We rarely went out, because heavy rain and violent storms came in mid-September.

We went back to Paris on September 22, and Sartre returned without pleasure to that dwelling where he "no longer worked." Sylvie went there to spend an evening and he said to her, "Have you come to see the dead man's house?" And a little later, when I questioned him, he replied, "Why, yes, I'm a living corpse." This was before he returned to any activity. Once he had done so he was much more living than dead. We went on with our dialogues, and he said that he was completely *happy*. Finally, he had resigned himself even to his half-blindness and he was proud of having adapted to it so well. One of the first steps he took was to send Giscard d'Estaing a letter asking that Benni Lévi (Pierre Victor) might be naturalized as soon as possible. On September 30 Giscard replied with a letter in his own hand —a letter in which he avoided calling Sartre *maître**—promising to obtain the desired naturalization very quickly, and ending, "Judging by your writings, everything seems to set us very far apart from one another. I am not so sure of that as you are. I have never thought that men were to be classified solely according to the conclusions that they arrive at. There is also their quest to be taken into account, as you know very well." The naturalization came through quickly, and Sartre wrote a short letter of thanks.† Victor celebrated the occasion by giving a party for all his close friends, and since Sartre and I intended to be there, Liliane Siegel lent her apartment, so that things should be easier for us.

Sartre went back to attending the *Temps modernes* meetings. All those who were present on October 2—Etcherelli, Pouillon, and Horst—thought he was completely transformed. He saw the *Libération* team once more. On October 15 *Le Monde* carried an appeal by Sartre and July, written by the latter and entitled "Save *Libération*." The paper, crushed by debts, had been obliged to suspend publication. Sartre and July appealed to the public for the seventy-seven million old francs‡ needed for its survival. He continued his discussions with Victor and had a great many appointments. In the afternoons and some evenings I read him the books he wanted to know about (Gramsci's political writings, a report on Chile, the most recent issues of *Les Temps modernes,* a work on surrealism and dreams, and Quentin Bell's biography of Virginia Woolf). He no longer dozed off, and he had almost perfectly adapted his motions as far as eating, smoking, and walking about were concerned. "Everything's fine, I promise you," he said to me kindly. "You read to me; we work; I can

* A compliment often paid to eminent writers and one that some of them find particularly irritating. (trans.)
† This was the full extent of the correspondence between Sartre and Giscard, which some papers referred to after Sartre's death.
‡ $110,000 at the time. (trans.)

see well enough to move about. Everything's fine." I admired him for the serenity of mind he had regained. (What serenity, in point of fact? Was it the proud acquiescence of the sage? An old man's indifference? The desire not to be burdensome to others? How can one tell? I know from experience that these states of mind cannot be put into words. Pride, wisdom, and care for those around him forbade Sartre to complain, even to himself. But in his heart of hearts, what did he feel? No one could have answered, not even he.)

On November 16 Sartre signed a declaration breaking with UNESCO, which refused to include Israel in any given region of the world. It was at this juncture that Clavel, acting as an intermediary, suggested that he should appear on television in a series of talks about himself. He began by saying no. Up until then, apart from one or two exceptions, he had declined to make any personal appearances on television, in order not to give a state organization his backing.* But when he had talked it over with Victor and Gavi, he had the idea of doing programs on the history of this century as he had known it or come close to it since his birth. I agreed. He hoped to influence the public, bringing about a renewal in depth of the way in which our recent history was seen. Marcel Jullian, the chief of Antenne 2, seemed to be in favor of the plan—with such a series Giscard's television would prove that it was becoming liberal. On November 19 Sartre gave *Libération* an interview on the subject. He had few illusions. "We'll see just how far we can go," he said.

For the moment there were other matters that interested him deeply. In the *Libération* of November 21 he published a letter protesting against the German authorities' refusal to let him see Andreas Baader. This was a matter in which he felt deeply committed. He had given *Der Spiegel* an interview in February 1973, and in it he had to some degree justified the Federal Republic's actions. Then in March 1974 *Les Temps modernes* published an article by Sjef Teuns on the "torture by sensorial deprivation" which was being inflicted on Baader and his companions; the same issue had an anonymous article on "scientific methods of torture" and another by Klaus Croissant, Baader's lawyer, entitled "Torture by Isolation." After that, Klaus Croissant had asked Sartre to go and see for himself the conditions under which Baader was imprisoned, and he had determined to do so. On November 4 he applied for permission to see Baader in his prison with

* He had made this decision at the time of the television and radio strikes.

Daniel Cohn-Bendit as interpreter. His determination was strengthened by Holger Meins' death in prison on November 9 after his hunger strike. Sartre's letter in *Libération* spoke of the German refusal as "merely playing for time." Shortly after its publication, Alice Schwarzer came and asked him, on behalf of *Der Spiegel,* for an interview on the subject. This appeared on December 2. Sartre had at last obtained permission to talk to Baader, and he now explained the reasons for his intervention. He disapproved of the Federal Republic's violent actions in the present German context, but he wished to show his solidarity with an imprisoned revolutionary militant and to protest against the treatment inflicted on him.

On December 4 therefore, he went to Stuttgart, and together with Pierre Victor, Klaus Croissant, and Cohn-Bendit he talked with Baader for about half an hour. The car that took him to the prison at Stammheim was driven by Bommi Baumann, a repentant terrorist who gave an account of his experiences in the *La France sauvage* collection.* The same day Sartre gave a press conference, extracts from which appeared in *Libération* and *Le Monde,* and together with Heinrich Böll he appeared on television to launch an appeal for the setting up of an international committee to protect political prisoners. His action provoked a violent campaign against him in the Federal Republic. He gave another press conference in Paris on December 10, at which Klaus Croissant and Alain Geismar were also present. Later, in the television program *Satellite* of May 22, 1975, he devoted an interview to Baader. He had no illusions about the consequences of his going to Stammheim. "I think the visit was a failure," he said. "German public opinion did not change. Indeed, the visit may even have turned it against the cause I meant to support. It was quite in vain for me to say that I was reflecting not upon the deeds for which Baader was blamed but only upon the conditions of his imprisonment —the journalists thought I was supporting his political activities. I think it was a failure, but in spite of that, if it were to be done again, I should do it." † Elsewhere he said, "What interests me is the motives behind the group's action, its hopes, its activities, and broadly speaking, its members' political idea."

On December 2, just before they left for Germany, Sartre, Victor, and Gavi introduced *On a raison de se révolter* (To Rebel is Justified)

---

* Some years later, under the name of Klein, he refashioned this narrative, finishing it off. The new book was called *La Mort mercenaire.* Both versions had a preface by Cohn-Bendit.
† In his conversation with Michel Contat, "Autoportrait à soixante-dix ans."

during a debate that took place at the Cour des Miracles. This was a meeting place financed by one of Georges Michel's friends, who had appointed him artistic director. Georges Michel had discovered the place and had adapted it with the help of some architect friends of his. There was a cinema, a theater, artisans' shops, and a very cheap cafeteria. On this occasion, and subsequently on many others, Georges Michel placed the theater at Sartre's disposal.

At this period Sartre was very busy. On December 17, at La Maison du Japon, he talked to students who wanted to understand the connection between his philosophy and his politics. Michel Contat recorded what he had said, and the text appeared in a Japanese periodical in 1975. He signed an appeal calling for the liberation of the soldiers imprisoned for having claimed democratic rights within the army. On December 28, after an accident that killed forty-three men in the Liévin mine, Sartre reprinted his Lens indictment of the Houillères in *Libération,* adding a short piece in which he passed this document on to Pascal, the examining magistrate. Together with Foucault he gave a press conference on the subject.

His chief occupation was talking over the programs we wanted to create for television. He discussed them three times a week with Victor, Gavi, and me. We had stopped working on our dialogues, and a typist had begun to transcribe them, though with great difficulty because of our rapid flow of words and the way the bells of Rome broke loudly into our conversaton. We were entirely taken up with planning these programs. Apart from the times when all met to work, Sartre and I talked about them a great deal, and in his almost illegible hand he noted down reflections and suggestions. For his part, between our meetings, Victor put his ideas down on paper and established contacts. We planned to produce ten programs on the history of the century, each lasting seventy-five minutes, followed by fifteen minutes devoted to present-day problems linked to the main theme. In less than two months we managed to outline six synopses; giving them their full substance would require the collaboration of historians, and we turned to young research workers, many of whom were friends of Victor and Gavi.

1975

The first question was who was to produce the series? Sartre would have liked Truffaut to work with him. Liliane Siegel knew Truffaut well, and on December 31 she brought him to see Sartre. Truffaut was not available. He advised Sartre to speak to Roger Louis, who had considerable means at his disposal. Roger Louis, a star reporter and producer on television, had resigned in 1968, giving his reasons in a very lively little book *O.R.T.F., mon combat.* He had then founded Scopcolor, an independent cooperative for productions that had vast premises at Belleville. He agreed to help us in our undertaking, which thus escaped official supervision. Negotiations with Edeline* allowed us to do without his team of technicians, and we became autonomous. We still had to choose directors. I thought of Luntz, whose *Les Coeurs verts* had pleased me very much. He arranged a showing of his latest film for us. It described the day of one of the heroes of *Les Coeurs verts,* Loulou, coming out of prison after five years inside. Sartre could see a little when he was very close to the screen and when he was helped by the text, and he liked the film very much; so did I. Gavi and Victor did not think it sufficiently political, but they were not against the idea. Roger Louis suggested Claude de Givray, and when we had seen some of the programs he had produced on television, we said yes. Both of them agreed to collaborate with us, though without the slightest guarantee on our part.

At the end of December Jullian had a little six-minute film made in Sartre's study in which Sartre, Victor, Gavi, and I announced our plan. It took us the whole morning. We were pleased with it when they gave us a showing a few days later. It was to appear on January 6 as part of a program in which Jullian would pompously introduce his plans for the year. It did not appear. A month earlier Gavi had made a blunder that neither Sartre nor I ever succeeded in understanding: in *Libération* he wrote that if Sartre agreed to work for television it was only so that he might make it appear ridiculous. Jullian told Sartre that he could not show Gavi on the small screen so short a time after

* President of the very important S.F.P. (Société Française de Productions).

this article. We asserted our solidarity with Gavi so strongly that Jullian gave up on the idea of cutting him out. In the end our introduction did appear, though censored, on January 20.

Meanwhile, on January 5, there had been a meeting of the historians, many of whom came up from the provinces. Since Sartre was not there, Victor presided. On the seventh we met Jullian and Wolfromm, his right-hand man, at Liliane's to clarify certain points. Among other things there was the question of money. Victor and Annie Chénieux were production secretaries and so far they had received nothing; Sartre had to pay them out of his own pocket. However, when the first six synopses were sent to Jullian January 20, he did produce a "lump sum of 13,500 francs" on the 22nd,* this being an advance on the transfer price of which the general conditions were still to be negotiated. It had needed fifteen telephone calls to get this money.

Apart from the thrice-weekly meetings of the "gang of four" at Sartre's apartment, many others took place. On January 28 Sartre had a talk with Luntz and Givray, and again on February 18. On February 1 the historians gathered, and thereafter they had a plenary session once a month in the Scopcolor premises. They were divided into several groups that worked separately on the various themes we had put forward. During these assemblies they set forth the results they had obtained. In particular, there was a group of women who wished to throw light on the part played by women in the course of these seventy-five years, a very important part but one that had been more or less kept secret. As we knew that the great wealth of material that the historians were bringing us could not all be used, we thought of publishing it in books that would accompany each program. It was agreed with Pathé that they would give us all the documents we required for nothing.

To deal with all the administrative and economic problems, we needed a lawyer. We chose Kiejman, whom we knew well, and on February 20 Sartre and Victor explained our problems to him. Among other things, he advised them to ask that a contract be signed as soon as possible. On March 6 Sartre met Jullian and Wolfromm at Liliane's, but he did not succeed in getting a contract drawn up; all he managed to do was extract another cheque from them, the whole of which was shared among the groups of historians whom Kiejman helped form

* A little more than $2,000 at that time. (trans.)

79

themselves into a *société civile*, a kind of company, that was to be regarded as the fifth author of the program.

As I have said, Sartre was hampered by not being able to *see* the people he was talking to, and when there were many of them he did not take much part in the proceedings. At these general assemblies it was chiefly Victor who spoke, and he did so with an authority that intimidated some and angered others. Yet on April 13 Sartre intervened at length. This was a somewhat stormy session.

It had been agreed that the programs should be centered on Sartre, and that if any dispute arose he should make the final decision. But the historians now called their relations with the "gang of four" into question again. They did not wish to be limited to the mere gathering of documents from which others would draw theoretical conclusions. Sartre tried to persuade them that since the aim was an "aesthetico-ideological" work it required a synthesis that could be carried out only by a very small group. The historians understood this point of view to some extent, but on the whole they felt frustrated. Fortunately, that day Scopcolor had produced a splendid buffet lunch that took the tension out of the atmosphere. As they ate and drank, the members were able to talk in little groups or in pairs. The afternoon proceedings were much friendlier.

Yet the meeting on May 10 had little life in it. At Scopcolor the next day we all had lunch together at little tables, but we did not return to the discussion. No one was filled with the sacred fire anymore, because the contract had still not been signed, and we were rather doubtful whether the whole thing would come off. However, the band of women historians did come to Sartre's apartment one morning to meet the "gang of four"; they were most cooperative and very interesting.

The question of money became pressing. On Monday, May 12, we all four met at Sartre's; Jullian was also there, and one after another we eagerly tackled him; it was only too obvious that he lacked good will. The whole business depended—or so it seemed—upon the classification of our work. If it was a dramatic program, we would be allowed the funds we needed; if it was a documentary we should only have a right to one-third of that amount. Jullian was to persuade Alain Decaux, the president of the Society of Television Authors and Composers, to class it as dramatic. We made an appointment with him for the following Wednesday, and Sartre defined his position in a letter to Jullian.

JEAN-PAUL SARTRE   *Paris, 15 May 1975*
                          MONSIEUR MARCEL JULLIAN
                            Président de Antenne 2
                            158, rue de l'Université
                                    Paris 7e

It was agreed between us that I should create a work for television: a work, that is to say a whole governed by one synthetic idea and brought into being by means of *pictures, dialogues,* and commentaries spoken by those who have *acted* in the history of these last seventy-five years (of whom I am one), or by actors playing historical roles.

It must be evident that we do not claim to give an account of all the facts of this history: we are not aiming at the documentary's kind of objectivity. We choose that part of the historical material that suits us and this is handled in relation to one particular subjective history—mine.

Rightly speaking, we are composing a narrative, and we hope that it will mean that on the basis of his own history, the viewer will distinguish between truth and falsehood. We mean to give the work an epic character, making it a saga of this century, as it were.

In order to accomplish this we employ aesthetic means:

—symbolic methods (for example, a sequence evoking the theme of *Nausea* in the third part);

—lyrical passages (for example, the evocation of Spain in the third part);

—reconstitutions (for example, a 1917 court martial in the first part);

—scenes (Sartre playing his part, actors playing theirs);

—diversion of material (for example, the diversion of Russian documents on Cronstadt from their primary destination in part two).

These instances of our way of dealing with the situation are given by means of example: they are not exhaustive.

In my opinion, therefore, the work can only be looked upon as a dramatic television program, and not at all as a documentary.

Decaux came to see Sartre on May 22; he was as agreeable as could be and thoroughly understanding. He classified the program as dramatic, which gave hopes that it would soon appear. Victor told the historians the good news by letter.

Meanwhile, the talks with Antenne 2 went on. On June 11, at Wolfromm's house, there was a conference in which at least fourteen people took part, including Jullian, Edeline, a man representing Pathé, Roger Louis, and Pierre Emmanuel, the director of the *Institut audiovisuel*. We came up against an awkward problem: if Contat's and Astruc's film, *Sartre by Himself,* were shown on the big or the small screen it might well put Antenne 2's programs out of the running.

The difficulty was resolved by means of a letter from Seligmann, the film's producer, to Jullian, undertaking not to bring it out before the showing of the ten programs that Sartre was to provide for Antenne 2. Then again, on June 18, our lawyer, Kiejman, met Antenne 2's lawyer, Bredin, and they drafted an agreement to be signed by Sartre and Jullian. The historians and those concerned with production were therefore very hopeful when they attended their last assemblies at the end of June. Sartre was less so when he left Paris on July 5; on June 30 he had written to Jullian, asking for an appointment, and Jullian had not replied.

Although this plan kept him busy, Sartre did many other things in the course of the year. I continued to read to him, generally speaking books that dealt with the history of the last seventy-five years. He listened; he tape-recorded. His intelligence was undiminished and for everything that interested him his memory was excellent. But he often lost his bearings in time and space, and often he paid no attention to the small routine of daily life, though formerly it had concerned him as much as it did me.

For an issue of *L'Arc* on "Simone de Beauvoir et la lutte des femmes," I questioned him on his relations with feminism. He answered with the greatest good will but rather superficially.

From March 23 to April 16 we were in Portugal, where a year earlier, on April 25, 1974, there had been what people called "the carnation revolution." After fifty years of fascism some officers, sickened by the war in Angola among other things, had risen in revolt. But it was not merely a question of a military coup d'état: it was an entire nation that had awakened and that supported the M.F.A., the soldiers' movement. Sartre wanted to know about this most uncommon event from closer at hand. To begin with he worried: "Shall I be able to *see* Lisbon?" But he soon forgot this anxiety. We were staying in a very noisy hotel in the center of the town, close to a huge open-air market. The weather was fine, but there was a very strong wind and we could not linger on our broad balconies. We walked about the streets among the happy crowds, and we sat on the terraces of the Rossio. As far as Sartre was concerned it was primarily a journey undertaken for the sake of information. Accompanied by Pierre Victor and sometimes by Serge July, he had many conversations with members of the M.F.A. He had lunch in the "red barracks," which officers attempting a putsch had tried to storm not long before. He gave a lecture to an audience of students who disappointed him by their lack of reaction to his questions. It seemed to him that they were undergoing the revolution rather than making it. On the other hand he had some very good encounters with the workers of a self-run factory near Oporto. He took part in a meeting of writers who, in a confused, puzzled manner, were wondering about the role that they would now have to play.

When he came back, Sartre gave a good talk on Portugal over the radio, and from April 22 to 26 *Libération* carried a series of conversations between Sartre, Victor, Gavi, and me, edited by July: (1) Revolution and soldiers; (2) Women and students; (3) The people and self-management; (4) Contradictions; and (5) The three powers. Sartre ended by expressing his critical support for the M.F.A.

In May the Czech philosopher Karel Kosik sent him an open letter denouncing the repression carried out against the intellectuals of his country. He spoke of the persecutions that he personally had suffered, including the confiscation of his manuscripts. Sartre assured him of his support in another open letter. "Pseudo-thought is what I call the theses maintained by your government," he wrote, "theses which have never been produced or examined by the thinking mind of a free man, but which are made up of words picked up in Soviet Russia and applied to activities to hide them, not to discover their meaning." He also published, in *Le Monde* of May 10, a statement on the past activity of the Russell tribunal. He had been asked for this in connection with the end of the war in Vietnam. He gave Tito Gerassi an interview that appeared in a Chicago magazine. Among other things he said, "Every one of my options has enlarged my world. So that I no longer see their implications as being limited to France. The struggles I identify myself with are worldwide struggles." He signed several documents during this year: an appeal for the Paris agreement on Vietnam to be respected (*Le Monde,* January 26–27); a warning against Jean-Edern Hallier, who was accused, rightly or wrongly, of having embezzled money intended for the defense of Chilean prisoners; an appeal in favor of the Basque nationalists (*Le Monde,* June 17, 1975).

We still had very pleasant evenings with Sylvie. One day we dined with Maheu at his house; for some years now we had resumed our relations with him—regular, agreeable meetings, though infrequent. We liked Nadine, his companion, and François, their son. She turned these dinners into positive celebrations. But at that time Maheu was seriously ill with a kind of leukemia and he knew that death was lying in wait for him. We once saw him at the clinic where he had been taken after a very bad attack; he was wearing a magnificent dressing gown, and he was nothing but skin and bone. On that particular evening, in his beautiful apartment, decorated with precious things brought back from his travels, we thought he looked even thinner and very much older. By contrast, I was struck with the youthfulness of Sartre, who had grown slim and alert once more. This was the last time we ever saw Maheu; he died shortly afterward.

That June Sartre felt full of life. Students came to see him, some bringing essays, theses, and books devoted to him. The papers spoke of him often. "It seems that I'm growing famous again," he said to me cheerfully. In March Contat had stayed with him at Junas for three days, and Sartre had given him a long and moving interview that *Le Nouvel Observateur* published in part on the occasion of his seventieth birthday and that brought him cordial congratulations—telephone calls, telegrams, letters. In this conversation,* which was entitled "Sartre par lui-même," Sartre reviewed his whole life on almost all levels, and he described his present ambiguous feeling with regard to himself and his relationship with the world. "How are things?" Contat asked him. And Sartre, "I can't say they're going well. But I can't say they're going badly either. . . . My calling as a writer has been completely destroyed. . . . In one sense that takes all reason for existence away from me. I have been and I am no more, you might say. I ought to feel very dejected, yet for some reason that I don't understand I feel pretty well. I'm never sad—I have no melancholy moments thinking about what I've lost. . . . That's just how things are and there's nothing I can do about it, so I have no call to be wretched. I have had some disagreeable moments. . . . Now all I can do is put up with myself as I am. What is forbidden to me from now on is . . . style; or let's say the literary fashion of setting out an idea or a reality."

Further on he spoke of his relations with death. "Not that I think about it—I never think about it; but I know it's going to come." He thought it would not come for ten years. One day, having made some abstruse calculations based on the longevity of his forebears, he said he reckoned upon living to eighty-one. Speaking to Contat he again said that he was satisfied with his life. "All right. I've done what I had to do. . . . I've written, I've lived; there's nothing to regret." He also said to him, "I don't have the feeling of old age." He said he was not indifferent to things, but he did admit that "There are not many

* Reproduced in its entirety in *Situations X*.

things left that excite me. I set myself on a rather higher plane." The interview as a whole gave the impression that he was sufficiently satisfied with his past to accept the present serenely.

Liliane Siegel gave a party in his honor on June 21. Among others there were Victor, Gavi, Geismar, Georges Michel, and myself. We were all very gay and Sartre roared with laughter. On the morning of June 25 together with many friends, we saw a private screening of the film, *Sartre by Himself*. And once again, as he sat there next to me, he seemed, in spite of his almost total loss of sight, the same as he was on the screen.

We were about to leave for our vacation. This year we were going to do something new—we were abandoning Italy for Greece, an idea that pleased Sartre very much. The contract with Jullian had not been signed, which vexed us, but we were hopeful; and we were pleased with the work we and our collaborators had done in the course of the year. With Victor, Sartre had roughed out a book that would probably be called *Pouvoir et liberté* (Power and Freedom) and that he intended to think about during the summer.

First he stayed with Arlette, then with Wanda in Rome; and in August, Sylvie and I, who had been traveling in Greece, went to meet him at the Athens airport. He seemed to be in excellent form. He was not walking very well, but even so, during the following days, he was able to go down the Hill of the Muses on foot and stroll about the little streets they call the flea fair. He saw his Greek friend again. She had been completely cured and she now worked as an assistant at the University. Because of the medicines she took she had gained over twenty pounds; furthermore, she was as silent now as she had been talkative before her illness. But she was still beautiful and Sartre liked being with her. When they were out together, I walked about Athens with Sylvie.

Almost at once we set off for Crete by ship, taking the car with us. I had booked comfortable cabins and we had a fine smooth crossing. It was poetic, finding ourselves on an unknown road by the side of the sea at seven in the morning with the sun coming up. The Elounda Beach hotel seemed to me a genuine paradise, with its whitewashed cottages scattered along the edge of the water or set a little back among scented plants and brilliantly colored flowers. The one Sylvie and I shared was right on the sea; Sartre's was some twenty yards inland. Inside they were comfortable and very pleasant, cooled by air conditioning. On most days Sylvie bathed in the morning, while

Sartre and I listened to music—we had brought a tape recorder and cassettes with us—or we read. Among other things I remember a fat book on Thorez and President Schreber's *Les Mémoires d'un névropathe*. We lunched in an open-air dining room sheltered from the sun; people helped themselves as they pleased from a sumptuous hot and cold buffet. We made a few excursions by car—a very beautiful one took us to the eastern tip of the island; another to Heraklion and Knossos; another, rather long and tiring, as far as Canea. In the afternoon we usually stayed at home with our books and cassettes. There was no agreeable bar, but we had refrigerators, and in the evening Sylvie made us delicious whiskey sours.* We had dinner in our rooms, eating almost nothing, or occasionally in a pleasant rustic tavern next to the hotel. Sartre was pleased with everything; he was wonderfully well and never so much as a cloud came over his cheerfulness.

After about twelve days we went back to Athens. The return voyage was wearisome; we had booked two cabins, but they refused to give us the keys. Amid hellish noise, heat, and crowds, Sylvie and I fought to get them at the reception desk, but in vain. In the end they shoved all three of us into a far from comfortable cabin with four bunks. We were asleep when late at night an officer opened the door: "You are M. Sartre; we didn't know. Your cabins are waiting for you." We refused to stir.

With joy we soaked ourselves in the calm of our Athenian hotel once more. We lunched at about two on a toasted sandwich and a cocktail in a bar icy with air conditioning. Then after going out on foot or by car we often had another cocktail on the sixth floor of the Hilton, which gave a sweeping view of the city and the distant sea. We dined here or there, often in an open-air restaurant at the foot of the Acropolis.

On August 28 I drove Sylvie to the ship that was to take her back to Marseilles. From there she would go back to Paris by car. Two days later Sartre and I took a plane for Rhodes. A mere hop. I could not believe my eyes when we began to come down again. We had two rooms with broad balconies next to one another on the sixth floor of a hotel on the edge of the sea, about a mile from the old town. The bar and the restaurant where we lunched every day were on a terrace opening onto the sea. As evening fell a taxi would take us to the gates of ancient Rhodes. We walked about the old streets, so beautiful and

---

* Dr. Lepresle had given Sartre leave to drink a little spirits.

so full of life. The joy of discovering new places with Sartre was one
that I had forgotten. We would stop in a little open-air café, shaded
by an enormous tree, of the kind one finds in Greek villages. Sometimes we ate a snack in a pleasant restaurant at the foot of the walls.
A taxi would take us back, and for an hour or two I would read aloud
to Sartre on my balcony. The weather was splendid, the sea dazzling;
the vast beach at our feet reminded me a little of Copacabana.

We made two excursions, both by taxi. The one to Lindos, a little
village with whitewashed streets, beautifully poised above the sea.
The place is particularly famous for its acropolis, but one had to ride
asses to get up to it, and we did not possess the energy. The other
expedition was to Kamiros, a large and fairly well-preserved ancient
town. On the way we saw a very beautiful monastery built on the
mountainside.

We returned to Athens and stayed there another ten days. The
weather was almost cool and walking was a pleasure. Sartre was still
capable of doing so; he even climbed up to the Acropolis. Sometimes
he had dinner with Melina, who never had any spare time during the
day. She would take him to a café where the Athenian intellectuals
gathered. When he came back, about eleven, he would have a glass of
whiskey in my room.

During this stay he gave two interviews, one to a left-wing daily
and the other to an anarchist bulletin.

At one point in the course of this summer Jullian sent Sartre a letter
in which he suggested putting on a "pilot-program," which was in-
sulting and absurd, since the series formed a whole which could not
be judged by a single fragment. On September 23, a few days after
having returned to Paris, Sartre, Victor, and I—Gavi was in the States
—met Jullian at Liliane Siegel's apartment. Sartre attacked him vig-
orously. He was no longer of an age to sit for examinations, he said.
But this suggested pilot-program was, in fact, an examination, one
that would be marked poor, average, or good. The only acceptable
judge would have been the public; yet it was not to the public that
this program was to be submitted but to "specialists." The question
of money that Jullian was trying to bring forward was not the real
question at all, since a budget of a million francs was usual for a
dramatic program lasting an hour and a half: many examples could be
cited. The truth of the matter was that the synopses had been laid on
the desk of Chirac, the prime minister, by André Vivien, a deputy
charged with relations with the O.R.T.F., who had been shown them

by Jullian. Since January, Vivien and Chirac had been radically opposed to our project, and Jullian, respectful of their authority, had merely been stringing us along. By the time everybody left, the break was complete.

On September 25 Sartre, accompanied by Victor and me, held a press conference at the Cour des Miracles. As soon as Jullian was told about this, on September 24, he telephoned Sartre to say that he would agree to four hundred million old francs.* Six months earlier there would still have been time enough to change the scenarios so as to diminish their cost;† now it was too late and Jullian knew it. He was only trying to prevent the whole thing from being made public. It *was* made public. There were a great many people at the Cour des Miracles. Sartre was in great form and he recounted the whole story, telling the exact truth and speaking in a wholly convincing manner. He had subtitled the press conference "A problem of television censorship." He observed, "It has been said 'Sartre is giving up.' No. I have been *made* to give up. It is a case of categorical indirect censorship." He stated that Jullian had promised him complete freedom of expression. When we put the first estimates to him he had said, "Even if it goes beyond eight hundred million [old francs] we'll still do it." Then he had had an altercation with the government on the subject, our synopses having inexplicably fallen into the hands of Chirac, who refused them. Then Jullian tried to win by wearing us down, and in the end he took refuge in the unacceptable suggestion of a pilot program. The journalists listened to this account with the utmost attention, and at the end some of them asked, "Why don't you work for foreign television?" Sartre replied, "This is the history of the French, and it's French people that I want to talk to." To another question, "Why not use the film distribution circuits?" he said, "Ten hours is a long time. Besides, this program was to be a dynamic approach on television for the first time. I suspected that it was not possible to work with this particular television network. Marcel Jullian had shaken my conviction. But now it's over. I won't appear on television again, either in France or elsewhere." Later he remarked, "For his part, Michel Droit had all possible freedom for his 1946 to 1970 chronicles."

On the whole, the papers gave an accurate account of this confer-

---

* About $600,000 at the time.
† A budget of a hundred million old francs had been foreseen for each part. The series of ten parts therefore came to a billion old francs. Jullian was offering less than half.

ence, and Jullian began a smear campaign against Sartre. At first he had acknowledged, "M. Sartre is not a money-grubber, but he wanted to have all possible means at his disposal to bring his dream into existence." In spite of this he later insinuated that Sartre wanted to earn enormous royalties, which was untrue, since these royalties were to be almost entirely shared among the many groups of historians. He also complained that Sartre left the undertaking to his young collaborators. This was equally false, for Sartre worked very hard within the "gang of four" and was present at all the general meetings. Lastly, the television people put out a rumor that echoed as far as Stockholm, whence a message was sent to the France-presse agency. According to this rumor Sartre was supposed to have asked for the money for the Nobel Prize for Literature, which he had refused in 1964. He sent the papers a very strong denial.

R.T.L.* suggested that Sartre should be interviewed on the *Journal inattendu* with Victor and me on October 5, 1975. He agreed and we prepared our pieces. But this whole business irritated him. In the course of the week Arlette told me on the telephone that he was extremely weary, and one evening, while with me, he found it really hard to speak; the corner of his mouth and the tip of his tongue were almost paralyzed. It was over in a quarter of an hour, but he told me that it often happened to him and I remained uneasy.

He had no life in him when we went to the R.T.L. studio, and he stumbled going upstairs. The journalist who received us was obviously hostile, and I felt tense. Sartre seemed harassed; he spoke slowly and with scarcely any variation of tone. I was horribly afraid that he might have a fit of abstraction during the program. In this emergency I took it upon myself to speak a good deal, even interrupting the R.T.L. man, to make our dealings with Jullian quite clear. And Cohn-Bendit, taking part by relay from Switzerland, spoke in a sharp and decisive manner. So on the whole this "journal inattendu" was a success.

From the studio we went to Liliane Siegel's apartment, where she had prepared a little buffet luncheon. Here we met a few of the historians, deeply disappointed over the break with Antenne 2. Toward five I took Sartre back to his own place and there he slept for a while. He admitted that he was tired out. "That makes more than five hours we've been working," he said in an exhausted voice. He spent the evening at Wanda's, and the next morning, on Sunday,

---

* Radio-Télévision Luxembourgeoise, an independent commercial station. (trans.)

October 5, Arlette called me. "It wasn't very serious," she said, "But even so . . ." Sartre had more or less fallen when he was at Wanda's. She had put him into a taxi; Michèle was waiting outside the Dôme to take him back to his apartment. Once there he had again lost his balance, and this occurred several times. She had driven him to Arlette's in the morning, and again he had fallen. On being called in, Zaidmann had given Sartre injections and prescribed a long rest in bed. I spoke to Sartre on the telephone; his voice was clear, but weary. He stayed to have lunch with Arlette, who took him home in a friend's car. They almost carried him up to his own apartment and there they put him to bed. I spent the afternoon with him, and Zaidmann came in the evening. Sartre's blood pressure had risen from 140 to 200. He had to be supported when he took the few steps from his room to the lavatory. I slept in the other bedroom with all doors open.

He stayed in bed on Monday and Tuesday. On Tuesday evening Dr. Lapresle came with Zaidmann. Sartre's blood-pressure was 215. They had a long conference. In addition to the usual medicines they prescribed a powerful tension reducer and Valium to help him smoke less. They advised him to get up and sit in an armchair, but to have a nap in the afternoons.

Life took on a pattern. Sartre ate his meals at home. On Sundays Sylvie took him his lunch, on Thursdays Liliane, on Mondays and Fridays Michèle, and Arlette the other days. As for dinner, I bought little things on those days when I stayed with him.

Zaidmann came again on the morning of Wednesday, October 15. The blood pressure had fallen to 160. He reduced the medications and told Sartre to go out a little, which he did. He looked almost as well as he had before his attack, but the medicines he had to take brought on his urinary incontinence again, and sometimes he even fouled his pyjamas at night. He looked upon these accidents with an indifference that I found hard to bear.

In spite of all this, he said, with an obstinate look, that he was going to go back to smoking. I protested strongly. If he became senile it would be I who suffered from it—he would not know what was going on. Did I persuade him? Or was he affected by an article Michèle read to him saying that in cases of arteritis, smoking might lead to the amputation of a leg? He almost stopped. He smoked no more than four cigarettes a day and sometimes he would forget the fourth.

There were times when he seemed to find his situation painful. One evening we agreed that one would not wish to live for a hundred years. "In any case," he observed, "I'm no longer anything but one of the extras." When I reminded him of the remark the next day, he told me why he had made it. He had been irritated because Gavi had dragged an interview on Spain out of him for *Libération*.

This interview appeared on October 28, 1975, while Franco was on his deathbed. Sartre spoke of his having "a Latin brute's abominable face." The expression had made many readers indignant. Sartre said "It was a mistake—words uttered in the heat of conversation acquire another meaning when they are literally transcribed—but it is a mistake I take upon myself entirely. Franco had the face he deserved; without any kind of doubt he was a brute, and no one will deny that he was a Latin."

His health was not improving and he realized it. "Physically I am not very well," he said to Liliane one morning, as he was having breakfast with her in a neighboring café, the Liberté. He complained that in the morning his mouth and above all his throat were half paralyzed, which explained why it was so hard for him to swallow. It took him at least an hour to get through a cup of tea or a glass of orange juice. His sugar level was what it ought to be, but his walking grew worse and worse. On Thursday, November 19, he had the greatest difficulty in reaching the Liberté, a hundred yards from his building, and then, at about two, in going to the Brazilian restaurant at the foot of the Tour Montparnasse, where we often had lunch. Zaidmann saw him the next day, and he found this regression disturbing. Dr. Lapresle came late in the afternoon; he thought Sartre better than the last time he had seen him, and even, on the whole, in good health. But as far as his motor activities (walking, swallowing) were concerned, he told me that "Sartre had moved down to a level from which he would never rise again." I remembered him, two months earlier, climbing the Acropolis; and I wondered whether the day would come when he could no longer move at all. And then, as he was in poor control of his reflexes, there was another accident with his bowels. It is horrible, your body betraying you while your mind is still sound.

For intellectually, Sartre had recovered entirely. "The great thing is to work," he said, "and fortunately my head's all right." He also said to me "I'm more intelligent than I have been for a long while." That was true. He worked steadily with Victor on their planned book, *Pouvoir et liberté* (Power and Freedom); he took a lively interest in the works I read him and in everything that was going on in the world, particularly the Goldman case,* which he knew in its smallest details. In the middle of November, when we thought that Goldman's appeal would be rejected, Sartre, with Victor's help, drew up a letter of protest for *Le Monde*. He did not publish it because the judgment condemning Goldman was quashed, to the great joy of all his friends.

Thanks to all his activities, Sartre was once more happy to be alive. One morning Liliane asked him, "It doesn't bother you much, being dependent on others?" He smiled. "No. There's even something rather agreeable about it." "Being coddled?" "Yes." "Because you feel we love you?" "Oh, I knew that already. But it's pleasant." On November 10 the European edition of *Newsweek* published an interview Sartre had given Jane Friedman. She asked him, "What is the most important thing in your life at present?" He replied, "I don't know. Everything. Living. Smoking." He was fully conscious of the beauty of this blue and golden fall, and he rejoiced in it.

Sartre was often asked to sign manifestoes and appeals, and he usually agreed. Together with Malraux, Mendès France, Aragon, and Francois Jacob, he signed an appeal to prevent the execution of eleven men condemned to death in Spain.† When they were executed he signed a protest and an appeal for a march on Spain. With Mitterand, Mendès France, and Malraux he protested against the United Nations' resolution likening Zionism to racism (in *Le Nouvel Observateur* of November 17). He signed an appeal in favor of imprisoned soldiers which was read at the Mutualité on December 15.

He had a new distraction. Arlette had rented a television set for him, and when there was a good Western or an entertaining film of any kind we watched it. By sitting very close to the screen Sartre could make out the picture pretty well. One Monday morning I went with him to see an excellent Greek film, *Le Voyage des comédiens*. The manager had put the theater at our disposal; only a few friends were there, so I could read Sartre the subtitles without bothering anyone.

On December 1 Sartre received a threatening letter signed G.I.N. . . . Gisèle Halimi asserted that it was to be taken seriously, the

---

* Goldman was a leftist who was accused and convicted of the holdup and murder of a pharmacist; on appeal he was cleared of the murder conviction but not of that for the holdup. During his incarceration he wrote a book, *Souvenirs d'un juif obscur*. He was subsequently assassinated, and his murderers were never apprehended. Goldman was a member of the staff of *Les Temps modernes*.

† This appeal, published in *Le Nouvel Observateur* on September 29, was carried straight to Madrid by Foucault, Régis Debray, Claude Mauriac, Yves Montand . . .

G.I.N. being an extreme right-wing group that boasted of having blown up Photo-Libération. She warned the neighboring police station and I had an armored door installed. I was really uneasy, but Sartre took little notice of it. His serenity never failed. "I've had an excellent three months," he told me, looking radiant, at the end of December. And when at the beginning of the year he was asked what people should wish him, he replied eagerly, "A long life."

Together with Sylvie we made a brief journey to Geneva which thoroughly entertained Sartre, in spite of the snow and the cold. We walked about the old town; we saw Coppet and visited Lausanne. Back in Paris, Sartre returned to his work with Victor. He even began writing again. It was an illegible scrawl, but Victor managed to make it out more or less. Sartre wrote on the limits of his adherence to his own values. "I don't *believe* in what I've written," he told me. But then he perceived that he was criticizing himself on the basis of *Being and Nothingness* and the *Critique,* thus proving that he did believe in it.

1976

At the beginning of March Sartre dictated an article on Pasolini to me. He had met him in Rome and he liked some of his films, particularly the first part of *Medea,* which he considered an extraordinary evocation of the *holy*. In this article he reflected upon the circumstances of Pasolini's death. He first wrote it in his illegible hand and then recited it to me by heart. It was a good article, and it appeared in the *Corriere della Sera* of March 14, 1976. He was pleased with having managed to produce it in less than three hours. Like me, Victor thought that Sartre had not been in such good form intellectually for a long while. To be sure, sometimes his light seemed to have gone out, but that was when the gathering was too large or when people bored him. He could be full of life and immediately present, as he was during the evening we spent with Alice Schwarzer, for example. It is also true that although he could listen, reply, and discuss, he was no longer inventive. There was a kind of emptiness within him, and that is why eating and drinking took on a much greater importance for him than they had had in earlier days. He found it hard to adapt himself, to new things. And he found being contradicted very hard to bear. I almost never did it, although he made enormous blunders about what had happened in the past.

On March 20 we set off with Sylvie for Venice, a city that the three of us never tired of. Taking very short steps, Sartre went for quite long walks with me. "Doesn't it bore you, being with a little creature who walks so slowly?" he once asked me. Quite sincerely, I said no. The fact that he could walk at all was already enough to make me happy. Sometimes in a melancholy voice he would still say, "I shall never get my eyes back." And it made him sad when a passenger in a vaporetto took his arm to help him get out at the stopping place. "Do I really look like a cripple?" he asked me. "You look as though you see badly," I said, "There's nothing to be ashamed of in that!" But these clouds soon vanished. As I was suffering from a kind of neuralgia in my right arm, I said to him, "Well, what of it? It's old age. One always has one damned thing or another." "Not, me," he said with conviction. "There's nothing wrong with me." That made me laugh, and after a moment's thought he laughed too. But on the spur of the moment he had felt that he was quite undamaged. He was much better adapted to his state than he had been the year before.

Back in Paris once more, he carried on his work with Victor. It was a beautiful spring—sun, greenery, flowers in his garden, and birds singing. Reading, music, and films filled our afternoons and evenings. At the beginning of the year *Life Situations* had come out. It brought together four political essays, a talk on *The Family Idiot,* the talk with me on feminism, and the long interview he had given Contat, "Self-Portrait at Seventy." Gallimard republished *Being and Nothingness* in the collection "Tel" and *Situations I* in the series "Idées." A translation of the *Critique of Dialectical Reason* appeared in London (it had been translated into German in 1967). Sartre's interviews on the Australian radio—on Marxism, on Laing, and on the role of the intellectual—were collected in a volume that was published in New York. On May 1 he gave an interview for the press book of the film, *Sartre by Himself* and in it he spoke of his differences with French television. In June he published a letter in *Libération* about the Larzac: he was sorry that he had not been able to be present at the meetings on the Larzac at Whitsun. In the same month *Le Nouvel Observateur* brought out a short piece that he had written on workers' safety in large concerns.

He also signed a manifesto of solidarity with the Marge group, which had occupied an annex of the Soviet embassy on January 20. In the *Libération* of January 28 he signed an appeal to the President of the Republic in favor of Jean Papinski, a primary-school teacher provisionally attached to a secondary school. In 1966, while Papinski was teaching a class in English, an inspector appeared; the inspector did not know English but he nevertheless made an unfavorable report that caused Papinski to be sent back to primary-school teaching. Papinski asked for redress; he did not obtain it. In 1974 he published a pamphlet entitled *Boui-Boui* in which he attacked the inspectors, the juries, and unfair promotion. His name was struck off the roll of teachers for life and he began a hunger strike (it was to last for ninety days).

In *Libération* on February 17 and *Le Monde* on February 18, Sartre, fifty Nobel prizewinners, and I signed an appeal for the liberation of Dr. Mikhaïl Stern. Together we conducted a campaign in his favor and in the end we won. On May 12 Sartre and some other intellectuals signed a communiqué in which they expressed their horror at the death of Ulrike Meinhof in a German prison.

That year, after a month's separation, which Sartre spent at Junas with Arlette and then in Venice with Wanda while I traveled in Spain with Sylvie once more, we all three, Sartre, Sylvie, and I, went to Capri. We stayed at the Hotel Quisisana and we spent nearly three weeks there very happily—Capri was a place that Sartre loved above all others. Early every afternoon we went to have a drink at the Salotto. Sartre even went for two long walks in the part of the island where cars are forbidden; he rested on a bench now and then, but his legs did not hurt him. He liked sitting in the sun as we lunched in an open-air restaurant. From his window he was aware of the beauty of the landscape running gently down to the blue of the sea.

We drove back to Rome—we had left the car in a garage in Naples —and returned to our customary terrace apartment. Sylvie left us the next day, and Sartre and I stayed on alone for a fortnight. It was the same pleasant routine as in other years. Part of the Pantheon square and the nearby streets were now reserved for pedestrians and we often walked there. We lunched in the Piazza Navona with Basso and his wife. Josée Dayan and Malka Ribowska, whom we had met by chance in Venice and whom I had seen since, came to talk to me about the adaptation of *The Woman Destroyed* for television. Sartre liked them and we had dinner together. At the end of our stay the Bosts came to see us and accompanied us to the airport, where we took off for Greece.

Sartre had in fact promised Melina to come to Athens to see her; we stayed there a week. He spent the days with me, the evenings with her. We could not get rooms in the hotel we liked, and those in which we did stay, next door, were utterly dismal. Although there was a dazzling sun, we had to have the lights on from morning till night. Fortunately, I had work to do. I went over the adaptation and wrote dialogues for *The Woman Destroyed*.

Paris once more in mid-September, and life began again in much the same way as the year before, apart from a few changes of timetable. Until mid-October the weather was magnificent, and this tended to make us feel optimistic. Furthermore, Sartre was very fit indeed and things were going well for him. He had given up attending the *Temps modernes* meetings, but he was working with Victor with great zest, and on all sides people were perpetually asking him to do things. In October he took part in a meeting in favor of the Soviet political prisoners and called for the liberation of Kuznetsov. Together with Le Bris and Le Dantec, he signed a foreword to Bommi Bauman's* book, *Tupamaros Berlin-Ouest,* which came out in the "France sauvage" series. This was the autobiography of a former German terrorist and the German police had seized it in 1975; Sartre had joined Heinrich Böll in calling for its republication. And now it was being brought out in French. "Bommi Bauman's tenets are not necessarily ours," wrote Sartre, "but they directly challenge untamed France."†

In September *Dirty Hands* was put on again at the Théâtre des Mathurins. There were a hundred and fifty performances, followed by a tour in the provinces. The reviews, apart from that of Marcabru, were excellent. The film, *Sartre by Himself,* came out at the end of October. Once again the critics praised Sartre enthusiastically and the public flocked to see it. *Le Magazine littéraire* published a long and very interesting conversation between Sartre and Michel Sicard on the subject of *The Family Idiot.*‡ Two issues of *Politique-Hebdo* were devoted to him; they contained articles by Châtelet, Horst, and Victor.

"What a splendid comeback!" I said. "A funerary comeback," he replied, but he laughed as he did so. In fact he was quite delighted. Sartre was much too proud ever to have indulged in vanity. Like all writers he was concerned for the success of his work and its influence.

---

* As I have said, he acted as Sartre's chauffeur at the time of his visit to Baader.
† This "untamed [or wild or unregimented] France" is of course the publisher's *France sauvage.* (trans.)
‡ A young teacher of philosophy who knew Sartre's work very well.

But for him, the past was left behind at once, and it was on the future that he staked everything—his next book, his next play. He now no longer expected much from the future. Yet he certainly did not brood anxiously over his past. Several times he repeated that he had done what he had to do and he was satisfied. But he would not have liked to feel cast aside and forgotten, even if it were only for a while. Since he was no longer able to engage in fresh plans with all his old energy, he and what he had already accomplished coincided. He looked upon his work as finished; it was by means of it that he could be known as he wished to be known.

On Sunday, November 7, at the Israeli embassy, he received the University of Jerusalem's degree of doctor honoris causa. In his speech (carefully prepared and memorized) he stated that he accepted the degree in order to promote the dialogue between Israel and the Palestinians. "I have been Israel's friend for a long while. Here I am concerned with Israel, but I am also concerned with the Palestinian people, who have suffered a great deal." The speech appeared in *Les Cahiers Bernard Lazare*. Soon after this Sartre gave Edith Sorel an interview which appeared in *La Tribune juive* at the end of November. *
He said that he would not write *Anti-Semite and Jew* in quite the same way at present. He spoke of his travels in Egypt and in Israel in 1967 and said that if the University of Cairo offered him a degree he would accept it.

In November the *New Left Review* began the publication of a long section of Volume II of the *Critique of Dialectical Reason*. In this Sartre reflected upon Soviet society and upon "socialism in a single country." These pages were more philosophical than historical and they were therefore a prolongation of Volume I, since the second was intended to move on to the subject of concrete history.

In the *Libération* of November 12 he published a letter supporting the five Corsicans detained in Lyons. On December 13, in an interview he gave *Politique-Hebdo,* he denounced the danger arising from the German-American hegemony in Europe. He then took part in the activities of the *Comité d'action contre l'Europe germano-américaine,* in which one of the moving spirts was J.-P. Vigier.

Melina came to spend a week in Paris and he saw a great deal of her. He enjoyed seeing her much less than he had in Athens, finding her "empty," but he still felt affection for her.

* The former wife of René Depestre. We had met her in Cuba.

The *Temps modernes* committee was much diminished. Bost, who could not hear well, no longer came, and all Lanzmann's time was eaten up by the film he was making on the holocaust. It seemed to us that we should co-opt some new members. We chose Pierre Victor, thanks to whom Sartre had started to come to the meetings again; François George, who had often contributed to the magazine; Rigoulot, a young teacher of philosophy who had also contributed and who had written a letter that touched us deeply; and Pierre Goldman, for whom we all had the greatest esteem. He came to see Sartre one evening with Lanzmann, and at once I felt a great liking for him; so did Sartre, but as it often happened if unknown people were present, he did not utter a word. When he and I were alone again he spoke of it with concern. I comforted him as well as I could. On the other hand, when Horst and his wife came to have a drink with us another evening, he was very much alive, because he was so used to them.

1977

On the whole he was remarkably well. No further trouble with his health. He did have difficulty in walking, and he smoked far too much for there to be any hope of an improvement; he also found it hard to swallow. But his mood was excellent. "At present I am thoroughly happy," he told me. Although he thought his "comeback" funerary, the articles about him gave him great pleasure. His intelligence was intact. If he had been able to read, and to reread his own writing, I am sure that he would have produced new ideas. For the moment he was working with Victor on a dialogue about the meaning of their collaboration and the reasons for it, a dialogue that appeared in the *Libération* of January 6, 1977.

He stated that the new form of his future book, *Pouvoir et liberté* (Power and Freedom), was due not only to his disabilities; it was due also to the fact that he very earnestly wished that a *we* should be apparent in it. For him this book was "the ethics and the politics that I should like to have finished at the end of my life." The prospect of its being a joint thought made him hesitate, because he still believed that one could think only by oneself, alone. But he hoped to attain a thought by the *we:* "It would call for a thought that is genuinely formed by you and by me at the same time, in the act of thinking, together with the changes in each of us that the other's thought brings about; and we should have to attain a thought that would be ours, that is, a thought in which you recognize yourself but at the same time recognize me and I recognize myself in recognizing you. . . .

"Yet after all, mine is a curious situation; broadly speaking, I've finished my literary career. The book that we are now working on is a book beyond the things that have been written. It's not altogether a living man, an older living man, who would be talking with you. I'm somewhat detached from my works. . . . With you I should like . . . to produce a work that is beyond my own works.

"I am not dead in fact; I eat and I drink. But I am dead in that my literary work is finished. . . . My relations with everything I've written hitherto are no longer the same—I work with you; you have ideas that are not mine and that will make me go in certain directions that I used not to take, so that I produce something new; I produce it as a last work and at the same time as a work set apart, not belonging to the whole, though naturally possessing some characteristics in common with it—the comprehension of freedom, for example."

Obviously, the ambiguity of the situation worried Sartre, but he tried to make the best of it: that is, he succeeded in convincing himself that it had positive aspects for him.

Meanwhile, he had become almost incapable of walking. He had pains in his left leg—calf, thigh, ankle. And he was unsteady on his feet. Dr. Lapresle assured us that his vascular troubles had grown no worse and that this was only sciatica. Sartre stayed in his room for two weeks, but at the end of that time he was no better. His leg hurt him in the night, and his foot during the day. Until December he had reached the nearby Brazilian restaurant quite easily; now in January he had to stop three times on the way, and he would arrive out of breath and in pain.

When either Arlette or I spent the evening with Sartre, we slept there. But on Saturdays Wanda was with him until eleven o'clock, and it was awkward both for Arlette and for me to go to his place so late at night. Michèle suggested that she should come after Wanda left and spend the night in the room next door. This arrangement suited everybody and we kept to it for a long while.

But one Sunday, when Sartre was having lunch with Sylvie and me at La Palette, we thought he appeared strange—half asleep. About nine that evening he felt so ill that I called a doctor, dialing S.O.S.: his blood pressure was 250. After an injection it dropped to 140. This sudden drop made him feel poorly the next day. Dr. Cournot came, and as Liliane was there he took her aside and asked, "Had he been drinking?" She said yes. She had not liked to let me know, but Sartre had told her that when Michèle was with him on Saturday evening, he had drunk half a bottle of whiskey. He admitted it to me as well. I telephoned Michèle, telling her why she was no longer to come to Sartre's on Saturdays. Some days later she said to him, "I wanted to help you die cheerfully. I thought that was what you wanted." But he did not want to die at all. From this time on, when I left him on Saturday evening I poured him out a ration of whiskey and hid the bottle. After Wanda had gone he would drink and smoke for a little while and then go quietly to bed.

At the beginning of January we had a splendid feastlike luncheon at Sylvie's home. Gallimard brought out the full text of the film, *Sartre by Himself,* with great success. He gave Catherine Chaine an interview on his relationship with women, and it appeared in *Le Nouvel Observateur* for January 31. He attended the *Temps modernes* assemblies, which now met two Wednesday mornings a month in his apartment, and took part in the discussions. Carried away by his habit of always saying yes, he agreed to sign an article that appeared in *Le Monde* on April 10, 1977, and that was in fact written by Vigier after a talk with him. In this he stated that "since its reestablishment in 1945, German social-democracy had been one of the most highly valued instruments of American imperialism in Europe," and he called upon militant socialists "to fight against German-American hegemony" by setting themselves against a certain way of building Europe. The style did not resemble Sartre's in the least, and an appeal to the socialists was very surprising, coming from him. Lanzmann, Pouillon, Victor, and others did not hide their disapproval.

He had promised Melina to go and give a lecture in the middle of February at the University of Athens, where she worked. He and Pierre Victor left by plane on Wednesday, February 16, and he stayed there a week, lunching with Victor, dining with Melina, mentally preparing his lecture. The subject was "What is philosophy?" and he presented it on Tuesday the twenty-second before fifteen hundred people in a hall meant for eight hundred. He spoke for about an hour and was thunderously applauded. Victor thought the lecture somewhat "facile," but since most of the students had a poor understanding of French, he admitted that it would have been pointless to attempt difficult concepts. I went to pick them up next day at the Orly airport. As I watched the passengers filing past, one of them told me in a reassuring tone, "They're coming." And indeed, there they were, the very last to appear, Sartre rather tired after his long walk from the plane, but delighted with his journey.

On March 9 Melina came to Paris. The next morning before nine she telephoned me in a panic. Sartre had taken her to dine at the Brazilian restaurant. On the way back his legs had given way under him, and twice he had nearly fallen; neighbors had practically carried him to the elevator. He was deathly pale, sweating, and out of breath. I telephoned Zaidmann and hurried over to Sartre's.* His blood pressure was 220. Melina assured me that he had not drunk too much, and I knew that from that point of view she always kept a close watch on him. Anyway his head was perfectly clear. I spent the afternoon with him. Dr. Cournot came that evening and spoke of a spasm in one leg. The next day Arlette called me to say that Sartre had fallen several times, particularly when going to bed.

Dr. Cournot returned. Although Sartre's blood pressure had gone down a great deal, Cournot asked him to go to the Broussais Hospital for a checkup. I slept at his apartment, as I did every Tuesday, and at half past eight in the morning Liliane came to fetch us. We helped Sartre cross the garden and go down in the elevator to the car. He could scarcely walk. At the hospital a male nurse took him away in a wheelchair. The doctors decided to keep him until the next afternoon. I stayed in his room and attended to the formalities of signing him in while he underwent a number of examinations. He was brought lunch and ate most of it. His blood pressure was good on the right-hand side, less so on the left; a very marked asymmetry. I stayed until half past three, sitting by Sartre and reading while he slept, until Arlette came.

I went back to the hospital the next morning. Sartre had had dinner, had watched a little television, and had slept well. They were now carrying out a long X-ray examination—thorax, legs, hands, and so on. They brought him back to his bed and Dr. Housset appeared. He spoke forcibly. Sartre could save his legs only by giving up tobacco. If he did not smoke anymore, his state could be much improved

---

* Dr. Zaidmann will no longer appear in this account. He suddenly collapsed in the Rue Delambre, struck down by a heart attack.

and he could be assured of a quiet old age and a normal death. Otherwise his toes would have to be cut off, then his feet, and then his legs. Sartre seemed impressed. Liliane and I took him home without too much difficulty. As for tobacco, he said he wanted to think it over. He saw Melina and Arlette and then the next day Pierre and Michèle. When I arrived late in the afternoon he was walking a little better. But the day after that, in the evening, he told me that his leg hurt every night for about an hour.

On Sunday Sylvie, he, and I went to see our friend Tomiko in her beautiful house at Versailles. We ate a stuffed duck and drank some excellent wine. As we drove back, Sylvie, who was a little tipsy, made ardent declarations to Sartre, who was delighted. (She was not always kind to him. She would not have it that he was ill, and some aspects of his behavior irritated her, while he would blame her for what he called her "ill temper." But none of this affected their relations in any way.)

We spent the evening reading and talking. He had made up his mind to stop smoking the next day, Monday. I said, "Doesn't it make you sad to think you're smoking your last cigarette?" "No. To tell you the truth I find them rather disgusting now." No doubt he associated them with the idea of being cut to pieces little by little. The next day he handed me his cigarettes and lighters to give to Sylvie. And that evening he told me that he was in an astonishingly good mood *because* he had stopped smoking. It was a final renunciation and he never seemed to find it burdensome. He was not affected even when his friends smoked in front of him—indeed, he even encouraged them to do so.

The following Thursday Liliane and I took him to a private consultation with Dr. Housset. The doctor looked through an immense file devoted to Sartre, congratulated him on having given up tobacco, and prescribed a series of intravenous injections. If he felt the slightest cramp, Sartre was to stop walking; otherwise there was the danger of a heart attack or a stroke. He strongly advised against the brief journey to Junas that Sartre had planned, and he handed us a thick envelope that I was to give Dr. Cournot. We took Sartre home, and as soon as we reached my apartment, Liliane and I steamed Housset's letter open. It was a highly detailed summary, little of which we understood. Liliane kept it to show one of her friends, a medical woman.

She telephoned me the next day. The friend thought the summary very disturbing—only 30 percent circulation in the legs. "With care he may live a few years more," she had said. A *few* years! For me, the word took on a tragic meaning. I was quite aware that Sartre would not live very much longer, but so vague was the period that lay between me and his end that it seemed far off. All at once it grew near. Five years? Seven years? In any event, a finite, definite time. Death, the inescapable, was already there and it had taken possession of Sartre. My general, unfocused anxiety gave way to a fundamental despair.

I tried to face up to it. I took the resealed letter back to Sartre's apartment, where in any case Dr. Cournot left it open on the table. He advised Sartre to walk very little during the next couple of weeks. We were about to leave for Venice, and I persuaded Sartre to order a wheelchair at the airport.

In Venice we had the same rooms that we had had in other years and Sartre was very pleased to be there again. But he rarely left the hotel. Every time we went to one of the restaurants he liked it was a laborious expedition. He found it hard to go even as far as Saint Mark's Square. Since the weather was damp and rather showery he could hardly ever sit on the café terraces. Still, when it was fine we lunched on the one belonging to the hotel, which overlooked the Grand Canal. Otherwise we crossed the street and sat at a table in Harry's Bar. For dinner we had a sandwich in the bar of the hotel. He spent most of the time in his room, where I read to him. When he slept in the afternoon or when he was listening to music on his transistor, I went out with Sylvie. Still, when we were leaving he told me that he was very pleased with his stay.

For a few days after our return to Paris Sartre saw a great deal of Melina. He liked her again. "When I'm with her, I feel as though I were thirty-five," he told me. Liliane, who had often seen them together, told me that he did indeed grow younger in her company. So much the better: there were so few cheerful things left in his life! Once again his legs were giving him a great deal of pain. One morning as he was getting up his right foot hurt him so much that he said, "I can see that they cut your feet off." Aspirin soothed his pain a little. Fresh injections took it away altogether. But it was still very hard for him to walk. When he was alone with me he was open and full of life. But when other people were there he often became withdrawn, closed in upon himself. Even with Bost one evening he did not say a word. Bost, overwhelmed, said to me, "How can one accept that such a thing should happen to *him*?"

It was precisely to him, I thought, that it had to happen. As far as he himself was concerned he had always carried out the policy of full employment, with no time off. If he felt tired, hesitant, or sleepy, he stuffed himself with Corydrane. An inborn, constitutional narrowness of his arteries did predispose him to the disease that struck him, but the least one can say is that he did nothing to avert it. He played ducks and drakes with his "capital of health." And he knew it, since he said in effect "I should rather die a little earlier and have written the *Critique of Dialectical Reason.*" Indeed, I have wondered whether, under the influence of Groddeck's books, he may not, more or less consciously, have chosen his condition. He did not really *want* to write the last volume of the Flaubert, but having no other plan for the time being, he would not renounce it either. What was to be done about it? For my part, I can put myself out to grass without life losing all its meaning. Sartre, no. He liked living—indeed, he loved it— but on condition of being able to work. As the reader will have seen in the course of this narrative, work was an obsession with him. When he found that he was incapable of carrying through what he had undertaken, he overdid the stimulants, and he so increased his activities and exceeded his strength that he made a stroke inevitable. One of the consequences that he had not foreseen and that horrified him was his near-blindness. But he had wanted to grant himself a rest, and for him, illness was the only way out.

At present I no longer fully believe this hypothesis—too optimistic a hypothesis in one way, since it makes Sartre the master of his fate. What is certain is that the tragedy of his last years was the consequence of his life as a whole. It is to him that one can apply Rilke's words: "Every man bears his death within himself, as the fruit bears its stone." Sartre's decline and death were those that his life had called for. And perhaps that is why he accepted them so serenely.

I have no illusions; this serenity of mind was obscured at times. More and more often he felt the need for a glass of spirits. Just before the vacation I asked Victor what he thought of Sartre's health. "He's getting worse," Victor replied. At the end of each conversation, Sartre angrily insisted on whiskey.

Yet he was full of smiles on that June 21, 1977, his seventy-second birthday, when together with many other intellectuals he welcomed the dissidents of Eastern Europe at the Théâtre Récamier. At the same moment Giscard was receiving Brezhnev at the Elysée. He sat next to Dr. Mikhail Stern, to whose liberation Sartre and I had contributed and who thanked him very heartily. Sartre had brief conversations with the other people present.

In this year, as in others, he signed many documents, all of which appeared in *Le Monde:* on January 9 an appeal in favor of *Politique-Hebdo*, which was in difficulties; on January 23 an appeal against the repression in Morocco; on March 22 a letter to the president of the court at Laval in support of Yvan Pineau, charged with having refused his military papers; on March 26 a protest against the arrest of a singer in Nigeria; on March 27 an appeal for civil liberties in the Argentine; on June 29 a petition addressed to the Belgrade conference against repression in Italy; and on July 1 a protest against the worsening of the political situation in Brazil.

In a different vein a conversation between Sartre and the musicologist, Lucien Malson, appeared on July 28. In this Sartre spoke about his musical tastes and deplored the new turning that France-Musique had taken. The director of the channel replied to his criticisms in the number dated August 7/8.

At the beginning of July Sartre set off by car for Junas with Arlette, Puig, and one of Puig's friends—a young woman Sartre liked very much. By the way of the usual relays he went to Venice with Wanda, and there he spent two weeks.* I often telephoned him, and he seemed well. But I was still overwhelmed by the verdict pronounced by Liliane's friend: *a few years to live.* As I traveled about Austria with Sylvie, her presence and my interest in the landscapes, towns, and museums helped me to get the better of my distress. But in the evenings, although I tried to bear up against it, I fell to pieces. I had taken a tube of Valium from Sartre's apartment; now I swallowed the pills in the vain hope of calming my mind, and I drank exaggerated quantities of whiskey. As a result my legs gave way and I staggered. Once I nearly fell into a lake and another time, reaching the hotel hall, I collapsed into an armchair and the proprietress gave me a very queer look indeed. Fortunately, I rallied in the mornings and we spent some lovely days.

We went down to Venice and Sylvie waited for me with the car in the Piazzale Roma while I took a motorboat to Sartre's hotel. As usual it was something of a shock, meeting him in the hall—his dark glasses, his awkward way of moving. We and Sylvie drove off under a

---

* Ever since he could no longer see, Liliane used to meet his plane when it reached Nimes; the next day Bost came for him at her house and drove him and Wanda to the airport, where they left for Italy.

magnificent sky. We stopped at Florence, where I had reserved rooms at the Excelsior, rooms flanked by terraces from which one could see the whole city. As we drank our cocktails in the bar, Sartre fairly beamed with pleasure, as he had so often done in former times.

At about two the next day we reached Rome, a deserted Rome. Unhappily, we no longer had our terrace apartment, which had been let to an American for the whole year. But I liked our new quarters— two bedrooms separated by a minute drawing room in which there purred a refrigerator. This too was on the fifth floor, and we had a magnificent view of Saint Peter's and saw fabulous sunsets.

I thought Sartre perfectly well (apart from his legs; he could scarcely walk) during the thirty-five days we spent together, at first with Sylvie, and then alone. He discussed the books I read aloud to him with great acuity—particularly those written by Soviet dissidents. Although Bost was inclined to be pessimistic where Sartre was concerned, he was astonished by his vitality when he and Olga came to see us. The day after Sylvie left, a little café opened ten yards from our hotel, where there had been a garage. Every day we had lunch on its terrace, eating a sandwich or an omelette. And sometimes in the evening, coming back from the restaurant where we had dined, having driven there in a taxi, we would stop and have a drink before going up to our rooms. It was there that we usually arranged to meet people.

In Rome that summer there was a great deal of nervous excitement in the air. A student had been killed at Bologna, whose mayor was a Communist. An enormous leftist demonstration was to be held there on September 23 to 25. Sartre, as I have said, had signed a manifesto against the repression in Italy. By doing so he had raised a storm in the Italian press, especially in the Communist press. *Lotta continua,* an extreme left-wing paper with which *Les Temps modernes* had excellent relations, asked Sartre for an interview on the question. M.-A. Macciocchi urged him to support the Bologna meetings. Rossana Rossanda begged him not to do so; she foresaw disaster. On September 15 and in the little café I have just spoken about, Sartre met several of the chief men of *Lotta continua.* They published the interview in four pages of their issue of September 19 under the heading *Libertá e potere non vanno in coppia.* Sartre set out his ideas on the Italian Communist party, the historic compromise, the Baader-Meinhoff band, the Eastern-European dissidents, the intellectuals' role with regard to the state and the parties, the new philosophers, and Marxism. He said, "Every time the state police fire on a young militant, I am on the young militant's side." He asserted his solidarity with the young, but hoped there would be no violence at Bologna. His words satisfied everybody, including Rossana Rossanda.

Sartre had indeed spoken very well. And in our own conversations too, I found him his old self entirely. We talked about our life, about our age, about everything and nothing.

He had grown older, certainly, but he was truly himself.

His heart had its whims. He no longer wanted Melina to come and see him in Rome or us to go to Athens as had been suggested. He said he would give her the money to live in Paris this year since he had promised it, but that he would not see her anymore. "She is too self-seeking; she's not worthwhile. She no longer means anything to me."

She reached Paris a little after our return. "I still have a good deal of affection for you," Sartre told her, "but I don't love you anymore." She wept a little. And he saw something of her from time to time.

There were many women in his immediate circle, old friends and newcomers. In a delighted tone he said to me, "I've never been so surrounded by women!" He did not seem at all unhappy. "Yes," he said, when I questioned him, "the world has a dimension of unhappiness now, but I am not unhappy." He was sorry that his sight was so bad, and above all that he could not see faces; but he felt thoroughly alive. His readings with Victor interested him; the television amused him; and at the *Temps modernes* meetings he took a much greater part in the discussions that he had in other years.

He also paid great attention to political events, especially to the case of Klaus Croissant, Baader's lawyer. On July 1 he signed an appeal against his extradition, and on October 11, together with the Committee against a German-American Europe, a fresh protest. On November 18 this same committee issued a communiqué on the Schleyer affair. On October 28 he, P. H. Halbwachs, Daniel Guérin, and I signed a warning against the use of force in connection with the Polisario Front. On October 30 he sent the Iranian intellectuals who were opposed to the régime a telegram of support. On December 10 he signed an appeal against the expulsion of the painter, Antonio Saura.

At the end of November he dictated to me a very happily conceived little preface to the American edition of his plays, taking an hour over it.

The T.E.P. intended to stage *Nekrassov* again; it had not been acted in Paris since it was first produced in 1955. In October Sartre had a talk about the play with Georges Werler, André Aquart, and Maurice Delarue, and in December he made a statement on the subject. He emphasized that his real purpose had been to denounce the behavior of the sensational press. "I would no doubt choose another pretext today," he said, "but just as I did before, I would willingly attack a certain kind of journalism that does not hesitate to abuse its readers' trust by fabricating completely untrue scandals." When some people criticized him for having allowed this revival, he replied that all his plays, including *Dirty Hands,* now belonged to the theater's repertory, and that he no longer saw any reason for stopping the production.

While we are on this subject, I should like to speak of the extraordinary misconception that attributed the slogan "Do not drive Billancourt to despair" to Sartre.* As his opponents saw it, out of loyalty to the Communist party (to which he did not belong) he had seen fit to remain silent about certain embarrassing truths: this he never did. He and Merleau-Ponty were the first to expose the existence of the Soviet camps in *Les Temps modernes.* And this integrity remained unaltered in later days. One has but to reread the play. Valéra, a swindler who passes himself off as Nekrassov, a Soviet minister who has "chosen freedom," is paid by the right-wing press to make revelations about the USSR, about which he knows nothing whatsoever. Véronique, a young left-wing militant, tells him that although he thinks he is deceiving the rich, he is in fact playing their game and that he will "drive the poor to despair," especially those of Billancourt. Valéra is apolitical, unscrupulous, and greedy for money. In a derisive tone he cries "By all means let's drive Billancourt to despair!" Neither of them speaks for Sartre.

The first performance was in February 1978. Maurice Delarue, who had been one of Dullin's pupils, came to Sartre's apartment to fetch him and Olga (a former comrade) and Bost and me. He drove us to the theater. Sartre liked the production and the acting. When the curtain came down we went to the green room, where he warmly congratulated Werler and the players.

Ever since his 1967 journeys in Egypt and Israel, Sartre had been particularly interested in the problems of the Middle East. Sadat's visit to Israel stirred him deeply. He wrote a short, striking article to encourage negotiations between Egypt and Israel; it appeared in *Le Monde* of December 4/5.

* Carefully kept up by Jean Dutourd and several other journalists.

Sylvie, he, and I ended the year very cheerfully, eating turkey at Dominique's. Sartre was satisfied with his work and his way of life. "All in all, we have had a good time since we came back to Paris," he said to me.

1978

He still saw many young women—Melina and several others. One day, when he was complaining of working too little with Victor, I said to him, with a laugh, "Too many young ladies!" "But it's useful to me," he replied. And indeed I believe that it was largely to them that he owed his taste for life. With a naive self-satisfaction he told me, "I've never been so popular with women before."

Other factors kept up his optimism. Liliane Siegel collected a number of photographs of him; I wrote brief commentaries on them, and they were published as an album by Gallimard. Michel Sicard was preparing an important issue about Sartre for the magazine *Obliques*, and they often discussed it together. Jeannette Colombel and many young people came to see him to talk about the works they were devoting to his philosophy. Gallimard was going to bring out all his novels in the *Pléiade* collection, prefaced by Michel Contat. The "comeback" was continuing, and he appreciated it very much indeed.

Yet he did have one grave anxiety: money. Ever since I had known him he had been unfailingly prodigal, and in the course of his life he had given away everything he earned to various people. At this point he was regularly paying out quite large sums every month to different recipients. His allowance from Gallimard was swallowed up at once; he had almost nothing left for his own needs. If I asked him to buy himself a new pair of shoes, he would reply, "I haven't the money." It was difficult to make him accept them as a gift. And he owed his publisher a sum he considered important. This position bred a positive anxiety in him, not for himself, but for all those who depended on him.

Since he wanted to see the results of Sadat's visit close at hand, he went to Jerusalem in February, accompanied by Victor and Arlette, who had become friends. I was afraid that although this journey was to be short it would tire him, but not at all. At Orly a wheelchair took him to the plane. When it landed Eli Ben Gal came to fetch him in a car. All four stayed in the comfortable guest house facing the old city of Jerusalem; they also spent a night in a fine hotel on the shores of the Dead Sea. For five days Sartre and Victor talked with Israelis and Palestinians. The temperature was in the high seventies and the sky a splendid blue. Sartre was enchanted. He loved moving about, learning things, and as far as his eyes would let him, seeing different countries. If, as some say, old age is the loss of curiosity, he was not old at all.

Of his own accord, Sartre would never have written an article after so brisk an investigation. Victor had fewer scruples. "You Maos always go too fast," Sartre had said to him during one of their first conversations. Yet he allowed his hand to be forced and they sent *Le Nouvel Observateur* a piece signed with both their names. Bost telephoned me in a state of great agitation: "It's horribly bad. Here at the paper everyone is appalled. Do persuade Sartre to withdraw it." When I had read the article, finding it indeed very weak, I passed on Bost's request. "Very well," said Sartre carelessly. But when I spoke to Victor he flew into a rage. Never had he been so insulted. He blamed me for not having told him about it. I had supposed that Sartre would look after that, but he had not done so, no doubt because he did not care. I told Victor all this and for some time we retained at least the appearance of being on good terms. But presently, at a *Temps modernes* conference that met at my apartment without Sartre, there was a violent quarrel between Victor, Pouillon, and Horst on the subject of the article—Pouillon and Horst thought it execrable. Victor insulted them, declaring later that we were all corpses, and he never took part in the meetings again.

His reaction astonished me. When we were young, Sartre and I had suffered many rejections, but never had we taken them for insults. Victor had been one of the leaders of the *Gauche prolétarienne* and he had retained the "little boss's" state of mind—everything had to give way before him. He moved easily from one conviction to another, but always with the same obstinacy. From the ill-governed intensity of his various enthusiasms he derived certainties that he would not allow to be called into question. This gave his words a vigor that some people found stimulating, but writing calls for a critical attitude of mind that he did not possess, and if anyone did adopt this attitude with regard to anything he had written, he felt injured. From that time on, he and I no longer spoke to one another; I avoided encountering him in Sartre's apartment. It was an unpleasant situation. Up until then, Sartre's real friends had always been mine too. Victor was the only exception. I did not doubt his affection for Sartre nor Sartre's for him. Sartre told Contat about it in one of their conversations. "All I wish is that my work should be continued by others. For example, I should like Pierre Victor to accomplish the work he wants to do, a work that is both that of an intellectual and a militant. Of all the people I have known he is the only one who gives me full satisfaction from that point of view." He appreciated the radical nature of Victor's ambitions, and the fact that like Sartre himself, he wanted everything. "Of course you don't attain everything, but you must want everything." Perhaps Sartre was mistaken, but if so it is of no great importance. That was how he saw Victor. At long intervals he went to have dinner in what Victor called his "community," a suburban house which Victor and his wife shared with another couple, friends of theirs. Sartre enjoyed these evenings. I should not have wished to take part in them, but I was sorry that from now on a part of Sartre's life was closed to me.

We were rather tired of Venice. For our Easter holiday I chose Sirmione, a charming little walled town on Lake Garda. Cars were not allowed in, unless one was staying there, which was the case with us. We had rooms in a hotel on the shores of the lake. As usual I read to Sartre in his room, and since he liked walking about the narrow and, except on Sundays, empty streets, we often went and sat on a café terrace in a nearby square. We had our meals in the little restaurants close at hand. Sylvie took us for some long drives. We went around the lake and we revisited Verona and then another day, Brescia. On our way back to Paris we stopped at the Auberge du Père Bise at Talloires. Generally speaking Sartre ate in a very monotonous, sparing fashion, but every now and then he did appreciate a really good meal.

During the months between this time and the summer vacation, he undertook few political initiatives. At the beginning of the year a false "Sartre's political will and testament" had been published in Sicily. The author upheld some old anarchist theses and attributed them to him. Sartre published a denial. In June he wrote to *Le Monde,* saying that now, ten years after the events of 1968, Cohn-Bendit should no longer be forbidden to come to France. In the same month he signed a document on the case of Heide Kempe Böltcher, a German girl who had been severely burned on May 21 in Paris during a police interrogation.

But what really interested him was carrying on with the book,

Pouvoir et liberté (Power and Freedom), that he was writing with Victor. A tape recorder registered their dialogues. In a piece that appeared in *Obliques* he told Michel Sicard how he looked upon this work. "If the book is carried right through to its end, it will be a new form . . . a genuine discussion between two living beings who have the ideas that they amplify in their writing; and when we are opposed to one another it will not be fiction but truth . . . in this book there will be moments of confrontation and moments of agreement and both are important. . . . This book with two authors is essential for me because contradiction, life, will be *in* the book. The people who read it . . . will adopt different points of view. That's what moves me so strongly."

Then summer came. As I had done in other years, I met Sartre in Rome, after a journey in Sweden with Sylvie; and there we spent six very happy weeks.

When we returned to Paris his health seemed stabilized. He talked with Victor; I read to him. He still took pleasure in his many female friendships. Melina had gone back to Athens, but she was replaced by others. After the "Love Letter to Jean-Paul Sartre" that Françoise Sagan had published in the press, they lunched together from time to time. He was quite fond of her. He took part in the film that Josée Dayan and Malka Ribowska made of me, and the issue of *Obliques* devoted to him came out.

On October 28 he received a delegation of peasants from the Larzac. There had been several articles in *Les Temps modernes* about their struggle. Sartre was interested in it for several reasons: their confrontation with the state; their fight against the expansion of the army; the discovery of new techniques of resistance; and their active nonviolence, which utterly confused the established order. He would have liked to talk these things over with them at the time of their Whitsun meeting in 1976, but the state of his health had not allowed him to attend.

In October 1978 several of them undertook a hunger strike at Saint Séverin's. Some came to ask Sartre to be present at a press conference that they were to hold the next day. He was not well enough to accept, but he wrote a statement that was read out to the journalists during the conference. "You believe that France has to be defended, but you do not think it right that the army should settle down in the very middle of the country, far from the frontiers, and there, over thousands of acres, set up a zone of extermination by new weapons; nor do you think it right that the government should hire out this inhabited stretch of country to the armies of other countries so that they should be able to come and exercise there. You are right. Turning the Larzac into the weird locus of a preventive world war, and that in time of deep peace, calls for the stupidity and the cynicism of those who govern us."

At about the same time he talked over a plan that Guillaumat, an actor from Lyons, had submitted to him—the staging of a work, *Mise en Théâtre*, that Jeannette Colombel had put together, based on historical and political passages in Sartre. The show had a great success, first in the two main theaters in Lyons and then for two years all over France.

1979

Sartre attached great importance to the Israeli-Palestinian conference that took place in March under the aegis of *Les Temps modernes*. Victor had cherished the notion ever since his journey with Eli Ben Gal; they often telephoned one another. One of our old Israeli friends, Flapan, had offered *Les Temps modernes* the minutes of an Israeli-Palestinian colloquy over which he had presided, but he asked for quite a lot of money, and the document added nothing new. Victor thought it would be better to arrange a similar meeting in Paris and to publish its results in *Les Temps modernes*. The expenses would no doubt be high, but Gallimard undertook to pay them. Over the telephone, Victor and Eli drew up a list of those they hoped would attend and sent out the invitations. Most of these people lived in Israel.

Numbers of practical problems arose, starting with where the meeting should be held, *Les Temps modernes'* office being a mere rabbit hutch. Michel Foucault kindly lent us his big, very well-lit, quietly and elegantly furnished apartment. Victor reserved accommodations in a little left-bank hotel for a few days and a private dining room in a nearby restaurant. Tables, chairs, and a tape recorder were set up in Foucault's living room. In spite of a few technical difficulties the first meeting was able to be held on March 14. Sartre opened the proceedings with a little speech that he and Victor had agreed upon. Apart from him, Claire Etcherelli, and me—and I did not go back the next day—no members of the *Temps modernes* team were present. All of them, including myself, looked upon Victor's undertaking with mistrust.

The members of the conference introduced themselves. A Palestinian living in Jerusalem, Ibrahim Dahkak, stated that this dialogue was meaningless. Did Sartre not know that in Israel Palestinians and Israelis saw one another every day and talked to each other? Since no Egyptians or North Africans had been invited, it would have been simpler and cheaper to hold the meeting in Jerusalem. Eli Ben Gal and Victor said that some of the Palestinians present would not have been able to enter Israel. Dahkak replied that some Palestinians had not been able to go from Israel to Paris. And he withdrew from the conference. The other members did in fact all come from Israel, except for the Palestinian, Edward Saïd, who taught in the United States, at Columbia University, and Shalim Sharaf, a Palestinian teacher in Austria. One or two spoke German and nearly all the rest English. There were voluntary translators. If an Israeli preferred speaking in Hebrew, Eli Ben Gal acted as interpreter. The conversations were tape-recorded and Arlette typed them. During the sitting Claire Etcherelli and Catherine von Bülow passed around coffee and fruit juice without enthusiasm. Apart from the official sessions, the Palestinians and Israelis lunched together in the restaurant Victor had chosen. At these times they talked in a more relaxed fashion. They expressed a certain amount of surprise at the modest nature of their hotel, but above all at Sartre's near-silence and the importance assumed by Victor, of whom they knew nothing whatsoever. A little fair-haired rabbi asked for kosher food. Schmuel Trigano, a friend of *Les Temps modernes,* took him to the Jewish restaurant in the Rue Médicis.

The speeches were more or less interesting, more or less touching, but in general it was always the same old story—the Palestinians wanted a territory of their own and the Israelis—all chosen from the Left—agreed, but they wanted their security guaranteed. In any event, all these people were intellectuals who possessed no kind of power at all. Victor was nevertheless exultant. "It's going to be an international scoop," he told Sartre. He had to eat his words. For various reasons the issue, entitled *Peace Now* after an Israeli pacifist movement that did not play any great part in politics, only appeared in October, and it fell flat. During the summer of 1980, Edward Saïd, whom Victor looked upon as the member of the conference with the greatest prestige, told some common friends that he did not understand why he had been made to come from America. The meeting had seemed to him a wretched affair while he was attending it, and even worse when he read the proceedings. But in March 1979 Sartre shared Victor's optimism, and I did not tell him about my doubts.

At the beginning of the Easter vacation we and Sylvie left for the South by car. We slept at Vienne, where we found Point's restaurant disappointing. On the other hand, reaching Aix was a delight. The hotel, half a mile out of the town, had a big garden that smelled of the sun and pine trees, and far away one could see the white ridge of Sainte-Victoire sharp against a pure blue sky. It was still too cool to sit out of doors. We read in Sartre's room, but often all three of us would go for drives, lunching at some pleasant spot in the neighborhood.

Shortly after our return to Paris Sartre was slightly wounded by a man who was half mad, Gérard de Clèves. He was a Belgian, a poet, and the protégé of our friends Lallemant and Verstraeten. At long intervals, between stays in the asylum, he would come to Paris, and there, day after day, he asked Sartre for money. During this last leave of absence from the asylum, Sartre gave him small sums on several occasions but then told him that he would not see him again. Clèves nevertheless returned. Sartre, who was at home with Arlette, refused to let him in, but he held the door ajar, with the chain still on. After a short discussion Clèves took a knife from his pocket and struck Sartre's hand over the chain. Then he began battering the closed door so violently that in spite of its armor it began to yield. Arlette telephoned the police, and after a long chase in the corridors of the building Clèves was arrested. Sartre was bleeding profusely. His thumb had been slashed, but fortunately not the tendon. For weeks it was bandaged.

On June 20 he took part in the "Un bateau pour le Vietnam" committee's press conference. This committee had already succeeded in carrying out the first part of its undertaking. A ship, the *Ile-de-Lumière*, was anchored off Pulo-Bidong and it had taken in a great number of refugees. Now the committee wanted to establish an airlift between the camps in Malaysia and Thailand and the transit camps in the western countries. For this, the press had to be alerted. The conference was held in the rooms of the Hotel Lutetia. Glucksmann went with Sartre, who for the first time in a great while shook hands with Raymond Aron. Foucault spoke, then Dr. Kouchner, who worked aboard the *Ile-de-Lumière*, and then Sartre, who left a little before Aron's speech. On June 26 they went to the Elysée together to ask Giscard to increase the help given to the boat people. They received promises that were mere hot air. Sartre attributed no importance to this meeting with Aron, although some journalists went on and on about it.*

This year too, the summer vacation was a delightful period. Aix had so pleased us in the spring that we went back there in August. This time we had rooms on the first floor with communicating terraces that looked straight down onto the garden. It was here that we usually sat to read and talk. Sometimes I went—by taxi, since it might almost be said that Sartre could no longer walk—to lunch with him on the Cours Mirabeau, which he had always liked very much. Or Sylvie would drive us to one of our favorite places. Now and then we saw smoke far off—forest fires. Sartre was very pleased with this stay. He was pleased too when Sylvie, who was going back to Paris, drove us to the Martigues airport, where we took the plane for Rome. Once again we had our old rooms, looking out over the dazzling or ghostly white of Saint Peter's, and once again we returned to our old peaceful habits. From time to time Sartre saw an American girl who lived in Rome and whose acquaintance he had recently made. We both met Alice Schwarzer and we saw Claude Courchay, who was staying in the city with a friend, Catherine Rihoit. Courchay was amazed at Sartre's good humor and his cheerfulness. He did not know him well, but he had pictured him as being more or less broken by his illness and his lack of sight, whereas there before him was a man filled with the joy of living. When Sartre appeared in public he usually made a painful impression. Writing to Claude Mauriac after the meeting at the hotel Lutetia,† Raymond Aron said in effect "I thought I was seeing a dead man." But in private life those who talked to him were struck by his unconquerable vitality.

He agreed to give M.-A. Macciocchi an interview, which she published in *L'Europeo*. He was not pleased with it.

Shortly before we left, Liliane Siegel telephoned us from Paris to give us the news of Goldman's murder. I was overwhelmed. Goldman attended the *Temps modernes* meetings with great regularity, and my liking for him had changed into a deep affection. I liked his intelligent irony, his gaiety, his warmth. He was full of life and unexpected

---

* They claimed that it was a political reconciliation, thereby implying that Sartre was now coming closer to the attitudes of the right wing. This was completely untrue.

† *Le Temps immobile*, Claude Mauriac, vol. 6.

turns; he was often funny; he was constant in his enmities and his friendships. That he should have been shot down in cold blood added to the horror of his death. Sartre was moved too, but he now looked upon everything that occurred with detachment.

Yet when we were back in Paris he wished to be present at Goldman's funeral. Claire Etcherelli drove us to the morgue in her little car. We did not go in, but we followed the hearse as far as the entrance to the cemetery. Here there was such a crowd that we found it very hard to get through, although people, recognizing Sartre, kindly moved aside. Cars were not allowed beyond a certain point. Etcherelli stayed at the wheel while Sartre and I slowly and with great difficulty made our way through the mass of people. After a few moments he felt exhausted. I wanted him to rest on a grave but someone brought a chair. Sartre sat on it and we stayed there for a while, surrounded by strangers who stared and stared. Fortunately, Renée Saurel caught sight of us; her car was drawn up just beside us. Having sent someone to tell Claire Etcherelli we were leaving, we got into it.

Sartre returned to his work with Victor. I was rather worried about it. On three successive days I asked him, "Has your work gone well?" On the first he said, "No. We argued the whole morning about . . . [some subject or other]." The next day he replied, "No. We don't agree." The third day he said, "We have managed to come to an understanding." I was afraid that he might be making too many concessions. I should very much have liked to know about these conversations directly, but they were taped, and Arlette, whose job it was to decipher and type them, worked slowly. Nothing was quite ready yet, Sartre told me.

In November he gave Catherine Clément an interview for *Le Matin,* and he lunched with the paper's team. In December he told Bernard Dort about his ideas on the theater. The conversation appeared in the magazine, *Travail théâtral,* and in the course of it he spoke of the dramatists he liked—Pirandello, Brecht, Beckett—and recounted the history of his own plays. In January 1980 he protested against the order that confined Andrei Sakharov to a given residence, and he supported the boycotting of the Moscow Olympic games. On February 28 he was interviewed by *Le Gai Pied,* a homosexual monthly. And he had a conversation with Catherine Clément and Bernard Pingaud for a coming issue of *L'Arc.*

1980

According to a fresh checkup at Broussais Hospital on February 4 he was neither better nor worse. He found his activities interesting, his relations with young women amusing. In spite of everything life was a joy to him. I remember one morning when a brilliant winter sun flooded into his study, full on his face. "Oh, the sun!" he cried in an ecstasy. We planned to go, Sylvie, he, and I, to Belle-Ile for the Easter vacation, and he often spoke of it in a happy voice. He was careful enough about his health to maintain his giving up of tobacco. And as far as I knew he only drank a very little. He was so slow with the half bottle of chablis he ordered when we had lunch together that he left as much as he drank.

Yet one Sunday morning at the beginning of March Arlette found him lying on his bedroom floor with a terrible hangover. We learned that he got his various young women, who knew nothing of the danger, to bring him bottles of whiskey and vodka. He hid them in a chest or behind books. That Saturday evening—the only night he had spent alone since Wanda's departure—he had got drunk. Arlette and I emptied the hiding places, I telephoned the young women asking them not to bring any more alcohol, and I scolded Sartre vehemently. In fact, since it had no immediate consequences, this outbreak obviously did not damage his health; but I was rather uneasy about the future. Above all I could not understand the return of this passion for drinking. It did not square with his apparent mental balance. He put my questions aside, laughing. "But you're fond of drinking too," he said. Perhaps he was not bearing the situation as well as he did before. It is not true that "in time you get used to it."* Far from healing wounds, time can on the contrary make them worse. Later it occurred to me that without clearly admitting it even to himself, he cannot have been altogether satisfied with his conversation with Victor, now soon to come out in *Le Nouvel Observateur*.

I read this conversation at last—it was signed by Sartre and Benni Lévi, Victor's real name—about a week before it was to appear. I was

---

* *No Exit:* "I suppose that in time you get used to it" (Garcin).

horrified. It had nothing to do with the "plural thought" that Sartre had spoken of in *Obliques*. Victor did not express any of his own opinions directly; he made Sartre assume them while he, by virtue of who knows what revealed truth, played the part of district attorney. The tone in which he spoke to Sartre and his arrogant superiority utterly disgusted all the friends who saw the document before it was published. And like me they were horrified by the nature of the statements extorted from Sartre. In fact Victor had changed a great deal since Sartre first met him. Like many other former Maoists he had turned toward God—the God of Israel, since he was a Jew. His view of the world had become spiritualistic and even religious. Sartre jibbed at this change of direction. I remember one evening when, talking to Sylvie and me, he gave vent to his dissatisfaction. "Victor absolutely insists that the whole origin of morals is in the Torah! But that's not at all what I think," he told us. And as I have already pointed out, he would struggle with Victor for days on end, and then, tired of contention, would give in. Victor, instead of helping him to broaden his own thought, was bringing pressure to bear on him so that he should repudiate it. How could he dare to claim that anxiety had been no more than a fashion for Sartre—for Sartre, who had never taken the slightest notice of fashions? How could he so weaken the notion of fraternity, so strong and firm in the *Critique of Dialectical Reason*? I let Sartre know the full extent of my disappointment. It surprised him. He had expected a certain amount of criticism, but not this radical opposition. I told him that the whole *Temps modernes* team was with me. But this only made him the more set on having the conversation published at once.

How can one explain this "abduction of an old man",* as it was put by Oliver Todd (who for his part did not recoil from the abduction of a dead one)?

Sartre had always thought it right to think against himself, but he never did so in order to sink into mere facility. This vague, yielding philosophy that Victor attributed to him did not suit Sartre at all.† Why did he concur? He who had never been open to any influence whatsoever was now subjected to Victor's. He has told us why, but it is a reason that has to be gone into more deeply. Sartre had always

---

* The French is *détournement de vieillard*, a variant of the very usual *détournement de mineur*— abduction of a young person, usually for immoral purposes. (trans.)
† This was very well said by Raymond Aron in a television confrontation with Victor after Sartre's death.

lived with his eyes fixed on the future; he could not live otherwise. Now that he was limited to the present, he looked upon himself as dead.* Old, threatened in his own body, half-blind, he was shut out from the future. He therefore turned to a substitute—Victor, a militant and a philosopher, would be the "new intellectual" of whom Sartre dreamed and whom he would have helped to bring into existence. To doubt Victor was to renounce that living prolongation of himself, more important to him than the praise of future generations. So in spite of all his reservations he had elected to believe in Victor. Sartre did have ideas and he did think; but he thought slowly. And Victor had a great flood of words; he stunned Sartre and he did not leave him the time he needed to bring things into focus. Finally, Sartre could no longer read. He could no longer reread what he had written. This, I believe, was very important. I am incapable of judging a text that I have not read myself. Sartre was like me. Yet he had checked this piece of writing only by ear. When he was speaking to Contat † he said, "The problem is that that factor of reflexive criticism, always there when you read a text yourself, is never very sharply present when somebody else is reading it aloud." Then again, Victor was supported by Arlette, who knew nothing whatsoever about Sartre's philosophical works and who sympathized with Victor's new tendencies—they were learning Hebrew together. Sartre was confronted with this alliance, and he lacked the perspective that only a thoughtful, solitary reading could have given him; so he gave way. Once the conversation was published, he was surprised and hurt when he learned that all the Sartrians and, even in a more general manner, all his friends shared my consternation.

On Wednesday, March 19, we and Bost spent an agreeable evening together without referring to the question. Just before he went to bed Sartre asked me, "At *Les Temps modernes* this morning, did anyone talk about the conversation?" I said no, which was true. He seemed rather disappointed. He would so much have liked to find some allies! The next morning I went to wake him at nine o'clock. Usually, when I went into his room, he was still dozing; this time he was sitting on the edge of his bed, gasping, almost unable to speak. Once when Arlette was there he had had what he called "an attack of aerophagia," but it had passed off quite soon. This one had been going on since five in the morning, and he had not had the strength to drag himself as

---

* As we have seen, he spoke of himself as "a living corpse" during his moments of depression.
† "Self-Portrait at Seventy."

far as my door and knock. I was frightened; I tried to telephone, but the service had been cut off, Puig having left the bill unpaid. I threw on my clothes and used the concierge's telephone to call a nearby doctor, who came at once. As soon as he had seen Sartre he telephoned the emergency service from a neighbor's apartment, and they arrived in five minutes. Sartre was bled, given an injection, and treatment that lasted for nearly an hour. Then he was laid on a kind of wheeled stretcher which was rolled down a long corridor; he was breathing oxygen from a mask that a doctor held over his head. They put him into an elevator and took him to an ambulance that was waiting at one of the entrances. It was not yet known to which hospital he would be taken; they would telephone the concierge. I went up to his apartment again to wash and dress properly. Now that he was in good hands, I thought the attack would quickly be brought to an end. I did not cancel my lunch with Den and Jean Pouillon. I never imagined when I closed the apartment door behind me as I set off to meet them, that it would never open for me again.

Still, when we had had our lunch and I took a taxi to go to Broussais Hospital—for I now knew that Sartre was there—I asked Pouillon to come too and wait for me. "I'm rather afraid," I said to him. Sartre was in the intensive care unit, breathing normally, and he told me he felt well. I did not stay long. He was drowsy and I did not want to keep Pouillon waiting.

The next afternoon, the doctors told me that Sartre had a pulmonary edema which was giving him a high temperature but which would soon be reabsorbed. He was in a big, light-filled room and he thought he was in the suburbs. The fever made him delirious. That morning he had said to Arlette, "You're dead too, my dear. What did it feel like, being cremated? Well, here we are, both of us dead now." * When I was there he told me he had just been to lunch at his secretary's house near Paris. Which secretary? He never used the word for either Victor or Puig. He called them by their names. As I seemed surprised he explained that the doctor had very kindly lent him his car to take him there and bring him back. He had passed through some very curious and very agreeable suburbs. Had he not dreamed it, I asked him? He said no, looking cross, so I did not press the point.

The fever lessened during the days that followed, and the delirium

---

* Arlette was a Jew and Lanzmann often used to talk to us about his film on the extermination of the Jews and therefore about the incinerators. We also spoke about the arguments of Faurisson, who denied their existence. Then again, Sartre wished to be cremated.

stopped. The doctors told me that the attack had been caused by a lack of irrigation in the lungs, the arteries not functioning properly. But now the pulmonary circulation was reestablished. We had thought of leaving for Belle-Ile quite soon and Sartre was delighted at the idea. "Yes, I shall like being down there; we'll be able to forget about all this." (*All this* was the Victor conversation and its repercussions.) As he was only allowed to see one person at a time, Arlette went to the hospital in the morning and I in the afternoon. I used to telephone at about ten to ask how he had passed the night, and the reply was always "Very well." He slept soundly and also dozed a little after lunch. We talked about unimportant matters. He sat in an armchair for his meals and when I came to see him. Otherwise he spent most of the time lying down. He had grown thinner and he seemed weak, but his spirits were good. He looked forward to leaving the hospital, but he was ill enough to put up with the situation cheerfully. Arlette came back at about six to be there when he had dinner, and sometimes she left for a little while so that Victor could come in.

Presently I asked Dr. Housset when he would be able to leave. Hesitantly he replied, "I can't say . . . he's frail, very frail." And two or three days later he said that Sartre would have to go down to the intensive care unit again. It was only in that part of the hospital that he could be watched twenty-four hours a day, so that he would not run the risk of any accident. Sartre did not like it there. When Sylvie came to see him he said, as though he were speaking of a hotel where he was staying for a holiday, "I don't care for this place. Fortunately, we'll be leaving soon. I love the idea of going to a little island."

There was in fact no longer any question of going to Belle-Ile. I canceled the rooms I had reserved. The doctor wanted to have Sartre within reach in case of a fresh attack. But they did bring him back to a room, bigger and lighter than the first. "This is fine," he told me, "because now I'm quite near home." He still had a vague belief that at first he had been taken to a hospital in a suburb of Paris. He seemed more and more weary; he began to have bedsores, and his bladder functioned badly. This had to be dealt with, and when he got up—which happened rarely now—he trailed a little plastic bag full of urine behind him. From time to time I left his room so that a visitor might come in—Bost or Lanzmann. When I did so I went and sat in a waiting room. It was there that I overheard Dr. Housset and another doctor talking, and they used the word "uremia." I understood that there was no hope for Sartre and I knew that uremia often brought hideous suffering with it; I burst into tears and flung myself into Housset's arms. "Promise me that he won't know he's dying, that he won't go through any mental anguish, that he won't have any pain!" "I promise you that, Madame," he said gravely. A little later, when I had gone back to Sartre's room, he called me. In the corridor he said "I want you to know that my promise was not mere words. I shall keep it."

Afterward the doctors told me that because his kidneys were no longer adequately supplied with blood, they no longer functioned. Sartre still passed urine, but without eliminating urea. An operation would have been needed to save one kidney, but he had not the strength to bear it; and even if it could have been carried out, the inadequate circulation would then have been transferred to the brain, bringing senile decay with it. The only answer was to let him die in peace.

He did not suffer during the few days that followed. "There's just one rather disagreeable moment," he told me, "and that is when they dress my bedsores in the morning. But that's all." These bedsores were horrifying to see (but fortunately they were hidden from him)— great purplish-blue and reddened patches. In fact, since the blood did not circulate properly, gangrene had attacked his flesh.

He slept a great deal, but he still spoke to me lucidly. At times it almost seemed that he hoped to get well. Pouillon came to see him during the very last days of his illness; Sartre asked him for a glass of water, saying cheerfully, "The next time we have a drink together, it'll be at my place and it'll be whiskey!" * But the next day he asked me "How are we going to manage the funeral expenses?" I protested of course, and branched off to the cost of the hospital, assuring him that the social security service would look after it. But I saw that he knew the end was near and that the knowledge did not overwhelm him. His only anxiety was the one that had tormented him these last years—the lack of money. He did not dwell on it; did not ask me any questions about his health. The next day, with closed eyes, he took me by the wrist and said, "I love you very much, my dear Castor." On April 14 he was asleep when I came; he woke and said a few words without opening his eyes, then he held up his lips to me. I kissed his

* Georges Michel's account is upon the whole correct, but he is mistaken in supposing that these were Sartre's last words.

mouth and his cheek. He went back to sleep. These words and these actions were unusual for him; they were obviously related to the prospect of his death.

Some months later I met Dr. Housset as I had hoped I should, and he told me that Sartre had sometimes asked him questions. "How will it all end? What is going to happen to me?" But it was not death that made him uneasy; it was his brain. He had undoubtedly felt the coming of death, but without anguish. He was "resigned" said Housset, or rather, correcting himself, "assured." No doubt the euphoria-inducing medicines they had given him contributed to this peaceful state of mind. But above all (except for the first days of his half-blindness) he had always borne what happened to him with moderation and constancy. He did not wish to trouble others with what troubled him. And revolt against a fate he could not alter seemed to him pointless. As he said to Contat* "That's just how things are and there's nothing I can do about it, so I have no call to be wretched." He still passionately loved living, but he was thoroughly used to the idea of death, even though he pushed back its time until he would be eighty. He accepted its coming without making a fuss, appreciative of the friendship and the affection that surrounded him and satisfied with his past. "I've done what I had to do."

Housset also asserted that the troubles and vexations that Sartre had suffered could in no way have affected his condition. A violent emotional crisis might have had disastrous immediate effects; but cares and worries, diluted in time, had no influence upon what mattered— the vascular system. He added that its state must necessarily have grown worse in the near future. In two years at the outside the brain would have been affected and Sartre would no longer have been Sartre.

On the morning of Tuesday, April 15, when as usual I asked whether Sartre had slept well the nurse replied "Yes. But . . ." I hurried over at once. He was asleep and breathing quite strongly; he was obviously in a coma, and he had been since the evening before. I stayed there for hours, watching him. At about six I made way for Arlette, asking her to telephone if anything happened. At nine the telephone rang. She said, "It's over." I came with Sylvie. He looked just the same; but he no longer breathed.

Sylvie told Lanzmann, Bost, Pouillon, and Horst. They came at once. We were allowed to stay in the room until five the next morning. I asked Sylvie to go and get some whiskey and we drank it as we

* "Self-Portrait at Seventy."

talked about Sartre's last days and his earlier times, and about what would have to be done. Sartre had often told me that he did not wish to be buried at the Père Lachaise cemetery between his mother and stepfather; he wanted to be cremated. We decided to bury him provisionally in the Montparnasse graveyard, from which he would be taken to the Père Lachaise for the cremation; his ashes would be brought back and placed in a permanent tomb in the Montparnasse graveyard. While we were watching over him, journalists besieged the building. Bost and Lanzmann went out to insist upon their going away. They hid. But they did not manage to get in. When Sartre was taken to the hospital they had also tried to take photographs; two of them, dressed as male nurses, had attempted to make their way into the room, but they had been put out. The nurses took care to draw the blinds and to put curtains over the doors to protect us. But still a photograph showing Sartre asleep, no doubt taken from a nearby roof, did appear in *Match*.

At one point I asked to be left alone with Sartre, and I made as if to lie down beside him under the sheet. A nurse stopped me. "No. Take care . . . the gangrene." It was then that I understood the real nature of the bedsores. I lay on top of the sheet and I slept a little. At five the male nurses came. They stretched a sheet and a kind of cover over Sartre and took him away.

I finished the night at Lanzmann's, where I also slept on Wednesday. For the days that followed I stayed with Sylvie, where I was better protected from telephone calls and journalists than in my own apartment. During the day I saw my sister, who had come from Alsace, and my friends. I looked at the papers and also at the telegrams that came flooding in at once. Lanzmann, Bost, and Sylvie took care of all the formalities. At first the funeral was fixed for Friday, but then it was changed to Saturday so that more people could attend. Giscard d'Estaing let it be known that he knew Sartre would not have wished for a national funeral, but that he offered to pay the expenses. We refused. He made a point of paying his respects to Sartre's remains.

On Friday I lunched with Bost. I wanted to see Sartre again before the burial and we went to the lecture theater of the hospital. Sartre was brought in his coffin, dressed in the clothes that Sylvie had brought for him to wear when he went to the opera. They were the only ones in my apartment, and she had not liked to go to his to find others. He was calm, like all dead people, and like most of them, expressionless.

On Saturday morning we gathered in the lecture theater, where

Sartre was laid out, his face uncovered, stiff and cold in his fine clothes. At my request Pingaud took some photographs of him. After quite a long time the men turned the sheet back over Sartre's face, closed the coffin, and took it away.

I got into the hearse with Sylvie, my sister, and Arlette. Before us there was a car covered with splendid sheaves of flowers and wreaths. A kind of minibus carried those friends who were old or unable to walk far. A huge crowd followed—about fifty thousand people, most of them young. There were some who rapped on the hearse windows; these were usually photographers leaning their cameras against the glass to take me unawares. Some of the friends of *Les Temps modernes* formed a barrier behind the hearse, and all around it people we did not know spontaneously linked hands, making a chain. All the way the crowd was orderly and warmly sympathetic, generally speaking. "This is the last of the 1968 demonstrations," said Lanzmann. For my part, I saw nothing. I was more or less anesthetized by Valium and braced taut in my determination not to collapse. I told myself that this was exactly the funeral Sartre had wanted, and that he would never know about it. When I got out of the hearse the coffin was already at the bottom of the tomb. I asked for a chair and I sat there at the edge of the open grave, my mind a blank. I saw people who had climbed onto walls, onto tombs; a vague swarming mass. I stood up to go back to the car. It was only ten yards away but the crowd was so dense that I thought I should be smothered. Then there I was at Lanzmann's house again with friends who had come straggling back from the graveyard. I rested for a while and then, as we did not wish to separate, we had dinner together at Zeyer's, in a private room. I remember nothing about it. Apparently I drank a great deal and had to be almost carried down the stairs. Georges Michel took me back to my apartment.

I spent the next three days at Sylvie's. On Wednesday morning there was the cremation at the Père Lachaise and I was too exhausted to go. I slept and—I cannot tell how—I fell out of bed and remained there in a sitting position on the carpet. When Sylvie and Lanzmann came back from the cremation and found me, I was delirious. They took me to a hospital. I had pneumonia. I got over it in two weeks.

Sartre's ashes were brought to the Montparnasse cemetery. Every day unknown hands lay little bunches of fresh flowers on his grave.

There is one question that I have not asked myself, I admit. It will perhaps occur to the reader. Should I not have warned Sartre of the imminence of his death? When he was in the hospital, weakened and without resilience, all I thought of was hiding the gravity of his condition from him. But before that? He had always told me that in the event of cancer or any other incurable disease he wanted to *know*. Yet his was an ambiguous case. He was "in danger," but would he hold out another ten years, as he had wished, or would everything be over in a year or two? Nobody knew. He had no arrangements to make; he could not have taken better care of himself. And he loved living. He had already found it hard enough to accept his blindness and his infirmities. If he had been more exactly aware of the threat that hung over him, it would only have darkened his last years without doing any good. In any case, like him, I wavered between dread and hope. My silence did not separate us.

His death does separate us. My death will not bring us together again. That is how things are. It is in itself splendid that we were able to live our lives in harmony for so long.

CONVERSATIONS WITH JEAN-PAUL SARTRE

AUGUST–SEPTEMBER 1974

PREFACE TO THE CONVERSATIONS

These conversations took place in Rome during the summer of 1974 and then in Paris at the beginning of the fall. Sometimes Sartre, when he was tired, gave indifferent answers; or it was I who lacked inspiration and asked pointless questions. I have omitted the conversations that seemed to me without interest. The others I have arranged according to their theme, at the same time keeping more or less to their chronological order. I have tried to give them a readable form—as everyone knows, there is a great difference between remarks recorded on tape and a properly written text. But I have not attempted to *write* them in the literary sense of the word—my intention has been to retain their spontaneity. Some rambling passages will be found, and some that mark time; and there are some repetitions and even some contradictions. This is because I was afraid of distorting Sartre's words or of taking away their finer shades of meaning. The conversations do not reveal any unexpected aspects of him, but they do allow one to follow the winding course of his thought and to hear his living voice.

DE BEAUVOIR: Let us talk about the literary and philosophical side of your work. Do you feel that there is something to be said on the subject? Does it interest you?

SARTRE: It doesn't exactly interest me. At present nothing interests me. But it did interest me enough over many years for me to want to talk about it.

DE BEAUVOIR: Why does nothing interest you at present?

SARTRE: I don't know. It's over and done with, all that stuff. I try to find things to say about it. I don't find them anymore; but I shall find them.

DE BEAUVOIR: In *The Words* you gave a very good explanation of what reading and writing meant to you and how, when you were eleven, you had a vocation to be a writer. You were destined for literature. That explains why you wanted to write, but it doesn't at all explain why you have written *what* you have written. What happened between the time you were eleven and the time you were twenty? How do you see the relation between your literary and your philosophical work? When I first knew you, you told me you wanted to be Spinoza and Stendhal, both at the same time. Not at all a bad program. Let's begin with the things you were writing when I first met you. Why was it that you were writing them—how did it come about?

SARTRE: One of the heroic works that I wrote when I was eleven or twelve was called *Götz von Berlichingen*. It was the forerunner of *The Devil and the Good Lord*. Götz was a remarkable hero. He beat people and set up a reign of terror, but at the same time his intentions were good. And then I read a piece about a man in the middle ages in Germany—I don't know whether it was Götz. In any case they wanted to execute him. They took him up into the steeple clock and in the clock they made a hole where the twelve was, a hole that went from the inside right out to the dial. They put his head through the hole and the hands cut it off as they moved from half past eleven to half past one.

DE BEAUVOIR: That was rather in the manner of Edgar Allan Poe.

SARTRE: It was a delayed-action beheading. In fact it impressed me very deeply. As you see, I was still doing what I had done for a long while—I was imitating.

DE BEAUVOIR: How long did you go on imitating and when did you begin to use writing as a form of self-expression?

SARTRE: I copied, or at least adapted, old newspaper stories and adventures until I was fourteen or fifteen. It was going to Paris that made me change my way of looking at things. I think I must have written one last novel—it was this Götz, by the way—at La Rochelle when I was in the fourth form. Then, when I was in the third and the second, I didn't write much. In the first, when I had come to Paris, I took to writing more serious things.

DE BEAUVOIR: The stories that you more or less copied—there was a choice governing that. You didn't copy just any story. Until you were fourteen you always liked adventure stories, heroic stories.

SARTRE: Yes. The heroism of a man stronger than the rest; to some extent the opposite of what I was—a man who killed the wicked fellows with a stroke of his sword and rescued kingdoms or saved young maidens.

DE BEAUVOIR: It could be said that until you were fourteen it was the process you described in *The Words*—playing at writing without actually writing. And why did coming to Paris change your relations with the written word?

SARTRE: Well, it was all connected with other people's literature. At La Rochelle I was still reading cloak-and-dagger novels, well-known novels like *Rocambole* and *Fantomas,* adventure stories, and then a whole mass of literature that was read by the lower middle class: Claude Farrère, for example. Writers who wrote tales about voyages, about ships; and there were sentiments, love, violence—but only minor violence, and even that was condemned. And then they showed the moral deliquescence of the colonies.

DE BEAUVOIR: When you came to Paris you changed your reading?

SARTRE: Yes.

DE BEAUVOIR: Why? Under whose influence?

SARTRE: Under the influence of the boys who were there with me— of a few of the boys. Nizan and the painter Gruber's brother, who were in my form.

DE BEAUVOIR: What was it that you took to reading at that time?

SARTRE: At that time we began to read serious things. Gruber, for example, read Proust, and I came to know Proust when I was in the first form—know him with delight. At the same time I became interested in classical literature, which we were taught by M. Georgin, a very able, very pleasant, very intelligent man. He used to say to us, as for this problem, this question, you must work it out for yourselves. So then we read. I would go to the Sainte-Geneviève library and read everything I could on the subject. I was very proud of myself. At that time I thought of joining the literary world, not as a writer but as a cultivated man.

DE BEAUVOIR: Apart from Proust, who were the writers who interested you at that time?

SARTRE: Well, Conrad, for example.

DE BEAUVOIR: Did you read Gide?

SARTRE: A little, but without much interest. We read *The Fruits of the Earth.* I found it rather boring.

DE BEAUVOIR: You read Giraudoux?

SARTRE: Yes, prodigiously. Nizan had a great admiration for him, and even wrote a short story in pure Giraudoux style; and I wrote one inspired by him too.

DE BEAUVOIR: So there was already a kind of philosophical content in what you were trying to do?

SARTRE: Yes: I don't know why. Anyhow, we'll come to that later. It was rather like what happened at the end of the nineteenth century, you see. People put philosophy in literature—Bourget did it. What I was doing was roughly the same.

DE BEAUVOIR: It was literature with a purpose.

SARTRE: The purpose was made up on the spot

DE BEAUVOIR: But still, what you were trying to express were your ideas rather than your experience of the world, wasn't it?

SARTRE: It was my ideas, which included experience of the world—but not mine: a fictitious imitation experience. A little later I wrote the story of a young hero and his sister who went up to the abode of the gods with just their petit-bourgeois experience. It was experience that was valid enough as far as mine was concerned but which in fact had nothing to do with it, since these were Greek children.

DE BEAUVOIR: Wasn't there a girl in *Er l'Arménien* (Er the Armenian)?

SARTRE: Yes, but scarcely anything was said about her. She merely gave the young hero his cue.

DE BEAUVOIR: What was the story? Wasn't it about soul weighers? And wasn't it the Armenian himself who weighed them?

SARTRE: No, it was the Armenian who was weighed. And there was a great battle with the giants, the great battle of the Oeta with the giants, with the Titans.

DE BEAUVOIR: But that was later than *Jésus la chouette* (Jesus the Owl) and *L'Ange du morbide,* (The Morbid Angel).

SARTRE: Oh yes. *Jésus la chouette* was before *L'Ange du morbide*; it must have been written in the first form or in philo.

DE BEAUVOIR: Can you tell me why you wrote it? What did it mean to you? *Jésus la chouette* was the life of a little provincial schoolmaster, wasn't it?

SARTRE: Yes, but seen by a pupil. The hero was a real master at the La Rochelle lycée. He had asked me to his house. I imagined his funeral, and in fact he did die in the course of the year. The boys did not go to his funeral, though they did in my tale. I imagined the funeral because perhaps after all I did really go, but nothing extraordinary happened. In my tale the boys kicked up a row and played the fool while he was being buried.

DE BEAUVOIR: But what made you want to write this story? Was it because you saw your own future foreshadowed in this teacher? Or was it just that he interested you for some reason or another?

SARTRE: What one should really look at is the way I moved from the cloak-and-dagger tales to a realistic novel. The hero is a pitiful creature. But I still kept my old tradition of a positive hero, embodying him in the boy, who did nothing outstanding but who was put forward as a critical, very intelligent and active witness in the tale.

DE BEAUVOIR: How did you pass from copying heroic stories to the making up of realistic ones?

SARTRE: I think that in spite of all I put into adventure stories, I knew that they were only a first stage—that there was another kind of writing. I knew it because I read other books at my grandfather's house: there was a heroic side in *Les Misérables,* but even so the book wasn't just that. I'd read France's novels; I'd read *Madame Bovary.* So I knew that literature did not always include that adventurous aspect, and that I would have to come to realism. Changing from the cloak-and-dagger tale to realism meant talking about people as I really saw them. Yet there still had to be something exciting in it. I could never have conceived some of the books of that time in which nothing happened. There had to be an event as important as a heroic event. In this tale it was the man's death that struck me. He died in the middle of the school year and a new master was appointed, a completely different kind of man. He was a young fellow who had just come back from the war, not bad at all.

DE BEAUVOIR: Was it Proust who led you to write about everyday life?

SARTRE: No. I think it came from the fact that I had an excellent teacher; and then there were all those novels that spoke about everyday things and that seemed to me natural. I'd read *Madame Bovary* when I was young, for example, and from my point of view that could only be seen as realistic. I saw that it was certainly not a cloak-and-dagger novel, so I knew that books unlike those I dreamed of writing were written and that I should come to them. So when I was in the first form I began writing *Jésus la chouette,* which I thought was realistic, since after all I was telling the story of one of my teachers, only changing the details.

DE BEAUVOIR: And perhaps you were rather tired of cloak-and-dagger. It was rather childish.

SARTRE: Oh, I've always been fond of it.

DE BEAUVOIR: And then later there was *L'Ange du morbide.* What did that story represent for you?

SARTRE: Realism. It happened in a place I know, in Alsace. There was a sanatorium not far away in the mountains. I used to see it as I went by. There was a slope with pine trees and on the other side you could see houses, quite far away. The sanatorium was there. I set a character in this sanatorium, a young schoolmaster, I think, who fell ill, and my description of him was utter nonsense, entirely made up. I put a certain amount of irony into it and then unconsciously something of myself.

DE BEAUVOIR: What, for example? Wasn't the story that he kissed a tubercular girl? Didn't he do it to catch the disease?

SARTRE: He slept with her, I think. No. He was sick. But she had a bad attack. She was much more deeply affected than he was. It happened in the sanatorium, and she was going back to her room having spent a rather unpleasant night with him. They hadn't made love because she had coughed too much. As for the end, I don't see it very clearly . . .

DE BEAUVOIR: Why this idea of morbidness? What made you tell morbid stories at that particular time?

SARTRE: It was morbid because it was consumptives sleeping together. I was as healthy as a herring. So I knew nothing about the tubercular side, and I knew nothing about the sexual side either. It was really playing with general notions. I think I should have liked writing horror stories. This wasn't a horror story, but the character was horrified. I can't really remember why—in a certain way it was still my own world, my own environment that I was describing, you see. It wasn't a question of strange, outlandish circles.

DE BEAUVOIR: And the other pieces that came out in the *Revue sans titre*, were they realism too?

SARTRE: Yes. And my first novel, *Une défaite* (A Defeat), which was not published, was also realistic. It was a rather odd realism—it was the story of Nietzsche and Wagner with me in the role of Nietzsche and a rather dim character as Wagner. Cosima Wagner, too. The hero fell in love with Cosima, Cosima being in love with Wagner, and as he was one of Wagner's very close friends. . . . It was what was left of the cloak-and-dagger tale carried over into a realistic novel.

DE BEAUVOIR: *Er l'Arménien* and even *La Légende de la vérité* (The Legend of Truth) went somewhat in the same direction. There was a change to Greek mythology, and a fairly stilted way of writing. How did the transition come about? Did your Greek and Latin studies mark you much?

SARTRE: Certainly. I think I used to look upon the ancient world as a storehouse of myths.

DE BEAUVOIR: Were you *very* keen on the Greeks and Romans?

SARTRE: Yes, ever since the sixth form. Egypt, Greece, and Rome. In those days ancient history was taught in the sixth and fifth, I think. Then I read books. I especially liked Duruy's Roman history, which was full of anecdotes.

DE BEAUVOIR: That had a heroic side. To some degree it was linked to the cloak-and-dagger tale. But how did it come about that whereas Nizan already possessed a style, even in the *Revue sans titre,* a very modern style influenced by Giraudoux, you on the contrary—and it lasted until *Nausea*—had a strongly academic and even stilted way of writing? You say you liked Proust and Giraudoux, but there's no feeling of them at all in what you wrote at that time.

SARTRE: No, but that's because I came from the provinces, where I'd been acquainted with all the literature of the bourgeois nineteenth century. They were stilted, academic, stupid authors. Nizan was in Paris. A Paris lycée was much more advanced than the La Rochelle lycée. We didn't live in the same world. I was living in the nineteenth century and Nizan, without being quite aware of it, was living in the twentieth.

DE BEAUVOIR: But when you came to Paris you read the same books as Nizan and the two of you were friends. Didn't that influence you?

SARTRE: It certainly did. It caused a crisis. An inner crisis. Oh, not very serious, but even so . . .

DE BEAUVOIR: It counted.

SARTRE: Yes. For a fellow who read Claude Farrère reading Proust was a complicated business. I had to change my outlook—I had to change my relations with people.

DE BEAUVOIR: With people or with words?

SARTRE: With words and with people. I had to understand that sometimes you were active with regard to people and at other times passive. It was important, all that. I tried to realize what a real circle, a real milieu, was, with the real relations that people have between themselves, that is, reacting or undergoing. All this was something I did not know about.

DE BEAUVOIR: Explain rather more clearly: real relations with people, undergoing, acting . . .

SARTRE: That's what people are like. They act and they undergo—suffer the action. But there are some who undergo and there are some who are active.

DE BEAUVOIR: But how did Paris make all this clear to you?

SARTRE: Because at that time I was a boarder, and relations between boarders were always trying.

DE BEAUVOIR: Why, exactly?

SARTRE: Because the dormitory is a whole world. You remember Flaubert in his dormitory when he thought about nothing but romantic literature? He read it there. It's a world in itself, the dormitory.

DE BEAUVOIR: When you were at La Rochelle you did after all know that people acted or underwent, didn't you? What about your relations with the other boys? Be clearer about the transition between La Rochelle and Paris.

SARTRE: I had been told a good many unpleasant things about being a boarder. Even my grandfather and my parents—"No, you can't be a boarder, because you'd be far away from the family—you might be victimized by a master or the head of the school." But I couldn't sleep at my grandfather's every night. For six days I slept at the lycée, never leaving it, with the evenings and those strange personal relations you have when you're a boarder. Then on Sundays I went to my grandparents. It was quite a different world from that of my own parents, since my grandfather was a teacher. And I was back in his library again. I lived in another world. A world of university people too, since I was preparing for the Ecole Normale and the *agrégation*.* I used to go and sing in church on Sundays. Just imagine that.

DE BEAUVOIR: Really? I never knew. Why did you do that?

SARTRE: Because I liked singing, and they had asked for people to make up a choir for Mass. An organ played in the Henri-IV chapel.

DE BEAUVOIR: Did you work well in those days?

SARTRE: I received the prize for excellence in the first form and perhaps in philo too: I don't remember.

DE BEAUVOIR: And why was it philosophy that you chose in the end? Since you were very fond of literature too.

SARTRE: Because when I followed the philosophy lessons of Cucuphilo, who taught us—his name was Chabrier, but we called him Cucuphilo—it became evident to me that philosophy was knowledge of the world. Then there were all the sciences that belonged to philosophy. In methodology you learned how a science was built up. As I saw it, as soon as you knew how to do mathematics or natural science, that meant you understood the whole of natural science and mathematics, so I thought that if I specialized in philosophy I would learn the entirety of the world that I was to talk about in books. It gave me the raw material, you might say.

DE BEAUVOIR: You say "the entirety of the world that I was to talk about." Did you think that the writer ought to give an account of the world?

SARTRE: Yes; perhaps it was talking with the other boys that gave me

---

* A competitive examination for admission to the teaching staff of lycées and universities. (trans.)

that idea. I thought the novel ought to give an account of the world as it was, both the literary and critical world and the world of living people. I didn't much care for Alphonse Daudet, but he filled me with admiration because he had written a novel about members of the Academy. He had taken a profession, if that can be called a profession, and he had made a whole novel out of it.

DE BEAUVOIR: But didn't you think that literature ought to consist of talking about yourself?

SARTRE: Oh not at all. Not at all. Because as I said, I began with cloak-and-dagger stories. I didn't think about them any more, but something remained. There was still cloak-and-dagger in *Road to Freedom*.

DE BEAUVOIR: Yes. But none at all in *Nausea*, nor in *The Wall*. All right. So you did philosophy because it was the discipline that allowed you to know everything, to believe that everything was known and that all sciences had been mastered.

SARTRE: Yes. A writer had to be a philosopher. As soon as I knew what philosophy was it seemed to me natural to insist upon that in a writer.

DE BEAUVOIR: But why was it absolutely necessary to write?

SARTRE: I belong to a period in which personal writing was held in low esteem, at least by the bourgeois and petit-bourgeois like my grandfather and the people around me. So one did not write personal things.

DE BEAUVOIR: But when you began to like Proust, what he was talking about was the very essence of personal things—how he slept, how he didn't sleep. Of course there's the world in it too, but still . . .

SARTRE: Yes, it was above all the world that I liked in Proust to begin with. It came little by little. Later I also thought that writing was for personal things. But you mustn't forget that from the time I began to study philosophy and to write, I thought that the aim of literature was to write a book that would reveal to the reader things he had never thought of before. For a long time that was my idea—the idea that I should succeed in saying things about the world, not just what anyone could see of it, but things that I should see. I did not know them yet, but I was going to see them, and they would reveal the world.

DE BEAUVOIR: Why did you feel yourself capable of revealing the world to people? What did you feel like inside? Very intelligent, very gifted, predestined?

SARTRE: Very intelligent, yes, of course. Although I did have some difficulties—rather unfortunate results in mathematics, for example, and in natural science. But I believed I was very intelligent. I did not think I had any special qualities. I supposed that style and what one had to say just came to an intelligent person who looked at the world. In other words, there was a positive theory in my head—we'll come back to it—according to which I was a genius, a theory totally contradicted by my way of writing and of thinking out what I had to write. I thought that in a certain fashion I was an ordinary man who was writing books, and if he wrote them as well as he could he would achieve something. He would be a good writer, and above all he would disclose the truth of the world.

DE BEAUVOIR: That idea of disclosing the truth of the world is interesting. But it arose because you had what are called ideas, theories. Even when you were very young you had views of your own about things.

SARTRE: Yes, I had views of my own for what they were worth. But I had had them since I was sixteen, in the first form and philo, when I conceived a whole mass of ideas.

DE BEAUVOIR: Yes, and these were ideas that were to be communicated in a literary form. A fine object had to be created, a book, but at the same time it had to reveal the ideas that were in you—in short, the truth of the world.

SARTRE: I didn't know the whole of that truth yet, far from it. I didn't know it at all. But I was going to learn it as I went along. I would learn it less by looking at the world than by combining words. By combining words I would get hold of real things.

DE BEAUVOIR: How could that come about?

SARTRE: Well, I didn't know. But I did know that the combination of words gave results. You combined them and then there were groups of words that provided a truth.

DE BEAUVOIR: I don't quite follow.

SARTRE: Writing consists of grouping words together—I was not yet concerned with grammar and all that. You combine by imagination; it's imagination that creates groups of words such as . . . "against the grain of the sun." Among these groups of words, some were true.

DE BEAUVOIR: You'd almost say surrealism. You group words and then all of a sudden, by some unknown magic, these words disclose the world?

SARTRE: Yes, that's how it was. Some unknown magic indeed, because I had no idea. It was faith in language.

DE BEAUVOIR: But you didn't write by mere chance, just putting words down in no particular order?

SARTRE: Certainly not.

DE BEAUVOIR: On the contrary it was carefully constructed, very much worked over.

SARTRE: Particularly when this writing had a certain philosophical content. For example, when I was in the first form or hypo-khâgne or philo I discovered the surrealists.

DE BEAUVOIR: Did they interest you?

SARTRE: Yes, a little. It was curious. There I was, with a very conventional education, coming up against all this. I wanted to be interested in it because it interested Nizan, and gradually I did grow more and more interested. At the Ecole Normale it was the prevailing tendency. But the people who were behind it were not much older than I was. I was eighteen when I went to the Ecole Normale. And the surrealists were twenty-five. There was no great difference of age. We read *The Immaculate Conception,* Eluard, Breton: it was very important to me I remember, since I tried my hand at writing pieces in the surrealistic style. Indeed, at that time I began reflecting upon mad people. They being surrealists, as you might say. One of the things I didn't give a damn about was beauty as an inner quality of a work. I didn't pay any attention to it. What mattered more than anything else was that the book should provide the greatest number of new perceptions.

DE BEAUVOIR: And how did you reach the first of your important ideas which has always remained in one shape or another—the idea of contingency?

SARTRE: Well, I find the first allusion to it in the *Suppositoires Midy* notebook.

DE BEAUVOIR: Tell me about this notebook.

SARTRE: I found it in the métro. It was completely blank. That was in khâgne. It was my first philosophical notebook and I took it so as to put down all the things I thought. It was a notebook put out by the Midy laboratories and given to a doctor—the pages were in alphabetical order. So that if I had a thought that began with A, I put it down. But what was curious was the beginning of the thought about contingency. I began thinking about it because of a film. I saw films in which there was no contingency and then when I left the cinema there I found contingency. It was therefore the films' necessity that made me feel that there was no necessity in the street when I went out. People moved about, they were ordinary . . .

DE BEAUVOIR: But how did that comparison take on the importance it had for you? Why did this fact of contingency affect you so that you really wanted to make it . . . I remember when we first met you told me you wanted to make it something that would be like *fatum* for the Greeks. You wanted it to be one of the essential dimensions of the world.

SARTRE: Yes, because I thought it was neglected. I still think so, by the way. If you push Marxist thought right through to the end, for example, you find a necessary world; there's no contingency. There are various forms of determinism and dialectic, but no contingent facts.

DE BEAUVOIR: Did contingency affect you emotionally?

SARTRE: Yes. I think the reason that I discovered it through my films and going out into the street was that I was made to discover it.

DE BEAUVOIR: And what did you write about contingency in the *Suppositoires Midy*?

SARTRE: That contingency existed, as could be seen by the contrast between the cinema, where there was no contingency, and the exit into the street, where on the contrary there was nothing but contingency.

DE BEAUVOIR: Did you talk to Nizan, for instance, or your other friends about your theory of contingency?

SARTRE: They didn't give a damn about it.

DE BEAUVOIR: Why not?

SARTRE: It didn't interest them.

DE BEAUVOIR: Because you hadn't yet given it a striking enough shape?

SARTRE: Maybe. I don't know. When you're at the Ecole Normale, you see, you don't give much of a damn for other people's opinions; you're looking for your own—you're trying to shift for yourself. Nizan moved very quickly from the Fascists to the Communists. In those days he had no time to think about contingency.

DE BEAUVOIR: Tell me more clearly about this connection between philosophy and literature. It struck me. You told me "I want to be Spinoza and Stendhal." But how did you look upon the relation? You didn't see two series of works, the one being philosophical and the other . . .

SARTRE: At that time I did not want to write books of philosophy. I did not want to write the equivalent of the *Critique of Dialectical Reason* or of *Being and Nothingness*. I wanted the philosophy I believed in and the truths I should attain to be expressed in my novel.

DE BEAUVOIR: That is to say that fundamentally you wanted to write *Nausea*.

SARTRE: Fundamentally I wanted to write *Nausea*.

DE BEAUVOIR: You already possessed a well-developed conception of life. Among your letters to Camille there's one that you wrote when you were nineteen and that is perfectly astonishing, since it already contains the embryo of a great theory you had later, concerning happiness, writing, the refusal of a certain kind of happiness and the assertion of your worth as a writer. What was your exact feeling about this worth?

SARTRE: It was absolute. I believed in it as a Christian believes in the Virgin, but I had not the slightest proof. Yet at the same time I had the feeling that those little bits of crap, the cloak-and-dagger stories and the first realistic novels were the proof that I had genius. I could not prove it by what was in them, since I was perfectly aware that they did not yet amount to anything, but the mere fact of writing proved that I had genius. It proved it because if the act of writing is perfect it necessarily requires an author who has genius. The fact of writing perfect things was the proof that one had genius. One can only wish to write in order to write perfect things. Which at the same time, it must be added, are not entirely perfect; they slightly exceed the limits of the perfect and go further. But the idea, "writing means writing perfect things," is the classic idea. I had no proof, then, but I told myself that since I wanted to write, and therefore to write perfect things, it had to be supposed that I should do so. Therefore I was a man who would write perfect things. I was a genius. It's all very comprehensible.

DE BEAUVOIR: But why did you think you were very intelligent?

SARTRE: Because people told me so.

DE BEAUVOIR: You weren't always at the top of the form. When you were at La Rochelle you didn't do so well at school.

SARTRE: It was the reputation I had, I don't quite know why. Certainly not because of my stepfather.

DE BEAUVOIR: Was it a reaction against your stepfather?

SARTRE: Probably. I thought my ideas were true. And that his were just confined to science.

DE BEAUVOIR: You haven't spoken about that at all. What influence did your relations with your stepfather have on you between, let's say, eleven and nineteen? You had this stepfather who was a scientist and whom naturally you didn't like for a whole lot of emotional reasons and because he'd stolen your mother from you. It's not that which sets you against science. In any case you had a childhood turned more toward literature. But can you give me some explanation?

SARTRE: It would take a long time to explain the nature of my relations with my stepfather.

DE BEAUVOIR: They were relations of childhood and adolescence.

SARTRE: Yes. Let's not talk about that now, chiefly because it hasn't the slightest importance as far as writing is concerned. Until I was fourteen I used to show my mother what I wrote, and she would say "Very pretty, very well imagined." She didn't show them to my stepfather, who didn't care about them. He knew I wrote, but he didn't give a damn. Furthermore, these pieces did not deserve that anyone should give a damn about them. But I knew my stepfather took no notice. So he was perpetually the person I wrote against. All my life. The fact of writing was against him. He didn't blame me, because I was too young—I was free to do that rather than play ball —but in fact he was against me.

DE BEAUVOIR: Did he think that literature was pointless?

SARTRE: He thought that you shouldn't decide to take to literature at the age of fourteen. To him that made no sense. As he saw it, a writer was a man who, when he was thirty or forty, had produced a certain number of books. But you had nothing to do with such things at fourteen.

DE BEAUVOIR: I come back to the question: why did you feel you were intelligent?

SARTRE: I didn't think I was intelligent because the word didn't exist for me. It existed, but I didn't use it. It's not that I thought I was stupid. I thought of myself rather as being profound, if a child can use that word. I thought, as you might put it, that I could turn things over in my mind that other boys could not turn over in theirs.

DE BEAUVOIR: Is that why you thought you understood more things than your stepfather did?

SARTRE: I thought that he was more intelligent than I was, because he understood mathematics.

DE BEAUVOIR: But you thought that you possessed something that he did not?

SARTRE: Yes. The fact of writing. The fact of writing put me above him.

DE BEAUVOIR: And the fact of thinking, too. Did you think what he said was nonsense?

SARTRE: No. It was very hard to judge what he said. He had ideas that weren't mine, ideas that missed the point, but I could not tell just when they went astray. He talked about mathematics and physics and technical knowledge and what happened in a factory. He had a completely organized world. He had read books that were of no great interest, but that were well known at that time.

DE BEAUVOIR: So he wasn't a mere engineer completely closed to other interests?

SARTRE: No. He had read books that I read and that I liked. Of course plenty of engineers do so nowadays. But as far as I was concerned it gave me a very uncomfortable feeling.

DE BEAUVOIR: To go back to that period you've talked about so little, from eleven to nineteen. Did you have any political attitudes then?

SARTRE: In 1917 we did take some interest in the Russian Revolution, the other boys and me . . .

DE BEAUVOIR: But how old were you?

SARTRE: I was twelve and we weren't much concerned. Our chief question was whether we could beat Germany in spite of the USSR's separate peace, and that was all.

DE BEAUVOIR: What were your feelings about society?

SARTRE: I was a democrat. My grandfather, who was a republican, brought me up to republicanism—I said so in *The Words*.

DE BEAUVOIR: Did that cause any conflict with your stepfather? Did the fact that you were a democrat and a republican show in any way?

SARTRE: No. My stepfather was a republican too. You might say we weren't the same kind of republicans, but that became apparent only little by little. Because to begin with my republicanism was words. An impulsive feeling for a society in which everyone should have the same rights.

DE BEAUVOIR: So at that time there was no particular conflict between him and you on those questions?

SARTRE: No. That was later, when I was at the lycée in Paris. And then I've forgotten one detail that helped in having me sent to Paris. When I was in the third form I stole money belonging to my step-father, who gave it to my mother.

DE BEAUVOIR: Tell this story again.

SARTRE: Well, I needed money.

DE BEAUVOIR: Yes, I know. You wanted to be on the same footing as the other boys and to be able to take them to the theater and treat them to things . . .

SARTRE: Treat them to cakes. I remember how we used to go to La Rochelle's big pastry shop and eat babas with my mother's money.

DE BEAUVOIR: So you were in need.

SARTRE: I was in need. My mother's handbag was kept in a cupboard. It always contained the whole month's money for her and for the things she had to buy—the food, for example. There were quantities of notes and I helped myself. I took single francs to begin with—they were worth much more than a present-day franc—and then I took notes, rather cautiously, five francs here and two francs there, and one day in May I found that I was master of seventy francs. In 1918 seventy francs was an enormous sum. Then one day I felt ill and went to bed quite early. The next morning my mother woke me, wanting to know if I was better, and I had put my jacket, which contained my whole treasure, notes and coins, over my legs to keep me warm. She picked it up and shook it, but without meaning anything, and she heard all the coins rattling about inside, ding, ding, ding. She put her hand in the pocket, found the notes and the coins, whipped them out and said, "What is all this money?" I said, "It's money I've taken from Cardino for a joke. His mother gave it to him, and I intend to let him have it back today." "Very well," said my mother, "but I'll give it back to him myself. You must bring him this evening so that I can ask him what it's all about." This was awkward, because the Cardino in question—I can't tell why I picked on him—was my worst enemy. I went to the lycée that morning, and it was the devil's own job to find Cardino, who then wanted to knock my head off. In the end some other boys stepped in and it was agreed that he should come, that he should take the money, that he should give me back three-fifths and keep two-fifths for himself. He came. My mother made him a positive speech, which he found very amusing—one should not allow oneself to be robbed like that, at his age one should take care, and so on. He took the money and left. He at once bought himself a huge flashlight. And Mme Cardino, his mother, discovered the whole thing two days later. Meanwhile, he had given the sum he owed me, that is, three-fifths of the money, to some friends who did not pass it on to me right away. There was a great scene with my mother and stepfather, I was blamed, and so on.

DE BEAUVOIR: Yes, but Mme Cardino, the boy's mother, came to ask what all this money meant.

SARTRE: Yes. So my mother understood everything. I was severely scolded and kept at arm's length for some time. And I remember—I was in the third form—my grandfather came down from Paris with my grandmother. He was told all about it and it vexed him extremely. One day I went to the chemist's shop with him, and going in he dropped a ten centime coin on the floor. It went ding. I hurried to pick it up. He stopped me and bent down himself, with his poor creaking knees, because I was no longer worthy to pick up coins from the ground.

DE BEAUVOIR: That must have wounded you somewhat. It's the kind of thing that wounds children.

SARTRE: Yes, it did wound me. And then my relations with the other boys weren't good.

DE BEAUVOIR: To what extent did your relations with the other boys in La Rochelle mark you, from the point of view of writing? You've sometimes said that they taught you about violence.

SARTRE: Yes, it taught me about violence. Normally, all I should have known about violence would have been a punch on the nose, given or received. That's how it was at the Paris lycée. But at the La Rochelle school they took the war seriously; the opponent was always a Boche. They were violent. Violence was an everyday reality. There was the violence of the war and then the minor violence of these boys without fathers. Above all, I was very often the object of it, as you are in a lycée, when you are knocked about. They don't knock you about as though you were an enemy, but like a comrade, and they do it to prevent you making a mistake or to oblige you to make friends again with someone or just for fun, it doesn't matter. We all belonged to the lycée, which had two chief enemies—the worthy Fathers' school, a religious establishment, and the boys we called the hooligans, young hooligans who did not necessarily belong to any school. They might be apprentices. They were boys like ourselves, of from twelve to sixteen, and when we met we fought with them, without knowing them, simply because their clothes were somewhat rougher than ours. They would come and look us right in the eye and we'd exchange punches. I particularly remember one day when I was going shopping with my mother after school. In a street that runs down the middle of La Rochelle, near a gate with a big clock on top of it, I found myself face to face with one of these hooligans. We rolled on the ground in the street, hitting and kicking one another until my mother, perfectly astonished, came out of the shop and found me lying there, inextricably tangled with my enemy. I felt her hand plucking me from his embrace. We used to fight wholeheartedly.

DE BEAUVOIR: When you fought with these boys, were you then at one with the lycée boys who ordinarily persecuted you?

SARTRE: Yes. If any of them had been going by, they would have joined me in beating up the hooligan. There was an alliance between the lycée boys. But I didn't fully belong to the lycée, because I was a Parisian and because I had a way of speaking and a way of being that was not the same as the other boys. I did have friends, nevertheless, but I used to tell them tall stories, and they didn't believe them. For instance, when I first went to the La Rochelle lycée I said I had a girl in Paris and that on Saturdays and Sundays we went to a hotel and made love. Seeing that I was twelve and somewhat below the average size, the tale seemed rather comic than otherwise. I was my own victim, since I had supposed that they would be plunged into admiration.

DE BEAUVOIR: Did this hostility affect you deeply or did it to some degree remain in the realm of play?

SARTRE: It remained in the realm of play only for them. Not for me. For my part I felt that some sort of ill-luck was at work upon me, and I was very unhappy. Very often I was the object of jokes and blows. And when that happened I felt inferior, which I was not at the Paris lycée, at Henri IV. There were difficulties, but they're inevitable at that age. I had friends, though there were also boys I did not get along with. However, at Henri IV there was a group of which I was an integral part. Whereas at La Rochelle, although I had friends, the affection came mostly from my side.

DE BEAUVOIR: And did that have an influence on your later development?

SARTRE: I think so. In the first place it seems to me that I've never forgotten the violence I learned there. It's in that light that I've seen people's relations with one another. I've never had tender relations with my friends since then. There were always ideas of violence between them or from them to me or from me to them. It was not a lack of friendship but rather the proof that violence was imperative in the relations between men.

DE BEAUVOIR: Yet this did not come into play in your relations with Maheu, Guille, or Nizan when you were at Henri IV or the Ecole Normale, did it?

SARTRE: With Nizan, no. As for Guille and Maheu, I never thought of knocking their heads off at any time. But I did feel a kind of distance, the possibility of violence between us.

DE BEAUVOIR: And did that have an influence on the part you played when you were at the Ecole Normale . . . ?

SARTRE: Yes, that was the continuation. I thought it was quite natural. It seemed to me normal to throw water bombs at fellows who came back at night, wearing evening clothes. At La Rochelle it was different. When we fought with the hooligans, the struggle made us bourgeois. I didn't think much about it for my part, but I could tell that it was certainly seen in that light by those around me. To knock hooligans about was to set yourself up as a bourgeois.

DE BEAUVOIR: But you were never a violent man in later days, were you?

SARTRE: I had my nose bloodied at the Ecole Normale from time to time.

DE BEAUVOIR: You used to have fits of anger. You were quite choleric when I first knew you, particularly in the morning. But it never turned to violence.

SARTRE: No.

DE BEAUVOIR: Was it related to a certain violence of language you had when we first met? You used pretty coarse words for things. Was there a connection?

SARTRE: It was a delicately shaded, abstract form of violence, but we all dreamed of a simple and violent philosophy that would be that of the twentieth century. When he was reading Descartes, Nizan conceived a positive world of violence.

DE BEAUVOIR: This kind of violence that made you fight with the hooligans had a right-wing, almost fascist aspect.

SARTRE: Fascist no, certainly not. But right-wing, yes. As I told you, we were bourgeois.

DE BEAUVOIR: And how did you get out of it?

SARTRE: I did not feel that I was really in it. And then I came to Paris . . .

DE BEAUVOIR: The transition from the provinces to Paris was very important to you, I believe?

SARTRE: I wasn't aware of it right away. I looked upon myself chiefly as an exile from that little world I was used to. It was the second form. There was no longer any question of fighting or my being knocked about, and I had normal though rather boring relations with the other boys. But in the end I'd grown quite fond of those surroundings; I'd adapted myself to La Rochelle. I was in Paris because my grandfather, a teacher of German, had colleagues there, headmasters who knew him and who would find me a place in a good lycée; and to turn me away from the appalling transgression I had committed with Cardino the previous year by stealing.

DE BEAUVOIR: Just now you said those years were very unhappy, but now you're saying that you had adapted yourself to La Rochelle.

SARTRE: Yes, the unhappy years were those of the fourth and third forms. But in the second I had adapted.

DE BEAUVOIR: And how did you feel about your arrival in Paris? You've said that the fact of your being a boarder was important to you, whereas before you had lived with your family. How did it affect you? Did you adapt yourself to life as a boarder easily?

SARTRE: I was frightened of it, because I had read a great many nineteenth-century novels in which there were boys who became unhappy when they were boarders. It seemed to me a set thing—you were a boarder, therefore you were unhappy.

DE BEAUVOIR: And in the event?

SARTRE: In the event I was not unhappy. I found Nizan and renewed my relations with him—deeper than those of the earlier days. We began an intimate friendship. We used to go and see the upper first form boys we knew and borrow their books. That was where I came to know Conrad and some others.

DE BEAUVOIR: Did Nizan also want to write in those days?

SARTRE: Ever since I knew him Nizan had wanted to write. He wanted to write even in the sixth form. It was a splendid thing for me, in the first form, to find someone of my own level who wanted to write, who had always wanted to write. Bercot was rather different. He too wanted to write, but he said less about it. He was more reserved. What mattered was that Nizan and I wanted to write; that bound us together. And the other boys knew we wanted to write and they respected us accordingly. I was in the first form A, of course. I did Latin and Greek with Georgin, whom I've told you about. I worked well, since I ended up with the excellence prize, which was very far from what I could have hoped for at La Rochelle.

DE BEAUVOIR: And did Nizan work well, too?

SARTRE: Nizan worked fairly well. He was not quite as steady as I was. He was more interested in going out, seeing the people he knew, in the friends of his family, in parties and girls and all that kind of thing. Yet he was very fond of intellectual work, of a writer's work.

DE BEAUVOIR: Did he too have the idea that he would be a great writer and let's say a genius, to a certain degree?

SARTRE: We didn't talk about it.

DE BEAUVOIR: What was this idea of genius, which according to you was inherent in the very fact of wanting to write?

SARTRE: What is inherent is that you write in order to create something worthwhile, to draw out of yourself something that has worth and that represents you. The man is to be found in his book. You and I know Proust only by his book; and it is from his book that comes our liking or our dislike for him. So the man is present in his book, and the man's value comes to him from the book.

DE BEAUVOIR: In short, it's rather Kant's idea: you must, therefore you can. You must produce a good book; it is your commitment, your choice. You must produce a great work, therefore you possess within you what is needed to do so.

SARTRE: That is quite obviously so. I elected to produce a work. I elected that which I was formed to do. It is indeed quite Kantian. But Kant's formal, universal ethics neglects contingent data. One has to act appropriately, allowing for the contingent characteristics of the people who are there and not only for their abstract existence.

DE BEAUVOIR: You were on that very plane, that abstract plane, and you still had a completely abstract vision of the future. Did this find expression in a kind of pride, self-satisfaction, contempt for others, exaltation? How did you experience it?

SARTRE: There certainly were moments of exaltation. I felt my genius only in flashes of intuition; the rest of the time it was merely a form without content. By an odd contradiction I never looked upon my works as works of genius. Although they were written according to the rules that in my opinion implied genius.

DE BEAUVOIR: In short, genius was always in the future?

SARTRE: Yes.

DE BEAUVOIR: You were perfectly well aware that your works at that time—*Jésus la chouette* (Jesus the Owl), *L'Ange du morbide* (The Morbid Angel), *Er l'Arménien* (Er the Armenian)—were not very good.

SARTRE: I didn't say it, but I knew it.

DE BEAUVOIR: And what about *Une défaite* (A Defeat)?

SARTRE: I began by seeing *Une défaite* as a novel that would express my particular way of feeling and my conception of the world. It was never finished, so it can't be compared with anything else. There again I didn't think I was a genius when I was writing it, but still this novel was more important for me.

DE BEAUVOIR: And *La Légende de la vérité* (The Legend of Truth)?

SARTRE: I thought *La Légende de la vérité* would be more important still because it contained my personal philosophical ideas. I thought that if these ideas were really well expressed they would strike people and they would explain what men were. You remember, there were men who thought in universal terms, and they were the learned, and there were others who had general ideas, that is to say the philosophers and the bourgeois. And then there were the thoughts of the man alone, a man such as I wished to be, a man who thought only by his own powers and who gave light to the city thanks to what he thought and what he felt.

DE BEAUVOIR: An extract from *La Légende de la vérité* was published. Was that the first time you appeared in print?

SARTRE: Yes.

DE BEAUVOIR: You had a few enthusiastic readers.

SARTRE: The manner was boring. Philosophy was discussed in the florid language of essays. It was rather absurd. It didn't have the technical vocabulary it should have had.

DE BEAUVOIR: And then you made the synthesis. You came to *Nausea*. There you really produced literature and at the same time you gave your philosophical view of the world, of contingency, and so on. But to go back to this question of genius, how have you changed in the course of your life?

SARTRE: I now think that style does not consist of writing fine phrases for oneself but of writing phrases for other people. It sets a boy of sixteen quite a problem when he tries to think what writing means and when he does not yet possess any notion of other people.

DE BEAUVOIR: Just how can one tell what are the words whose association will act on the reader? Must one trust in the void? Take the plunge?

SARTRE: Yes, you chance it. After all, you have reasons for chancing it.

DE BEAUVOIR: You used to have the idea of a kind of salvation according to which a literary work had a reality that went beyond the moment, being something absolute. That doesn't mean that you were thinking directly of posterity, but of a kind of immortality nevertheless. What did you mean by salvation?

SARTRE: When I originally wrote "Pour un Papillon" (For a Butterfly) I wrote something absolute. I created something absolute which was, in short, myself. I carried myself over into an everlasting life. An artistic creation outlives mundane things. If I bring one into existence, it outlasts mundane things and therefore I, the author that it embodies, I outlast mundane things. Behind this there was the Christian idea of immortality—I passed from mortal to immortal life.

DE BEAUVOIR: And it was that notion which came to an end when you reached your committed writing?

SARTRE: It came to an end entirely.

DE BEAUVOIR: There was no idea of salvation anymore? It's never come again? I imagine the very notion has faded away? Not that that means you haven't kept an eye, a rather sideways eye, on posterity.

SARTRE: Until after *Nausea* I had only dreamed of genius, but after the war, in 1945, I'd proved myself—there was *No Exit* and there was *Nausea*. In 1944, when the Allies left Paris, I possessed genius and I set off for America as a writer of genius who was going for a tour in another country. At that point I was immortal and I was assured of my immortality. And that meant I no longer had to think about it.

DE BEAUVOIR: Yes, because in fact you were not one of those men who say, "I'm writing immortal works; I'm immortal." Nothing like that about you.

SARTRE: And it's complicated, too, because the moment you're immortal and you're writing immortal works, everything is already decided. Yet you have the feeling that you're creating something that did not exist before. You must therefore place yourself in everyday time. So it's better not to think about immortality, except out of the corner of your eye, but rather to stake everything on life. As a living man I write for other living men, supposing that if I succeed in what I'm doing, I'll still be read after my death, and that people my message is not aimed at, people to whom it is not addressed, will find it valid.

DE BEAUVOIR: Which do you think will make you live on—insofar as you do think you will live on—literature or philosophy? Would you rather people liked your philosophy or your literature, or would you choose to have them like both?

SARTRE: Of course my answer is let them like both. But there is a hierarchy, and the hierarchy is philosophy second and literature first. I should like to achieve immortality through literature, and philosophy is a way of reaching literature. Philosophy does not possess an absolute value in itself, since circumstances change and bring philosophical changes with them. A philosophy is not something that is valid for the present moment; it is not something you write for your contemporaries. It speculates upon timeless realities, and since it speaks of eternity it will necessarily be overtaken and left behind by others. It speaks of things that go far beyond our individual point of view of today, whereas literature, on the contrary, catalogs the present world, the world one discovers through reading, conversation, passion, traveling. Philosophy goes further. For instance, it considers that the passions of today are new passions, passions that did not exist in the ancient world; love . . .

DE BEAUVOIR: Do you mean that in your opinion literature has a more absolute character, philosophy depending much more on the course of history and being much more subject to revision?

SARTRE: It necessarily calls for revision, since it always goes beyond the present age.

DE BEAUVOIR: Certainly. But is there not an absolute in the fact of being Descartes or Kant even if, in a certain manner, they are to be outstripped? They are outstripped, but the outstripper only moves on from what they have already contributed. There is a reference to them that is an absolute.

SARTRE: I don't deny it. But that doesn't exist in literature. People who love Rabelais wholeheartedly read him as though he had written yesterday.

DE BEAUVOIR: And in an absolutely direct fashion.

SARTRE: Cervantes—Shakespeare—you read them as though they were here now. Romeo and Juliet or Hamlet are works that seem to have been written only yesterday.

DE BEAUVOIR: So you give literature the first place in your work? Yet in your reading taken as a whole, and in your education, philosophy has played an enormous part.

SARTRE: Yes, because I look upon it as the best means of writing. It was philosophy that gave me the dimensions necessary for creating a tale.

DE BEAUVOIR: But still, it can't be said that for you philosophy was nothing more than a means.

SARTRE: To begin with, that's what it was.

DE BEAUVOIR: To begin with, yes, but afterward, when one considers the time you spent writing *Being and Nothingness* and then the *Critique of Dialectical Reason,* one can't say that it was simply in order to be able to create literary works. It was also because you were passionately fond of philosophy for its own sake.

SARTRE: Yes, it interested me, that's certain. I wanted to express my vision of the world while at the same time making the characters in my literary works or my essays experience it in their lives. I was describing this vision to my contemporaries.

DE BEAUVOIR: In short, if someone said to you, "You're a great writer, but as a philosopher you don't convince me," you would prefer him to one who said, "Your philosophy is prodigious, but as a writer you don't amount to a row of beans."

SARTRE: Yes, I like the first hypothesis better.

DE BEAUVOIR: Perhaps you think that your philosophy doesn't belong exclusively to you, and that someone else could hit upon the idea of the practico-inert or of recurrence, just as even the most original scientists are only the first to find out what others would have discovered sooner or later. Could it not also be said that literature is absolute, but that it is also closed and brought to an end, whereas although philosophy is outstripped it is at the same time carried on. Descartes lives on in you, for example, and it is not at all the same kind of survival that Shakespeare or Tacitus might have for you, or anyone else you read with great pleasure. They may influence you in a certain way, but they do so by sympathetic vibration as it were, or by reflection, whereas Descartes has become an integral part of your way of living.

SARTRE: When I was little I wanted to write a novel that would be like *The Hunchback of Notre Dame* or *Les Misérables,* a work that would be recognized in other ages, an absolute that nothing could modify. And as you know, philosophy came into my life in a rather sideways fashion.

DE BEAUVOIR: Why did philosophy come into your life, insofar as you considered yourself a creator?

SARTRE: I was a creator of novels in my imagination. When I began philosophy I didn't know what it was. I had a cousin who was in the elementary mathematics course and like all elementary mathematics boys he did philosophy. He wouldn't talk about it in front of me. I knew he was learning things I didn't know and that aroused my curiosity. But I already possessed fixed, settled ideas of novels and essays—nonphilosophical essays—and they were too strong for philosophy to overturn when it appeared.

DE BEAUVOIR: Why did you become a creator in philosophy?

SARTRE: It's rather odd, because in philosophy I didn't want to be a creator, I didn't want to be a philosopher—I thought it was a waste of time. I was fond of learning philosophy, but as for writing it, that seemed to me absurd. It's hard to understand, I may say, since as I wrote I was also inventing and I might just as well have amused myself with the thought that one could write philosophical works. But philosophy had a relation to truth and to the sciences that bored me, and then again it was too early. In khâgne the subject for my first essay was "What is duration?" So I came into contact with Bergson.

DE BEAUVOIR: Then afterward, during the years when you were preparing for your degree and the *agrégation,* did it interest you?

SARTRE: Yes. I wrote works that benefited or rather "malefited" from my philosophical knowledge. Indeed, I remember that *Er l'Arménien* (Er the Armenian) contained a description of Plato's cave. I'd thought it was my duty to put it together again and describe it.

DE BEAUVOIR: Even so you were deeply interested in philosophy at the same time, since you produced a most uncommonly well-polished essay for your degree, a very thoroughgoing essay on the imaginary.

SARTRE: It was Delacroix who said to me, "Well, then, write a book on the imaginary for my series."

DE BEAUVOIR: Why did you agree, since you were so taken up by *Nausea* and various literary plans?

SARTRE: The prohibition against writing philosophy was not absolute. Doing so might be useful to me. The imaginary was linked to literature, since works of art have a relation to the imaginary, and then earlier on I had had ideas about images and I wanted to clarify them.

DE BEAUVOIR: You also had ideas about contingency that were philosophical ideas. When we first met, you said to me, "I want to be Spinoza and Stendhal." So you also had a vocation to be a philospher?

SARTRE: Yes, but you see I chose sensitive men, accessible to a twentieth-century mind. For me, Spinoza was more a man than a philosopher. I liked his philosophy, but above all I liked the man. Now it's his work that interests me—that's the difference.

DE BEAUVOIR: There were two books, *Psychology and the Imagination* and *The Psychology of the Imagination.* Which one was commissioned?

SARTRE: *Psychology and the Imagination.*

DE BEAUVOIR: Then why did you write *The Psychology of the Imagination?*

SARTRE: Because it followed from *Psychology and the Imagination.*

DE BEAUVOIR: Was there a kind of dialectic involved?

SARTRE: I remember having had the idea of *The Psychology of the Imagination* while I was writing the other. They did not form two separate volumes but one complete work, the first part being *Psychology and the Imagination* and the second, *The Psychology of the Imagination.* As I had to give Delacroix something for his collection, I let him have the first.

DE BEAUVOIR: And then, later on, why *Being and Nothingness?*

SARTRE: That was during the war. I conceived it during the phony war and in the prison camp. I wrote it in that period—you either wrote nothing or you wrote things that were essential.

DE BEAUVOIR: That idea of nothingness already occurred in *The Psychology of the Imagination.* You couldn't help going into it more deeply.

SARTRE: In it I expressed my essential idea. Since my philo year I had decided in favor of realism. I had turned thoroughly against idealism when I was taught it. I had two important years of philosophy, in the first form and the year in the upper first, the khâgne. In hypo-khâgne, on the contrary, I had a master I did not understand. I had two good years of philosophy before going to the Ecole Normale, and there I had only one idea—that any theory which did not state that consciousness perceived exterior objects as they were was doomed to failure. In the end it was that which made me go to Germany, when I was told that Husserl and Heidegger had a way of grasping the real just as it was.

DE BEAUVOIR: Philosophy interested you enormously then, since you spent a year in Germany to make a thorough study of Husserl's philosophy and to get to know Heidegger.

SARTRE: This is how I spent my time in Germany. Philosophy in the morning and until two in the afternoon. Then I had something to eat, came back at about five, and worked on *Nausea,* that is, a literary work.

DE BEAUVOIR: But even so, philosophy counted a great deal. I remember when you had read Levinas's book on Husserl you had a moment of utter dismay and confusion because you said to yourself, "Oh, he's already discovered all my ideas." So they mattered a great deal to you, your ideas.

SARTRE: Yes, but I was mistaken when I said he'd already discovered them.

DE BEAUVOIR: You had a certain intuition, and you didn't want anyone else to have had it before you. You were therefore banking on philosophical creation too. Once you had lived in Paris and had matured a little, what did you think of your chances of success when you talked to Nizan or thought about it by yourself?

SARTRE: In my novel based on the relations between Nietzsche and Wagner, I saw myself as a man who would have an eventful life and who, after each catastrophe, would write a book that would be published. I imagined a romantic life and a man of genius who would die unrecognized but to whom fame would come later. These are old memories. I used to set the character there before me and dream about everything that would happen to him. But fundamentally, I already foresaw writing in a much more reasonable fashion. I would write my books, they would be good, and I would have them published—that was how I saw things. The proof is that when Nizan had had one or two books published, I gave him extracts from *La Légende de la vérité* (The Legend of Truth). *Bifur* published one piece.

DE BEAUVOIR: When you thought reasonably about being published and read, what kind of success did you look forward to? Did you think about fame and celebrity? I mean when you were eighteen or twenty?

SARTRE: I thought that the public capable of understanding me would be a very limited élite.

DE BEAUVOIR: That was the Stendhal tradition you liked so much—the "happy few."*

SARTRE: Those readers would recognize and like me. I would be read by fifteen thousand people, and fame would consist of fifteen thousand others and then fifteen thousand more.

DE BEAUVOIR: Then what you wanted was to last. Being Spinoza and Stendhal meant being someone who had marked his century and who would be read in the centuries to come. Is that what you thought when you were twenty?

SARTRE: Yes, when I first met you.

DE BEAUVOIR: In one way you were very arrogant. You took to yourself little Hippias's remark, "I have never met any man who was my equal."

SARTRE: I'd written that in a notebook.

DE BEAUVOIR: How have your relations with fame and celebrity evolved? What have been your inner feelings about your career?

SARTRE: Fundamentally, it was something very simple—you wrote and you became well known. But there were certain ideas of the time that made it all more complicated than that.

DE BEAUVOIR: And then you had some cruel blows when at the beginning you thought *Nausea* had been rejected. That did shake you!

SARTRE: What's more it proved how important I thought publishers were. A real genius, such as I imagined him, would have laughed, saying, "Why, so I'm not in print. Well, well . . ."

DE BEAUVOIR: Yes, but while you were arrogant you were also—the word modest doesn't suit you—but let's say reasonable and long-suffering. You did not look upon your books as works of genius, and

* In English in the text (trans.)

although you'd put a great deal into *Nausea* you did not feel you'd written a masterpiece. You did not see things in that light, it seems to me. That's what I'd like you to explain more clearly.

SARTRE: It varied. In the beginning the work was only potential, it was unrealized. I sat down at my table and then I wrote, but the work was not there, since it was not yet written. My relation to the work was therefore abstract. Yet I was writing, and that was a real act.

DE BEAUVOIR: Once you had written a book, *Nausea,* for example, you really looked upon it as a book. *La Légende de la vérité* too. And you were perfectly willing to have it criticized; you were aware of its faults. In the case of *Nausea* you were supported by me—I liked it very much—and you really banked on that book. You were dreadfully taken aback when it was rejected.

SARTRE: That was part of everyday life. But still I looked upon myself —though in all modesty, if I may say so—as a genius. I talked to my friends as a genius talks to his friends. Quite unpretentiously, but seen from within, it was a genius who was speaking.

DE BEAUVOIR: To go back to the first refusal of *Nausea,* did you think you were a genius who had not yet found the way of gaining recognition?

SARTRE: I thought *Nausea* was a good book and that it had been rejected just as good books are rejected in the history of literature. You've written a book; you've offered it. Later on it will be a masterpiece . . .

DE BEAUVOIR: As it was for Proust, by the way.

SARTRE: That's how I saw things. I didn't stop thinking of myself as a genius, but this would become apparent only in the future. I was to be a genius. I was one already, but above all I was to be a genius. I'd staked a great deal on *Nausea.*

DE BEAUVOIR: You were with me at Chamonix just after the rejection, and you were extremely sad. I believe you even shed a few tears, which is something very rare for you. It really was a blow.

SARTRE: Yes, but I thought the book had been rejected because it was good.

DE BEAUVOIR: As for me, I was entirely behind you. I thought it was very good.

SARTRE: That was what I thought. But there were sad moments, moments of loneliness, when I said to myself that it was a failure and I would have to begin again. But the notion of genius was not wiped out.

DE BEAUVOIR: And when it was accepted, and when very soon after that you wrote some short stories that were published right away, did you feel satisfied?

SARTRE: Oh, it was splendid!

DE BEAUVOIR: I know, because you wrote me very cheerful letters at the time. You told me how it had been accepted and how you had been asked to make a few little alterations and how you had agreed because you thought them reasonable. Brice Parrain asked you to tone down the Populist aspect somewhat. You didn't play the genius who never accepts any advice.

SARTRE: No.

DE BEAUVOIR: You were perfectly ready to take advice. It was almost the relation between the transcendental and the empirical characters.

SARTRE: That's right.

DE BEAUVOIR: From a transcendental point of view you were a genius, but it was a question of making that evident in empirical life. You were not absolutely certain you would be able to do so right away.

SARTRE: No, because when I referred to my guides, who were the famous men of earlier times, I saw that you didn't really become a person of any importance before the age of thirty. The lives of Victor Hugo, Zola, and Chateaubriand meant a great deal, even if I wasn't so keen on Chateaubriand. Those lives formed a synthesis, producing a single life that was to be mine. I really behaved according to these patterns, and I thought I should dabble in politics when I was fifty.

DE BEAUVOIR: Because all the great men had gone in for politics.

SARTRE: I didn't think that politics was life, but in my future biography there had to be a political period.

DE BEAUVOIR: I wish you would say something on this subject.

SARTRE: On the subject of genius?

DE BEAUVOIR: On the way you felt it and thought about it. Did you think that *Nausea* was a masterpiece?

SARTRE: No. I thought, "I've said what I had to say, and that's fine. I've corrected the faults that Mme Morel and Guille pointed out. I've done as well as I could and it has a certain value." But I didn't go much further than that. I didn't think, "It's a masterpiece begotten by my genius." Yet there was something of that about it too. Not "it's a masterpiece" but "it's a genius who has produced this." It was there somewhere, though I can't exactly place it. I didn't trifle with my works. They stood for something important. And yet as a genius I had the right to laugh at them or make jokes about them, though at the same time they were of the first importance. And at the same time a genius doesn't allow himself to despair if he isn't recognized.

DE BEAUVOIR: But on the other hand he's not fully satisfied if a book is successful?

SARTRE: No. He goes on. He has other things to say.

DE BEAUVOIR: And how did things develop afterward?

SARTRE: Well, what was awkward about this idea of genius was that I believe in a kind of equality between different intelligences. It follows that a work can be defined as good because it suits the author who wrote it and because he has acquired a certain technical skill, but not because he has a quality that other men do not possess.

DE BEAUVOIR: You've told me that one must distinguish between genius and intelligence, that you did not consider yourself particularly intelligent, but what seemed to set you apart from the other boys at La Rochelle was a certain depth and also the idea of a mission—you were to reveal truths. So you did have an uncommon destiny, after all.

SARTRE: Yes, but it didn't make sense. That idea of mission had to be given up. But it's true I used to think, "I have a mission."

DE BEAUVOIR: Yes, and you've already spoken about it in *The Words,* and in connection with Michel Strogoff. But even so, until the war, didn't you feel much more intelligent than all the people around you?

SARTRE: Yes, without a doubt.

DE BEAUVOIR: You once said to me—and I thought it very sound—"Fundamentally, intelligence is an exacting requisition." It's not so much quickness of mind or finding the connections between a whole mass of things, but a requirement, that is, a requirement not to stop but to go farther on, always farther on. I think you had that requirement. Did you feel that it was stronger in you than in others?

SARTRE: Yes, but I shouldn't put it like that now. I should not say that because I'd written books I was superior to a fellow who's built houses or traveled a great deal.

DE BEAUVOIR: When you and Nizan were together you used to say you were supermen for fun, and at the end of *The Words* you say that you are just anyone at all. It's a very equivocal phrase—you both think it and do not think it. To begin with, how did you pass from the idea of the superman to the idea of just anyone at all? And quite honestly what does it mean for you, that idea of being just anyone at all?

SARTRE: I think I may have a little more talent than another man, a slightly more developed intelligence. But these are only phenomena whose origin remains an intelligence equal to my neighbor's or a sensitivity equal to my neighbor's. I do not think I have a superiority of any kind. My superiority is my books, insofar as they are good, but the next man also has his superiority—it may be the bag of hot chestnuts he sells at a café door in the winter. Each man has his own superiority. For my part, I've chosen this one.

DE BEAUVOIR: You don't believe that entirely since you think there are some people who are fools or swine . . .

SARTRE: But I don't think they were so to begin with. They have been made so. In my notebooks I've written about the nature of stupidity and the way some people have been forcibly taught it. The essential comes from outside. It is an oppression from outside imposed upon the intelligence. Stupidity is a form of oppression.

DE BEAUVOIR: Did your feelings about genius change between the days before the war and those after it?

SARTRE: Yes. I think the war was useful to all my ideas.

DE BEAUVOIR: In one way you had a certain satisfaction when you were a prisoner of war, because starting from a completely anonymous basis you made them acknowledge that you were someone. In other words you might indeed have been just anyone at all. What pleased you was that you were not lost among all those men and isolated by your culture, your books, or your intelligence, but on the contrary you were on an equal footing with them. It was being on an equal footing, being just anyone at all, that made you attribute a value to this anyone at all.

SARTRE: You may be right.

DE BEAUVOIR: It was something you were pleased about. You arrived there, empty-handed, unknown, nameless, without any superiority visible to the people around you, because they weren't very keenly aware of intellectual superiority, and you established good relations with them. There was *Bariona,* which not just anyone at all could have written; and you were friends with the intellectuals and the priests. You made yourself a place there and you shifted for yourself like an ordinary second-class private.

Speaking of the wave of fame that burst over you after the war, you said you had not had the least expectation of this international celebrity. What impression did it make on you? Was it the fulfillment of a wish and the recognition of your genius, or was it no more than an empirical happening that had no great influence on the transcendental truth that you were clinging to in any event?

SARTRE: I should say the second. Of course it did have a certain effect on me, being fairly well known and having people come from far off and say, "You are M. Sartre, and you have written this and that." But I did not attach any great importance to it. Seeing these people who said, "Oh, you wrote this, you wrote that," left me comparatively indifferent. And it seemed to me that the time for fame had not yet come. It comes at the end of your life. You are famous at the end of your life, when you have completed your work. But really I did not see things clearly. It's more complex than that. At the end of your life you have a transitional period that goes on for a few years after your death, and fame comes after that. Yet what is quite sure is that I looked upon it all as a kind of unimportant game, a sort of shadow of fame to show what fame really was; but it was not fame itself. I had no fellow feeling for all those people who crowded into my lectures in 1945. I did not like them. They were packed together and there were women who fainted. I thought it was ridiculous.

DE BEAUVOIR: You knew that there was something of snobbery in it, something of misapprehension, something that arose from the political situation, since at that time French culture was being exported, there being nothing else to send abroad.

SARTRE: I did not take much part in the whole affair. It was thought that I did, because the papers said, "he does this and he does that in order to be talked about."

DE BEAUVOIR: Yes, you were accused of seeking publicity, whereas on the contrary you were . . .

SARTRE: I didn't take any notice of it. I wrote. Of course I had to have an audience when I wrote a play, but I did nothing to make people come. I wrote the play, I had it acted, and that's all.

DE BEAUVOIR: And after the war, how did your relations with your books evolve? Did you ask yourself from time to time, "What does it amount to in the end, all these things I've written? What level have I reached? Will I last?"

SARTRE: Yes, but rarely.

DE BEAUVOIR: Yes, what really mattered was writing those books, being pleased with them yourself and having the approval of certain people. Working to satisfy yourself and to satisfy some given readers is the best thing in life. As for fame, you may have it during your lifetime, but it did not prevent Chateaubriand from having terrible fits of bitterness. Though to be sure they were connected with political affairs.

SARTRE: Yet fame is never pure. It has to do with art, but also with

163

politics and many, many other things. The celebrity I had after the war prevented me from wanting anything else, but I've never mistaken it for the fame that comes after, the fame that I may or may not have.

DE BEAUVOIR: In other words, what you mean by fame is the verdict of posterity?

SARTRE: Unless the world changes entirely, I shall be granted a place in the twentieth century. The textbooks of literature will mention me as a successful writer. They may say that the success was owing to a mistake on the part of the public, or on the contrary they may say that I was important, and so on. Then again, fame goes with a certain superiority—superiority over other writers. And it must be admitted that that's not very pretty, since I think two contradictory things. I think that good writers are better than the others and that a very good writer is better than anyone, than anyone, that is to say, except other very good writers, who are rare. And that is the class in which I would put myself. But I also think that readers differentiate between people who follow the profession of writing, who produce literature, only according to the circumstances. This writer will be thought better than that one, perhaps not all the time but only during a certain period. And indeed, even though he may be dead, his books will in fact be more valuable, more useful, because for one reason or another they happen to suit the epoch. I think that after his death a writer who has written a worthwhile book will have a life that changes according to the period, according to the century. He may be quite forgotten. And I also think that a writer who has embodied the essence of literature in his work is neither more nor less able than his neighbor. The other man has also embodied the essence of literature. You may prefer one to the other, according to whether he is nearer to or farther from your ideas and your range of sensitivity, but in the end they are the same.

DE BEAUVOIR: You mean that you see the writer's superiority both as something absolute and as something relative to history.

SARTRE: Just so. Or else you think you'll be a writer and you'll write various things, and if they're good there you are—you're a good writer. But I also think that being a writer means attaining the essence of the art of writing. And when you have attained the essence of the art of writing you've attained it neither more nor less than the next man. You can of course stay on the edge, but that's not what I'm talking about; I'm talking about people who are real writers—Chateaubriand, for example, or Proust. Why should I say that Chateaubriand did not have as clear an understanding of what literature was as Proust?

DE BEAUVOIR: I agree. When writing is concerned there's no order of rank, as though there has been a competitive examination. It's each separate person at each separate period who prefers this writer or that. But do you think about posterity at present? Does it exist for you? Or has it no relation to you at all, like the crabs in *The Condemned of Altona?*

SARTRE: I don't know. I've sometimes had the feeling that we were living at a time that would be followed by immense upheavals, entirely changing the idea of literature. There would be other principles and our works would no longer mean anything to the people who came after. I've thought that. I still think it sometimes, but not always. The Russians have taken on all their earlier literature, but the Chinese have not. So one wonders whether the future will keep the writers of former times or only a few of them.

DE BEAUVOIR: As far as you do think about it, do you think it is your strictly literary or your philosophical work that has the greater chance of surviving? Or is it both?

SARTRE: I think it's *Situations,* articles related to my philosophy but written in a very simple style and speaking of things that everybody knows about.

DE BEAUVOIR: In short a kind of critical reflection upon all aspects of the period? Upon the political aspects? The literary and artistic aspects too?

SARTRE: That's what I should like to see Gallimard bring together in one volume.

DE BEAUVOIR: What are your subjective relations to your work as a whole?

SARTRE: I'm not very pleased with it. The novel's a failure.

DE BEAUVOIR: No. It's not finished, but it's not a failure.

SARTRE: Generally speaking, it's been less highly thought of, and I think people are right. As for the philosophical works . . .

DE BEAUVOIR: They're wonderfully good!

SARTRE: Yes, but what do they lead to?

DE BEAUVOIR: I think the *Critique of Dialectical Reason* has advanced thought splendidly!

SARTRE: Isn't it still rather idealistic?

DE BEAUVOIR: I don't think so at all. I believe it can be immensely useful in making the world and people understandable, just like the Flaubert, though in another way . . .

SARTRE: I didn't finish the Flaubert, and I never shall.

DE BEAUVOIR: You haven't finished it. But then the style of *Madame Bovary* wasn't something that interested you all that much.

SARTRE: Still, there were things to be said about it.

DE BEAUVOIR: Yes, but you've already said so much about Flaubert; it amounts to such a mass of work on the way one can reflect upon a man and on the methods of that reflection! And a point one mustn't overlook is the strictly literary side of the book; it's fascinating to read the Flaubert as one reads *The Words*.

SARTRE: I never tried to write the Flaubert well.

DE BEAUVOIR: Yet there are places where it's wonderfully well written; there are places where it's really literature, like *The Words*.

SARTRE: As for *The Words*, that I did try to write well.

DE BEAUVOIR: Still, modesty apart, you're not dissatisfied when you compare your work with what you wanted to do, are you? I know the indefinite dreams of youth don't coincide with the realization, which is always finite, but even so that was what you wanted to do?

SARTRE: I'm not fully satisfied. I'm not dissatisfied. And then there's one very big question mark. What will become of it all?

DE BEAUVOIR: That's what we were saying just now. What will posterity make of it?

SARTRE: If we have a posterity of the Chinese kind, they won't make much of it.

DE BEAUVOIR: The circumstances aren't the same at all.

SARTRE: This really is a time of change, there's no telling in what direction. But the world we live in isn't going to last.

DE BEAUVOIR: Still, we're not in the eighteenth century and yet we still read eighteenth-century books. We're not in the sixteenth, but we read sixteenth-century books.

SARTRE: But in the eighteenth there was no revolution of this kind. The '89 revolution was nothing in comparison.

DE BEAUVOIR: We read the Greeks and the Romans although the world has changed.

SARTRE: We read them as beings not of the present time, and that's something else again.

DE BEAUVOIR: Has literature always kept the same value in your eyes, or did it diminish somewhat once you became politically active?

SARTRE: No, politics hasn't made it lose in value.

DE BEAUVOIR: How do you conceive the relations between the one and the other?

SARTRE: My view is that political action ought to build up a world in which literature would be free to express itself—the opposite of what the Soviets think. But I've never approached the question of literature politically. I've always looked upon it as one of the forms of freedom.

DE BEAUVOIR: Haven't there been times when literature, compared with political questions, has seemed if not more pointless, then at least of secondary importance?

SARTRE: No, I've never thought that. I don't say that literature must come first, but rather that I am designed to produce literature. Politics too, like everybody else, but particularly literature.

DE BEAUVOIR: Yes. And it was for that reason you protested in your recent conversations with Victor and Gavi when they wanted to prevent you from writing your Flaubert.

There was a time round about 1952 when you more or less stopped writing in order to read enormously. That coincided with your drawing closer to the Communist party and with a wish to "break the bones in your head" as you put it. But at that time literature still kept its . . .

SARTRE: I didn't ask myself about it, but if I had done so I should have told you that I was dedicated to literature.

DE BEAUVOIR: During that period the essential part of your work was no longer writing.

SARTRE: It was reading.

DE BEAUVOIR: And reflecting.

SARTRE: It was the time of *The Communists and Peace*.

DE BEAUVOIR: Those were pieces much more of a political than a literary nature.

SARTRE: Yes. The break with Camus was essentially political too.

DE BEAUVOIR: The approval of your own circle or of people like Paulhan or of the critics properly so called—what part has that played? Did you despise reviews entirely, or did you on the contrary take notice of them? How have you experienced your relations with the critics and your readers?

SARTRE: As far as I have seen the readers have always been more intelligent than the critics. I've learned virtually nothing about my writing from the critics, except from those who have written a book about some aspect or other. They have sometimes taught me something, but most of the critics have brought me nothing at all.

DE BEAUVOIR: Yet like everybody else you're eager enough, when a book comes out . . .

SARTRE: I want to know what people think of it, that goes without saying. Yes, when a book is published I read all my reviews. Not all. That can't be done. When I see a list of the criticisms written in the course of the year I'm amazed. I've missed half of them. Yet I try to read them all. But the critic says it's good, or it's less good, and that's all he tells me. The rest . . .

DE BEAUVOIR: Have there ever been comments from your readers that have suggested something for your future work or that have on the contrary rather paralyzed you? Has that had an influence on the development of your writing?

SARTRE: I don't have that impression. No. I had one special reader and that was you. When you said to me, "I agree; it's all right," then it was all right. I published the book and I didn't give a damn for the critics. You did me a great service. You gave me a confidence in myself that I shouldn't have had alone.

DE BEAUVOIR: In one way it's the reader who gives a text its truth.

SARTRE: But I didn't know the reader. And then again, the reviews didn't satisfy me. There was only you. That's how it always was. If you thought something was good, then it was fine as far as I was concerned. The critics did not think much of it. All right, they were fools.

DE BEAUVOIR: Still, you were affected when your work had the approval of intelligent people or even success in the true sense of the word.

SARTRE: At present the critics are rather different. There's one I'm really fond of—Doubrovsky. He's intelligent, he's subtle, he sees things. And there are some others like that, because nowadays criticism has a meaning. Earlier, it had none.

DE BEAUVOIR: It's certain that the very enthusiastic praise that greeted *The Words* did not persuade you to write a sequel.

SARTRE: No. Why should it have persuaded me? They said, "There's going to be a continuation." Well, there wasn't one.

DE BEAUVOIR: Still, to some extent writing is an answer to a call. Besides, you've very often written pieces for the occasion, and generally speaking, you've found it answers very well. The whole of *Situations* is . . .

SARTRE: The whole of *Situations* is made up of pieces written for the occasion.

DE BEAUVOIR: So there is a fairly direct relation with the public, after all.

SARTRE: There is a relation. Something happens. A given section of the public wonders what Sartre thinks about this happening, because they like me. So sometimes I write for them.

DE BEAUVOIR: When I first knew you as a very young man you lived for posterity. But wasn't there a period when you said it meant nothing at all to you? Can you tell me how you saw the relation between writing in a committed manner for your contemporaries and the approbation of the centuries to come?

SARTRE: When you're engaged in committed writing you're concerned with problems that will no longer have any meaning in twenty years time—problems that have to do with present-day society. If you have some degree of influence and if you handle the question well, you've succeeded when you persuade people to act or to look at things from your point of view. Posterity's point of view won't exist until after the problem's been resolved either well or badly—in either case certainly not by the writer himself. Since the business has been settled, there is a way of looking upon the work some twenty or thirty years later from a strictly aesthetic point of view! That is to say, all right, you know the story, you know that a writer has written the piece at a given moment—that Beaumarchais, for example, wrote certain very important pamphlets. But you can no longer make use of them for a contemporary problem. You look upon the literary object as something that is valid for everyone, but without taking its anecdotic content into consideration. The details become symbols. A given specific fact is valid for a series of facts that are characteristic of a given society or of several kinds of society. What was a limited object becomes universal. So that when you are writing a committed text you are primarily concerned with the subject you have to deal with, the arguments you are to provide, and the style that will make things more understandable, more striking for your contemporaries. You're not going to spend time wondering about what the book will amount to at a period when it will no longer move anyone to action. Yet, still, there's a vague notion at the back of your mind that makes you feel that if the work succeeds in doing what it's meant to do, then in the future it'll have repercussions in a universal form. It will no longer be operative. It will to some degree be looked upon as a gratuitous object; it will all be as though the writer had written it gratuitously and not for its stated operative value with regard to a stated social fact. Thus one

169

admires Voltaire's works for their universal value, whereas in Voltaire's day his tales derived their value from a certain social outlook. So there are two points of view, and the author is conscious of them both when he writes. He knows that if he writes something specific he is taking part in an action, and he does not look as though he were using words just for the pleasure of writing. Yet, fundamentally, he thinks he is creating a work that possesses a universal value, a value that is its real meaning, even though it has been published to realize a particular action.

DE BEAUVOIR: There are still two or three things we must look into. In the first place, not all your works are equally committed. Some, like *No Exit* and *The Words,* are more distinctly aesthetic. You didn't write them in order to carry out an action. They are the sort of works that are called works of art, truly literary works. Then again, in pieces where you are making an appeal or trying to persuade people, you're always very careful about style and composition, both in order to reach your contemporaries and at the same time with the idea of some kind of seal of universality that will make the work valid at a later date.

SARTRE: Perhaps so.

DE BEAUVOIR: So you've never said be damned to posterity.

SARTRE: No, I didn't trouble about it. But behind my dream, which was always that of writing for the neighbor who would read me, there was the notion of a posterity—a posterity that can only come into existence together with a complete transformation of the work, which stops being active but which becomes a work of art like almost all objects which belong to the past.

DE BEAUVOIR: And which are grasped as belonging to the past. Obviously you did think about posterity, since you've often told me—and I think you even wrote it in *The Words*—that literature hid the idea of death from you entirely. You did not mind dying, since you were to survive; so you thought a book lived on.

SARTRE: I had a very strong belief in posterity, above all when I was little, at the period when *The Words* comes to an end, and then in the years that followed and when I was twenty. It was only gradually that I came to understand that I was primarily writing for my readers of today. So then posterity turned into something that shimmered from behind, like a kind of vague fluorescence that accompanied what I was writing essentially for contemporary readers.

DE BEAUVOIR: You weren't at all one of those writers who settle into the future with a calm contempt for their contemporaries, like

Stendhal—though you're very fond of him—who thought, "But I shall be understood in a hundred years time; so today is nothing to me."

SARTRE: Absolutely not.

DE BEAUVOIR: You hadn't the least contempt for your contemporaries nor the least notion that your books would provide you with a revenge. Perhaps on the other hand you thought that it was insofar as you had succeeded in touching your contemporaries that you would represent your century and move on to posterity, and not insofar as you were set apart from them.

SARTRE: I thought that this recognition by my contemporaries was something that happened in my life, something that was the stage one had to pass through in order to reach fame or death.

DE BEAUVOIR: It was the objectification of your work that gave it its reality. There was an important notion, one that you also spoke of in *The Words*, by the way, and that was the idea that literature brought a certain salvation.

SARTRE: Certainly, because as I said in *The Words*, my understanding of literary survival was obviously a kind of transfer from the Christian religion.

DE BEAUVOIR: Even when you were reading philosophy in Germany, it didn't prevent you from writing *Nausea*. You divided yourself between the two.

SARTRE: *Nausea* was the more important.

DE BEAUVOIR: But even so, reading philosophy was important enough to make you go and live in Germany for a year. I asked you how you came to write *Being and Nothingness*, and you answered, "It was the war."

SARTRE: Yes.

DE BEAUVOIR: But that's not an adequate explanation.

SARTRE: Well, as for *Being and Nothingness*, I wrote a good deal of it in my notebooks. The ideas were based on a notebook written during the phony war, and they came directly from my years in Berlin. When I wrote in the notebook I had none of the texts at hand, so I rediscovered it all myself. I don't know why the Germans made me a present of Heidegger in the prisoner-of-war camp. It remains a mystery to me.

DE BEAUVOIR: How did it come about?

SARTRE: When I was a prisoner a German officer asked me whether I was in need of anything, and I answered, "Heidegger."

DE BEAUVOIR: Perhaps because Heidegger was in favor with the government . . .

SARTRE: Perhaps. At all events, they gave it to me. A thick, expensive volume. It's odd, because they didn't shower favors on us, you know.

DE BEAUVOIR: Yes, it remains rather mysterious. Still, it does mean that at that time you read Heidegger.

SARTRE: I read Heidegger while I was in the prison camp. I understood him much better through Husserl than through himself, I may add. I'd already read something of him in '36 . . .

DE BEAUVOIR: Oh, yes, I remember you made me translate long pieces. We talked about him when I was still at Rouen I think. Good. But at the same time *Being and Nothingness* arose from the discovery you had made in *The Psychology of the Imagination.*

SARTRE: Yes. That's right. The discovery of consciousness as nothingness.

DE BEAUVOIR: Later you used to say you'd never again have the ideas and intuitions you had for *Being and Nothingness.*

SARTRE: But for all that, I did write some books that are related to philosophy. *Saint Genet,* for example.

DE BEAUVOIR: Yes.

SARTRE: As I saw it, it was a long essay, not philosophical. But in fact I made use of philosophical concepts all the time.

DE BEAUVOIR: Yes.

SARTRE: It might be called a philosophical work. . . . And then with the *Critique of Dialectical Reason* certain things occurred to me.

DE BEAUVOIR: Oh, yes. And that too came in an episodic fashion, born of a conjuncture of circumstances, since the Poles asked you . . .

SARTRE: The Poles asked me where I stood philosophically. That produced *Questions of Method.* The Poles published it. I wanted to show it —and you advised me to show it—to the readers of *Les Temps modernes.*

DE BEAUVOIR: Yes.

SARTRE: The original text wasn't very good. I set myself to rewriting it and I published it in *Les Temps modernes.*

DE BEAUVOIR: Yes, but wasn't there another motivation? From 1952 on you had taken to reading an enormous amount about Marxism, and philosophy became something—it wasn't mere chance that it was the Poles who asked you for it, by the way—something political.

SARTRE: Yes. For Marx, philosophy should be suppressed. For my part, I didn't see things that way. I saw philosophy dwelling in the city of the future. But there's no doubt that I looked toward Marxist philosophy.

DE BEAUVOIR: Yet a fuller explanation might be important. It was suggested that you write *Questions of Method*. But why did you agree to do it?

SARTRE: Because I wanted to know where I stood philosophically.

DE BEAUVOIR: In your relations with Marxism . . .

SARTRE: Superficially, yes. But above all with dialectic, because if you were to look at my notebooks—and unhappily they no longer exist—you'd see how dialectic was making its way into what I wrote.

DE BEAUVOIR: Yet in *Being and Nothingness* there's no dialectic at all.

SARTRE: Exactly. I moved from *Being and Nothingness* to a dialectical idea.

DE BEAUVOIR: Yes. When you'd written *The Communist and Peace* you began working out a philosophy of history. To some degree it was that which produced *Questions of Method*.

SARTRE: Yes.

DE BEAUVOIR: But how did you move on from *Questions of Method* to the *Critique of Dialectical Reason?*

SARTRE: *Questions of Method* was methodology alone; but there was philosophy behind it, the philosophical dialectic that I was beginning to define. And as soon as I'd finished *Questions of Method*, three months or six months later, I began the *Critique of Dialectical Reason*.

DE BEAUVOIR: And how did you find out you had fresh ideas, since for years you'd been saying to me, "No, I don't know whether I'll ever write another philosophical book. I have no more ideas."

SARTRE: Well, I think when I said, "I have no more ideas," I had none consciously, but nevertheless there was something there . . .

DE BEAUVOIR: Something was working itself out.

SARTRE: Yes. And when I'd written *Questions of Method*, which I did very rapidly, my ideas fell into order again. They were the ideas I'd jotted down in my notebooks over three or four years . . . those notebooks, you know . . .

DE BEAUVOIR: Oh yes, I can see those fat notebooks quite clearly. . . . But still it doesn't seem to me that they contained the very important ideas of recurrence and the practico-inert.

SARTRE: No. But I'd been far enough on the dialectical plane to have a certain foreknowledge of them.

DE BEAUVOIR: In practice, when you're actually at work, what difference does it make if you're dealing with literature or with philosophy?

SARTRE: When I'm writing philosophy I don't make a rough draft.

Whereas ordinarily I make seven or eight drafts, seven or eight sections of a page for a single text. I write three lines, draw a stroke
under them, and then the fourth line is on another sheet. In philosophy, nothing of the kind. I take a sheet, I begin writing the ideas
that are already there in my head—ideas that perhaps I've not had for
long—and then I carry them on to the end. Perhaps not as far as the
end of the page, but quite far. And then toward the bottom of the
page I stop because I've written something badly. Then, having made
corrections, I start again on the next page and so on until the end. To
put it in another way, philosophy is words I address to someone. It's
not like a novel, which is also addressed to someone, but addressed in
another manner.

DE BEAUVOIR: Yes.

SARTRE: A novel I write so that it will be read by someone. In philosophy I'm explaining to someone—I'm doing it with a pen but it might
just as well be with my tongue, my mouth—I'm explaining my ideas
just as they come to me today.

DE BEAUVOIR: In short, you couldn't write literature on a tape recorder, but perhaps you could philosophy.

SARTRE: That's right.

DE BEAUVOIR: I saw you working on the *Critique of Dialectical Reason*.
It was quite terrifying. You scarcely reread at all.

SARTRE: I reread the next morning. I used to write about ten pages.
That was all I could do in a day.

DE BEAUVOIR: It was like watching an athletic feat, seeing you write
the *Critique of Dialectical Reason*. And you wrote under the effect of
Corydrane.*

SARTRE: All the time.

DE BEAUVOIR: Whereas with literature you never used Corydrane.

SARTRE: Literature wouldn't have gone with Corydrane, because the
stuff induces facility. I remember having tried to write with it after
the war. It was a passage in the novel where Mathieu is walking about
in the streets of Paris before going home. It was horrible. He walked
about in these streets, and every single one of them gave rise to
comparisons.

DE BEAUVOIR: I remember. It was dreadful. I'd like to ask you another
question. Even if one is not a narcissist one has a certain image of
oneself. We've talked about yours when you were a little boy and

* An amphetamine, easily obtained at that time. (trans.)

when you were somewhat older. What about the present? You are sixty-nine. How does it affect you, being the object of so many theses, bibliographies, biographies, interviews, and pieces about you, and with so many people wanting to meet you? What is the effect of all that? Do you feel as though you've been classed as a historical monument or . . .

SARTRE: A historical monument to some extent, yes. But not entirely. It's as though I were rediscovering that character I used to set up before me at the beginning. The character there is not myself, and yet he is myself, since he is the person addressed. People create a certain character for themselves who is me. There is a me-him and a me-me. The me-him is the me that people create and that in a certain manner they bring into relation with myself.

DE BEAUVOIR: Does it mean anything, this coincidence between the character of today and the character you dreamed of when you were young?

SARTRE: It does not. I never say to myself, "Well, that's roughly what I wanted when I was young, and so on." It means nothing. I've never thought about myself much, and for some years now I've completely stopped doing so.

DE BEAUVOIR: Since when? Since you became politically committed?

SARTRE: That's about it, yes. The ego reappears when I do individual or personal things, when I go to see someone or when I do something for someone. Then the ego reappears. But in literature, when I'm writing, the me no longer exists. When I was about fifty or fifty-five —before *The Words*—I now and then dreamed of writing a story that would take place in Italy and that would describe a fellow of my age in his relations with life. It would have been subjectivist.

DE BEAUVOIR: I vaguely remember it. But come, there's something we must go back to—all the books you haven't written.

SARTRE: Yes.

DE BEAUVOIR: Why you planned them, why you gave them up . . .

SARTRE: I did write long sections of *La Reine Albermale ou Le dernier touriste* (Queen Albermale or the Last Tourist) and many notebooks too.

DE BEAUVOIR: One last question. You say you're not interested in your image, or in yourself. Yet you enjoy having these conversations?

SARTRE: Yes. But, you know, if I'm treated badly I react; if I were insulted, I'd be angry.

DE BEAUVOIR: Of course.

SARTRE: And since I've not a great deal to do at present, I have to take some notice of myself . . . otherwise I'd have nothing at all . . .

DE BEAUVOIR: Above all since you've said very little about yourself.

SARTRE: True enough . . .

DE BEAUVOIR: You did speak about yourself in *The Words,* then a little in connection with Merleau-Ponty and with Nizan. But since the time you were eleven you've never written anything autobiographical. You've never kept a diary. You used to write down the ideas that came into your head, but you've never kept a diary day by day. You've never even thought of doing so.

SARTRE: Except during the war. Every day during the war I wrote whatever passed through my mind. But I looked upon it as a task of an inferior kind. Literature begins with choice, the refusal of certain aspects and the acceptance of others. It's an undertaking that's not compatible with diary-writing, in which the choice is virtually spontaneous and can't very well be explained.

DE BEAUVOIR: Yet in the kind of writing that might be called raw literature, there was one side in which you were outstanding. You had a well-deserved reputation as a great letter-writer, particularly when you were young. When we were apart you used to write me letters of enormous length, and not only to me. You sometimes wrote twelve-page letters to Olga, telling her about our journeys. And when you were doing your military service or when I was on a walking tour, you'd write me very, very long letters, sometimes every day for two weeks. What did those letters mean to you?

SARTRE: They were the transcription of immediate life. A day in Naples, for example. It was a way of making it exist for the person who received the letter. It was done spontaneously. Privately, I thought those letters were fit to be published, but actually they were letters meant for the person I wrote them to. I did have a faint notion at the back of my mind that they might be published after my death. But I no longer write letters of that kind because I know that a writer's letters are published, and I think they are not worth it.

DE BEAUVOIR: Why not?

SARTRE: Because they're not sufficiently worked over, except in a few cases. Diderot's letters to Sophie Volland, for example. In my case I dashed them off, crossing nothing out, never troubling about any reader other than the one I was sending the letter to. So it doesn't seem to me a valid literary work.

DE BEAUVOIR: Yes, but after all you did thoroughly enjoy writing letters.

SARTRE: I liked it very much.

DE BEAUVOIR: They'll certainly be published later, because they're so amusing and full of life.

SARTRE: Fundamentally, my letters played something of the part of a diary.

DE BEAUVOIR: The other day you said that you'd been much influenced by the lives of well-known writers. Was it the fact that the correspondence of Voltaire, Rousseau, and others was important and that it was published—was that what impelled you to write letters?

SARTRE: I had no literary aims when I wrote them.

DE BEAUVOIR: Yet you say you had a sly notion that perhaps they would be published.

SARTRE: Oh, at the moment of writing them, perhaps I put in a little more gaiety or lyricism than would have been found in a letter written to just any reader if one weren't a writer. I did try to phrase my letters pleasantly, but without overdoing it or I would have been a pedant. And I would have been claiming to turn out spontaneous literature. Nowadays I don't believe in spontaneous literature, but at that time I did. To put it briefly, my letters were the equivalent of testimony about my life.

DE BEAUVOIR: Let's go back to the books that you haven't published, that you didn't finish. I'd like you to talk about them.

SARTRE: I believe it's the case with all writers.

DE BEAUVOIR: Oh, I don't think so. Can you give a rough list of the books you haven't published?

SARTRE: *La Légende de la vérité* (The Legend of Truth).

DE BEAUVOIR: That was different. It was rejected. Only a section of it was published . . . But there was one quite considerable work, *The Psyche*. What was it, exactly?

SARTRE: *The Psyche* was written when I came back from Germany, after a year there, reading Heidegger and above all Husserl.

DE BEAUVOIR: Then you wrote *The Transcendence of the Ego*, which was published.

SARTRE: Which was published, which was forgotten, which then disappeared, and which has been republished by Mlle Le Bon.

DE BEAUVOIR: There was a relation between *The Transcendence of the Ego* and *The Psyche*.

SARTRE: It was from that point that I had the idea of *The Psyche*. *The Psyche* is the description of what's called the psychic. How, philosophically speaking, does one experience subjectivity? That's explained in *The Psyche*. It also deals with emotions, feelings . . .

DE BEAUVOIR: You treated them as psychic objects lying outside consciousness. That was your main idea, wasn't it?

SARTRE: Yes. That's right.

DE BEAUVOIR: Just as the ego is transcendent, so are . . .

SARTRE: The feelings.

DE BEAUVOIR: The feelings, the emotions. It was a pretty considerable
essay covering the whole of the psychical field.

SARTRE: It should have been a book of the size of *Being and Nothingness*.

DE BEAUVOIR: And didn't *Emotions: Outline of a Theory* form part of
The Psyche?

SARTRE: Yes, it did.

DE BEAUVOIR: Why did you keep *Emotions*—you were quite right to
do so, by the way: it's very good—and not the rest of *The Psyche?*

SARTRE: Because the rest repeated ideas of Husserl's that I had assimilated. I expressed them in a different manner, but it was still pure
Husserl—it wasn't original. Whereas the *Emotions* were, and that is
why I kept them. It was a sound study of certain *Erlebnisse* that might
be called emotions. I showed that they were not produced in isolation
but had a relation to the consciousness.

DE BEAUVOIR: That they were actuated by intentionality.

SARTRE: Yes. It's an idea I still retain, an idea that I did not produce
myself, but one that is necessary to me.

DE BEAUVOIR: The originality was in applying the intentionality to
the emotion, to the expression of the emotions, and to the manner of
experiencing them, and so on.

SARTRE: Husserl would no doubt have seen emotion as preceding
intentionality.

DE BEAUVOIR: Certainly; but he did not deal with it.

SARTRE: At least, not as far as I know.

DE BEAUVOIR: So *The Psyche* was one of the first books you gave up.

SARTRE: Yes, just keeping a part of it. . . . And then at about the
same time I wrote a long short story about a female orchestra's journey
from Casablanca to Marseilles.

DE BEAUVOIR: The female orchestra that appears again in *The Reprieve.*

SARTRE: It was a female orchestra that I heard at Rouen and that had
not the least connection with Casablanca.

DE BEAUVOIR: There was this orchestra, and then there was a zouave
or a soldier who thought he was handsome. And what happened to
the story?

SARTRE: God knows. It's like the tale about the midnight sun that I lost when I was on a walking tour with you.

DE BEAUVOIR: Oh yes, in the Causses. That was after *Nausea,* and you thought of including it in a collection of short stories . . . which came out later. Suppose you were to tell the story of "Le Soleil de minuit" (The Midnight Sun)?

SARTRE: It was about a little girl who saw the midnight sun in a childish way, but I can no longer remember quite how she did so.

DE BEAUVOIR: She'd formed a mental picture of an extraordinary sun that would be there in the sky in the depths of the night. And then she sees the real midnight sun which is like a long-drawn-out twilight with nothing extraordinary about it. You didn't think much of the tale.

SARTRE: No. I never rewrote it. In the end it amounted to a description of a journey that I had made, and this little girl's impressions were more or less my own.

DE BEAUVOIR: There was another story connected with that long letter you wrote to Olga about Naples.

SARTRE: Yes, some of it was published.

DE BEAUVOIR: Under the title of *Nourishment.*

DE BEAUVOIR: Could you tell the story?

SARTRE: Wait a moment. I was in Naples with you, and we'd been to Amalfi.

DE BEAUVOIR: I left you at Naples because Amalfi did not interest you very much, and I went by myself. So you spent an evening alone in Naples.

SARTRE: And I met two Neapolitans who offered to show me the town. Everyone knows what that means. It was seeing a hidden Naples, that is, the brothels, more or less. And in fact they did take me to a brothel, rather a special one. We went into a room with a couch running round the wall—the room was circular—and another couch in the middle, a round couch that surrounded a pillar. The assistant madam sent the young men out, and then a young woman came in with another not so young, both of them naked. They did things to one another or rather they pretended to do them. The older woman, who was very dark, acted the man, and the other, who was about twenty-eight and quite pretty, the woman.

DE BEAUVOIR: You told me they displayed the various positions one sees in the famous Villa of the Mysteries at Pompeii.

SARTRE: That was exactly it. They first announced them and then very discreetly they imitated the various postures. I left, rather astonished. Downstairs I met my two young fellows, who had been waiting for me. I gave them a little money. They went and bought a bottle of red Vesuvian wine and we drank it there in the street. We had something to eat and then they said goodbye. They went off with the small sum of money I'd given them, and I with my not very interesting visions.

DE BEAUVOIR: But after all you'd had a pretty good time on the whole. You were much amused next day when I came back and you told me about it. Was it that particular night you spoke of in the story?

SARTRE: Yes. I wanted to tell about the fellow's visit to the brothel and then his vision of Naples.

DE BEAUVOIR: And why didn't you publish the story in the end? It was called "Dépaysement" (Exiles).

SARTRE: I've no idea. I believe you advised against it.

DE BEAUVOIR: Why? Wasn't it good?

SARTRE: It can't have been good.

DE BEAUVOIR: Perhaps we considered that its structure was inadequate—that it didn't come up to the other tales.

SARTRE: Probably.

DE BEAUVOIR: Then after *Being and Nothingness* you began writing a work on ethics.

SARTRE: I meant to write it, but I put it off till later.

DE BEAUVOIR: That was the book in which you wrote an important, long, and very fine study of Nietzsche.

SARTRE: That formed part of it. What is more, I wrote on Mallarmé too—about two hundred pages.

DE BEAUVOIR: Oh yes! There were very highly detailed explanations of all Mallarmé's poems. Why has that not been published?

SARTRE: Because it was never finished. I used to drop it and then go back to it again.

DE BEAUVOIR: But as for the whole—which you didn't call your *Ethics* but which was a phenomenological study of human attitudes, a critique of certain attitudes, connected with your essay on Nietzsche— why did you abandon it?

SARTRE: I didn't abandon it. Those notes were made to be treated at greater length.

DE BEAUVOIR: It seems to me that you thought the phenomenological side too idealistic.

SARTRE: Exactly so.

DE BEAUVOIR: Writing an analysis seemed to you too idealistic . . .

SARTRE: Not an analysis, a description.

DE BEAUVOIR: A phenomenological description of various human attitudes. There were other things you didn't finish. You wrote a long essay on Tintoretto, but you only published a small part of it in *Les Temps modernes*. Why did you give it up?

SARTRE: In the long run I found it boring.

DE BEAUVOIR: In any case, I think the essential is there in what you did write.

SARTRE: It was commissioned by Skira.

DE BEAUVOIR: Yes.

SARTRE: It wasn't Skira who chose Tintoretto: it was I who said to him I'll take Tintoretto. I abandoned it because it bored me.

DE BEAUVOIR: There was another book you worked on for quite a long time and then dropped: *La Reine Albermale ou Le dernier touriste* (Queen Albermale or The Last Tourist). When was that?

SARTRE: It was between '50 and '59. I wrote perhaps a hundred pages of it. I believe there were twenty about the plashing sound that gondolas make.

DE BEAUVOIR: Yes, you've written a great deal about Venice. Besides, you did publish that piece on Venice. You published some of it.

SARTRE: Yes, in *Verve.*

DE BEAUVOIR: The idea was to catch Italy in the net of words; but it was a self-destructive account of a journey.

SARTRE: Self-destructive insofar as it was a tourist's account.

DE BEAUVOIR: That's right.

SARTRE: And what remained to be explored was a more important Italy that was not for tourists.

DE BEAUVOIR: It was very ambitious, because you wanted it to be both historical—you wanted for example to talk about the monument to Victor Emmanuel seen throughout the whole of Italian history—and at the same time to be subjective.

SARTRE: Yes.

DE BEAUVOIR: It had to be objective-subjective.

SARTRE: It was very ambitious and I gave it up because I couldn't hit upon just the right point of view.

DE BEAUVOIR: You had fun writing it, though.

SARTRE: Yes, I had great fun.

DE BEAUVOIR: Are there any other literary or philosophical writings that you thought about but did not bring into being?

SARTRE: There was a work on ethics I prepared for that American university which invited me. I began by writing four or five lectures that I was to deliver over there and then I went on for myself. I have piles of notes. I don't know what has become of them, by the way: they must be in my flat. Piles of notes for a work on ethics.

DE BEAUVOIR: Wasn't it essentially on the relation between ethics and politics?

SARTRE: Yes.

DE BEAUVOIR: So it was completely different from what you wrote around '48 or '49?

SARTRE: Completely different. I have some notes on it. The whole book would in fact have been very considerable.

DE BEAUVOIR: Why did you abandon that one?

SARTRE: Because I'd grown tired of writing philosophy. It always happens like that with philosophy, you know. At least it does with me. I wrote *Being and Nothingness* and then I grew weary. In that case too there was a possible continuation, but I did not produce it. I wrote *Saint Genet,* which can be looked upon as something between philosophy and literature. Then I wrote the *Critique of Dialectical Reason,* and there again I came to a halt.

DE BEAUVOIR: Because it would have called for an enormous amount of historical reading?

SARTRE: Just so. I should have had to study a period of some fifty years and try to look into all the necessary methods of getting to know about those fifty years, not only as a whole but in their separate details.

DE BEAUVOIR: You did think of studying an event that took up less time, such as the French Revolution. You did an immense amount of work on the French Revolution.

SARTRE: Yes, but I had to have other examples too. I wanted to go really deeply into the nature of History.

DE BEAUVOIR: You spoke of Stalinism.

SARTRE: Yes, I began speaking of Stalinism.

DE BEAUVOIR: There's another side of your work that we haven't touched on at all, though it's very important, and that's your plays. . . . How do you explain your coming to write plays, and how important has it been for you?

SARTRE: I'd always thought I would take to it. When I was a little boy of eight and I played in the Luxembourg Gardens I used to put on those puppets you wear like gloves and make them act.

DE BEAUVOIR: But did you go back to the idea of writing plays when you were an adolescent?

SARTRE: Oh, yes. I wrote parodies and operettas. I discovered the operetta at La Rochelle, where I used to go to the municipal theater with my school friends, and under its influence I began one myself, *Horatius Coclès*.

DE BEAUVOIR: Oh yes, of course.

SARTRE: I remember two lines: I'm Mucius Scaevola, and I stand here/ I'm Mucius, Mucius, and that is clear. Then later at the Ecole Normale I wrote a one-act play called *J'aurai un bel enterrement* (I Shall Have a Fine Funeral). It was a comic piece about a fellow who describes his death agony.

DE BEAUVOIR: Was it staged?

SARTRE: No, of course not! I also wrote an act for an Ecole Normale revue. Every year there's a revue showing the principal, his underlings, the pupils, and the parents. I wrote one act. The show was repulsively obscene.

DE BEAUVOIR: And you acted in it too.

SARTRE: I took the part of Lanson, the principal.

DE BEAUVOIR: All that was just for fun. Did you go on afterward?

SARTRE: I wrote a play that was called *Epiméthée*, I think. The gods came into a Greek village that they meant to punish, and in this village there were poets, story-tellers, and artists. In the end it was the birth of tragedy, and Prometheus expelled the gods. After that he came to no good. But I thought the drama a somewhat inferior form of expression. That was how I looked upon it to begin with.

DE BEAUVOIR: And later? I think we must talk about *Bariona*.

SARTRE: When I was a prisoner of war I belonged to a group who put on plays in a large barn every Sunday. We made the sets ourselves, and since I was an intellectual who wrote, they asked me to provide a play at Christmas. I turned out *Bariona*, which was thoroughly bad but which did have a dramatic idea. In any event it was that which gave me a liking for the theater.

DE BEAUVOIR: You wrote me letters about it, telling me that from then onward you would write plays. *Bariona* was committed drama. You used the pretext of the Roman occupation of Palestine to refer to France.

SARTRE: Yes. The Germans didn't understand that. They just saw it as a Christmas play. But the French prisoners got the point, and my play interested them.

DE BEAUVOIR: It was what gave you such power—acting before an audience that was not made up of people from outside, as it is in bourgeois theaters.

SARTRE: Yes, *Bariona* was acted before an audience that was involved. There were men there who would have stopped the play if they had understood it. But all the prisoners knew what it was about. It was real drama in that sense.

DE BEAUVOIR: After that came *The Flies*. Say something about the circumstances in which you wrote it.

SARTRE: Like you I was friends with Olga Kosakievitch. She was learning how to be an actress under Dullin, and she needed an opportunity to act in a play. I suggested to Dullin that I write one.

DE BEAUVOIR: What did it mean to you, *The Flies*?

SARTRE: *The Flies?* It was like my old themes—a legend to be treated at greater length, a legend to be given a present-day application. I kept the story of Agamemnon and his wife, Orestes' killing of his mother, and then the Furies, but I gave it another meaning. In fact I gave it a meaning that had to do with the German occupation.

DE BEAUVOIR: Explain rather more clearly.

SARTRE: In *The Flies* I wanted to speak about freedom, about my absolute freedom, my freedom as a man, and above all about the freedom of the occupied French with regard to the Germans.

DE BEAUVOIR: You were saying to the French, "Be free, regain your liberty, and banish the remorse they're trying to load you with." And how did you feel when you saw your play acted? There was an audience and there was your work. What was the difference between that and the publication of a book?

SARTRE: I didn't like it much. Dullin and I were friends and I'd talked about the production. I didn't know a great deal about it, but I'd talked it over with him. Yet the producer's work is so important that I didn't really feel that I was there on the stage at all. It was something that was being done on the basis of what I had written, but it was not what I had written. Later, with other plays, I no longer had that feeling, and I believe that was because I took a hand in the work myself.

DE BEAUVOIR: How did it go with the other plays? With *No Exit* to begin with?

SARTRE: Rouleau made a good job of it, a fine production that served as a model for those that came after. What he brought into being was what I had seen in my mind's eye when I wrote the play.

DE BEAUVOIR: And what about the next one?

SARTRE: That was *The Victors*. I intended to show the French public's indifference to the members of the Resistance after the war and the way people were gradually forgetting them. At that point there was a massive resurgence of the bourgeoisie, a bourgeoisie who had been more or less accomplices of the Germans. They were irritated by a play about the Resistance.

DE BEAUVOIR: Yes, it caused a scandal, particularly the scenes of torture. Why exactly did you write the play?

SARTRE: To remind people who the resisters had been, and that they had been tortured, that they had been brave, and that the way they were being spoken of at that time was rather base.

DE BEAUVOIR: We won't go through all your plays one by one. What I'd like you to tell me is the distinction you make between dramatic and strictly literary work.

SARTRE: To begin with, the theme is very hard to find. I usually sit there at my desk for two weeks, a month, six weeks. Sometimes I have a phrase in my head.

DE BEAUVOIR: Oh yes! You once said to me "The four horsemen of the Apocalypse."

SARTRE: From time to time a vague theme appears.

DE BEAUVOIR: It must be said that your plays have often been works written for a particular occasion. It was not a question of a theme that you wanted to deal with. For instance, you wanted to give Wanda a play to act in.

SARTRE: Yes.

DE BEAUVOIR: She hadn't acted for a long while. She wanted to act and you wanted to have her act. So you said to yourself, I'll write a play.

SARTRE: Just so. There was one theme I've always thought about and that I've never handled. A fellow whose mother is pregnant—she's furious about it.

DE BEAUVOIR: Ah, yes.

SARTRE: She sees his life, and the spectators, watching the stage, see "mansions" that light up one after another. They see all the events in his life including his torture and death at the end. And she's confined, the child is born, grows up and passes through all the scenes that were foretold, but in the end he's a great man, a hero.

DE BEAUVOIR: Yes, you've thought over that play a great deal. But it's never really jelled.

SARTRE: Never.

DE BEAUVOIR: Let's go back to your way of working for the stage.

SARTRE: To begin with, I work on a theme, then I drop it. I hit upon phrases or replies and I make a note of them. It all assumes a more or less complex form which I then simplify. I did that for *The Devil and the Good Lord*. I remember everything I thought up and that I then abandoned so as to come at last to the . . .

DE BEAUVOIR: Final version.

SARTRE: Yes. At that point I don't find writing very difficult. It's a question of a conversation between people who toss what they have to say to one another back and forth.

DE BEAUVOIR: I've seen you working and it seems to me that where the stage is concerned there's a great deal of preliminary work that goes on in your head, whereas for short stories and novels it's done on the paper.

SARTRE: Yes.

DE BEAUVOIR: Does a book's success please you more than a play's?

SARTRE: Oh, as for plays, you're happy when they're successful, of course. You know whether a play's a flop or a success very soon. But the fate of plays is bizarre. They can fall flat, or on the contrary they can recover even if the first night was a failure. Their success is always in doubt. Not for a book. If a book is going to do well it takes a long time over it, perhaps three months, but then you can be sure of it. Whereas with a play, a success can turn into a flop or a flop can turn into a success. It's very strange. And then the big successes usually end badly. Brasseur, for example, made a mess of it for me twice—he acted in the play for a certain number of performances, and then he either took a holiday or went off to have an operation and the play came to an end.

DE BEAUVOIR: Another thing. It rarely happens that you reread one of your books. But you often see one of your plays again, because it's being staged abroad or with a new production. Do you see one afresh when you see it again? Do you have the feeling that it's a play written by someone else?

SARTRE: No. While the play is going on it's the production you watch.

DE BEAUVOIR: What has given you most pleasure in the theater? Was it seeing the play acted and thinking it was good or well staged, or was it being happy because it was a success? In short, what moments have given you most pleasure in your career as a playwright?

SARTRE: Well, it's strange, but a book is dead. It's a dead object. It lies there on a table and you're not intimately connected with it— there's no solidarity between you. For a certain period a play is different. You live and you work, but every evening there's a place where a play of yours goes on being acted. It's a very curious thing to live on the Boulevard Saint Germain and to know that at the Théâtre Antoine around the corner . . .

DE BEAUVOIR: . . . the play is being acted. You found it very disagreeable for *The Victors.* Did you like it on other occasions, though?

SARTRE: Yes. *The Devil and the Good Lord.* I liked that. It was a great success.

DE BEAUVOIR: And then it was put on again at Wilson's . . .

SARTRE: Oh, yes, I liked that too.

DE BEAUVOIR: And I think it must also have pleased you when you saw *The Flies* in Prague.

SARTRE: Yes, when the play went well I've had strong, vivid pleasures from the theater. You don't have an immense amount of pleasure the first night, not the first night. There's no telling how it's going to turn out.

DE BEAUVOIR: Indeed, one's rather distressed. Out of solidarity with you, I've never been to a first night of yours without being horribly anxious.

SARTRE: And even if it's gone well, that only shows the probable trend. . . . But when it goes on and continues to do well, then you are really happy—then the whole thing holds together. You have a real contact with the audience, and if you like, you can go to the theater any evening, settle down in a corner, and see how the audience reacts.

DE BEAUVOIR: You've never done so.

SARTRE: I've never done so. Or almost never.

DE BEAUVOIR: And which of your plays do you like best?

SARTRE: *The Devil and the Good Lord.*

DE BEAUVOIR: I'm very fond of it too, but I'm also very fond of *The Condemned of Altona.*

SARTRE: I don't like it so much, but still I'm pleased with it.

DE BEAUVOIR: But you wrote it in circumstances that . . .

SARTRE: I wrote it at the time of my crisis in '58.

DE BEAUVOIR: Perhaps it was that which made you sad.

SARTRE: You remember that when we heard of de Gaulle's coup d'état we left for our holiday. We went to Italy, and in Rome I wrote the last scenes of the *Condemned.*

DE BEAUVOIR: With the family council . . .

SARTRE: Yes.

DE BEAUVOIR: . . . It was a very bad scene.

SARTRE: Very bad. Besides, the first acts were only roughed out. I worked over them afterward, during the whole year. . . . You remember?

DE BEAUVOIR: Very well. We were in the Piazza Sant' Eustacchio, near the hotel where we were staying.

SARTRE: Yes.

DE BEAUVOIR: I had gone down to read the last act and I was appalled. You agreed. You saw that it was not a family council that was called for, but only something between the father and the son.

SARTRE: Yes.

DE BEAUVOIR: And what are your relations with the theater at present?

SARTRE: I don't write plays anymore. That's finished.

DE BEAUVOIR: Why?

SARTRE: You reach an age when you detach yourself from the theater. Good plays aren't written by old men. There's something urgent about a play. Characters come on and say, "Good morning. How are you?" and you know that two or three scenes later they'll be caught up in an urgent affair, one that will probably end badly for them. That's something that is rare in real life. One's not in a state of urgency. A serious threat may be hanging over one, but one's not in a state of urgency. Whereas you can't write a play without urgency in it. And this urgency comes back to you because it's felt by the audience. They'll be living a time of urgency in their imaginations. They'll wonder whether Götz is going to die or whether he's going to marry Hilda. So that when it's acted, the play you've written puts you into a kind of state of urgency every day.

DE BEAUVOIR: But why, just because you're old, can you no longer revive that feeling of urgency? On the contrary, you ought to think, "After all, I haven't very much longer to live. I must say the last things I have to say, and say them quickly."

SARTRE: Yes, but I've nothing to say in the theater for the moment.

DE BEAUVOIR: Are you influenced by the fact that at present the French theater is scarcely a writer's theater any longer?

SARTRE: Certainly. Mnouchkine's *89,* for example, was created by actors, actors who themselves composed the text.

DE BEAUVOIR: Is that a factor that really influences you, or not?

SARTRE: Yes. My theatrical writing has become something that belongs to the past. If I were to write a play now—which I won't—I'd give it another shape, so that it would be in harmony with what's being attempted today.

DE BEAUVOIR: There's one annoying thing about the theater—the audience, which is almost always bourgeois. You once said, "But really, I've nothing to say to these bourgeois who'll come to see my play."

SARTRE: I did have one experience of a working-class audience. It was for *Nekrassov*. I was on good terms with *L'Humanité*, with the Communist party, at that time, and they sent people from the great factories and the Paris suburbs to see *Nekrassov*.

DE BEAUVOIR: Did they like the play?

SARTRE: I don't know. I know they came. There were also popular companies who acted *The Respectful Prostitute* in factories and that went well.

DE BEAUVOIR: There is a question that I would like to ask you and it is this: In *The Words* you said a great deal about reading and then about writing. You gave a very good explanation of what reading meant to you—the two levels of reading, that in which you understood nothing but were still fascinated, and that which you did understand. You also spoke, though in a more cursory fashion, of what the discovery of other books meant when you were older. But it seems to me that we should return to what reading meant to you from, let's say, the age of ten. What was reading for you at La Rochelle? What was it when you came to Paris? What was it later on? What was it during your military service? During the years when you taught at a lycée? And up until these last years?

SARTRE: One has to distinguish between two kinds of reading. The one, which came after a certain length of time, was the reading of books or documents that were to be directly useful for my literary or philosophical works. The other is a free, independent reading—the reading of a book that has just come out or that someone has recommended or of an eighteenth-century book that I did not know. This is committed reading insofar as it is linked to my whole personality, my whole life. But it has no exact part to play in the book I'm writing at that time. In disinterested reading, the reading of all cultivated men, I've passed through periods that brought me first to adventure stories at about the age of ten, as you know. To Nick Carter and Buffalo Bill and their like, who in a certain fashion showed me the world. Buffalo Bill and Nick Carter were set in America, and seeing Nick Carter in the pictures that illustrated each number of the magazine was in itself a discovery of America. He looked exactly like the Americans who were to be seen when one went to the movies. He was big, strong, clean-shaven, and he was accompanied by his henchmen and his brother, equally strong and tall. And the tale described New York life to some extent. In fact that's where I first came to know about New York.

DE BEAUVOIR: You spoke about that in *The Words*. But I'd like you to go on to the period you did not speak about in *The Words*. What did reading mean to you at La Rochelle?

SARTRE: At La Rochelle I belonged to a lending library; that is to say I took over my grandmother's role. I had known about lending libraries, as I said in *The Words*, through my grandmother, who used to go to one and take out novels. So I began going to the lending libraries in La Rochelle and to the town hall library, which also lent books.

DE BEAUVOIR: But what did you read and why? That's what matters.

SARTRE: It was a mixture of books that carried the adventure stories on, making them continually nobler and more specialized. It was there that I read Gustave Aymard, for example.

DE BEAUVOIR: Fenimore Cooper also?

SARTRE: A little Fenimore Cooper, but I found him rather boring. Others too, whose names I've forgotten but who came out in books rather than in periodicals.

DE BEAUVOIR: And what was there apart from these adventure stories?

SARTRE: Apart from those books, I made something of a return to the ways I had had in my grandfather's time, when I used to read books in his library. They were finer books but they were also less interesting. I was a little boy when I discovered adventure stories, whereas my grandfather's novels came at a later time.

DE BEAUVOIR: But at La Rochelle it was no longer your grandfather's books. What were they, then?

SARTRE: To some extent it was my mother's and my stepfather's books —books they advised me to read. And then I found myself better oriented. My mother was no great reader, but still now and then she did read a book, one of those that were being read at the time.

DE BEAUVOIR: And your stepfather, did he read?

SARTRE: My stepfather *had* read. He no longer did so. But he *had* read.

DE BEAUVOIR: Did he give you advice about reading? Did he guide you a little?

SARTRE: No, no.

DE BEAUVOIR: Not at all?

SARTRE: Not at all. Nor my mother. I wouldn't have had it.

DE BEAUVOIR: Yet you say you read the books they read.

SARTRE: Yes, because I came to them myself. I'd see the books in their bedroom or in the drawing room and I'd get them, particularly after the war, because they were books that had to do with the war and I wanted to learn.

DE BEAUVOIR: There were no prohibitions? You could read whatever you liked?

SARTRE: There were no prohibitions, none at all. In any case I didn't take particularly forbidden books. I took ordinary books. Some of them provided a link between academic and bourgeois culture. There were books that actually presented themselves as doing so.

DE BEAUVOIR: Did the teachers recommend books to you?

SARTRE: That wasn't done in those days. It was strictly textbooks that they mentioned. There was a library, of course, but Jules Verne was what one mostly found there.

DE BEAUVOIR: And didn't you have an intellectual exchange with the other boys at school? At La Rochelle?

SARTRE: They didn't read much. I was almost the only one who did. They were chiefly interested in games.

DE BEAUVOIR: So it was very much a matter of chance.

SARTRE: It was not exactly governed by that. There was a certain amount of choice. Claude Farrère, for example. I read him because there was one of his books on my stepfather's shelves. It was books of that kind that I lighted on. I came across them because they were there in the lending libraries. Those were the books one saw.

DE BEAUVOIR: Were there any books that particularly struck you at that time? Were there books that you liked, in spite of those middle-class restrictions?

SARTRE: Oh, at that time it was mainly detective and adventure stories that I liked. I did read Claude Farrère's books. They certainly interested me. And I read others of the same sort, though I found them less interesting.

DE BEAUVOIR: There was nothing that gripped your imagination.

SARTRE: Nothing.

DE BEAUVOIR: What was the nature of the change, from the point of view in reading, when you came to Paris?

SARTRE: It was a total change, because my friend Nizan and the three or four top boys in the class, Bercot and then Gruber, the painter's brother, were readers. And when I met him in the first form at Henri IV, Guille was a reader too. Their essential reading was Proust. And that was a great discovery. It was Proust who made a transition from the novel of adventure to the novel of culture, to the cultivated book.

DE BEAUVOIR: Whom did you like at that period? Proust? Giraudoux?

SARTRE: Giraudoux, whom Nizan made me read. Paul Morand, also recommended by Nizan. I was brought into this literary life by Nizan, who did not read adventure novels but who did read a great many more modern books.

DE BEAUVOIR: You read Gide too? Anyhow, you discovered modern writing.

SARTRE: I must have read *The Fruits of the Earth*, but nothing else. After all, those days were long ago. There were lots of modern writers, and speaking of them, Nizan used to say, "Have you read this one? Have you read that one?" And so I read them. From that time on, from the first form to philo, reading transformed the world. It wasn't so much philosophy but rather books by the surrealists, by Proust, Morand, and others.

DE BEAUVOIR: You read partly to be in harmony with Nizan and not to be surpassed by him, to know as much as he did, to be in the swim.

SARTRE: Primarily because of him, but also because of the few others at the school who read too.

DE BEAUVOIR: You say "it transformed the world." Could you speak of that at somewhat greater length? Could you to some degree describe this transformation of the world?

SARTRE: Where adventures were concerned, it was perfectly clear that certain novels were situated in America, a world that I did not know. But I wasn't particularly interested in geography. I had no distinct notion of what America was like. Whereas the books, let's say Morand's books for example, opened the world to me from the first form and philo on. That is, things didn't happen simply outside the world I was living in. They happened in this place or in that, in China or New York or on the Mediterranean . . . all of which astonished me. I was discovering a world . . .

DE BEAUVOIR: On the planetary, geographic level?

SARTRE: Yes, and that was of the greatest importance. So although I was bad at geography in class, I was beginning to understand it.

DE BEAUVOIR: I believe that's a very general phenomenon. At that time writers discovered exoticism. Morand, Valéry Larbaud, and many others were leaving France and describing the world. But you also had other openings onto the world. Giraudoux or Proust don't go in that direction at all.

SARTRE: Giraudoux is tense, on edge. I didn't like him much. Of course the essence of what Proust brought me was the subjective psychology of his characters. But he also gave me the idea of milieu, of environment. One thing Proust taught me was that there are different social environments just as there are different animal species. You are as it were a petit bourgeois or a noble or a member of the haute bourgeoisie or a teacher, and so on. All that is seen and acknowledged in the Proustian world. And that's something I've thought about a great deal. It seemed to me almost at once, or shortly after, that a writer should know everything about the world, that is, he should be at home in several milieus. And I've seen that idea elsewhere among people I don't care for much—among the Goncourts, who wanted to frequent all environments and make sketches of the types they would put in their novels. They wrote one about domestic servants because they had a maid they were fond of who died, and who had had quite an interesting sexual life.

DE BEAUVOIR: But wasn't it also something of a revelation of another kind? You came from a very provincial and bourgeois milieu—didn't all this open up the possibilities of life to you—feelings, ethics, psychology? Wasn't it that too?

SARTRE: Yes, certainly. It opened contemporary life to me, since my parents were living fifty years behind the times as far as culture and life were concerned. Whereas in Paris on the contrary all these young fellows were living day by day in the cultural life of the moment. Especially the surrealists. As I've said elsewhere, it was a godsend to us, a source of influence. Then I discovered *La Nouvelle Revue française* —the magazine and the books. It was a real discovery. At that time the *Nouvelle Revue française* books had a smell, a certain papery smell. The books published then have still kept something of it. I remember it. You might say it was the smell of culture. And the *N.R.F.* really stood for something. It was culture that was there.

DE BEAUVOIR: Modern culture.

SARTRE: It was in that series that I read Conrad. Conrad was the *N.R.F.* for me, since they brought out all his books.

DE BEAUVOIR: Why were you so fond of Conrad? That's the second time you've mentioned him.

SARTRE: I wasn't so fond of Conrad. But there I was at school at Henri

IV, in the class of philo and as a boarder, and in the study rooms I was in contact with boys in khâgne who were preparing for the Ecole Normale with well-known teachers, such as Alain. They talked to us, which was a great honor, since they belonged to a class much above us. They were special people whom we did not know well and whom we tried to know. Now and then they let us read a few books from their library, and in particular, one of Conrad's.

DE BEAUVOIR: Did anything of Alain's influence reach you through these boys or through anything else? Did you read Alain when you were in philo?

SARTRE: Not when I was in khâgne, but later yes. At the Ecole Normale.

DE BEAUVOIR: And all the great classics, let's say Zola, Balzac, Stendhal, and so on, when did you read them?

SARTRE: Zola and Balzac didn't interest me much. I did come to Zola later on, but I've never really gone deep into Balzac. I built up a library of the classics as the opportunity offered. Stendhal right away. I began reading him in philo, and I went on till the Ecole Normale. He was one of my favorite authors. That's why I was astonished when I learned that he should not be read between seventeen and eighteen because he takes young people's freshness away, gives them gloomy ideas, and disgusts them with life—that's what was said around me. I still don't understand, I may add . . .

DE BEAUVOIR: No, because on the contrary he's very cheerful.

SARTRE: Yes. There are love affairs, there's heroism, adventures. I really don't understand the resistance that Stendhal arouses.

DE BEAUVOIR: Very well. Now what next?

SARTRE: An author like Stendhal, then, I read him with people of my own age and against those who were older, even the teachers.

DE BEAUVOIR: In short, reading was a way of seizing the cultural world and at the same time a pleasure, of course . . .

SARTRE: That's it, a pleasure. But I was also making the world my own. That is, essentially the planet. And since I was ambitious (I wanted to live in lots of milieus with lots of people in lots of countries) that gave me a foretaste. I read a great deal until my third year in the Ecole Normale. I stopped reading when I was preparing for the *agrégation,* though I failed the first time.

DE BEAUVOIR: You'd worked a great deal. But you astonished me when I first met you because you'd read authors who aren't generally read. You'd read Baour-Lormian and Népomucène Lemercier. You had an all-embracing culture.

SARTRE: Yes, I followed the advice of history and literature. The history master and the French master mentioned these people during their lessons. So I got them and read them.

DE BEAUVOIR: And when you were in Paris, how did you get hold of books?

SARTRE: Some Nizan lent me and some I bought. And then, as I said, the boys in khâgne at Henri IV lent us books from time to time.

DE BEAUVOIR: And what did reading mean to you once you had passed the *agrégation?* I know that during your military service it was primarily an amusement.

SARTRE: Yes.

DE BEAUVOIR: Because you were deeply bored.

SARTRE: Yes.

DE BEAUVOIR: But there was something else too, wasn't there?

SARTRE: Reading has always been contact with the world. A novel, a book of history or geography—it told me about the world. A specific thing was happening in a given place, or it had happened a hundred years ago, or it would happen if I were to go to a certain country. It was information about the world that I was gathering, information that filled me with enthusiasm.

DE BEAUVOIR: I know you read many foreign books after the *agrégation*. Many American books—Dos Passos, for example.

SARTRE: Yes. I found American literature fascinating.

DE BEAUVOIR: Russian literature too.

SARTRE: I'd been reading the old Russian books, Dostoievski, Tolstoy, and so on, for a great while. They had been recommended to me at the lycée. I didn't care for Tolstoy, by the way, but in that I've changed. Dostoievski I did like, of course.

DE BEAUVOIR: And when you were teaching at Le Havre, did you read much?

SARTRE: Yes, I used to read . . .

DE BEAUVOIR: Did you still have time for reading once you had started to write really seriously, and what did it mean to you?

SARTRE: I read a lot on the train. Le Havre-Paris, Le Havre-Rouen. It was then that I found something new—I took an interest in detective stories.

DE BEAUVOIR: Ah, yes.

SARTRE: Before, it was adventure stories. There was nothing to do on the train. You watched people go by and you read. Read what? Something I should have called noncultural, not realizing that I was absorbing culture from the detective stories.

DE BEAUVOIR: We used to take the train a great deal.

SARTRE: To a prodigious extent. So I read detective stories.

DE BEAUVOIR: And why did you like detective stories?

SARTRE: I was certainly attracted by the importance they'd assumed. It was about then that everybody began reading them.

DE BEAUVOIR: Yes, but you could have ignored them.

SARTRE: I could have, but still there was that old strain of adventure that amused me.

DE BEAUVOIR: Wasn't it also the construction that interested you?

SARTRE: Yes. I've often thought it was a form of construction that could be used for novels dealing with more serious, more literary subjects. That is to say, given the construction of a puzzle that yields its own solution at the end, I thought that producing something rather hidden—not a crime, but just some happening in a life, relations between men or between men and women—might provide a theme for a novel. The fact would gradually be revealed. People would make hypotheses about it. I thought there was the possibility of a novel there. Afterward I gave up the method. Yet in the first volume of *Roads to Freedom* there are still aspects somewhat reminiscent of the detective story. Boris's relations with Lola, for example.

DE BEAUVOIR: Even in *Nausea,* there's a kind of suspense, because the hero wonders, "What is it? What's happening? . . ."

SARTRE: Yes.

DE BEAUVOIR: I think the kind of necessity that exists in a well-conceived, well worked-out detective story was something that appealed to you.

SARTRE: It was a particular necessity. A necessity that most of the time was expressed through dialogue, because when an investigator discovers something in a detective story there are . . .

DE BEAUVOIR: Interrogations.

SARTRE: It's above all the dialogue, in which the fact appears or reappears and causes anxiety or emotional attitudes. This therefore implied that dialogue could be very . . .

DE BEAUVOIR: Could have the value of action, as it were.

SARTRE: Yes. It could inform people and make them act. The adventure was in the dialogue, and it was the dialogue as adventure that seemed to me important.

DE BEAUVOIR: What then? Apart from the detective stories? When you were at Laon and when you came back to Paris—in short, during your prewar years as a teacher?

SARTRE: I read American literature mostly. It was mainly there that I came to know it. Faulkner? I still remember—it was you who read him first and you showed me the short stories, telling me I had to read them.

DE BEAUVOIR: Ah!

SARTRE: I was in your room one afternoon and you had this book. I asked you what it was and you told me. I already knew Dos Passos.

DE BEAUVOIR: Kafka. We discovered him together quite late.

SARTRE: In Brittany, if I remember rightly.

DE BEAUVOIR: Yes. In the *N.R.F.* someone spoke of the great writers, Proust, Kafka, and Joyce. And Joyce, did we know him then? I can't remember.

SARTRE: We knew him quite early, yes. First by hearsay and then we read him. The whole environment and everything that was strictly Bloom's interior monologue interested me a great deal. I even gave a lecture on Joyce at Le Havre. There was a hall where the teachers gave paid lectures. It was arranged by the municipality and the library. And I lectured the bourgeois of Le Havre on the modern writers, whom they did not know.

DE BEAUVOIR: Who, for example?

SARTRE: Faulkner.

DE BEAUVOIR: You gave a lecture on Faulkner?

SARTRE: No, but I spoke of him during a lecture and they asked me who he was.

DE BEAUVOIR: And who did you give lectures on? It seems to me you gave one on Gide, didn't you?

SARTRE: Yes, and I gave one on Joyce.

DE BEAUVOIR: Those lectures were earlier than your first critical articles.

SARTRE: They were less exhaustive than my articles, but they went in the same direction.

DE BEAUVOIR: Did you already have the idea that a technique was a system of metaphysics?

SARTRE: Yes, I'd had that idea quite early.

DE BEAUVOIR: So in short, you read to give yourself pleasure, to keep abreast of the times, and to know what was being published throughout the world?

SARTRE: I read a great deal. It interested me very much. Reading was my most important amusement. Indeed, I was crazy about it.

DE BEAUVOIR: And among all the books you read, were there any that influenced you for your own work?

SARTRE: Oh, quite obviously. Dos Passos influenced me enormously.

DE BEAUVOIR: There wouldn't have been *The Reprieve* without Dos Passos.

SARTRE: Kafka influenced me too. I can't say exactly how, but he influenced me profoundly.

DE BEAUVOIR: Had you read Kafka when you wrote *Nausea*?

SARTRE: No. I didn't yet know Kafka when I wrote *Nausea*.

DE BEAUVOIR: After that came the war, and I think that during the phony war you read a great deal.

SARTRE: Yes, you sent me lots of books. They were brought to the school where we meteorologists were stationed during the day, doing nothing but allegedly correcting or studying the wind observations that had been made that morning or during the last few days. It was no use to anybody, since no one took any interest in the wind readings.

DE BEAUVOIR: I dare say you don't remember what you read? It must have been as the books appeared.

SARTRE: Yes.

DE BEAUVOIR: Did you only read novels? No, of course you read philosophy.

SARTRE: Or history.

DE BEAUVOIR: A lot of history even by then?

SARTRE: Yes, but history as it was written in those days. Anecdotal and biographical history. I read various works on the Dreyfus affair, for example. I read a good deal of history. In any case it went with the philosophical concept that one ought to be interested in history, that it formed part of philosophy.

DE BEAUVOIR: You read many biographies.

SARTRE: Yes.

DE BEAUVOIR: We shared the same tastes in that. There were many books that we read together—basically the same list as those I give as having read myself in *The Coming of Age*.

SARTRE: One copy would often do for both of us, and we'd talk it over a great deal. There were characters from novels or from real life that we used as points of reference.

DE BEAUVOIR: Everything we read was very much part of our lives.

SARTRE: Yes, and that ought to be pointed out, because the fact that we shared a book at that particular time gives reading still another aspect.

DE BEAUVOIR: When you were in the prisoner-of-war camp, I suppose it was hard to get books.

SARTRE: I had a few. Books that a prisoner had brought in his pack.

One or two that reached me from the Germans below. Very few in fact. But I did have *Being and Time,* which I asked for and which I got.

DE BEAUVOIR: As far as that's concerned, it wasn't reading, it was work. We ought to set the books that meant work for you to one side. Heidegger, for example, and Husserl.

SARTRE: You know, it's hard to distinguish between work and reading. Were Husserl and Heidegger work or only a somewhat more systematic reading than the rest? It's very difficult to say.

DE BEAUVOIR: And didn't the reading undertaken for pleasure form part of a kind of immense task—the task of assimilating the world?

SARTRE: Later, yes, when I needed it to write my books. But when I wrote *Nausea* I needed almost no books. Nor for the short stories.

DE BEAUVOIR: And when you came back to Paris, during the war and immediately after, what did reading amount to? Even before the war you had begun to write criticisms. So in that case there was reading with rather different views.

SARTRE: Yes.

DE BEAUVOIR: Whom did you criticize before the war? Mauriac?

SARTRE: Chiefly Dos Passos

DE BEAUVOIR: And Brice Parrain? You did write on Brice Parrain, didn't you?

SARTRE: Yes, during the war. What did we read during the Occupation?

DE BEAUVOIR: I know we read *Moby Dick* at that time. But generally speaking we had no American books anymore.

SARTRE: No more American books, no more English books, no more Russian books.

DE BEAUVOIR: What did we read then?

SARTRE: We read French books.

DE BEAUVOIR: Nothing much came out.

SARTRE: We read things we hadn't read before or else we reread.

DE BEAUVOIR: That's right, we no longer read new books.

SARTRE: We read quite a lot, nevertheless.

DE BEAUVOIR: For my part, I believe it was then that I read—I don't know whether you read it too—the whole of the Arabian Nights in Dr. Mardrus's edition.

SARTRE: Yes. We read out of time; we read in the nineteenth century —Zola. I reread him during that period.

DE BEAUVOIR: And after the war?

SARTRE: There was one book that was important for me during the war, and that was Jaurès' *Histoire de la Révolution.*

DE BEAUVOIR: After the war there was a flood of American and English books. We then discovered another form of the adventure novel. And quantities of books that showed us what the war had been like on the other side of our curtain of darkness.

SARTRE: That was more interesting for you than for me.

DE BEAUVOIR: Why?

SARTRE: Because I . . . I don't know. I read them, of course, but I did not possess the kind of experience that would provide a starting point for reading of that sort.

DE BEAUVOIR: From '45 onward, didn't you read rather less, because of the fact that you were writing a great deal and that you were pretty well committed to political battles?

SARTRE: Yes, but then I had nothing else to do. Before, I was at the lycée. It was at about this time that I formed up a library for myself. I took books from it, read them and reread them.

DE BEAUVOIR: You kept your library in your mother's apartment, where you were living. There was a time when you didn't possess a single book. When we were at the Hotel de la Louisiane, someone came to see you and he was dumbfounded. He said, "But haven't you any books?" You said, "No, I read, but I don't own any books. " But the moment you began living in the Rue Bonaparte you formed a library.

SARTRE: Yes. It was out of love for books and a desire to touch them and look at them. I used to buy books in the Rue Bonaparte, and in the Rue Mazarine too. There are immense numbers of bookshops all over that part of Paris. I used to buy complete editions . . .

DE BEAUVOIR: You had the complete edition of Colette. And Proust's complete works . . .

SARTRE: Yes. From the time I settled in my mother's home I accepted the possession of certain things, such as a library, for example. The fact of not having owned books before that was the result of a clearly defined decision. I did not want to possess anything. And I stuck to it until I was forty . . .

DE BEAUVOIR: It must be admitted that our material conditions were not very favorable to ownership, since we always lived in hotels . . .

SARTRE: Yes, but I could have if I had wished. No. I didn't want to possess. I possessed nothing. Neither at Le Havre nor at Laon . . . Then in '45 I changed my life in certain ways.

DE BEAUVOIR: You engaged a secretary and you lived more comfortably than you had before. To some extent it was the force of circumstances.

SARTRE: It was because after my stepfather's death my mother wanted me to live in her apartment.

DE BEAUVOIR: Yes, I know. All right, then, to come back to reading, did you read as much after '45 as before? And did you read the same things? It seems to me, though I may be mistaken, that you did less uncommitted reading, that you read fewer novels.

SARTRE: There were novels published that were good and that I did not read. It was historical works that I read mostly.

DE BEAUVOIR: When was it that you began to read vast numbers of books on the French Revolution and even to buy volumes of memoirs on it? About '52, I think.

SARTRE: Yes, it was toward '50, '52.

DE BEAUVOIR: And that was already with a view to the *Critique of Dialectical Reason?*

SARTRE: Yes and no. At that time I wanted to write more philosophy, but it remained vague. A strong desire, but vague reading. And then I was making notes in my notebook.

DE BEAUVOIR: But you were reading very systematically and in books that were sometimes rather heavy going. You read books on crops and on agrarian reform in England. Above all, things to do with French history—many, many of them.

SARTRE: It was essentially the history of the Revolution and of the nineteenth century.

DE BEAUVOIR: A great deal of economic history. All that was documentary reading directed toward an end that was not yet clearly seen but that was nevertheless outlined.

SARTRE: In my notebooks I wrote down the ideas I drew from these books or the knowledge they provided me with.

DE BEAUVOIR: You read Braudel's book on the Mediterranean. Another you thought very important was Soboul's *Les Sans-Culottes.* For relaxation you went on reading detective stories and novels about spying.

SARTRE: Above all, novels about spying. There was a period when spy stories appeared and I read them. And then things in the *Série Noire.* *

DE BEAUVOIR: The *Série Noire* had just come into existence, Duhamel's *Série Noire.* It was good at the beginning. Afterward it declined badly.

SARTRE: It became rather tired.

---

* A popular collection of thrillers and crime-stories. (trans.)

DE BEAUVOIR: Once again I'd like to ask you what literature has been for you throughout your life. In *The Words* you explained what it meant to you during your earliest years. But what did it become, and what is it for you at present?

SARTRE: To begin with, for me, literature meant telling—telling fine tales. Why were they fine? Because they were well worked out. There was a beginning and an end and inside there were characters that I brought into existence by means of words. Within this simple idea there was also the idea that this telling did not mean the same thing as recounting to a school friend what I had done the day before. It meant something else. It was creating with words. The word was the means of telling a tale—a tale, furthermore, that seemed to me independent of the words. But the word was the means of telling it. Literature was a narrative made with words. It was complete when there was a beginning of the adventure and when the adventure was carried to its end. That lasted until my lycée studies made me see that there was another kind of literature, since there were any number of books that did not tell stories.

DE BEAUVOIR: So at La Rochelle, for example, you wrote things that were more or less narratives. Telling in writing was very different from telling things to a friend. You say it was very different because there were words. But there were words too when you told things to a friend.

SARTRE: Yes, but they were not experienced for their own sake. If it's a question of letting the friend know what happened the day before, one gives the objects that were present the names that refer to them, but one does not give those words any privilege at all. They are there because they are the words with that meaning. Whereas in a tale the word itself has a certain value.

DE BEAUVOIR: Isn't it also because at that point one moves into the imaginary?

SARTRE: Yes, but I don't know whether at the age of ten I made a very clear distinction between what was true and what was imaginary.

DE BEAUVOIR: Still, you must surely have realized that the tales you wrote had not actually happened.

SARTRE: Oh, I knew very well that those stories were inventions, but since on the other hand they were all rather like—even wholly like— the tales I'd read in comic books, I had the feeling that they possessed at least the reality of belonging to the world of those tales, which existed outside myself. I did not then possess the idea of the purely imaginary, though it came quite soon afterward. You might say that the imaginary raised no problem at all. All right, the tale didn't exist, it was invented. But it wasn't imaginary. It wasn't imaginary insofar as it wasn't a tale that seemed credible but that in fact was not so.

DE BEAUVOIR: But still wasn't there a certain feeling for what might be called the beauty and the necessity of the tale?

SARTRE: I didn't tell just anything. I told something that had a beginning and an end that had a strict relation to the beginning. So that one made an object whose beginning was the cause of the end and whose end referred back to the beginning.

DE BEAUVOIR: An object closed upon itself?

SARTRE: Yes, the whole tale was made up of things that were in relation to one another. The beginning created a situation that was cleared up at the end with the elements of that same beginning. The end therefore reechoed the beginning and the beginning had already a conception of the end. For me that was very important. In other words, there was the narrative which called invention into play. That was one of the elements. The other element was that what I invented was the tale, which was self-sufficient and whose end corresponded to the beginning and the other way around.

DE BEAUVOIR: Without using the word, you mean it was necessity.

SARTRE: It was a necessity that one revealed only in the telling of the tale. That was the essential feature, you might say. A necessity was revealed in the telling, a necessity that was the linking together of words chosen so that they might be linked. . . . And then, but very vaguely, there was also the idea that there were good words, words that looked well when they were being linked together and that made a fine phrase once they were joined. But all that was vague. I certainly felt that words could be beautiful, but I did not worry about it much. I was concerned with saying what there was to be said. That lasted until I was about twelve. Then we began reading works of the great seventeenth- or eighteenth-century writers at the lycée, and I saw that not all of them were romantic tales, but that there were also discussions, essays, and so on. And this kind of writing resulted in a work in which time no longer appeared in the same manner. Nevertheless, it seemed to me that time was of the essence in literature. It was the reader's time that was called into being. That is, the reader had his own time to begin with, and then he was set in a duration that was created for him and that took place within him. During the time he read he became the object he was making.

DE BEAUVOIR: So you then had a conception of literature that still reckoned on the reader's time but that was no longer necessarily a tale. What had it become at that point?

SARTRE: There was a before and an after. The reader began the essay with ideas that were not those which the writer was setting out. Slowly, he became aware of the writer's ideas. It took time, starting at two o'clock in the afternoon and going on until six and then beginning again the next day. So it was by means of time that he learned the author's ideas. There was an outline in the first chapter, and then it all built up and the reader finished by possessing a temporal idea. It was temporal because it took time to form itself. That's how I saw things.

DE BEAUVOIR: But did you write what could strictly be called essays when you were really young, in khâgne or the first form?

SARTRE: Not before khâgne in any event. And did I write any even then? At that time Nizan and I each worked on his own, but we showed one another what we had written and the novels were at the same time essays. That is, we wanted to put our ideas into them, and then the novel's length of time simultaneously became the duration in which the idea was expressed. And Nizan's short stories in the *Revue sans titre* were rather like essays. While for my first essay I wrote *La Légende de la vérité* (The Legend of Truth).

DE BEAUVOIR: And *Er l'Arménien* (Er the Armenian)—how did you look upon that?

SARTRE: More or less as an essay. As an essay but with characters to whom meaningful things happen. In their conversation they deal with them at length and explain them. And so it becomes a symbol.

DE BEAUVOIR: But the other day you said that one of the things you wanted to do was reveal truths. To reveal the truth of the world to others.

SARTRE: Yes, that came slowly. It didn't come at the beginning. Yet it was there. One had to have a subject. For me, it was the world. What I had to say, to talk about, was the world. Furthermore, I think it's the same with all writers. A writer has only one subject, and that's the world.

DE BEAUVOIR: There are some writers who reach the world by way of themselves, writers who go in for intimacy and speak of their own experiences.

SARTRE: Everyone has his own way of seeing things. I don't know why, but I did not write about myself, at least not as a subjective character, as one having a subjectivity and ideas. It never occurred to me to write about myself, about something that had happened to me. Yet naturally it was still entirely a question of me. But in the stories I wrote the aim was not to represent myself.

DE BEAUVOIR: That is to say it was the world that was apprehended through you.

SARTRE: There's no doubt that the subject of *Nausea* is primarily the world

DE BEAUVOIR: It's a metaphysical dimension of the world that has to be revealed.

SARTRE: Just so. It's an idea other than that of literature. Literature reveals the truth about the world, but in a way unlike that of philosophy. In philosophy there's a beginning and an end and therefore a duration; yet philosophy refuses that duration. You have to take up the book. You don't understand it until you've finished it, and so at that stage there's no duration. You don't inject into the book the time you've taken to make it out and understand it. And the thought you get out of it is an ideal thought. You keep it in your head as a well-organized whole. The book may speak of duration—there may be a chapter or two on it—but at that point it is a concept, not a dimension of the object. I've changed as far as that is concerned, because now I think on the contrary that my philosophical works contain the notion of temporality, not only as the necessity that each person may have in reading the book, starting at the beginning or the end, which means an expenditure of time, but also insofar as the time taken in the exposition and the discussion makes part of the philosophy itself. The one determines the other.

DE BEAUVOIR: At the time of writing *Nausea*, did you have an idea of necessity?

SARTRE: Yes.

DE BEAUVOIR: For you, was the idea of beauty linked with the idea of writing a book?

SARTRE: Lord, no! I thought that beauty was something you had into the bargain if you took care of your phrases, your style, and the way the tale was told. But those were formal qualities and I didn't take much trouble with them. For me what mattered was finding the world at the bottom of the tale.

DE BEAUVOIR: Yet just now you told me that even when you were young, you already attributed an importance to words.

SARTRE: Yes. It was a kind of element of beauty, but also of precision, of truth. A phrase with well-chosen words is a true, accurate phrase.

DE BEAUVOIR: Yet at the end of *Nausea*, when the hero hears "Some of These Days" he says he'd like to create something like that. And it touches him by what might be called its beauty.

SARTRE: Yes, but the reason why "Some of These Days" moves Roquentin is that it is an object created by man, by a man a great way off, who touches him by means of his verse. It's not that he's a humanitarian; it's a man's creation that strikes him and that he likes.

DE BEAUVOIR: In other words it was a question of communication rather than of beauty?

SARTRE: Those objects that survived once they had been produced were to be found in libraries as material realities. But they were also in a kind of intelligible heaven that was, not an imaginary heaven. It was a reality that remained. And I remember that *Nausea* lagged somewhat behind my own ideas. That is, even then I was no longer concerned with creating true or beautiful objects outside the world, as I supposed before I knew you. I had gone beyond that. I didn't know exactly what I wanted, but I did know that it wasn't a beautiful object, a literary object, a bookish object that one created. It was something else. From that point of view, Roquentin marked the end of one period rather than the beginning of another.

DE BEAUVOIR: I don't quite see what you mean. Flaubert thought a book was an object that stood perfectly well on its own feet, that had, as it were, no need of a reader, whom he would like to look upon as totally useless. Is that what you thought before *Nausea*?

SARTRE: More or less, though I did not think it had no need of a reader.

DE BEAUVOIR: Well then, when *Nausea* was finished and even while you were writing it, how did you see the book?

SARTRE: I saw it as a metaphysical essence; I had created a metaphysical object. It was like a Platonic idea, you might say, but a particularized idea and one that the reader would discover as he read the book. I began *Nausea* believing that, and by the end I no longer believed it.

DE BEAUVOIR: What did you believe at that point?

SARTRE: I wasn't sure.

DE BEAUVOIR: And when you wrote short stories? What did you think you were doing when you wrote a short story?

SARTRE: The short story had a more immediate necessity, since a short story is thirty to fifty pages long. So not only did I conceive the necessity, but when I read the story I practically saw it. Where the stories were concerned I had a more obvious vision of the literary object than when I was writing *Nausea*, which is long.

DE BEAUVOIR: Yes; but what exactly did writing these short stories mean to you? With *Nausea* it's quite clear. There's a revealing of the world, essentially accompanied by that dimension of contingency which you valued so. But what about the stories?

SARTRE: The stories. It's odd. They changed their meaning. I intended to write a story to render certain spontaneous impressions by means of words. "Le Soleil de minuit" (The Midnight Sun), the story I lost, was of that kind. I meant to write a volume of stories . . .

DE BEAUVOIR: Of atmosphere, as it were.

SARTRE: . . . of atmosphere. Naples, for example. I wanted the story to help one see Naples.

DE BEAUVOIR: What then? Did it change?

SARTRE: Yes. It changed, I can scarcely tell why. "Erostrate" was one of Bost's dreams.

DE BEAUVOIR: Yes, but why did you choose that dream?

SARTRE: My plan took on a broader character. The story might be the vision of a moment that mattered a good deal to me, or it might also be something more important, like the Spanish war. There was one about madness. So it was a question of situations that were pretty serious and completely different from what I had meant at the beginning. At the beginning my idea was more to write a tale about an evening on the Paris boulevards, about a garden, a tale about Naples, or a crossing by sea.

DE BEAUVOIR: Those are the very stories you did away with, those stories of atmosphere. There was one that was lost, and you did not try to rewrite it. You did away with the female orchestra's sea crossing, although you took it up again later. All right. But throughout all this what was the nature of that which you called the very "essence" of literature the other day? Here it was still recounting.

SARTRE: Certainly recounting. Even an essay recounts.

DE BEAUVOIR: But still, writing an essay on Giacometti is not the same thing as "The Wall."

SARTRE: It's not the same thing. But even so time is needed to enter into Giacometti's pictures. And there is the time of the reading. It's not quite the same as the time of the creation, but the two are interconnected. And when the reader reads the essay, insofar as he is a reader he creates, and he will bring about the apparition of the object as it was laid down for him.

DE BEAUVOIR: Let's go on to the essays, then. You began writing criticism before the war, didn't you?

SARTRE: Yes.

DE BEAUVOIR: And you went on during the war . . .

SARTRE: I went on during the war in a review published in Marseilles. It was called *Confluences*.

DE BEAUVOIR: And you continued after the war. In your essays there are lots of different things—literary criticism, artistic criticism, and then political comments. And sometimes biographies. Portraits of Merleau-Ponty and Nizan. What were your views on criticism then? And why did it interest you? I remember at the beginning, when I had the idea that you were made to write novels, it seemed to me that it was rather a waste of time. I was completely mistaken, because it is one of the most interesting parts of your work. But what prompted you to take to criticism?

SARTRE: The world still. Criticism is a discovery, a certain manner of seeing the world, a way of discovering how the fellow whose work you're reading and criticizing saw the world. How Faulkner saw the world, for example. The way events are narrated in his books, the way characters are presented. It was a way of yielding up his own manner of reacting to the people around him, the landscapes, the life he led, and so on. All that could be seen in the book, but not right away. It had to be seen through great numbers of signs, of notations that had to be studied.

DE BEAUVOIR: There was one thing that interested you very much in the novels you've been speaking about, and that was the technique.

SARTRE: Technique. I think it came to me from Nizan. He took a great deal of trouble with it. For his own novels and for other people's.

DE BEAUVOIR: But it was in the most direct fashion that you became interested in Dos Passos's technique.

SARTRE: Yes, of course. But the idea of studying a book's technique and finding out whether it was worth anything came to me from Nizan.

DE BEAUVOIR: I know that when Nizan talked to us about Dos Passos, his first and main concern was Dos Passos's technique.

SARTRE: That's so.

DE BEAUVOIR: But there was one idea that was entirely yours and that was highly important—the idea that the technique at the same time reveals the man's metaphysics.

SARTRE: That was what I said to you just now. Fundamentally, my criticism searched for the metaphysics, searched for it by means of the technique. And when I'd found the metaphysics I was happy. I truly possessed the entirety of the work.

DE BEAUVOIR: Yes.

SARTRE: For me that was the critical idea. Finding out how the men who wrote saw the world, each separately. They described the world, but they saw it in different ways. Some in its plenitude, others from the side, narrowly.

DE BEAUVOIR: Some in a dimension of freedom, others in a dimension of necessity, of oppression. . . . Yes.

SARTRE: It's all that which has to be grasped.

DE BEAUVOIR: But you had another idea as well, and that was that an essay was also an object, an object that was necessary and that ought to have its own literary quality. To begin with, you found it quite hard to write an essay that was not like a treatise but that should have, let's say, elegance if not beauty.

SARTRE: The danger of elegance is that it may separate the object from its truth. If it's too elegant it no longer says what it wants to say. If a criticism on Dos Passos contains overelegant passages, if it makes sacrifices to beauty, it no longer says exactly what you meant it to say . . .

DE BEAUVOIR: In other words, the problem is to find the right balance between the object to be grasped and the personal way of speaking of it.

SARTRE: That's right. What one had to say had to be said, but said in a manner that should possess necessity, be well worked out . . .

DE BEAUVOIR: And in your opinion what constituted an essay's elegance?

SARTRE: Oh, they were very Cartesian ideas—lightness, clarity, necessity.

DE BEAUVOIR: Yes.

SARTRE: The quality of the essay came of itself, since I brought in metaphysics. So there was always criticism at one level. A study of the particular author's words—why he chose a given adjective or a given verb, what his tricks amounted to, and so on—and then behind that the metaphysics were brought into question. As I see it, criticism is a double process. It must be an exposition of the author's methods, rules, and techniques insofar as these techniques show me his metaphysics.

DE BEAUVOIR: Yes, but at the same time it was a question of saying all that in what we might call an artistic fashion. The idea of art is there, since your criticism of Mauriac runs, "God is not an artist; nor is M. Mauriac." So you certainly thought there was a literary art, an art of writing. Besides, the other day you were talking to me about the essence of the art of writing. So you thought there was a particular art of writing an essay?

SARTRE: Yes. . . . And one that I did not hit upon easily. I found it hard to begin with. Although in the end I confined myself to writing essays and nothing else.

DE BEAUVOIR: How do you mean?

SARTRE: After the novel stopped there were the plays, but apart from the plays, which don't belong to the same literary species, what was I writing? Articles, books . . .

DE BEAUVOIR: Ah! Then came books of philosophy. I don't call books of philosophy essays, for the very good reason that in books of philosophy you didn't worry about literary art.

SARTRE: No.

DE BEAUVOIR: There are highly literary passages, particularly in *Being and Nothingness,* whereas the *Critique of Dialectical Reason* is really harsh, both in style and tone.

SARTRE: In a novel you're not quite sure what you will do with the characters, or what they'll say to one another. You can twist the dialogue and cut its head off in order to write it differently, because you have an intuition that it would be better that way. As I did with Götz, for example.

DE BEAUVOIR: Yes, when you turned the scene around. Whereas in an essay you are continually led by what you have to say.

SARTRE: So naturally from time to time one may indulge oneself a little, but one must not do so too often. If any of the indulgences tend to drag it's no longer a good essay.

DE BEAUVOIR: Which were the essays you wrote most easily, letting your pen run on, and which were those you worked over most?

SARTRE: I've never let my pen run on with my essays. I've always worked in a literary fashion.

DE BEAUVOIR: Even the essay on Lumumba?

SARTRE: I was just thinking of Lumumba. At that very moment I was thinking you might raise that objection. But it's not so. I did try to work over Lumumba. For instance I discuss the books he had read. I might not have done so, or I might have spoken about them differently. So there is a whole inventive side to the essay. I mean, you don't have a clearly defined plan when you begin an article, and if you choose to include the books he'd read and what he said about them it's because that's important. But you are the one who defines it as important.

DE BEAUVOIR: Still, it seems to me that you paid less attention to art when you were writing the political essays.

SARTRE: Perhaps rather less.

DE BEAUVOIR: As with *The Communists and Peace,* for example.

SARTRE: Ah! Yet I'd particularly wanted that to be well written.

DE BEAUVOIR: Yes, of course. Well written, not too lengthy. But even so it did not lend itself to a concern about the style as much as some others.

SARTRE: To sum up what we've said. For me, a literary work is an object, an object that has a duration of its own, a beginning and an end. This particular duration is rendered evident in the book by the fact that everything one reads always refers to what went before and also to what will follow. It is that which is the work's necessity. It is a question of aligning words that have a certain tension of their own and that by this tension will bring into being the tension of the book, which is a duration to which one commits oneself. When you begin a book you enter into that duration. You cause your own duration to be determined in such a manner that it now has a certain beginning, which is the beginning of the book, and which will have an end. There exists therefore a certain relation between the reader and a duration that is his own and that at the same time is not his own, a relation that lasts from the moment he begins the book until he finishes it. This supposes a complex relation between the author and the reader, since the author is not simply going to narrate, but to form his narration in such a manner that the reader really conceives the duration of the novel and reconstitutes the causes and the effects himself, according to what is written.

DE BEAUVOIR: I think you might say more about this, because after all it's your conception of literature, the conception of your relations with your reader.

SARTRE: The reader is a person there in front of me, a person on whose duration I act. That's how I'd define him. And in the course of that duration I cause the appearance of feelings intimately connected with my book, feelings that correct themselves, argue with one another, combine and leave the finished work confirmed or done away with.

DE BEAUVOIR: The other day you spoke of an attempt at seducing the reader.

SARTRE: That's right, an attempt at seduction. But not an unlawful seduction, not as you might seduce someone with arguments that are not true but that sound good—no, seduction by the truth. To seduce, a novel has to be an expectation, a waiting, that is to say a duration that stretches out.

DE BEAUVOIR: In a certain fashion there's always suspense.

SARTRE: Always. It's resolved at the end.

DE BEAUVOIR: One always wonders what's going to happen. And even in an essay the reader is always asking himself, "What is he going to say now? What is it he wants to prove?"

SARTRE: And "What does he mean now and how does he reply to these objections?" So time steps in too. And through this time, through this construction of the object, I read the world, that is, the metaphysical being. The literary work is someone who is rebuilding the world as he sees it by means of a narrative that is not directly aimed at the world but which has to do with imaginary works or characters. And that's roughly what I wanted to do.

DE BEAUVOIR: You ought once more to explain—you've already done so very well, but it was so misunderstood—you ought to explain your move on to committed literature.

SARTRE: I've written a whole book on it.

DE BEAUVOIR: Yes, of course. But after all what relation is there or what difference is there between the works you produced before having the theory of engaged works and those that came after? Are the same things finally to be found in the committed works or not?

SARTRE: It's the same thing. In a committed book it's not a modification of the technique but rather of the idea of what one wishes to create by means of words. But that doesn't bring about a change, since the committed work will be connected with a certain political or metaphysical concern that one wishes to express and that is present in the work. Even if it doesn't call itself "committed."

DE BEAUVOIR: It's rather a question of the choice of subject.

SARTRE: Just so. Even if there had been a Lumumba in 1929, I shouldn't have written about him then.

DE BEAUVOIR: But when you want to convey the feeling of contingency, as you do in *Nausea,* or when you want to convey the feeling of the injustice and cruelty inflicted upon Lumumba, they're fundamentally the same techniques, it's the same relation with the reader.

SARTRE: Exactly. One simply has a wish to enlist him in a cause that will show him certain aspects of the world.

DE BEAUVOIR: Besides, you've often said that it was the entirety of a man's work that should be committed. And that each particular book . . .

SARTRE: Each book is allowed not to be.

DE BEAUVOIR: You wrote *The Words,* for example.

SARTRE: Just so. Yes, a man's commitment is in the body of his work as a whole.

DE BEAUVOIR: We haven't said much about *The Words.* Perhaps we could go back to it for a while. It's a book that took you ten years to write. How did the first idea come to you and then why was it laid aside?

SARTRE: I'd always had the idea when I was eighteen or twenty of writing about my life when I'd lived it, that is to say at fifty.

DE BEAUVOIR: What happened then in about '52?

SARTRE: Well, I said to myself Here we are, I'm going to write.

DE BEAUVOIR: But why did you say that just in '52?

SARTRE: There was a great change in '52 . . .

DE BEAUVOIR: Yes, I know that. But it was a change that made you more politically conscious. So how does it come about that it led you to write about your childhood?

SARTRE: Because I wanted to write my whole life from a political point of view, my childhood, youth, and middle age, giving it the political sense of arriving at communism. And when I'd written *The Words* in its first version, I found that I had not described the childhood I had meant to describe. Not at all. I'd begun a book that would have had to go on, showing my stepfather marrying my mother, etcetera. Then at that point I stopped, as I had other things to do.

DE BEAUVOIR: Tell me about this first version. Nobody knows about it.

SARTRE: That was the one I worked over. . . . It was more ill-natured about me and my milieu than the second. I wanted to show myself perpetually eager to change, uneasy with myself, uneasy with others, and then changing and at last becoming the communist I ought to have been to start with. But of course that's not true.

DE BEAUVOIR: You called it *Jean-sans-terre,* didn't you? What did that title mean?

SARTRE: *Sans terre* meant without inheritance, without possessions. It meant what I was.

DE BEAUVOIR: And what point in your life did it reach?

SARTRE: The same as *The Words.*

DE BEAUVOIR: In short, it really was a first version of *The Words.*

SARTRE: A first version of *The Words,* but a version that had to continue.

DE BEAUVOIR: And how long was it before you went back to it?

SARTRE: That was . . . in '61, wasn't it?

DE BEAUVOIR: Yes, I think so.

SARTRE: I went back to it because I had no money left and I'd borrowed some from Gallimard as an advance.

DE BEAUVOIR: An Englishman asked for something of yours that had not been published but in the end you gave it to Gallimard. You went back to it, and you changed it a great deal.

SARTRE: I wanted it to be more literary than the others because I felt that it was a way of saying goodbye to a certain kind of literature, and that I should produce it, explain it, and take my leave of it. I wanted to be literary in order to show the error of being literary.

DE BEAUVOIR: I don't quite understand. What kind of literature did you mean to say farewell to with *The Words?*

SARTRE: The literature I'd pursued in my youth and then in my novels and short stories. I wanted to show that it was over and done with, and I wanted to emphasize the fact by writing a very literary book about my childhood.

DE BEAUVOIR: What did you intend to write afterward? Since you no longer wanted to produce literature as you had done before.

SARTRE: Committed and political writing.

DE BEAUVOIR: You'd already produced committed writing.

SARTRE: Yes, but political, more especially political.

DE BEAUVOIR: It's curious, because in the end what you did produce was the Flaubert and not especially political writing.

SARTRE: A little, nevertheless.

DE BEAUVOIR: Not much. But let's go back. What do you mean by a work that's more literary than another? How can there be degrees in literature?

SARTRE: You can work more over the style, for example. *The Words* is heavily worked over. It contains some of the most worked-over phrases I've ever written. And I spent a lot of time over it. I wanted there to be hints, implications in every phrase, one or two implications, so that it would strike people at one level or another. And then I wanted to present each thing, each character in a particular manner. It's heavily worked over, *The Words.*

DE BEAUVOIR: Yes, I know, and it's very successful. But I wanted to get you to say exactly what you mean by "literary."

SARTRE: It was full of tricks, of clever dodges, of the art of writing, almost of plays on words.

DE BEAUVOIR: That is to say that the desire to charm the reader by words, by the turn of phrase, is greater than in any other of your works?

SARTRE: That's it.

DE BEAUVOIR: So that's what you call "literary." But according to all you've said, one just can't conceive a work that has no desire to charm.

SARTRE: I've always had that desire. And when I feel I've succeeded, why, that produces something for which I've a special affection or regard.

DE BEAUVOIR: And you do have regard and affection for *The Words?*

SARTRE: Yes.

DE BEAUVOIR: And at present how do you see literature?

SARTRE: At present I've finished. I'm on the other side of the door.

DE BEAUVOIR: Yes, but what do you think of it?

SARTRE: I think I've done what I've done, and there you are.

DE BEAUVOIR: At times, quite a long while ago, you were disgusted with literature. You used to say, "Literature is crap." Exactly what did you mean by that? And more recently you've sometimes said, "After all it's stupid to labor to express yourself." You seemed to be saying that all that had to be done was to write just anyhow, as one might put it. Then again you've sometimes told me you wrote the Flaubert like that, which wasn't strictly true.

SARTRE: It wasn't true.

DE BEAUVOIR: You wrote drafts and you made corrections. And then you had some felicitous expressions, even if you weren't trying for them. There are many felicities in the Flaubert.

SARTRE: I write faster. But that comes from practice.

DE BEAUVOIR: What did you mean when you said, "It's crap" or when you said, "But there's no point wasting your time in writing well?" To what extent did you think it? Do you still think it?

SARTRE: It's a queer thing, style. We'd have to talk it over to see whether a work is worth the trouble of being written stylishly, and we'd have to ask ourselves whether the only way of having style is to correct what one's written so that the verb agrees with the subject and the adjective's well placed, and so on, as I've done. Whether there's not a way of letting things slide that would be successful. For example, I write faster because I'm used to it now. Well, might there not be a way of writing fast from the very beginning? But, you know, many left-wing writers think that style, taking too much care of words and all that, is an infernal bore, and that one ought to go straight for the object, not worrying about the rest.

DE BEAUVOIR: But very often the result is disastrous.

SARTRE: I don't agree with them. I don't mean style's not necessary. I only wonder whether great labor over words is necessary to create a style.

DE BEAUVOIR: Doesn't that rather depend on the people, the period, the subject, the temperament, the opportunities?

SARTRE: Yes, but fundamentally I believe that the best-written things have always been written without too much effort.

DE BEAUVOIR: Why is it that you read much less literature now?

SARTRE: From my childhood and for quite a long time, until 1950, I looked upon a book as something that presented the truth. The style, the way of writing, the words, all that was a truth, and it brought me something. I didn't know what and I didn't express it to myself in words, but I thought it brought me something. Books were not only objects, not only a relation with the world, but a relation with truth, a relation difficult to put into words but one that I felt. So that was what I asked from literary books, this relation to truth.

DE BEAUVOIR: The truth of a certain view of the world other than your own.

SARTRE: I couldn't have said exactly what truth. Criticism was rather useful to me as far as that was concerned. Trying to extract the meaning of the author's truth, and what it could bring us. That was very important.

DE BEAUVOIR: And have you lost that idea, and if so why?

SARTRE: I have lost it, because I think a book's much more common-place than that. Now and then, with great writers, I recover something of that feeling.

DE BEAUVOIR: But when did you lose the feeling?

SARTRE: About '50, '52, when I went into politics to some extent. When I grew more interested in politics, when I had relations with the Communists. It's vanished. I think it was an idea that dated from a hundred years ago.

DE BEAUVOIR: You mean a rather magical idea of literature?

SARTRE: Yes, rather magical. That particular truth wasn't suggested to me by scientific or logical methods. It came to me from the beauty of the book itself, from its value. I believed in it profoundly. I believed that writing was an activity that produced a reality, not exactly the book, but something beyond the book. The book belonged to the imaginary, but beyond the book there was truth.

DE BEAUVOIR: And you stopped believing it when you had read a great deal of history and when you plunged deeper into committed writing.

SARTRE: Yes. As a man gradually gains his experience so he loses the ideas he used to have. That was around '52.

DE BEAUVOIR: It seems to me that the last work you read with a great deal of pleasure was *Moby Dick*. Then came Genet's books, I think. It was not by mere chance that you wrote about him. You were charmed by his work. After '52, I don't think you had any great literary enthusiasms.

SARTRE: No.

DE BEAUVOIR: At that time reading was either study or mere amusement.

SARTRE: Or else books of history.

DE BEAUVOIR: I know you haven't read the books that I've liked these last years. I've mentioned them to you, but we haven't talked about them together, even when I told you I thought them very good, like Albert Cohen or John Cowper Powys. Reading them didn't interest you at all. There's a kind of disenchantment with literature in the strict sense.

SARTRE: Perhaps. Besides, generally speaking, I no longer really see why people write novels. I'd like to talk about what I once thought literature was, and then about what I've abandoned.

DE BEAUVOIR: Do, by all means. It's very interesting.

SARTRE: To begin with I thought that literature was the novel.

DE BEAUVOIR: Yes, a narrative, and at the same time the world was seen through it. It gives you something that no sociological essay, no table of statistics, or anything else can give.

SARTRE: It gives the individual, the personal, the particular. A novel would give this room, for example, the color of this wall, these curtains, the window, and it's only the novel that can give it. That's what I've liked in it, the fact that these objects were named, that they were very close in their individual character. I knew that all the places described did exist or had existed, and that in consequence the truth was certainly there.

DE BEAUVOIR: Though you weren't particularly fond of literary descriptions. There are descriptions in your novels from time to time, but they are always closely linked to the action and to the way the characters see them.

SARTRE: And short.

DE BEAUVOIR: Yes. A little metaphor, three little words to hint at something. Not really a description.

SARTRE: Because a description—well, it isn't time.

DE BEAUVOIR: No. It comes to a halt.

SARTRE: It comes to a halt. It doesn't give the object as it appears at the moment but as it has been for the last fifty years. It's absurd!

DE BEAUVOIR: Whereas hinting at the object in the movement of the action, that's fine! But may there not be another reason? Isn't it because you've read practically all the great books of literature? And it must be admitted that what comes out from one day to the next is rarely of an astonishing quality.

SARTRE: It was like that before the war.

DE BEAUVOIR: Oh, no, before the war you hadn't yet read Kafka or Joyce or *Moby Dick*.

SARTRE: No. I had read Cervantes, but I'd read him badly. I often say I should reread *Don Quixote*. I've tried once or twice. I've been prevented, not because I didn't like it—on the contrary, I liked it very much—but circumstances have turned me aside. There are lots of things to reread, or to read. I might set myself to it.

DE BEAUVOIR: But perhaps you think it would no longer bring you anything much, would not enrich you, would not give you any new views on the world. And there again, you know, you're in agreement with the general opinion, as has so often happened during your lifetime and mine. On the whole, people read fewer novels and like them less than they did at one time. It has to be said that there's been the attempt of the *nouveau roman,* which was so boring that people would rather read biographies, autobiographies, sociological or historical studies. One has a much stronger feeling of truth than when one reads a novel.

SARTRE: Those are in fact the things I read.

DE BEAUVOIR: Yes, that's what interests you at present. But there are things other than literature that have filled you with enthusiasm during your life. Music and painting. Sculpture too. One thing I've observed and that rather intrigues me is that although you've always been very fond of music, although you've played the piano, although you come from a musical family, and although you still listen to a great deal, either on records or on the radio, you've practically never written about music, apart from an introduction to a book by Leibowitz on committed music.

SARTRE: That's true.

DE BEAUVOIR: Whereas painting, on the other hand. . . . To begin with, you weren't so very fond of it when I first knew you. Then gradually, having educated yourself, you came to love and understand painting and you've written a greal deal on the subject. Could you tell me something of the part it's played in your life? And the reason for this contrast?

SARTRE: I'll begin with music, because that's something I came into contact with very early. As for painting, I saw reproductions. I didn't go to museums when I was five, six, seven years old, but I did see reproductions of pictures, especially in the splendid Larousse dictionary, which provided engravings of them. Like many children I had a pictorial culture before I'd ever seen a picture. But I was born in the midst of music. A curious thing happened. My grandfather became deeply interested in music.

DE BEAUVOIR: Your grandfather Schweitzer himself?

SARTRE: Yes. He was interested in it, and he wrote a thesis on a singer, a musician—Hans Sachs.

DE BEAUVOIR: And then there was Albert Schweitzer's work on Bach.

SARTRE: My grandfather had a great regard for that book and he often reread it. And sometimes my grandfather composed. I remember having seen him compose music when I was fifteen, at the house of his brother Louis, a pastor. He sat down at the piano and he composed. He composed things that sounded rather like Mendelssohn.

DE BEAUVOIR: What relation was he to Albert Schweitzer?

SARTRE: He was his uncle. He was his father's brother.

DE BEAUVOIR: And did your grandfather esteem Albert Schweitzer?

SARTRE: Yes, but he didn't understand him very well. He didn't have the same problems and tended to make fun of him.

DE BEAUVOIR: So it was Albert Schweitzer who was the great musician of the family.

SARTRE: Yes. When I was a child I was present at an organ recital that he gave in Paris. My mother took me and my grandmother.

DE BEAUVOIR: And your mother herself—she was musical.

SARTRE: Yes, very musical. She played well. She'd taken fairly advanced lessons in singing and she sang very well. She played Chopin, she played Schumann; she played difficult pieces. She certainly had less musical experience than my uncle Georges, but she was fond of it, and in the afternoons—I told about this in *The Words,* by the way —she used to play the piano to herself.

DE BEAUVOIR: Did you have piano lessons?

SARTRE: Very early. I had piano lessons when I was about ten, I think. Nine or ten.

DE BEAUVOIR: And until what age did you go on?

SARTRE: When I left Paris for La Rochelle I gave them up.

DE BEAUVOIR: So how does it happen that you were really quite good at the piano?

SARTRE: I taught myself. From the time I was in the fourth form my mother's piano was in the drawing room of my stepfather's house, and when I had nothing to do, I used to slip in and try to play the tunes I remembered. And then there were the operettas that I had bought or rented from the music shops in La Rochelle. At first my learning was slow and difficult; but I was sensitive to rhythm. When my mother remarried she played much less because of my stepfather, who really didn't like music. Still, she did play when I came back from the lycée and before my stepfather returned. I'd sit beside her and listen, and when she left I'd play myself. At first I played with one finger, then with five, and then with ten. In the end I succeeded in training my fingers to some extent. I didn't play fast, but I did play all the pieces.

DE BEAUVOIR: Did you play four-handed with your mother?

SARTRE: Yes, quartets and Franck's symphony.

DE BEAUVOIR: All arranged for the piano?

SARTRE: Yes. I provided myself with a musical culture not unlike my mother's. And I played the piano until two years ago, at Arlette's.

DE BEAUVOIR: There was a time when you played a great deal. It was when you lived in the Rue Bonaparte, in your mother's apartment. I can still see the sort of little gilt latticed bench; you used to sit there and sometimes play for an hour before settling down to work.

SARTRE: So I did, sometimes.

DE BEAUVOIR: You'd very often play from three o'clock until five, and then at five you'd begin work. At the beginning, when I could still play the piano a little—I always played very, very badly, but there was a time when I could still play a little—we played four-handed pieces together.

SARTRE: Yes, occasionally.

DE BEAUVOIR: But not often, because you played infinitely better than I did. You used to play Chopin. And then when you were no longer living with your mother, you no longer had a piano.

SARTRE: We must distinguish between the various stages. I played at my mother's home and at my stepfather's at Saint-Etienne until I was thirteen or fourteen. Then when I came to Paris, where I was a boarder, I played at my grandparents' house. They had a piano that was scarcely used anymore. Though my grandmother did play a little —she would sometimes sit at the piano and run off a few notes. My grandfather didn't play at all. So when I came back from the lycée on Saturdays and Sundays, the piano was a great delight. I played badly, I made mistakes in the time, and as soon as I came to a brilliant passage my hands were not quick enough, but I did manage fairly well with Chopin, Franck, and Bach.

DE BEAUVOIR: You didn't play badly at all. Not like a virtuoso of course, but not badly.

SARTRE: It came gradually, as I played more and more. My mother made me work at it a little, and so did my grandmother. I used to play at my grandmother's house. I still remember a four-handed piano version of Beethoven's piano and violin sonatas. And some Schubert: a little Chopin. It took me quite a while to learn to play them. But music gave me a very real pleasure.

DE BEAUVOIR: Did you go to concerts? Did you have records?

SARTRE: I had no records. In those days they were not very good, and then it wasn't my family's way to listen to records. But I did go to concerts on Sundays, sometimes with my grandmother, sometimes with my grandfather. There were those famous *concerts rouges* that were given in the Rue de Seine, I believe. I went with my grandfather. It was a place where cherries in brandy were passed around during the intermission.

DE BEAUVOIR: Was it classical music?

SARTRE: Yes, and the performers were good. They played well. At that time I knew only classical music.

DE BEAUVOIR: Operetta too, you said.

SARTRE: Yes, but what I mean is that I scarcely knew the more recent music at all. A trifle of Debussy.

DE BEAUVOIR: Almost every year once we'd met, we used to attend the series of Beethoven quartets at the Salle Gaveau.

SARTRE: We went at least twice.

DE BEAUVOIR: We were very much taken up with the question of whether there might not be some great composer unknown to us. In fact there were some of whom we were completely ignorant, particularly the Viennese school.

SARTRE: And Bela Bartók.

DE BEAUVOIR: I believe you discovered Bela Bartók in America.

SARTRE: Yes.

DE BEAUVOIR: And a little later, or at the same time, Leibowitz made us understand something about atonal music. After the war we discovered Bartók and Prokofiev.

SARTRE: I was never very fond of Prokofiev.

DE BEAUVOIR: Nor was I; but after all he was one of the first moderns we ever heard.

SARTRE: It was chiefly Bartók and the atonalists that we discovered.

DE BEAUVOIR: When I lived in the Rue de la Bûcherie I bought a huge phonograph. It was Vian who helped me choose it. It still played seventy-eights, records that lasted five minutes. We listened to a great many things. Monteverdi among others. Then the long-playing records came in and I bought another phonograph.

SARTRE: And you have a fine collection of records.

DE BEAUVOIR: Then we began to listen seriously to Berg, Webern, and others. Then to the men who were still more modern. I say *we* because we usually listened together. It was then that we began to listen to Stockhausen and then Xenakis and then all the great moderns. Music means a very great deal to you. So how does it come about that you've never been tempted—thought you gave me a very good explanation of atonal and particularly dodecaphonic music—how does it come about that in spite of loving, understanding, and living in music you've never really been tempted to write about it?

SARTRE: I feel that it's not for me to talk about music. I can talk about things to do with literature that are quite remote from me, but after all I write, it's my calling, my art, so I have the right to reflect publicly about a literary work. But with music I think it's for musicians to do so, or musicologists.

DE BEAUVOIR: Besides, it must be very difficult to write about music. Almost everybody does it so badly. There's nothing more boring than musical criticism, generaly speaking. Leibowitz did it fairly well in *Les Temps modernes*. The Massins wrote a very good book on Mozart. But on the whole it's rather hit or miss, as though the language of music could not be transcribed.

SARTRE: Music is a language of its own.

DE BEAUVOIR: Did you know the rudiments of theory?

SARTRE: I learned some of them.

DE BEAUVOIR: Solfeggio? Harmony?

SARTRE: Yes, when I was eight or nine I learned all that. And later I read theorists' works on counterpoint.

DE BEAUVOIR: How do you explain that you understood atonal music and dodecaphony so well? Was your ear accustomed to it? Because as for me, I could make nothing of it at all.

SARTRE: Did I understand it as well as all that?

DE BEAUVOIR: Well in any case you explained many things to me.

SARTRE: I did understand the rudiments, but it took me a long time to grasp their meaning.

DE BEAUVOIR: I come back to my question: why did you write the article on committed music?

SARTRE: Since I listened to music I wanted to say where I stood. I wanted to write something about music, yes. When Leibowitz asked me to write the preface I thought it quite natural to agree.

DE BEAUVOIR: You tell me, "I don't feel that it was for me to talk about music; it was for musicians to do so." But at a given point, why did you think it was for you to talk about painting?

SARTRE: That came much later. I became acquainted with certain pictures the first time I went into the Louvre. I was sixteen, I was in Paris, and my grandfather took me to the Louvre. He showed me pictures and made interminable, rather boring remarks about them. But still it interested me. I went back alone when I was in the first form and in philo. I even took a girl, a cousin of Nizan's, a little blond, and I already knew how to talk pictures to her. The way I did so was comic, I dare say, yet I did know how to talk about them. But behind me I had no family with sure values in painting as they had sure values in music. My family did not care about painting.

DE BEAUVOIR: And what about your friends? Nizan in particular, but Gruber too, since his brother was a painter?

SARTRE: Gruber never talked about it.

DE BEAUVOIR: Nizan never really took to painting.

SARTRE: At all events Nizan studied painting in much the same way I did. That is to say, at fifteen he knew nothing about it. At sixteen he went to the Louvre, he looked at pictures, and he tried to understand them. But we didn't go together, or very rarely. I used to go alone.

DE BEAUVOIR: In any case you only saw classical painting. You never went to exhibitions of modern pictures.

SARTRE: Never. I knew modern painting existed, but . . .

DE BEAUVOIR: How late did you go? Naturally you went as late as Impressionism. Cézanne? Van Gogh?

SARTRE: Cézanne and Van Gogh, yes. My grandfather must have talked to me about Cézanne.

DE BEAUVOIR: Gradually you educated yourself; you traveled, you saw great numbers of things. In that respect we coped with a good deal of our education together.

SARTRE: It was you who showed me modern painting.

DE BEAUVOIR: I didn't know much about it, but still, influenced by Jacques, I did know something of Picasso, a very little about Braque . . .

SARTRE: I knew nothing about them whatsoever, so I learned about them through you.

DE BEAUVOIR: Italy and Spain helped us educate ourselves. Fernand Gérassi was beginning to paint. At Madrid he wasn't entirely in agreement with us—he said we thought too much of Bosch and not enough of Goya. I'm still just as fond of Bosch, by the way, but now I have a much higher opinion of Goya than I had—I didn't like him in those days. Gérassi thought there was something in Goya that we hadn't grasped. He was right. So gradually, then, you came to attach a great deal of importance to painting. We went to lots of exhibitions —Picasso, Klee, etcetera. But how did you, not being a painter, come to have the nerve to talk—and in my opinion talk very well— about painting? Who did you talk about, by the way? Let's recapitulate a little. Wols, Giacometti.

SARTRE: Calder too. Klee. Not in a special article, but in the pieces on Giacometti and Wols. Tintoretto.

DE BEAUVOIR: I come back to my question. Why did it seem to you perfectly normal and easy to write about painting while music was taboo?

SARTRE: I thought that for music you needed a musicologist's training —to understand counterpoint and know all that lay behind a work before discussing it. It was possible to delight in music and to profit by it, as I did, but to know what it all meant called for a greater degree of culture than I possessed.

DE BEAUVOIR: And how did it come about that you wanted to speak of painting?

SARTRE: I'd had experience of painting without relation to the history of painting. I'd seen a picture that seemed to me to need explaining. It was at Colmar, when I was . . .

DE BEAUVOIR: Ah, yes! It was one of the pictures you liked best, by Grünewald.

SARTRE: Yes.

DE BEAUVOIR: There was another picture you were very fond of, the Avignon Pietà.

SARTRE: And I knew it, too, before knowing anything at all about painting, because it was in a room I used to pass through in the Louvre. I saw the painting and I liked it very much. That was even before I knew you.

DE BEAUVOIR: As for Grünewald, it was you who showed him to me.

SARTRE: And I saw what could be said about the picture when I read one of Huysmans's books.

DE BEAUVOIR: Did Huysmans talk about Grünewald?

SARTRE: Yes, and at length, in *Against the Grain.*

DE BEAUVOIR: That's interesting. Because you never found anything written in books that made you want to talk about music.

SARTRE: Never.

DE BEAUVOIR: There's only one person who's spoken quite well about a piece of music and that's Proust; but it's very subjective. In my opinion much better books have been written on painting than on music. All right. So you read Huysmans's book. And you thought a man of letters could talk about painting.

SARTRE: Yes, he talked about it well, at least for those days. He raised questions; he described the pictures. Even before seeing Grünewald's picture I'd read Huysmans on Grünewald. I had therefore read about Grünewald without knowing him. It was during the war, when it was not possible to go to Alsace. I did not see the picture until after the war. Meanwhile, I'd read the Huysmans piece on Grünewald, pages and pages of it.

DE BEAUVOIR: Which was the first article that you wrote on painting? We mentioned some just now, but not in order. Which was the first?

SARTRE: It must have been Calder.

DE BEAUVOIR: Yes. Your article on Calder must have been written in '46 or '47. You wrote it for a Calder exhibition in Paris. Calder is not exactly a painter, but that doesn't matter. Then who came first, Giacometti or Wols?

SARTRE: Giacometti. Giacometti was long before Wols.

DE BEAUVOIR: Did you write about his sculpture first or his painting?

SARTRE: His sculpture. For a long while I looked upon Giacometti as a sculptor only. It was not until later that I came to appreciate his painting.

DE BEAUVOIR: Still it must be said that the most beautiful things he produced were certainly his sculptures.

SARTRE: Certainly. But there are pictures of his that I'm very fond of.

DE BEAUVOIR: Giacometti and you were friends. You often used to talk to him; and in his way of understanding sculpture there was something that went along with your own theories on perception and on the imaginary.

SARTRE: Yes, we understood one another. And as he explained his own work to me he explained sculpture as a whole. So I wrote about him.

DE BEAUVOIR: You were inspired by him, as it were. Yet it was wholly personal. But what about Tintoretto? You told me that it arose upon a particular occasion. But even so, the idea of writing a long book on a painter . . . ?

SARTRE: It tempted me. And I thought Tintoretto interesting because his evolution was Venetian, independent of Florence, which was so important, and of Rome. There was a Venetian painting I liked much more than that of Florence. And in the course of explaining who and what Tintoretto was, one could also explain Venetian painting. And then it seemed to me that in his pictures Tintoretto had studied the three dimensions. That was new to me, for after all a picture is flat and the dimensions are imaginary. What induced me to write a study on him was the fact that Tintoretto was so deeply and tenaciously concerned with space, with three-dimensional space.

DE BEAUVOIR: What you've just said gives me an idea. Did you prefer writing on painting to writing on music because, although music does in fact reflect its time, the society of its time, it does so in such a remote and indirect fashion, so difficult to grasp, that it seems almost independent of it, whereas painting is truly an image of society, almost an emanation from it? Was that one of the reasons?

SARTRE: Yes. Tintoretto is Venice, although he didn't paint Venice.

DE BEAUVOIR: To some extent that may be why you wrote about painting.

SARTRE: Certainly. Music is much harder to place.

DE BEAUVOIR: All right: what else is there to be said on the subject, do you think?

SARTRE: Painting and music have always existed for me and they exist still. Painting is forbidden to me now. I can no longer see it.

DE BEAUVOIR: Not for this last year.

SARTRE: I can no longer play music for the same reasons. But I can listen to it. Radio. Records.

DE BEAUVOIR: There's another thing that belongs to culture—we've spoken about music, painting, sculpture to some extent—and that is travel. You've made a great many journeys. You dreamed about them often when you were young, and you've made many with me, many without me. Short ones, easy ones, on foot, by bicycle, by plane, and so on. I'd like you to talk to me about them.

SARTRE: My life was to be a series of adventures, or rather one adventure. That was how I saw it. The adventure took place more or less everywhere, but rarely in Paris, because in Paris you don't often see a Redskin leap out with feathers on his head and a bow in his hand. So the necessity of adventures compelled me to conceive of them in America, Africa, and Asia. Those were the continents made for adventure. As for the European continent, it provided little opportunity. So I began to dream that I would go to America, where I'd fight with roughnecks and come out of it safely, having knocked around a fair number of them. I often dreamed of that. In the same way when I read adventure stories with young heroes in planes or dirigibles going to countries that I could scarcely imagine, I dreamed of going there too. I dreamed of going to shoot blacks, those eaters of their own kind, or yellow men, guilty of being yellow.

DE BEAUVOIR: So at that time you were racist?

SARTRE: Not exactly. But they were yellow and I'd been told that they'd committed dreadful massacres, atrocities, tortures, so I saw myself bravely defending a European girl from the yellow men, she being in China against her will. What these adventure stories brought me, and I'm deeply grateful to them for it, was an appetite for the whole earth. I rarely thought of myself as French. I did think it now and then, but I also thought I was a man to whom the whole earth— I won't say belonged, but was the place he lived in, a place that was familiar. And later on I should be there in Africa or Asia, I thought, taking possession of those places by what I did. So the idea of the whole earth, which is very important, was to some degree connected with the idea that the function of literature was to speak about the world. The world was larger than the earth, but it was roughly the same thing. And the journey would only strengthen me in these possessions. I say "possessions" because I'm thinking of the child that I was, but I wouldn't use the word at present. Besides, I think it wasn't exactly possession but rather a certain relation between the man and the place where he is at a given moment, a relation that is not one of possession, but a certain way of causing the soil and the landscape to yield things I'd never seen and that I would see as being there for me and I being changed by them.

DE BEAUVOIR: An enrichment of the experience, in short.

SARTRE: Yes. So that was the beginning of the idea of traveling, and from that moment on I was a potential traveler. When you first knew me . . .

DE BEAUVOIR: You wanted to go and see the slums of Constantinople.

SARTRE: Yes.

DE BEAUVOIR: But had you traveled at all before meeting me?

SARTRE: Never abroad, apart from Switzerland. We went there because my grandparents and my mother had to go to various resorts for the waters. Montreux, for example.

DE BEAUVOIR: But that didn't give you the feeling of a journey. It gave you the feeling of being on a holiday. Was the fact of your having asked for a post in Japan connected with that?

SARTRE: Why, of course! That post in Japan was vacant. It was being offered. It was not that I asked to go to Japan just like that. What happened was that the head of the school was asked to choose a pupil who was willing to go to Japan to fill the position of French teacher in a Japanese school at Kyoto. I put my name down for it. That seemed to me absolutely natural. When we met . . .

DE BEAUVOIR: Yes, there was a question of our parting so that you could go and spend two years in Japan. And you were very sad at not going.

SARTRE: It was Péron who went, because for teaching French they preferred a specialist in languages, which I quite understand. So the first journey I made was the one we made together, in Spain. And that was an immense delight, a treat for me. It was the beginning of my travels . . .

DE BEAUVOIR: It was thanks to Gérassi. Because influenced by Nizan —he had advised it—we had thought of a modest journey to Brittany. But Gérassi said, "But listen, you can stay with me in Madrid; it's very easy. Do come. It's not so dear as all that—you can manage." Crossing a frontier—what did that do to you?

SARTRE: It turned me into a great traveler. Once I had crossed a single frontier I could cross them all. Consequently, I had become a great traveler. What was that frontier called?

DE BEAUVOIR: I think we crossed at Figueras. It's not quite the frontier, but it was there that we got out of the train.

SARTRE: It was there that we saw our first *guardia civil* and we were delighted. We were so very happy to be at Figueras.

DE BEAUVOIR: Ah! I remember that as a wonderful evening, although

Figueras is ghastly and the surrounding country far from pleasant—I passed through it again this year. We stayed in a little *posada* and we were very happy. Still, it wasn't at all the journey you'd dreamed about. Because it was a journey with me . . .

SARTRE: Oh, that side of it was fine.

DE BEAUVOIR: But there was nothing of the adventurous aspect that you had hoped for. It was a very prudent sober journey, a journey of two young teachers with little money.

SARTRE: The adventurous side was in my dreams. I progressively eliminated it. As early as the second journey it was over and done with. And when I went to Morocco, where my little heroes had had so many terrific battles, I had completely lost the idea that anything might happen to me. And in fact nothing did happen to us.

DE BEAUVOIR: Well then . . . ?

SARTRE: I'd say that traveling meant primarily the discovery of towns and landscapes. People came afterward. People I didn't know. I left a France I didn't know either, or very slightly. I didn't know Brittany in those days.

DE BEAUVOIR: You knew almost nothing of France, nor did I.

SARTRE: The Côte d'Azur.

DE BEAUVOIR: You knew Alsace.

SARTRE: Yes, slightly. I did know Saint Raphaël.

DE BEAUVOIR: During those first years we went to Spain, then to Italy, then we traveled in France. At the end of the second Spanish journey we went to Spanish Morocco and then to Morocco. Those were our journeys before the war. Greece, too. What did it all bring you?

SARTRE: To begin with it was cultural. For instance, when I went to Athens or Rome, why, Rome was the city of Nero and Augustus, Athens was Socrates and Alcibiades. We settled on a journey from the cultural point of view. In Spain there was Gérassi, who was our friend and who had invited us. That had a different importance. But even so the essential was what was meant by Seville, by Granada, the Alhambra, a bullfight, and so on. A whole mass of things like that. And I wanted to understand and discover everything I'd been told, not at the lycée, but by the writers I liked. I didn't like Barrès all that much, but still he had talked about Toledo and about El Greco. I had to see what I had gathered about El Greco from reading Barrès, for example.

DE BEAUVOIR: You're mixing things somewhat. Bullfights aren't the same as a Greek temple or as painting. It was a way of plunging into the country, into the crowds, and that counted too.

SARTRE: The bullfight counted enormously.

DE BEAUVOIR: You had the idea that one should be "modern" in one's way of traveling.

SARTRE: Yes.

DE BEAUVOIR: I mean when Guille stayed in the Alhambra at Granada, for example, you thought—and rightly—that we should also go down into the lower town.

SARTRE: And see the Spaniards.

DE BEAUVOIR: See life in the present tense. I remember the arguments with Guille at Ronda. You were irritated because we only saw dead things belonging to the past—aristocratic palaces—and for you, the town had no life in the present tense. So you were happy in Barcelona, because there we plunged into a swarming, living city.

SARTRE: We saw Spanish strikers in the act of striking. Yes. I remember General San Giorgio's coup d'état at Seville.

DE BEAUVOIR: It didn't last long. He was arrested the next day.

SARTRE: Yes, but we did see the general in an open car. He was being taken away by the mayor.

DE BEAUVOIR: That rather linked up with your dreams of adventure.

SARTRE: Ah, yes. There was something adventurous about it.

DE BEAUVOIR: Yet we were in no danger.

SARTRE: For the moment we were caught up in the event. In any case we were in contact with people.

DE BEAUVOIR: We ran along with the crowd. There was that woman who held out her arms crying, "It's too stupid, it's too stupid." Did that shift of country, that change of skies mean anything to you?

SARTRE: The bullfights and things like that weren't merely cultural. They were something much more mysterious and much stronger than a simple meeting in the street or an accident I might have seen there. They made a synthesis of a lot of the country's aspects. We had to reflect on the bullfight, and try to find out its meaning.

DE BEAUVOIR: Then there was also the kind of change of skies that can come from different tastes—from what we ate and drank.

SARTRE: Of course. In Italy I remember the Italian cakes. We talked about them at enormous length. I even wrote about them.

DE BEAUVOIR: Yes, I recall that you compared the palaces of Genoa, for example, with the taste and color of the Italian cakes. I remember that in London, too, you tried to make a synthesis of what constituted London. Too hurriedly, of course. . . . But you were trying to grasp the whole. We differed very widely. For my part I always wanted to see, to see everything. You thought it was a good thing to soak yourself in the atmosphere, doing nothing, sitting smoking your pipe in a square, for example. And that you would have just as good a grasp of Spain in that way, as you would by seeing a couple of extra churches.

SARTRE: Absolutely. What's more, I still uphold my point of view.

DE BEAUVOIR: Now it's more or less mine too.

SARTRE: Yes indeed. I thought smoking a pipe in the Zocodover square was a delightful occupation.

DE BEAUVOIR: And in Florence, for example—I was really crazy in those days, and I was the one who was a bad traveler. In Florence, after lunch at about two in the afternoon, you wouldn't stir before five o'clock. You were studying German, because you meant to go to Berlin the year after. But I went out. I went to see four or five more churches, more pictures, more things—I never stopped. Still, when all is said and done, you were pleased to make those journeys that you called journeys of a cultural nature. But there is a dimension we've not spoken about: all these journeys did nevertheless possess a political dimension.

SARTRE: Oh, it was vague in those days.

DE BEAUVOIR: Very vague. But still we were aware of the atmosphere. The journey to Spain was the republic, the coming of the republic. The journey to Italy on the other hand was fascism. Germany, where you went to stay and where we traveled together, was nazism. And in Greece it was Metaxas. We didn't feel it a great deal, but after all it did exist for us.

SARTRE: Yes, it existed. We'd meet a citizen on a street corner who had not at all the same basis for his ideas as we had, and indeed it might sometimes have gone far along the road to dissension. I felt it above all in Italy. Fascism was really very strongly present. I remember one night in the Piazza Navona, where we were sitting and dreaming, and two Fascists dressed in black, with their little caps, came and asked us what we were doing there and angrily told us to go back to our hotel. We saw Fascists everywhere on the street corners.

DE BEAUVOIR: And I also remember that in Venice we saw German brown shirts. We found that very disagreeable. All the more disagreeable because you were thinking of going to Germany the next year.

SARTRE: Yes, I can still see those brown shirts quite clearly. And we felt Metaxas too. But as we lacked information we didn't really know a great deal about his intentions. He didn't worry us much.

DE BEAUVOIR: Still I do remember that we saw a prison, at Nauplia. We saw a Greek and he told us, "All the Greek Communists are rounded up in there." With a great deal of pride. And it was a prison. It was surrounded with cactus. What are your most striking memories of those days? We went to Italy twice.

SARTRE: Yes, twice. And Spain too.

DE BEAUVOIR: We thought Spain more alive.

SARTRE: Because of the Fascists, Italy was stiff, unnatural, awkward. The former values had disappeared or had been set aside for a while. And then again the Italians seemed ill-natured. Since they had rallied around fascism we had no liking for them, and they did nothing to arouse it. We didn't have much contact with the people in the towns or in the countryside. There were always those Fascist shackles.

DE BEAUVOIR: What else do you recall from those early journeys?

SARTRE: They made me wild with delight, that's for sure. They gave an extra dimension. There was the feeling of having another dimension, an outside dimension, a dimension in the world. France became a constricting enclosure.

DE BEAUVOIR: Yes, it was no longer the absolute center. I think the trip to Morocco impressed you too.

SARTRE: It was an entirely different world, different cultural concepts, different values. There were Lyautey's heirs, and then the sultan . . . Generally speaking, we French had contacts with other Frenchmen. We didn't live in the Arab town.

DE BEAUVOIR: We were very much cut off. But at Fez, for example, we scarcely left the Arab town except to sleep.

SARTRE: Wasn't it at Fez that I was ill?

DE BEAUVOIR: Yes.

SARTRE: Just what happened?

DE BEAUVOIR: Well, we'd been to eat a native meal, an excellent meal, and as we left we said, "It's extraordinary how we managed to eat four courses or even six. It ought to have been heavy, it ought to have made us feel poorly, but it's had no effect on us at all." We even reasoned about it, saying, "It's because we drank no wine—it's because we ate no bread." Thereupon you went back to lie down and you had a liver attack that kept you in bed something like three days.

SARTRE: I remember.

DE BEAUVOIR: Can you find any other memories that you find amusing?

SARTRE: We traveled in Greece with Bost. It was a very agreeable journey. We often slept in the open—at Delos, for instance. And on an island where we saw a Greek Punch and Judy show.

DE BEAUVOIR: I think you mean at Syra.

SARTRE: At Syra. And then in the Greek countryside. We often slept in the open.

DE BEAUVOIR: Oh, every other night, I think. Without a tent, without anything. And particularly in that very pretty town near Sparta where there are Byzantine churches with frescoes. We slept in a church, and when we woke up in the morning there were all kinds of peasants around us. But I'm the one who is talking; it ought to be you.

SARTRE: Not at all, we're talking together—it's a time we lived through together. They were journeys without incident, on the whole. We did what was to be done quietly and peacefully. We saw people from the outside. They were journeys that looked rather bourgeois seen from Paris, but they were less so when we were in the country. We slept out, for example.

DE BEAUVOIR: Yes, because we had no money.

SARTRE: People felt that, and it put us more nearly into a working-class category right away.

DE BEAUVOIR: But we were very much cut off by not knowing the language. Indeed it was only in Spain that we had someone belonging to the country who led us about, told us stories, showed us cafés, and pointed out Valle Inclan. Our first journey in Spain was like that.

SARTRE: Thanks to Gérassi. In Italy things were fairly easy; I had begun learning Italian.

DE BEAUVOIR: Yes, we managed, but we didn't have any real conversations. We met neither intellectuals nor politicians, and of course we were cut off from the Fascists. And then what about America, later on? That was something else again.

SARTRE: Yes. You could say there's a third category of journeys. The first—the kind I never made—is the adventurous journey. Those that our status made suitable for us were cultural trips and we made many of them. And then, because of the historical events that took place from 1945 onward, we began making journeys not strictly political but political in part. That is to say, journeys in which we tried to understand the country, whatever it might be, on the political level.

DE BEAUVOIR: Journeys in which we were no longer just isolated tourists but in which we had contacts with the people of the country. That was something very important. So let's talk about that trip to America.

SARTRE: America—we'd thought about it to an enormous extent, because . . . to begin with, when I was a child, Nick Carter and Buffalo Bill and their kind showed me a certain America, one that the films told us more about later on. We'd read the novels of the great modern period, Dos Passos as well as Hemingway.

DE BEAUVOIR: There was jazz too. Why, we didn't mention it when we were talking about your love for music. Jazz meant a great deal to you.

SARTRE: A great deal.

DE BEAUVOIR: It was the first trip you made with a group. Not with a group of tourists, but with a band of journalists. And then it was the first trip you made with a distinct mission—to write articles. You were to send articles to *Le Figaro*. One might say you undertook the journey as a reporter.

SARTRE: Yes, I set off with experienced newspapermen who were used to reporting. There was André Viollis with us.

DE BEAUVOIR: And wasn't it the first time you'd ever taken a plane?

SARTRE: Yes, it was the first time. I took a military plane, flown by a military pilot.

DE BEAUVOIR: And what effect did that have on you? Were you at all frightened?

SARTRE: Not at all at the taking off and landing. I was rather uneasy in the air, but not very. It didn't have any great effect on me. The plane the Americans put at our disposal, the plane that took us all over America, didn't frighten me much either.

DE BEAUVOIR: But what different dimensions did traveling like that give to your trip?

SARTRE: For me, it was an absolutely different kind of journey. A journey—it was something you made by train; you passed from one country to another. That sort of glass cage in which I flew over the ocean made a prodigious difference. It was of a nature entirely different from an ordinary crossing of a frontier. And the ferocity of the American customs men was not to be compared with the free and easy ways at most European frontiers.

DE BEAUVOIR: But didn't the fact that you were an invited group make things easier?

SARTRE: No. They looked at our bags and asked all the usual questions.

DE BEAUVOIR: What was different about this journey?

SARTRE: It was a conducted tour. Not only in the sense that we were a little convoy of seven members, but also because it was run by the War Department.

DE BEAUVOIR: It was a question of showing you the American war effort.

SARTRE: As far as I was concerned, I didn't give a damn for the American war effort. It was America I wanted to see.

DE BEAUVOIR: Of course.

SARTRE: And I was quite grateful to them because they did show us the whole of America, with the war effort coming second.

DE BEAUVOIR: What did they show you of the war effort?

SARTRE: An armaments factory, for example.

DE BEAUVOIR: So it was a journey in which you mainly saw a living country, a country in movement.

SARTRE: Mainly because when I was shown Roosevelt's TVA, it wasn't particularly important to understand it from the point of view of the war effort.

DE BEAUVOIR: Yes, but it was a piece of economic knowledge. It was no longer a matter of pictures, monuments, or landscapes, as the earlier trips had been.

SARTRE: And then in New York they took us to a projection room and there over several days they showed us the great American movies that had been made since the beginning of the war and that we hadn't seen. That was more like something cultural.

DE BEAUVOIR. It must have been fascinating too.

SARTRE: It *was* fascinating.

DE BEAUVOIR: Where did you stay in New York?

SARTRE: At the Plaza.

DE BEAUVOIR: You were very well treated, then?

SARTRE: We arrived at New York in the evening, at ten o'clock in the evening, and nobody expected us at that time. We went through the customs, and there was no one there to tell the people it would be better not to push us around too much. We were given back our luggage and told to sit in the corner of a big waiting room. There we were, the seven of us, at ten o'clock at night, in the darkness, sitting by our bags—there weren't many of them, by the way, since each man had only one case—and we waited. At last the man responsible for the group, who tried to be as little responsible as he possibly could, said, "I'm going to telephone." He had a telephone number that he'd been given in Paris. He called and they welcomed him with a great deal of amusement and surprise since no plane had been expected that evening, seeing we had had a long, complicated flight.

DE BEAUVOIR: Yes, it was rather haphazard.

SARTRE: As it happened we arrived that particular evening, though we could just as well have arrived another day. So for that reason there was no one waiting for us. They sent cars to the airport at once and brought us back to New York. Our car drove us into the city. As we left the airport and traveled toward the hotel, we passed through great crowded streets. At half past ten at night there were masses of people about. It all shone and it was full of shops that were lighted. At night the electricity was turned down a little but it was still there. I remember my amazement, sitting there in our car, at seeing open, lighted shops with people working in them—they were barber shops—at eleven o'clock at night. You could have your hair cut or washed or you could be shaved at eleven o'clock at night. And the town seemed to me astonishing because what I saw was chiefly shadow. I saw shops below and then I saw shadows above, enormous shadows. They were the skyscrapers I saw next day. We arrived on a Saturday.

DE BEAUVOIR: Didn't you think the hotel overwhelmingly luxurious?

SARTRE: The hotel. . . . The first thing we saw was a swinging door with a crowd of white-haired women in low-cut evening dresses coming out of it. Men in dinner-jackets too. There was some festival or other.

DE BEAUVOIR: It happens all the time. They aren't festivals . . .

SARTRE: People meet for one reason or another, and they are in evening dress. It was absolutely as though I were rediscovering peace. They didn't realize that there was a war on.

DE BEAUVOIR: Since we usually went to unpretentious hotels, didn't the Plaza seem to you astonishingly sumptuous?

SARTRE: No. But we did have a wonderful breakfast the next morning. It reminded me of our London breakfasts—they were modest, of course, but even so they were very good.

DE BEAUVOIR: Yes, but in contrast with France, which was still utterly poverty-stricken, wasn't it astonishing?

SARTRE: To me it just meant that America was far from the war. The country hadn't been invaded.

DE BEAUVOIR: That's true. It was largely because of that. Whereas France was in a state of terrible poverty. When I was in Spain and

Portugal at the same period I had a staggering impression of wealth. So what must it have been in New York!

SARTRE: Yes. But in fact it didn't particularly strike me.

DE BEAUVOIR: You told me a story about your clothes.

SARTRE: Yes. First thing the next day the people in the department whose guests we were sent us shopping, particularly to buy jackets and trousers. I bought a pair of striped trousers.

DE BEAUVOIR: You bought me a tailor-made suit as well.

SARTRE: Yes. And in three days I had a suit too. I set off wearing it. I already possessed a lumber jacket.

DE BEAUVOIR: Yes, a wretched thing. Cartier Bresson photographed you in it. What about your contact with New York the next day?

SARTRE: They left us free to go and walk along Fifth Avenue to begin with. It was a Sunday, I remember. I went out with the other people in my group.

DE BEAUVOIR: You didn't always stay together, all seven of you?

SARTRE: No, but there, that first day, the men all walked around together on Fifth Avenue. In the morning we saw people going into a church. That avenue moved us deeply. Yet I liked it less than some others that came later—Sixth, Seventh, and then the Bowery and Third Avenue. I began to find my way about these avenues—it's as easy as can be! And I was absolutely enchanted. We were between the sixties and the fifties, that is to say, near the middle.

DE BEAUVOIR: At the Plaza you were close to Central Park. Where did you eat?

SARTRE: We were often asked out to lunch or dinner.

DE BEAUVOIR: I think what made a great difference between this trip and our others was that you met people.

SARTRE: Yes. Not exactly the people of the country. People who were all in this War Department—people who spoke on the radio, for example. Talking to France, to England.

DE BEAUVOIR: There were Frenchmen?

SARTRE: Yes. And English.

DE BEAUVOIR: But even so you must have met some Americans.

SARTRE: Yes, of course.

DE BEAUVOIR: It was there that you came to know the group who looked after the war effort on the radio.

SARTRE: That was how I met numbers of people. As for the Americans, I met them more on the spot, as it were. I mean there were Americans in the places they took me to, and these Americans talked to me. I remember a factory that had been set up in a village of prefabricated houses standing in the middle of debris and rubble. It was extremely curious to see these prefabricated houses put together as a village, surrounded by all this rubbish and upturned soil.

DE BEAUVOIR: Broadly speaking, what did you see? How long did you stay? Three months? Four months?

SARTRE: Three or four months, yes.

DE BEAUVOIR: Did you stay mostly in New York?

SARTRE: Oh, no. The journey, the official journey, had us staying a week in New York on the way out and then five or six days on the way back. I stayed two weeks. Besides, I left America from Washington. I left later than the others. We all left at different dates, because we had differing amounts of money to spend. I stayed at least six weeks after the end of the official journey.

DE BEAUVOIR: In New York?

SARTRE: In New York, yes.

DE BEAUVOIR: Did you go to Hollywood?

SARTRE: Yes, I went there almost immediately. We did Washington, the TVA, and then New Orleans. Not Miami. I saw Miami much later. From New Orleans we crossed America, still by plane. We saw the Colorado gorges and then we traveled on.

DE BEAUVOIR: Did you see Chicago too?

SARTRE: Yes, of course. We went to Hollywood, and from Hollywood to Chicago. From Chicago I think we went to Detroit.

DE BEAUVOIR: Yes, what with the war effort they must have shown you some appallingly boring towns.

SARTRE: Yes, I saw Detroit, and then from Detroit we came back to New York.

DE BEAUVOIR: And there you met quantities of French people. You saw Breton.

SARTRE: Yes, naturally I came into contact with French people there. And I must have seen Lazareff once, or at least his wife. ·

DE BEAUVOIR: There were many French who had left for America, either because they were Jewish or because they didn't want to stay under the Occupation. André Breton had left.

SARTRE: So I met André Breton. I also met Léger. I called on him. He was very kind. I saw him several times, and he would not let me leave without presents, that is to say without having chosen some of his pictures. I kept them for a long while. I chose them in America and he brought them to me later.

DE BEAUVOIR: Léger, Breton. Rirette Nizan was there too.

SARTRE: And Lévi-Strauss. Yes, I saw Rirette Nizan again. Who else? There were people around Breton. There was Jacqueline Breton and her future husband, David Hare. She was about to divorce.

DE BEAUVOIR: He was an American.

SARTRE: He was a young American sculptor. He doesn't seem to have had much of a career.

DE BEAUVOIR: There was Duchamp too.

SARTRE: Yes, but Duchamp wasn't one of the refugees.

DE BEAUVOIR: He's been living there for a long while.

SARTRE: I had lunch with him.

DE BEAUVOIR: Who did you meet among the real Americans?

SARTRE: There was Saint-Exupéry's wife. And then I knew Calder well.

DE BEAUVOIR: You didn't meet any writers?

SARTRE: I had met some writers in Paris. I met Dos Passos there.

DE BEAUVOIR: Richard Wright, did you meet him over there?

SARTRE: Yes, him and his wife. And then some American critics. We haven't mentioned Hemingway. Hemingway I met in France too.

DE BEAUVOIR: Oh, yes! We met him at the Liberation. It didn't worry you too much, not speaking English?

SARTRE: No, because those Americans I saw spoke French. The others dropped me, naturally enough, as someone who didn't know the language. Over there I was known, slightly known, among the foreign refugees in America because I'd written an article on France under the Occupation in Aron's magazine.

DE BEAUVOIR: We said we'd talk about the moon.

SARTRE: Yes, because the moon accompanies everyone from his birth to his death. And during these last fifty or sixty years it has pretty well stamped the evolution of the environment, of the milieu, and therefore our inner and outer revolution. When I first saw it, it looked like a night sun. It was a disk very far away in space like the sun; a weak but positive source of light. In the disk you could make out either a man with a burden on his back or the features of a head, or whatever you liked. It was more homely than the sun and we were told it was closer, more nearly connected with the earth. We looked upon it as something we owned—it was an object in the sky yet, as it were, linked to us.

DE BEAUVOIR: Which in fact it is, since it's a satellite.

SARTRE: Exactly. But to begin with one knew from experience that it was always there, that there was a full moon and that it stood for something like a terrestrial sign in the heavens. That's how I knew it in the beginning. I saw it at night and it was important to me in some way; I couldn't tell exactly how. It was the light of the night, the light that showed like a comfort in the darkness. When I was a child I was rather afraid of the dark and the moon comforted me. When I went out into the garden and there was the moon overhead I was happy. Nothing much could happen to me. As other children do, I sometimes imagined that it spoke, that it told me things, and I imagined that it saw me, too. It really represented something for me, there in the sky. I remember too that I used to draw the moon, and in it I put things I claimed to see there, things that were not the man with a bundle of sticks on his back or the head, but faces or landscapes in the moon that I made up—things I didn't really see but that I pretended to.

DE BEAUVOIR: And when you were older, did it still have an importance for you?

SARTRE: For a very long while, yes. The sun—I didn't necessarily like it, not all the time. It dazzled me. The sky was an expanse inhabited by the sun and the moon.

DE BEAUVOIR: Do you speak about the moon in your books? At any rate you do speak of it in the prologue to *Nekrassov*. A man and a woman are on the quay. He says, "Look, look at the moon." She says, "It isn't pretty. You see the moon every day," and he replies, "It is pretty because it's round." I don't remember whether there's any moonlight in your novels.

SARTRE: It seems to me that the moon's just touched upon in *The Wall*. I used to think of the moon as something personal. Fundamentally, for me, the moon stood for everything that is secret in contrast to what is public and freely admitted, which was the sun. I had an idea that it was a nocturnal copy of the sun.

DE BEAUVOIR: Why did you want to talk about it particularly?

SARTRE: Because I'd said to myself that one day I would write about the moon. Then afterward I learned roughly what the moon was, and that it represented a satellite. I was taught that and I took it personally —it wasn't the earth's satellite, it was my satellite. That's how I felt about it. It seemed to me that I had thoughts that came because I was looked at by the moon. I was very fond of it: it was poetic—it was pure poetry. The moon was completely separated from me, up there, outside, and at the same time there was a link between us, a shared destiny. It was there like an eye and like an ear; it conversed with me. I'd written dissertations on the moon.

DE BEAUVOIR: Why do you speak in the past?

SARTRE: Because the moon means less to me since people go there. The moon was all that I've said up until the time they started going to it. I was intensely interested when it was decided that men should go and when they did go. I kept myself fully informed about the voyage. I remember that at Naples I even rented a television to watch Armstrong's flight.

DE BEAUVOIR: To see the first men on the moon.

SARTRE: To see how they looked, what they did there, and what the moon was like, how the earth looked from the moon—all that filled me with enthusiasm. But at the same time it changed the moon into a scientific object, and it lost the mythical character it had had up until then.

DE BEAUVOIR: Had you imagined that people would go to the moon?

SARTRE: No. I'd read Jules Verne's tales about it and then Wells's *The First Men in the Moon*. I was well acquainted with all that, but it seemed to me legendary, impossible. Wells's way of going there wasn't really scientific.

DE BEAUVOIR: Jules Verne's was rather more so. . . . There was also Cyrano de Bergerac's *The Voyage into the Moon*.

SARTRE: Yes, but that . . .

DE BEAUVOIR: It wasn't very interesting. Still, people have often had the dream of going to the moon.

SARTRE: I never did.

DE BEAUVOIR: The other day we touched upon the idea you expressed at the end of *The Words*, that no matter who was as good as no matter who, and that you were no matter who yourself. I'd like to know just what that assertion means to you. But how did these ideas of equality between men, or those of superiority, of hierarchy come into being to begin with—how did they form in your mind? On the one hand you say that when you were young you felt you were a genius, and on the other you say, more or less, that you had always thought that men were equal. Could you do something toward untangling this for us, starting with your childhood and youth?

SARTRE: When I was a little boy, in the days when at the age of eight I wrote my first stories, my grandfather called me prince and to some degree he really looked upon me as a little prince. So at that juncture I was adorned by him with the inward quality, the intimate, subjective quality of the little prince, which was, I may add, nothing but his own kindness and generosity that he saw reflected in me. If a being possesses this subjective reality of princehood it does not lead to equality, for a prince is superior to those around him. Yet there was a kind of equality at the bottom of all this, because I believed that I was a human being and that all human beings were therefore princes. That was roughly how I saw things. As for the common crowd, it was made up of semihuman beings, human beings who had not turned out very successfully, and they were all around me. But there were other human beings I discovered, people who had turned out successfully, who were close at hand and who were certainly princes. So there was one kind of world made up of equals, who were princes, and then a rabble. It wasn't equality of course, yet in the idea of these princes who recognized one another and who were equals there was already the notion of an equality, an equality that I have always wished to establish, have always dreamed of establishing, between other people and myself. Every time I've had close relations with anyone, man or woman, I've come to see that the person was entirely my equal, and that although I might perhaps handle words better, the other's first intuitions were in every case exactly the same as mine and that things were seen from the same viewpoint as mine.

DE BEAUVOIR: Let's go back to your boyhood. When you were at the lycée didn't certain gradations between good pupils and bad take place?

SARTRE: A gradation did occur. But since it didn't favor me much—I wasn't a very good pupil: I was among the middling boys, sometimes a little higher than the average, sometimes lower—I didn't look upon it as being on my side. And I looked upon it as something that did not concern me. I didn't think that coming first, coming before or after young Brun or young Malaquin gave a true view of my being. My being was that deep subjective reality which was beyond everything that could be said about it and which could not be classified. In fact it was then that I began saying that you can't classify. A subjectivity is something that doesn't take the form of first or second. What is there, in itself and before itself, is a total, profound reality, one that is in a certain manner infinite. It is the being, the person's being.

And there's no question of grading that in relation to some other given being, which may be less evident, less positive, but which in its depths is just as true. It is not a question of classifying these individuals but of leaving them as wholes, as entireties that represent the man.

DE BEAUVOIR: In a way what you were asserting before all other aspects was the absolute side of consciousness.

SARTRE: That's right. I asserted the absolute side first in myself. I began asserting it as the little prince, but in fact that meant consciousness, the consciousness of what I saw, what I read, what I felt. And then deep consciousness connected with the objects around me and at the same time possessing a depth that was hard to convey and that was myself. And that could not be inferior to anyone at all, nor superior. The others were like that too, and this was something I felt when I was young, when I was a child.

DE BEAUVOIR: Yet when you and Nizan were in the first form and during the years that followed, you said that you looked upon yourselves as supermen; and at the same time you've told me you had the intuition that you were a genius. Wasn't this notion of genius and of supermen in contradiction to that of equality?

SARTRE: No, for the very reason that, as I saw it, the genius and the superman were just beings who showed in their full reality as men. The mass of people who graded themselves according to figures and hierarchies were a raw material in which there might be found supermen who would emerge later, who would break free. This raw material was not really made up of supermen, however, but was formed by submen and in fact corresponded to a set of hierarchies, hierarchies rarely directed at the man himself but rather at his qualities—directed at the railway inspector, the inspector of public works, the teachers. In short, the calling, the activities, the objects they surrounded themselves with—all these things were susceptible of gradation. But if you reached the depths there was no gradation possible. And that was what I gradually clarified for myself.

DE BEAUVOIR: But still, when you were at the Ecole Normale there were rivalries, places in class, ranks.

SARTRE: No, there was no rivalry or precedence, absolutely none.

DE BEAUVOIR: There was to get into the school, for example.

SARTRE: There was an examination to get into the school and one had a place in the order; and then on leaving school there was the *agrégation*.

DE BEAUVOIR: Yes.

SARTRE: So there again there was a competitive examination in which one had a place, but between the two there was nothing. Hitherto I've shown you the notion of subjectivity as genius and that of hierarchy as a classification connected with particular qualities. At the Ecole Normale there were these two classifications. One classification, which was the same thing as an absence of classification; and then the absence of classification which was pure subjectivity, conceived as infinite and characterized by genius. I looked upon myself as a genius. It was an idea that came to me very young. It arose from the idea of my elder brothers, the writers, I myself being a writer. I thought that I should equal a Balzac, a Bossuet, and that therefore I should be what was called a genius. So at the Ecole Normale there was on the one hand my subjectivity, which was that of a genius, and on the other the ranks brought into existence by seniority. When I joined the Ecole Normale, for example, I was in the first year and I joined a *turne,* a kind of study group, with five or six friends I knew and liked. On either side there were other *turnes* of the same sort. On the floor above there were the *carrés,* the second-year students, also gathered in *turnes,* but fewer of them in each; then came the *cubes,* the third-year men; and after that one was an *archicube.* All this was a differentiation according to the years. And indeed, it corresponded to something, since you were acquiring knowledge that finally gave you a value as teacher of a given subject. For example, in four years I learned the essential of what had to be known in order to teach philosophy. Another would have learned French. In short, there was this classification by school years that meant nothing to us. We didn't think they were superior to us; they were just classified.

DE BEAUVOIR: Yes, it was a hierarchy in equality, since each one was to reach it almost mathematically.

SARTRE: Obviously the equalities were not exactly the same, since at each step more knowledge was acquired and a greater number of examinations passed. But still they were equalities. The equality of the first-year men who had no exams behind them but who were the same insofar as they were all embarking on the four years of school. Then the equality of the other years which had an exam behind them —a degree obtained in the course of the year, for example—and which therefore had additional attainments and qualifications. But it was the same equality in the end.

DE BEAUVOIR: Yet you distinguished between your school fellows.

You didn't at all have the notion that everybody was worthwhile. A man like Merleau-Ponty, for example, had a very open, welcoming attitude. You were not in the least like that.

SARTRE: On the contrary, I made violent distinctions between the good and the bad. And very soon Nizan and I, and Guille to a certain extent, joined Alain's pupils, who were violent and brutal in those years and who wanted to create something of a reign of terror in the school. I admit that this doesn't go very well with hierarchy and the subjectivity of genius. Yet still I think there was some connection with the subjectivity of genius. I believe that when we hid at the top of the stairs in order to throw water bombs at the boys who came back about midnight wearing dinner jackets, having been dining out, we were thereby indicating that the dining out, the dinner jacket, the distinguished air, the well-brushed hair were wholly exterior things, nonvalues, of no worth. That these were things those boys ought not to have possessed, ought not to have desired, because what one ought to desire was the inner brilliance of genius, and certainly not success at a fashionable dinner party.

DE BEAUVOIR: Couldn't it be said that like everyone else you were living on two levels at the same time? That there was a certain metaphysical level on which the absolute quality of all consciousness was asserted, but that there was also a moral, practical, and even social level on which this absolute of consciousness did not interest you if the person endowed with it had a way of behaving, of living and thinking that you were fighting against. At the Sorbonne you, Nizan, and Maheu had the reputation of being extremely contemptuous of the world in general and of the Sorbonne students in particular.

SARTRE: That was because the students represented beings who were not quite men.

DE BEAUVOIR: It's very serious to say that some men are not entirely men. It goes dead against the notion of equality.

SARTRE: I got rid of it later, but there's no doubt that it was there to begin with. I began with the idea that those people weren't worth much. Some of them might perhaps become men, but the majority never would. And this corresponded to the fact that I had no friendship for them, no connection, no relations with them. We saw one another . . .

DE BEAUVOIR: You say you had hierarchical relations with them.

SARTRE: I had relations on account of the work they were doing or I was doing. At that point we were classified and therefore stood on an objective basis. There were twenty-five of us. I was graded fifth, tenth, first, and thus it was possible to compare us. But that never reached the being that was myself and that also wrote pieces which were, I thought, the product of genius and which could in no way be compared on the hierarchical level.

DE BEAUVOIR: So the fact is that you were very selective in your friendships, and you've been very selective all your life. Yet not feeling friendship for someone and rejecting him, amounts to setting up an inequality with those for whom on the contrary you do feel friendship and whom you do accept.

SARTRE: Yes. I think that in fact everyone possesses within himself, in his body, in his person, in his consciousness, what is necessary to be, if not a genius, then at all events a real man, a man with the qualities of a man. But that is something that most people do not want. They stop at some level or another, and in the end they are nearly always responsible for the level at which they remain. So I think that in theory every man is the equal of every other man and that relations of friendship could exist. But this equality is destroyed by people because of stupid impressions, stupid research, stupid ambitions and impulses. So one is concerned with men who would be equal if they would make a slight change in their attitude, but who in their present state are countermen, people who have made themselves men in virtually inhuman situations.

DE BEAUVOIR: Especially those you call the swine.

SARTRE: The swine are people who commit their freedom to being acknowledged as good by others, whereas in fact, because of their very activity itself, they are bad. I truly, sincerely love a man who seems to me to possess the sum total of a man's qualities—self-awareness, the power of judging for himself, the power of saying yes and that of saying no, and strength of will. I value all these things in a man, and they lead toward freedom. At that point I can feel friendship for him, and I often do feel it for people I know very slightly. And then there was the majority, the people beside me in a train, in the métro, in a lycée—people to whom I quite genuinely had nothing to say. At the utmost it was just possible, placing oneself on the plane of the hierarchy, to discuss the fifth or tenth place awarded to a pupil or a teacher.

DE BEAUVOIR: And when you were at the lycée did you find that the relations of age brought about relations of inequality between you and your pupils, or on the contrary were relations of equality possible?

SARTRE: Oh, yes! Relations of equality were quite possible. It might be said that at the lycée, and particularly the Ecole Normale, the relation of age allowed the existence of an obvious hierarchy, but one that absolutely did not possess a value of an essential, subjective nature for any one of us. It was merely a way of arranging people in a certain order so that they could be easily referred to, but it did not correspond to a reality. To put it in another way, there was a genuine reality, which was the reality of each person for each person, but which was not evident and which remained what it was. Then there was a great universal classification which agreed with other classifications conceived in the same way and which gave a person a rank on a phenomenal plane, a level on which the person's reality was wholly obliterated. This produced a society in which man's reality was suppressed, in which there were above all people who were capable of carrying out a certain kind of activity that defined them; but there was no self-aware subjectivity, no essential reality that might be reached either by another or by the one who possessed that subjectivity, that reality. There was nothing of that. It was all left out.

DE BEAUVOIR: Is is because of this feeling of equality between men that you have always refused everything that might set you apart? Your friends have often noticed your rejection of what are usually called honors—one might even say your disgust. Is it more or less linked with that? And then again just what are the circumstances in which you have shown this disgust?

SARTRE: The one is certainly linked to the other, but it's also linked to the idea that my deep reality is above honors. These honors are given by men to other men, and the men who give the honor, whether it's the *légion d'honneur* or the Nobel prize, are not qualified to give it. I can't see who has the right to give Kant or Descartes or Goethe a prize which means *Now you belong in a classification. We have turned literature into a graduated reality and in that literature you occupy such and such a rank.* I reject the possibility of doing that, and therefore I reject all honors.

DE BEAUVOIR: That explains your refusal of the Nobel prize. But there was an earlier refusal on your part, the refusal of the *légion d'honneur* after the war.

SARTRE: Yes. The *légion d'honneur* seems to me a reward that's given to the mediocrities wholesale. It's said that a given engineer deserves the *légion d'honneur* and that another, who is much the same, does not. And really they are not judged for what they're worth, but for a piece of work they've done or because of their chief's recommendation or other circumstances of that kind. That is, nothing that corresponds to their reality. That particular reality is not quantifiable.

DE BEAUVOIR: You've just used the word "mediocrities." So even with your theory of equality you do now and then come back to very aristocratic epithets and expressions.

SARTRE: Oh no, not at all, because as I've already told you, freedom and equality are there at the beginning, and in a human process, that is, in a man's development, equality ought to be there at the end. But man is also a being submitted to a hierarchical system, and it is as a graded being that he may grow stupid or that he may come to prefer the hierarchy to his own profound reality. On that level, on the hierarchical level, he may deserve pejorative epithets. You understand?

DE BEAUVOIR: Yes.

SARTRE: I think that most of the people around us still have too high an opinion of a *légion d'honneur,* a Nobel prize, and things like that, whereas in fact they correspond to nothing. They correspond only to a distinction given in the hierarchy to a being that is not real, that is abstract, that corresponds to the being that we are but that corresponds without really understanding why.

DE BEAUVOIR: Yet there are recognitions that you accept. You don't accept the recognition of, let's say, the worth of your philosophical work by certain men so that they give you a Nobel prize. But you do accept recognition from your readers, from the public, and you even desire it.

SARTRE: Yes, that's my function. I write, so I want the reader for whom I write to think the things I write good. Not that I think they are always good—far from it—but when they do chance to be good, I do wish them to be immediately rated as good by my reader.

DE BEAUVOIR: Because your work is yourself, and if your work is acknowledged, you are acknowledged in your reality.

SARTRE: That's right.

DE BEAUVOIR: Whereas the exterior quality that would cause you to be given the *légion d'honneur* is not you yourself.

SARTRE: No, it's abstract.

DE BEAUVOIR: Do you remember what happened with the *légion d'honneur?*

SARTRE: Well, it was in '45, and the London people who had come to establish themselves in Paris . . .

DE BEAUVOIR: The London people. You mean de Gaulle.

SARTRE: De Gaulle, yes. He appointed ministers and under secretaries of state, and there was a ministry of culture, with Malraux as its minister and my friend Raymond Aron as its under secretary of state. And they began handing out *légions d'honneur*. That gave my friend Zuorro,* whom I've talked about elsewhere, the idea of making me have the *légion d'honneur* against my will, thinking that I should be profoundly embarrassed by it.

DE BEAUVOIR: Because, as it must be admitted, Zuorro loved playing tricks on you.

SARTRE: He went to see my mother, spent a long time with her and extracted her consent. The poor woman knew nothing about it at all. Her father had had the *légion d'honneur,* her husband had the *légion d'honneur* . . .

DE BEAUVOIR: She thought it was all very fine.

SARTRE: It seemed to her that her son should have it. He told her to accept the award of the *légion d'honneur* in my name, and said they would give it to me as a surprise. She willingly agreed.

DE BEAUVOIR: That is, she signed a paper.

SARTRE: It was indeed irregular, because it ought to have been signed by me. But I only knew that afterward. Then one day someone telephoned, a friend who had a relation in the ministry, and said, "Did you ask for the *légion d'honneur?*" I howled with surprise and then he said, "Well, you're going to get it." So I flung myself on the telephone and called Raymond Aron. I said to him, "My dear friend, they intend to give me the *légion d'honneur.* You must prevent it." Aron took it much amiss; he thought me thoroughly unpleasant. But nevertheless he did manage things so that I escaped the *légion d'honneur.*

DE BEAUVOIR: On the whole we liked the government. There were people who were real friends of ours in it. It brought the resisters of France together, and as with Camus, for he was offered it too, by the way, the distinction was to come to you rather in your capacity as a resister-intellectual.

SARTRE: There was a gulf, even if the conditions had been the very best. The fact remained that accepting a decoration was something unimaginable for me.

DE BEAUVOIR: Because at the same time the *légion d'honneur* was part

---

* Whom I call Marco in my memoirs.

and parcel of a bourgeois hierarchy. And it therefore made you belong to that society.

SARTRE: It wasn't the bourgeois society, it was the hierarchy. There are similar hierarchies in the USSR or the socialist countries.

DE BEAUVOIR: Yet there are certain prizes that you have accepted. And it would be interesting to know why. I'm thinking of a particular Italian prize . . .

SARTRE: I have accepted others. I first accepted a Populist prize in '40, a small sum that was given me and that allowed me to live rather better. I was mobilized. I gave you some of the money and kept a little for myself at the front, and with it I lived rather better. I think in that case I was perfectly cynical, feeling that the war took away all value from prize or nonprize, that if you were given one while you were fighting it was a joke, and that I could accept it. To tell the truth I had nothing whatsoever to do with a Populist prize, since I had absolutely nothing in common with the Populist writers. So I accepted.

DE BEAUVOIR: Yes, you took the money cynically. But there were prizes that you accepted without any notion of advantage.

SARTRE: The Italian prize, that was because I was on good terms with the Italian Communists and because I was very fond of some of them. At that point I was not on good terms with the French Communists. I liked the Italian Communists, and just at that time they were organizing this little festivity. It was a matter of giving a yearly prize to the person who had displayed courage or intelligence during the Occupation, and they gave it to me. Obviously, that cannot possibly be reconciled with my theory.

DE BEAUVOIR: But it was a prize related to the Occupation?

SARTRE: It was a prize connected with the Resistance. I had it— though God knows that my resistance . . . I was a resister, and I knew resisters, but I never suffered much for it. Yet they gave it to me. I think I didn't look upon this prize as the outcome of a period, of a hierarchy. I was too clearly aware that there was absolutely nothing in common between my attitude during the Occupation and that of the resisters who had been taken prisoner by the Germans, who had been tortured, who had died in prison. We were resisters, so all right. But for a writer, resistance chiefly meant writing in little clandestine magazines and minor activities of that sort. I saw the prize rather as an acknowledgment on the part of the Italians of a certain kind of intellectual resistance during the Occupation. That was what interested me. That is, they emphasized the kind of refusal that we writers, or at least all those I knew, put first and foremost. So I looked upon myself not as personally worthy of this distinction, but worthy insofar as other writers might, like me, have had the award. Someone had this prize and it happened to be me. It stood for a kind of French intellectual resistance.

DE BEAUVOIR: In short you and the Italian Communists were friends. They offered you a certain acknowledgement of your own and your friends' activities during the war, and you accepted it, also in friendship. It had nothing to do with hierarchies, honors, distinctions.

SARTRE: Absolutely not.

DE BEAUVOIR: It was really a reciprocal relation between you and those who . . .

SARTRE: They gave me some money.

DE BEAUVOIR: Which you in your turn gave to support I can't remember what social movement. Now let's turn to another honor that was offered to you. An honor you were pressed to accept, even by some people who were close to you—that of being a professor at the Collège de France.

SARTRE: Yes, but I couldn't see why I should be a professor at the Collège de France. I had written some books of philosophy, but philosophy has been looked upon as a subject to teach since the eighteenth century. You can call it a subject to teach as long as it's a question of the philosophical systems of the past, but if you are trying to think out the present in a philosophical manner, I don't think you can do so through what you teach your pupils. They may become aware of it, but there's no reason why a teacher should teach something that is not completely worked out, something whose value he does not know exactly. In short, I couldn't see why, as a philosopher, I should go to the Collège de France. It seemed to me completely foreign to what I was doing.

DE BEAUVOIR: You thought it would be better to write books and for people to read them at leisure, having time to reflect, rather than give them ex cathedra lectures on the subject.

SARTRE: Just so. And I should add that I was very busy at that point. I was fully occupied with writing books and it would have meant cutting down my time for work, since I would have taken a certain number of hours in the week to prepare lectures on things I felt I knew. So giving a series of lectures at the Collège de France would not have advanced me at all. Merleau-Ponty took the position because to some extent he looked upon philosophy from within the professorial system. I don't know why, I may say. His books weren't particularly academic books. Yet I think we differed in that, from the beginning, he accepted the university as a means of dealing with philosophy, and I did not.

DE BEAUVOIR: Yes. Besides, Merleau-Ponty had written a thesis. He had made his career in the university. It must also be said that there were practical considerations. As a successful writer you were earning a lot of money at that time, whereas clearly for Merleau-Ponty his university career was his living. So that counted a greal deal. And then for him, on the contrary, being at the Collège de France meant more time available, since he had less to do than if he had been just a professor at the Sorbonne. I think that's an aspect that influences many of the people who are at the Collège de France. But obviously, since you had no practical or financial motive, in your case it would only have been a question of honors.

SARTRE: I didn't look upon being a professor at the Collège de France as an honor.

DE BEAUVOIR: You've never looked upon anything as an honor.

SARTRE: No. I've thought myself above any honors that could be offered to me because they were abstract and because they were never directed at me.

DE BEAUVOIR: They were directed at the Other in you. Let's go back to the Nobel prize, which was then the most notorious of your refusals, the most widely known and talked about.

SARTRE: I am entirely against the Nobel prize because it amounts to classifying writers. If it had existed in the fifteenth or sixteenth centuries we should know that Clément Marot had had the Nobel prize, that Kant had missed it—he ought to have had it, but it had not been given to him because there had been a mixup or because some members of the jury had done something or other—that Victor Hugo had had it, of course, and so on. At this point literature would be completely ordered, arranged in a hierarchy. You would have the members of the Collège de France, then others who had had the Prix Goncourt, and then others who had had still other awards. The Nobel prize consists of giving a prize very year. What does this prize correspond to? What does it mean, saying that a writer had it in 1974, what does it mean in relation to the men who had it earlier or to those who have not had it but who also write and who are perhaps better? What does the prize mean? Can it really be said that the year they gave it to me I was superior to my colleagues, the other writers, and that the year after it was someone else who was superior? Does one really have to look at literature like that? As people who are superior one year, or who had been superior for a long while but who are to be acknowledged as such this particular year? It's absurd. It is perfectly obvious that a writer is not someone who at a given moment is superior to the rest. At the utmost he is the equal of the best. And "the best" is another bad way of putting it. He is the equal of those who have written really good books, and he is their equal forever. He'd written these books maybe five years before, maybe ten. There has to be a little fresh spurt for them to give you the Nobel. I'd published *The Words*. They thought it worthwhile and they gave me the prize a year later. For them it gave my work a fresh value. But must one draw the conclusion that the year before, when I had not published the book, I was worth much less? It's an absurd notion. The whole idea of arranging literature in a hierarchical order is one that is completely contrary to the literary idea. On the other hand it is perfectly suitable for a bourgeois society that wants to make everything an integral part of the system. If writers are taken over by a bourgeois society they will be taken over in a hierarchy, because it is in an ordered fashion that all social forms appear. Hierarchy is what destroys people's personal value. Being above or below is absurd. And that's why I refused the Nobel prize, because on no account whatsoever did I wish to be looked upon as the equal of Hemingway, for example. I was very fond of Hemingway, I knew him personally, and I'd been to see him in Cuba. But the idea of being his equal or of holding any rank at all in relation to him was very far from my mind. There is an idea here that I think naive and even stupid.

DE BEAUVOIR: I'd like to go back to your pride. The fact that you are proud emerges very clearly from our conversations. But how would you define your pride?

SARTRE: I think it's not a pride that concerns me myself, Jean-Paul Sartre the private individual, but rather one that has to do with the characteristics common to all men. I am proud of performing actions that have a beginning and an end, of changing a given part of the world insofar as I carry out the act of writing, of producing books—in short, it's my human activity I'm proud of. Not that I think it superior to any other activity, but it *is* an activity. It's the pride of consciousness expanding in the form of an act. No doubt it also has to do with consciousness as subjectivity insofar as it produces ideas and feelings.

It's the fact of being a man, a creature born and condemned to die, but between the two, acting and setting himself off from the rest of the world by his action and by his thought, which is also an action, and by his feelings, which are an opening onto the world of action. It's by means of all this, whatever his feelings and thoughts may be, that I think a man should define himself. In a word, I don't understand that other men are not as proud as I am, since it seems to me a natural characteristic, part of the structure of conscious life, of life in society . . .

DE BEAUVOIR: The fact is that they usually are not proud. How does it come about that you have managed to be?

SARTRE: I suppose that in the immense majority of cases it's poverty and oppression that forbid them to be proud.

DE BEAUVOIR: You feel that all men tend to have a certain pride?

SARTRE: That's what I think. This pride is connected with the very fact of thinking, of acting. It is that which reveals the human reality, and it is accompanied by a consciousness of the act one performs, the act with which one is pleased and of which one is proud. I think that is the sort of pride that should be found in everybody.

DE BEAUVOIR: And why are there so many people who are not at all proud?

SARTRE: Take a boy who lives in a more or less disunited family in an atmosphere of poverty, a boy with no education, who hasn't reached the level at which society asks him for truly human proofs and qualities, a boy who in these conditions comes, when he is eighteen or nineteen, to a job that calls for hard, low-paid, subordinate work. This boy may be proud of his physical strength, but that's no more than vanity. He does not possess pride properly so called, because he's perpetually alienated, perpetually thrust out of the sphere in which he ought to be able to act with others, asserting, "I've done this, I've done that. I have the right to speak."

DE BEAUVOIR: So pride seems to be a class privilege?

SARTRE: No! I don't say that. I say that at present the possibilities of having pride are available more to one class, the oppressing class, the bourgeoisie, than to another, the class of the oppressed, the proletariat. But in fact it seems to me that any man can be endowed with this pride. Because of social circumstances it's easier for some bourgeois to have it than for proletarians who are humiliated and oppressed. So they, the proletarians, have something other than pride, they have an urgent need for it. They feel the emptiness where the pride they ought to possess should be, and in revolutions they are crying out for the pride of being men. You can see by their words and actions that there are some proletarians and peasants who have retained their pride. Those people will be the revolutionaries. If their backs are bent, if they are bowed down as one says, it is against their will.

DE BEAUVOIR: Don't you think that family and upbringing are of great importance here? If people belonging to the unfavored classes are lucky with their family, they will keep their pride even under oppression and exploitation, the direct opposite of the wealthy bourgeois, who are completely ruined by an overprotected childhood. In that context, how do you explain that you managed to be proud?

SARTRE: I had a childhood in which a great deal was said, and improperly said, about my intelligence and about the fact that I was the grandson of my grandfather, who mistakenly believed that he was a great man. I was led to think of myself as a little prince. In the petit-bourgeois world I lived in, I was already a privileged creature, and because of my grandfather I was looked upon as possessing some inestimable quality. That doesn't correspond to what I say about pride, because I don't think I do possess an inestimable quality. I just think I have human possibilities—it's the human being in me that I'm proud of. But it did come to me from my first pride, which was that of a child.

DE BEAUVOIR: You were encouraged to have pride in being a man.

SARTRE: Yes. I think my grandfather had it too, but in another way . . . based more on personal qualities, connected more with teaching —diminished. But he was certainly proud.

DE BEAUVOIR: When you were writing about Genet, you were pleased with his remark, "Pride comes later." Do you think it's sound for yourself?

SARTRE: Pride is called pride, is felt as pride later. By later I mean after I was twelve, after an earlier life in which it existed but in which it was not named.

DE BEAUVOIR: It seems to me that there was one thing you liked very much at the Ecole Normale, and that was all of you being together.

SARTRE: Yes, we saw one another very often. We formed groups—we went to the movies together, we had lunch together. Most of the time we had lunch and dinner at the school itself. There were conversations from table to table between the scientists and the literary men.

DE BEAUVOIR: You've often said that the years at the Ecole Normale were among the happiest of your life.

SARTRE: Yes, I was perfectly happy.

DE BEAUVOIR: So you took great pleasure in living among other men? It really was among men, because you were a boarder, and as you say, you ate together, and so on. So you found men's company very agreeable.

SARTRE: Yes, but still I did have relations with women.

DE BEAUVOIR: Yes, I know. There was Camille; there was the fiancée.

SARTRE: There were quite a lot.

DE BEAUVOIR: In another way, through Guille, there was Mme Morel.

SARTRE: But generally, I spent my days among men. Mind you, Guille, Maheu, Nizan, and I formed a group that people made fun of.

DE BEAUVOIR: Yes, because you were very standoffish with people you didn't like. Merleau-Ponty, for example. You were on very bad terms with him, weren't you?

SARTRE: Yes, but even so I once protected him from some men who wanted to beat him up.

DE BEAUVOIR: You were singing obscene songs, and being pious he tried to stop you?

SARTRE: He went out. Some fellows ran after him—there were two of them—and they were going to beat him up because they were furious. So I went out too. I had a sort of liking for Merleau-Ponty. There was someone else with me. We overtook them and said, "Come on. Don't beat him up. Leave him alone and let him go." So they didn't do anything; they went off.

DE BEAUVOIR: There was another time in your life when you were happy when you were living in a community of men. That was in the prison camp.

SARTRE: Yes, but I was not so happy.

DE BEAUVOIR: Naturally, because of the circumstances. But what I mean is, you did not dislike the fact of living a communal life with men at that period. It wasn't that which made your being a prisoner somewhat painful. The painfulness was already there, objectively. But you liked being among men, being accepted by them and working with them, didn't you?

SARTRE: I liked it.

DE BEAUVOIR: That's amusing, because if we now go back chronologically, it's plain that your friendships with men have been quite rare, in any case very selective, and that upon the whole you haven't been so fond of living among men. I mean, let's take your military service . . .

SARTRE: Military service. There was a first part, which was during a course at Saint Cyr, the meteorological course. I had nothing much in the way of relations with the other soldiers apart from Guille, who had chosen the same speciality, and with Aron, who was an instructor. There were one or two others I talked to, but very little. It was really the instructor and Guille who were my best friends. Then afterward, at the Villa Polovnia, I was with two fellows, one who came from Toulouse and one who was a seminarian whose feet smelled horribly, who did his work badly, and who had what relations with me he could manage, seeing that I did not believe in God and did not hide it from him.

DE BEAUVOIR: So in that case it was enmity?

SARTRE: As soon as anything went wrong it turned into enmity. I didn't like the man from Toulouse at all, either. He was a thief and a grafter; but I had little to do with him. As far as our relations in the kitchen went, or strolling around Tours for a day, he was bearable.

DE BEAUVOIR: And when you were a teacher you necessarily had close relations with the whole group of teachers.

SARTRE: No, I didn't have close relations with them.

DE BEAUVOIR: I mean you were there and there were other teachers around you. Did you keep them entirely at a distance? You did after all have some friendships! At Le Havre you had Bonnafé.

SARTRE: I had Bonnafé, and then I had the English teacher, although Bonnafé and I looked upon him as a buffoon. We used to have lunch together in the restaurant I described in *Nausea*.

DE BEAUVOIR: Why were you friends with Bonnafé?

SARTRE: Because he was a good-looking fellow and a boxer. It was essentially that.

DE BEAUVOIR: When you were teaching at Le Havre you were friendly enough for us to go on a walking tour for a few days with him, his girl, you and me.

SARTRE: Yes, I was quite fond of him at that time.

DE BEAUVOIR: Afterward, at your various posts at Laon and Paris, did you never have friendly contacts with your colleagues?

SARTRE: I used to see them when I went to the meetings for giving the pupils places on the honor roll—that is, *when* I went, for I was often reproved for not going. But I can't say I had relations with them. Yet it's true I did with Magnane and Merle. I was at the Lycée Pasteur for two years, and I knew them both there.

DE BEAUVOIR: But you weren't friends with Magnane, were you? Surely you were acquainted with him, but it didn't amount to anything?

SARTRE: Yet I saw more of him than of Merle. But that was because Merle had his own life and he didn't have much spare time, whereas Magnane did.

DE BEAUVOIR: What other contacts did you have? When you were at Le Havre Bost and Palle were there. You used to box with them. It would be amusing to talk about your relations with your pupils.

SARTRE: Generally speaking I was quite fond of them, and when Bonnafé thought up the idea of giving boxing lessons I persuaded them to come to the gymnasium myself. There were ten or twelve of us; the others wouldn't follow, as they were afraid of making fools of themselves or hurting somebody. There were about ten of us and we boxed without doing one another much harm.

DE BEAUVOIR: There were other pupils you liked—Morzadec, for example. On the whole, did you like them better than your fellow teachers?

SARTRE: I didn't know my fellow teachers. I wished them good day, I asked them how they were and how their wives and family were, but it stopped there. I wasn't unpleasant with them, but we didn't know one another, and they didn't make any effort to know me, either. They had their own lives. There were one or two who had a vague liking for me.

DE BEAUVOIR: A priori you were in sympathy with the pupils. Why?

SARTRE: A priori.

DE BEAUVOIR: Yet these were still relations with men. But there was a difference—these were young. You weren't so old yourself, but even so . . .

SARTRE: When I first went to Le Havre the difference was very slight . . .

DE BEAUVOIR: You had passed the *agrégation* at twenty-three, you had done your military service, so you were twenty-six, twenty-seven . . .

SARTRE: And they were eighteen or nineteen. I liked them. I wasn't so fond of the top boys, the ones at the very top, but I was interested in those who had ideas. They were often rather different from the top boys—they were beginning to think for themselves.

DE BEAUVOIR: Why did you like them? Because they weren't yet set in their ways, because they didn't yet feel they had rights, because they weren't yet swine?

SARTRE: I was very like them as far as thought and way of life were concerned. I was a little freer since I didn't live with my family, but after all it was pretty well the same thing. There really was a link, so that I was friends with Bost and Palle, much as I was with Guille and Maheu.

DE BEAUVOIR: There's someone we haven't mentioned, and that's Zuorro, with whom you had a strange connection.

SARTRE: I had a certain liking for him, a liking that arose from his appearance. He was quite good-looking.

DE BEAUVOIR: He was even very good-looking.

SARTRE: He was fairly amusing, ironic, fairly intelligent.

DE BEAUVOIR: Very much of a mythomaniac.

SARTRE: He was homosexual and he had a certain amount of trouble at the Cité universitaire.* I was there too at that time. It can't be said that he and I got on well together. He got on better with Guille, for example.

DE BEAUVOIR: Let's go back to the young. Why did you like them?

SARTRE: I think it was because I recognized myself more in them than in older people or those of my own age. Insofar as they were interested in philosophy they had an unmethodical way of looking for ideas that corresponded with the way I looked for my theories and truths. I often used to say, "I've discovered three theories this week." Well, there was something of that in them. Their way of thinking was a kind of discovery—they weren't yet formed; they were forming themselves. I wasn't yet formed either, and I was well aware of it. I felt that I was changing, and as for them, they were in a state even earlier than the change I felt in myself. And I did after all see a good deal of them, partly by pressing them to box and then by not pressing the daily contacts.

DE BEAUVOIR: There was also a gym teacher you saw now and then.

SARTRE: Rasquin. He and his wife asked me to lunch at their house, and she cooked a special meal for me, a meal that I didn't like because there were oysters.

---

* A group of student hostels in Paris. (trans.)

DE BEAUVOIR: Why him rather than the others?

SARTRE: He was a big fellow, quite good-looking and powerfully built, and he told stories. What I liked were stories about men's lives with sex and fighting in them.

DE BEAUVOIR: In short you liked Bonnafé and Rasquin because they weren't pedants and they didn't try to have intellectual contacts with you, and because they were handsome, full of life, and told stories.

SARTRE: Both of them were good at gymnastics. Well, anyway, Bonnafé went in for boxing.

DE BEAUVOIR: Although Bonnafé taught Latin?

SARTRE: Yes, Latin, French, and Greek. But you must realize that for me Le Havre wasn't the center of my contacts. In fact I had much deeper relations with Guille, Maheu, and that lady—less so with Nizan in those days.

DE BEAUVOIR: Things had cooled very much since his return from Aden. Then he got married. You still saw one another but it was no longer an intimate friendship. Whereas Guille and you were very intimate. He was rather touchy where friendship was concerned. To begin with, when you always brought me with you, he took offense and once or twice he asked to see you by yourself and to stay at Le Havre with you alone.

SARTRE: So he did.

DE BEAUVOIR: Guille always had a rather easily offended and jealous side.

SARTRE: That's true. That was not at all the case with Maheu, who was far more remote in his friendships, by the way. Maheu was very much bent on succeeding, succeeding at any price.

DE BEAUVOIR: He has succeeded!

SARTRE: But that's exactly what he wanted.

DE BEAUVOIR: What happened next?

SARTRE: I began working on *Nausea*. Then I left for Berlin.

DE BEAUVOIR: There too you lived in a male group.

SARTRE: Yes, but there was a woman too.

DE BEAUVOIR: The one you called the moon woman. But on the whole yours was a life among men.

SARTRE: It was a life of solitary walks in Berlin and then of work.

DE BEAUVOIR: In fact you didn't have many contacts with those Berlin comrades of yours?

SARTRE: No. We met for the evening meal. We were free to go out for the midday meal and we had enough money to treat ourselves to it elsewhere, but in the evening we all dined together. There were six or seven of us.

DE BEAUVOIR: You mostly saw Susini and Brunschwig?

SARTRE: Yes, but there were others. Some came to study a particular German poet about whom they then wrote theses.

DE BEAUVOIR: Were there people you disliked?

SARTRE: There was one teacher whose name I no longer remember. A tall fellow with spectacles and a black moustache. I must have pointed him out to you. And then there was another, a young fellow too.

DE BEAUVOIR: What were the relations like with the men you didn't like? Aggressive or polite?

SARTRE: Polite, on the whole, yet rather aggressive too. I had quarrels with that black-moustached teacher. There were quite violent quarrels in the evening at dinner. Yet generally speaking, my contacts with those people were pretty civil. We saw one another. We used to go to the movies together.

DE BEAUVOIR: I think there was one you rather liked, wasn't there? A man called Erhard?

SARTRE: He was an odd creature.

DE BEAUVOIR: It was he who took us to night clubs when I came to see you. You used to go out with him.

SARTRE: No, I didn't go out with anyone. I used to go and lunch by myself in the Kurfürstendamm, which was quite a fashionable part in those days. I went and had my lunch either in a beer hall or over near the station. . . . Contacts with the other boarders didn't interest me.

DE BEAUVOIR: Your relations with the moon woman interested you much more. Was she more important than the men?

SARTRE: Yes, obviously.

DE BEAUVOIR: After that you began having your books published. Did you know many people at that period?

SARTRE: Before the war? Oh, yes, a fair number.

DE BEAUVOIR: You knew Paulhan, Brice Parain, Gaston Gallimard, Claude Gallimard. They were all in publishing.

SARTRE: And then I knew some writers. I remember a dismal gathering at Gallimard's one afternoon. It was a cocktail party, a year before war was declared. That was in June 1938, and the end came in July–August 1939. Everybody felt that something was going to happen, and that day the atmosphere was far from gay. It was the only thing people talked about. So yes, at that time I did know a few of Gallimard's writers and colleagues.

DE BEAUVOIR: Was it that day you met Jouhandeau? Wasn't it he who asked you, "Have you ever been in hell?"

SARTRE: Yes, that was Jouhandeau.

DE BEAUVOIR: Still, it didn't go far. They were never friendships; they were just encounters.

SARTRE: Yes. I had nothing more than encounters with people in the writing world.

DE BEAUVOIR: Did you meet Gide?

SARTRE: Yes. Adrienne Monnier gave a dinner and she invited me and Gide. I no longer remember that dinner very clearly, but we didn't dislike one another, Gide and I.

DE BEAUVOIR: Did seeing writers amuse you?

SARTRE: Yes, there was one very amusing meeting when Adrienne Monnier had writers' photographs taken. I met lots of them that way —Valéry, for instance. I saw Valéry again later, after the war, in the bar of the Pont Royal; we made an appointment to meet again. I don't recall what we had to say to one another—it can't have been much.

DE BEAUVOIR: Still, none of all that went beyond an amused or interested curiosity. You didn't form any close friendships?

SARTRE: No friendships at all.

DE BEAUVOIR: You didn't meet the surrealists. Neither Aragon nor any of the others.

SARTRE: No. I must have met Aragon after the war.

DE BEAUVOIR: Very well, let's go back to the war. There again you were in a community of men. What were your relations with your meteorological colleagues?

SARTRE: I got along well with Pieter, who was a Jew. I remember how anguished he was in June '40.

DE BEAUVOIR: You were all taken prisoner. Was he taken too?

SARTRE: Yes.

DE BEAUVOIR: It wasn't known that he was a Jew?

SARTRE: No.

DE BEAUVOIR: How did he manage?

SARTRE: Why should it have been known? He had no papers.

DE BEAUVOIR: His name . . .

SARTRE: He kept his name but he didn't say he was a Jew.

DE BEAUVOIR: It seems to me that we saw him again after the war.

SARTRE: I saw him again even during the war. He got out; I think he managed to escape.

DE BEAUVOIR: So you got along pretty well with him?

SARTRE: Yes. Very badly with the corporal, but quite well with a Paris working man, Muller.

DE BEAUVOIR: But you did see other soldiers too?

SARTRE: Yes, I met the secretaries of the general's HQ, and we used to talk.

DE BEAUVOIR: On the whole they liked you?

SARTRE: Pieter did. Corporal Pierre not at all. We were both teachers. He vaguely felt that that ought to have been a bond between us; I didn't. As far as I was concerned the bond didn't exist, so he wasn't pleased.

DE BEAUVOIR: You've already spoken about your experiences as a prisoner, but have you perhaps some little things to add?

SARTRE: I met Bénard in the prison camp. He lived at Le Havre and he had married the daughter of the man who owned *Le Petit Havrais*. He was on the staff of the paper before the war, and he was very fond of his wife, who had been my pupil at Le Havre.

DE BEAUVOIR: But why did you make friends with him?

SARTRE: He was so amusing. He spoke well, and then what was more important, in the camp we had strange relations which were both those of work and at the same time of resistance against the collaborationist officers and soldiers. He helped me and he looked after the food very well. I became friends with him and even more so with a priest, the Abbé Leroy. I was in constant touch with the priests, who had a hut of their own.

DE BEAUVOIR: Why this choice of priests?

SARTRE: Because they were intellectuals. And that was also the reason why they had recruited me and why they had recruited others. For if an intellectual could get along with priests in circumstances of that kind, the priests adopted him. There was also the Abbé Perin. I was on good terms with him too.

DE BEAUVOIR: But you had contacts with the others, didn't you? The ones who were not intellectuals.

SARTRE: Yes, it was with them that I was most frequently in contact, since we were in the same hut.

DE BEAUVOIR: But what feelings did you have with regard to them?

SARTRE: Mine was the performers' hut. There were some who played the trumpet; there were some, like Chomisse, who organized the theater on Sundays. Others were singers or more or less makeshift actors.

DE BEAUVOIR: In short, the fact of being among men didn't displease you? You didn't live in contempt, disgust, solitude, withdrawal?

SARTRE: There was withdrawal insofar as I thought things they didn't. But in the evening, for example, I was entirely with them—I'd tell stories, I'd sit at a table in the middle of the hut and talk and they were very much amused. I told them any old crap, playing the fool.

DE BEAUVOIR: You sought contact with them and you established it. Among them some fellows you disliked individually, I suppose.

SARTRE: Yes, there were some I was not very fond of.

DE BEAUVOIR: But what was it that made you like or dislike someone?

SARTRE: On the whole, I was not fond of the fellow who didn't play the game. There's always a game in relations between men. In that prison camp, for instance, there was a way of living with the others, you confided in one another, you asked one another's advice, and so on. Well, those who profited from that for their own advantage—those were the ones I disliked in the first place, and they might become real enemies. Chomisse, for example, you didn't know where that sort of fellow came from. They said he used to open the doors of taxis outside the Gaumont Palace cinema. It's not impossible.

DE BEAUVOIR: But that's not what made you dislike him?

SARTRE: I didn't like him because he wouldn't admit it, and because he told tall stories about the life he had led.

DE BEAUVOIR: You didn't like phonies.

SARTRE: I didn't like phonies. It was basically that.

DE BEAUVOIR: Mythomaniacs at a pinch . . .

SARTRE: Mythomaniacs didn't worry me.

DE BEAUVOIR: I know you really liked Leroy, for example, because he was very straightforward and very brave. He didn't see fit to change to another camp, taking advantage of being a priest; he preferred to stay. You liked men who had character, men who resisted.

There were many important friendships that were formed during the war when you came back to Paris. You were in contact with the intellectual Resistance. Whom did you know at that time?

SARTRE: Men whose names I've forgotten.

DE BEAUVOIR: There was Claude Morgan.

SARTRE: Yes, Claude Morgan. Claude Roy a little later.

DE BEAUVOIR: What work did you do?

SARTRE: We worked on little publications, particularly *Les Lettres françaises*.

DE BEAUVOIR: Did you feel a solidarity with those people, as you had with the prisoners of war?

SARTRE: Yes, to some degree.

DE BEAUVOIR: I think you met Camus after the article you wrote about him. What friendships did you have during this period?

SARTRE: There was Giacometti, but he very soon left for Switzerland. He came back after the war.

DE BEAUVOIR: We knew him during the first years.

SARTRE: And then he very soon left for Switzerland, in '42.

DE BEAUVOIR: During the war your relations with him didn't really exist yet?

SARTRE: No, they were less intimate than they became later.

DE BEAUVOIR: Well, who did you know during the war, then?

SARTRE: Leiris and his wife.

DE BEAUVOIR: How did you meet him? Through *Les Lettres françaises*, perhaps?

SARTRE: Through the Resistance. At that time I read all his books. I felt a very simple, very great, very strong friendship for him. His wife and he very often used to invite us to dinner. The kind of knowledge he had, his knowledge as a sociologist for example, did not correspond to mine; and his researches and his interests were different from mine. But that did not prevent us liking the pair very much indeed.

DE BEAUVOIR: There's someone we haven't mentioned, someone who also has his place in your life before the war and during it—Dullin.

SARTRE: I was very fond of Dullin.

DE BEAUVOIR: There was Queneau too.

SARTRE: We met Queneau and his wife at the Leiris's.

DE BEAUVOIR: About '43 there were those fiestas . . .

SARTRE: Where we met Bataille, Leibowitz, Jacques Lemarchand, a whole literary world. During that period this literary world did not appear in the papers, nor did they any longer produce books. They maintained their reserve. But they did still meet. One saw Picasso at the Flore, for example, and there were restaurants where the people close to Picasso and Leiris were to be seen—the restaurant that was called Les Catalans.

DE BEAUVOIR: Yes, but we didn't go. It was too expensive for us.

SARTRE: But we were invited there two or three times.

DE BEAUVOIR: Maybe. And then we acted in Picasso's *Le Désir attrapé par la queue.*

SARTRE: Which made us somewhat better acquainted with Picasso's friends.

DE BEAUVOIR: What were your relations with Picasso?

SARTRE: Fairly slight, but still most amiable up until the Liberation.

After that he was taken over by the Communist party. And then again he lived in the South and I only saw him rarely. My relations with Picasso were quite superficial. They were no more than polite social relations, but they were always cordial.

DE BEAUVOIR: Let's talk about people you were more friendly with. There was Camus.

SARTRE: There was Camus, whom I met in '43. I saw him at the first night of *The Flies*. He came up to me and said, "I'm Camus."

DE BEAUVOIR: Yes. You'd written a critical but very appreciative article about *The Stranger*.

SARTRE: Which obviously implied that I thought the book important.

DE BEAUVOIR: Would you speak about your relations with Camus? Their beginning, the way they continued.

SARTRE: Their beginning, yes. But to describe their continuation after the war would be very complicated. . . . We had curious relations and I think they did not quite tally with those he would have liked to have with others. In the same way ours with him were not the kind we liked having with people.

DE BEAUVOIR: That was not so at the beginning. For my part, I was very pleased with the relations we had with Camus.

SARTRE: For a year or two things went quite well. He was amusing: extremely coarse, but often very amusing. He was very deeply committed to the Resistance, and then he edited *Combat*. What we found engaging was his Algerian side. He had an accent like that of the South of France and he had Spanish friendships, friendships that went back to his contacts with the Spaniards and Algerians . . .

DE BEAUVOIR: Above all our contact wasn't stiff, solemn, intellectual. We drank, we ate . . .

SARTRE: In a certain way intimacy was lacking. It didn't lack in conversation, but it wasn't deep. One had the feeling that there might be a clash if we touched on certain things, and we didn't touch on them. We had a great liking for Camus, but we knew we shouldn't go too far.

DE BEAUVOIR: He was the one in whose company we enjoyed ourselves most and had most fun. We saw a very great deal of one another—we exchanged innumerable stories.

SARTRE: Yes, we had a real friendship with him, but it was a superficial friendship. People thought they would please us by calling all three of us existentialists and that enraged Camus. In fact he had nothing in common with existentialism.

DE BEAUVOIR: How did your relations with him evolve? He thought of staging *No Exit* and acting the part of Garcin. So you were very close to one another in '43.

SARTRE: And in '44 too. I joined his Resistance group a little before the Liberation; I met people I didn't know who together with Camus were looking into what the Resistance could do in this last stage of the war. Many of them were arrested during the following weeks, in particular a girl called Jacqueline Bernard.

DE BEAUVOIR: Then Camus asked you to write articles on the liberation of Paris for *Combat,* and after that it was largely for *Combat* that you went to America.

SARTRE: It was Camus who registered me as a reporter in America for *Combat.*

DE BEAUVOIR: And when did it all begin to go sour? I remember the great row he had with Merleau-Ponty.

SARTRE: Yes, that separated us to some degree. He was at Boris Vian's one evening in '46. He had recently spent a few days with a charming woman, who had since died, and because of this love affair and separation he was rather closed up and morose. He greeted everyone and then all at once he attacked Merleau-Ponty, who was there, about his article on Koestler and bolshevism.

DE BEAUVOIR: Because at that time Merleau-Ponty was somewhat inclined toward communism.

SARTRE: It was in my review, *Les Temps modernes,* that the article had appeared, so I was against Camus. At that juncture Camus was certainly not angry with me, but he couldn't bear Merleau-Ponty. He didn't really hold with Koestler's argument either, but he was furious; and he had personal reasons for being very much on Koestler's side.

DE BEAUVOIR: In any case his relations with you were very odd. He often used to say that when you actually met he was filled with liking for you but that at a distance there were a great many things about you he disapproved of. When he made a tour in America he spoke of you in a pretty disagreeable way.

SARTRE: Yes, his was an ambivalent attitude.

DE BEAUVOIR: He wouldn't join us in the review, and I think it irritated him very much when people thought he was more or less your disciple, he being very young and you being better known. He was extremely touchy, and he didn't much care for that. But how did things come to get worse and worse, to the point of reaching a break?

SARTRE: There was a personal episode that didn't make me in the least angry with him but that he found disagreeable.

DE BEAUVOIR: The business of the woman you'd had an affair with yourself?

SARTRE: It was rather awkward. And as this woman had broken with him for personal reasons, he held it against me to some extent. In fact it's a complicated story. He'd had an affair with Casarès and had fallen out with her. He broke it off and he told us confidentially about this break. I remember an evening with him in a bar at the time when we often used to go to bars; I was alone with him. He had just made it up again with Casarès and he had letters of hers in his hand, old letters that he showed me, saying, "Well, there you are! When I found them again, when I was able to read them again . . ." But politics separated us.

DE BEAUVOIR: That argues a certain intimacy on the private level.

SARTRE: Yes, it was always there as long as we were on good terms. Even our political differences didn't worry us much in conversation. For example, he went back to Casarès and he came to see her rehearse *The Devil and the Good Lord,* you remember?

DE BEAUVOIR: Yes, indeed. What were these political differences, and how did it all end by blowing up? When there was the R.D.R., did he belong to it?

SARTRE: No.

DE BEAUVOIR: Well, what did cause the final break, then?

SARTRE: The final break came about when he published his book *The Rebel.* I tried to find someone who would be willing to review it in *Les Temps modernes* without being too harsh, and that was difficult. Jeanson wasn't there at that time and no one among the other members of *Les Temps modernes* wanted to deal with it, because I wanted there to be moderation and everybody loathed the book. So that for two months, three months *Les Temps modernes* did not mention *The Rebel.* Then Jeanson came back from his travels and he said to me "I'm quite willing." It must be added that Jeanson's attitude was somewhat complex. He was trying to get in touch with people like Camus to see whether, with their help, he could not found a review that would be the counterpart of *Les Temps modernes* but further to the left, *Les Temps modernes* being a reformist review while the other would be revolutionary.

DE BEAUVOIR: It was strange to want to do that with Camus, who had nothing of the revolutionary about him.

SARTRE: He had asked various people. He had asked Camus, but obviously that would not do. So probably to have his revenge on Camus, who had not wished to work with him, he wrote the article in the way I had not wanted, that is to say, it was violent and slashing, and it pointed out the book's faults, which was not difficult to do.

DE BEAUVOIR: Above all it pointed out the book's philosophical poverty. That wasn't difficult either.

SARTRE: I wasn't there. I was traveling—in Italy, I think.

DE BEAUVOIR: In any event you wouldn't have censured a contributor's article.

SARTRE: No, but it upset Merleau-Ponty very much and he felt—he was alone in charge in Paris—that I wouldn't like it to appear. He tried to get Jeanson to change his mind—they had quite a violent quarrel—and then all he could do was let the article appear. It did appear, but under special conditions—Jeanson had consented, and it was the only reservation that he did consent to, to show Camus his article before it was published and ask him whether he agreed. Camus was furious and he wrote an article in which he called me Monsieur le Directeur, which was comic, for although we didn't say *tu* to one another we did speak very freely—there was no Monsieur between us. So I wrote an article replying to the insinuations he had flung in my teeth. Camus had not said much about Jeanson in his piece—he attributed all Jeanson's ideas to me, as though I had written his article. I answered quite harshly, and at that point our relations came to a stop. I retained a liking for him although his politics were completely foreign to mine, particularly his attitude during the Algerian war.

DE BEAUVOIR: That was later. At the same time he assumed the part of an important person, he became pompous, he became someone quite different from the cheerful, amusing young writer whose head had been slightly turned by fame but in a naive fashion. Well now, Merleau-Ponty and Koestler—what were your relations with them?

SARTRE: There were no deep relations with either one or the other. With Merleau-Ponty it's clear enough. I had a great esteem for him, and I was perfectly sincere in my article at the time of his death, but he was not someone it was easy to be with often.

DE BEAUVOIR: In any case I think we never dined or had a drink with him. He never came to our parties. He never was part of our private life.

SARTRE: What's more he made it obvious.

DE BEAUVOIR: Except absolutely by chance, when we met him at Saint-Tropez. But quite exceptional circumstances were called for.

SARTRE: We didn't get along very well in conversation.

DE BEAUVOIR: What about Koestler, then? He was much more amusing.

SARTRE: We met Koestler at the Pont Royal—he introduced himself. He stood up and he said "I am Koestler."

DE BEAUVOIR: You liked *The Spanish Testament* very much.

SARTRE: Yes. We said how do you do to him very warmly. We stayed with him a while. From then on we had more frequent encounters and almost at once he bored us on the anti-Communist level. Not that we were wildly in favor of the Communists, but Koestler's anti-Communism seemed to us worthless. He had been a Communist and he had broken with them; he never said exactly why. He did give theoretical reasons but these theoretical reasons were connected not with theoretical but with practical events. What events? No one knew; or at least you and I didn't. He talked about his anti-Communism at enormous length. He went to Italy to write a series of articles and he came back frightened by the Italian Communist movement. And the arguments for his anti-Communism were the arguments to be found in every paper.

DE BEAUVOIR: And then there was something else that irritated us, and that was his going on and on about science.

SARTRE: His scientific stuff annoyed us very much because he knew little about it and because he made use of thoroughly popularized notions to write popular books.

DE BEAUVOIR: There was also the way he found the young repulsive. I remember once an evening turned out very badly because we had brought Bost. Koestler was much put out. Very well, then—all this amounted to encounters of no great importance, but there were two men with whom you had really cordial bonds, Giacometti and Genet. I think that after the war it was for them that you had the warmest feelings. Why?

SARTRE: Well, they both had one thing in common: they excelled, the one in sculpture and painting, the other in writing. From that point of view, they were certainly among the most important people I've known. We used to see Giacometti for dinner, usually once a week or thereabouts. We had dinner in restaurants in '45 and '46, more or less anywhere. And we talked more or less about everything. He would talk about his sculpture and I didn't really understand what he meant; nor did you, either.

DE BEAUVOIR: You came to understand him in the end, since you wrote articles about him.

SARTRE: Yes, several years later. He tried to explain the nature of a sculptor's perception, he talked about his statues, he described the progress he had made between his first, which was very thick and very heavy, and the long, thin statues he made later and that he was still making. We did not always understand, but it seemed to me important and interesting. And then we also talked about just anything— about his contacts, his love affairs.

DE BEAUVOIR: He talked much about his life and he told a great many stories—he told them very amusingly.

SARTRE: We were very fond of his wife, Annette, who always came with him.

DE BEAUVOIR: Indeed, it could almost be said that you never met Giacometti alone, just the two of you.

SARTRE: Well, not to put too fine a point on it, never! There was always Annette and you, or in any event you, if Annette wasn't there. I did once see Giacometti and Annette without you, because you were away traveling.

DE BEAUVOIR: Why, that's a funny thing, and it's something we haven't yet talked about—you shared all these friendships you had with men after the beginning of the war with me. You almost never saw Camus or Leiris or Giacometti alone, did you?

SARTRE: Yes, Camus I did. I remember seeing Camus alone, because I used to leave my mother's apartment and go down to the Deux Magots. I quite often used to see him at the Deux Magots in the morning the first year. You were living in the Hotel de la Louisiane and I would see you later.

DE BEAUVOIR: Yes, but you never made an appointment with one of these friends, saying, "We'll both have dinner together." And that wasn't just a matter of not leaving me in the lurch, but because you didn't particularly want to have a one-to-one friendship of the kind you had had with Nizan or Guille.

SARTRE: No, there was no question about it.

DE BEAUVOIR: And what about Genet?

SARTRE: The relations were more unpredictable. I remember having met him here, for example, here, in Rome, with a young homosexual.

DE BEAUVOIR: And how did your relations with Genet begin?

SARTRE: I knew Cocteau at that time, and he was very fond of him. My relations with Cocteau didn't end very well, I've never been quite sure why, but end they did in the year of his death. Still, we did have lunch together three weeks or a month before he died. In any case Genet certainly helped to make this connection with Cocteau something that was not quite properly balanced.

DE BEAUVOIR: But you had many more affinities with Genet. You never had any with Cocteau.

SARTRE: Many more. I didn't really have affinities with Cocteau at all. I used to call on him, or I dined with him. He was intelligent.

DE BEAUVOIR: He was intelligent, he was brilliant, he was very kind. He was one of the few men who didn't enter into rivalry with you. He came out strongly in favor of *No Exit*. All right, but to go back to Genet.

SARTRE: There was no trace of meanness in Cocteau, and he had the sense of friendship. When he was fond of anyone—and it seems that for a while he was fond of me—he was warmhearted and he could do kind, charming little things. But his relations with Genet were in opposition to mine, because he saw Genet simply as a remarkable character who should be helped, whereas I thought he was managing by himself perfectly well and that he had no need of anyone like Cocteau. I thought that Genet's relations with Cocteau were something of a stratagem. Let him manage by himself, I thought, and things would go better. So our relations with regard to Genet were quite different. For my part, I encouraged him to be alone as I was alone—I don't mean abandoned by everybody, but not looking for any sponsor to get into the writing world—whereas Cocteau would willingly have sponsored him. Genet already knew me a little through my books when he met me at the Flore. At the Flore I saw a little fellow like a boxer come up to me.

DE BEAUVOIR: I was with you, by the way.

SARTRE: A lightweight or even a featherweight. And at that time he was thinking mainly about his books and how to make them known.

DE BEAUVOIR: We had already read *Our Lady of the Flowers* and we liked it very much.

SARTRE: The conversation was most agreeable, although it was a very special sort of conversation. One had to listen to a long speech on some given subject, a speech that was often interesting, though sometimes rather wearisome, because it was about writing, and he had his own opinions . . .

DE BEAUVOIR: In those days he was something of a pedant. That quite stopped later on, but with him it wasn't the same kind of daily contact in which one talked about everything, as it was with Giacometti.

SARTRE: No, but still they were good relations. We used to go and have dinner together, and he even dined at your apartment. You made one of those meals that you were in the habit of making at that time.

DE BEAUVOIR: So it was at the end of the war?

SARTRE: It was at the end of the war that I met Genet.

DE BEAUVOIR: About '43?

SARTRE: Or perhaps '44, during the last months of the Occupation. In any case he told me stories about his life, and he introduced his young friends, who were often good-looking youths who seemed to be compensating for their homosexuality with a somewhat forced toughness. He liked talking about homosexuality with us, because he knew that we were quite ignorant of it and that we had minds open enough to understand what he told us.

DE BEAUVOIR: What gave you the idea of writing a book about Genet?

SARTRE: He was published by Gallimard. At that time he was on good terms with me and he suggested that I should write a preface for him.

DE BEAUVOIR: Oh, that's how it was! He asked you for a preface, and you turned the preface into a book. How did he take the book?

SARTRE: In a very odd fashion. To begin with he didn't take much notice of it. He talked about the subject a little with me and he told me a few small things. When I had finished I gave him the manuscript. He read it, and one night he got up and went over to the fireplace with the intention of burning it. I believe he did throw some pages in and then plucked them out. It disgusted him because he felt that he was as I had described him, and although he was not disgusted with himself, yet . . .

DE BEAUVOIR: Yet he was disgusted that a book should be written about him. It was like a funerary monument.

SARTRE: He did not argue about the ideas. He thought that on the whole the things I said about him were true, and indeed sometimes their truth surprised him. But at the same time it irked him that I should have written this book, examining his books and sifting them through and through, especially because he looked upon himself as a poet. He took himself for *the* poet and me for *the* philosopher, and he made great use of this distinction, a distinction that he did not express, but that could be felt. He said things about poets, he said things about philosophers, so that it should all be neat and compact, so that it should be like a book; and at the same time he regarded the book with profound distrust. As far as I'm concerned, I don't think it was one of my worst books.

DE BEAUVOIR: No, it's a very good one. And what happened to your relations after the book? Did it have an effect on them?

SARTRE: They diminished. After that we would meet by chance at Gallimard's, where he came to hand in a manuscript or ask for money. We'd spend a short time together and make an appointment for the next day or the day after that. But it should be pointed out that two things happened just then—he was much attached to Abdallah, who killed himself more or less because of him, and at that moment Genet decided not to write anymore. And in fact he never did write anything much after that death. Besides, he was no longer living in Paris. When I met him it was after an absence of six months or a year.

DE BEAUVOIR: One last thing. How did all the friendships we have talked about finish? We've spoken of the prewar friendships, Guille, Nizan, Maheu, etcetera.

SARTRE: With Guille it came to an end because his life had rather soured him. He lost his wife, who meant a great deal to him and with whom we got along very well, and he married another woman whom he did not see fit to introduce to us. Gradually he withdrew from our life.

DE BEAUVOIR: As early as 1950 he was no longer on really good terms with you. He was very conservative, very bourgeois, very much taken up with the past; on that level things did not go well between us, so we stopped seeing one another. Now what about Maheu?

SARTRE: I quarreled with Maheu over something that happened to a Czech who was a friend of ours, a man we were looking after and . . . it's complicated.

DE BEAUVOIR: It must be said that there had been ups and downs—there had been eclipses. There were years during which we never saw him and then afterward we did see something of one another again. Zuorro?

SARTRE: He was killed in a car accident in Algeria.

DE BEAUVOIR: In rather suspicious circumstances.

SARTRE: That's not certain; we know nothing about it.

DE BEAUVOIR: As for Aron, you broke with him after the war for political reasons.

SARTRE: Not immediately, but quite soon. For political and for more essential reasons—our way of looking upon not only man's world but also the philosopher's were entirely different.

DE BEAUVOIR: All right. We're still very fond of Leiris, but we scarcely see him anymore. As for Queneau, there was an odd quarrel the meaning of which we could hardly figure out.

SARTRE: But which was final.

DE BEAUVOIR: In fact, of all these friends you've had there wasn't one you've liked so much as you liked Nizan or Guille, for example, when you were young.

SARTRE: Certainly not.

DE BEAUVOIR: Perhaps the closest was Giacometti. There was never any quarrel with him.

SARTRE: There was never any quarrel, but there were periods of coldness.

DE BEAUVOIR: Because of an affair that you spoke of in *The Words* and which wasn't exactly what he thought was the truth.

SARTRE: Things went very well with Giacometti until almost the very end, but because of that business he was more or less estranged from me for the last months.

DE BEAUVOIR: Many of your friendships have ended in estrangement. With Camus it was a downright quarrel; with Queneau too. And with Aron, and with Guille.

SARTRE: Maheu, that was an estrangement too.

DE BEAUVOIR: Entirely so at the end. Why were things like that?

SARTRE: Breaking off doesn't affect me in the least. A thing is dead —that's all.

DE BEAUVOIR: Can you tell me why it doesn't affect you?

SARTRE: I think I did not feel a deep friendship for some of the men who were among the closest of my friends. Guille and I did not belong to the same world. He had a much more bourgeois way of living than I did. He wasn't a philosopher, and that meant something. I used to expound my theories to him, as I've said, and he replied; but it didn't really interest him.

DE BEAUVOIR: But it's not only that which spoiled your friendship.

SARTRE: Still, these were things that came up again and again until the end. For example, the reason he married again without telling us was that he had a certain image of me.

DE BEAUVOIR: He had an image of the image you had of him. That was what he didn't like. The image was false, I may say. But what do you mean when you say, "I didn't feel a deep friendship"? Who have you had a deep friendship with?

SARTRE: With some women. With Nizan, yes. Up until his marriage, and even a little beyond. When I first met you I still felt quite a deep friendship for Nizan, although there was the whole length of his stay at Aden that had separated us.

DE BEAUVOIR: And when I first met you, you had a great deal of affection for Guille. I think that if anything had caused a break between you and Guille at that time, it would have wounded you.

SARTRE: Certainly. But generally speaking, there weren't deep, sensitive elements between the other fellows and myself.

DE BEAUVOIR: Do you mean that what existed was rather a certain intellectual understanding, and that if this understanding came to an end either for political reasons, as it did with Aron, or for others, then everything fell to pieces?

SARTRE: Yes, that's right.

DE BEAUVOIR: The emotional bond that makes one overlook certain divergences did not remain . . .

SARTRE: Exactly.

DE BEAUVOIR: Even so, there were cases where you had quite violent conflicts that were overcome right away, with Bost, for example. There was a conflict because he was on Cau's side.

SARTRE: There was a conflict. I threw him out of your apartment that evening, and then I followed him and we went and had a drink in a nearby café. That particular dispute doesn't count. But I've had violent quarrels with people. The breaks have usually come about from a want of vigor in the relationship.

DE BEAUVOIR: Bost would have done anything not to remain on bad terms with you. And there's someone else who had done a great deal not to break with you when there were disagreements, and that is Lanzmann. Whereas there are many who've let things drift, perhaps because they felt your indifference.

SARTRE: Because they were indifferent themselves.

DE BEAUVOIR: They were because you were.

SARTRE: I've very often broken off relations, but I don't think I've done so without cause. On the other side there was someone who led me to the break—to a difference in any case—always to a distance!

DE BEAUVOIR: There's no doubt that Aron and Camus, for example, led you to assume that distance.

SARTRE: Camus wrote a letter breaking off relations.

DE BEAUVOIR: When he called you Monsieur le Directeur, obviously.

SARTRE: As for Aron, it was the whole business of Gaullism and a dialogue on the radio. We had one hour on the radio every week to discuss the political situation, and we had been very violent against de Gaulle. Some Gaullists wanted to reply to me face to face, particularly Bénouville and another whose name I forget. So I went to the studio. We were not to meet until the dialogue began. Aron appeared —I think I'd picked him to arbitrate between us, being sure, I may say, that he would take my side—and he pretended not to see me. He joined the others. It was comprehensible that he should join them, but not that he should drop me. It was from that moment that I realized that Aron was against me on the political plane. I looked upon his solidarity with the Gaullists against me as a break. There has always been a strong reason behind my breaks, but in the end it was always I who made the decision to part. Aron, for example. I had been seeing him since his return from London, but gradually you and I came to feel that he wasn't at all on our side. My last try was this business on the radio, but for some while we had not been at all in agreement with him in our conversations. A separation was called for. That separation was brought about by a quarrel. For example, he didn't work on *Les Temps modernes* with us.

DE BEAUVOIR: He had begun by doing so. But come, that brings us to something we haven't spoken about at all. Among your relations with men there have been those with the team of *Les Temps modernes*.

SARTRE: That team now represents my best friends.

DE BEAUVOIR: Today's team. But what about when it began?

SARTRE: At the beginning there were people I knew only slightly, people who had come because I had a certain fame.

DE BEAUVOIR: And because of links formed during the Resistance.

SARTRE: There was Aron, there was a Gaullist . . .

DE BEAUVOIR: There was Ollivier, Leiris, you and I . . .

SARTRE: Camus refused to join us, which I understand perfectly well. He wasn't required to form part of a collective body.

DE BEAUVOIR: It was after all a very odd, uneven group and it broke up fairly quickly in the end. But later on there were times when there were a great many of us, and we used to meet in your bedroom.

SARTRE: Ah, later on it was not only the leaders who met, but a whole team of people who wrote in every number or who chose the texts for every number.

DE BEAUVOIR: How did you feel about those meetings, then?

SARTRE: I felt them as something very free, in which agreeable people came to explain their point of view on this or that, or on some given part of the review.

DE BEAUVOIR: Would you like to say something about your relations with the present *Temps modernes* team?

SARTRE: Most of the people on the present team have been with the review from the beginning. Bost and Pouillon were there at the start. Lanzmann came later, at the time of the Sunday meetings in my apartment.

DE BEAUVOIR: He came in '52. What about Horst?

SARTRE: Horst, from the beginning.

DE BEAUVOIR: And then there was—it wasn't a quarrel—but let's say a parting from Pingaud and Pontalis. Why did they leave?

SARTRE: We disagreed about psychoanalysis. That was always a rather delicate subject.

DE BEAUVOIR: Nowadays we accept a great many things from psychoanalysis, but we don't like the way psychoanalysts work at present or the kind of oppression that they make the patient undergo. That was one of the reasons, but there was another behind it. Your attitude was much more radical than theirs.

SARTRE: Certainly more radical than Pontalis's and Pingaud's. We disagreed when the piece on "L'Homme au magnétophone" (The Man with the Tape Recorder) was published.

DE BEAUVOIR: But there were also Horst's lead articles on the state teaching system for which they didn't like to accept responsibility, finding them far too radical.

SARTRE: Yes, and in any case Pontalis was not suited to this kind of review. He was too bourgeois. In politics he maintained a much more bourgeois theory, and he considered that what radicalism he possessed should go into psychoanalysis and his studies of it. And then Pingaud was politically hostile.

DE BEAUVOIR: Earlier he had been right wing. He and Boutang wrote a book against you. Then he moved to the Left, but even so something of his past still clung to him. But to come back to the team as a whole, you said, "They are my best friends." Could you be more specific?

SARTRE: Well, there's Bost, whom I've known forever—well over thirty years, nearly forty. They are old friends there.

DE BEAUVOIR: They are old friends, but they are all at least ten years younger than you. That has evened out a little now, but at the beginning it made a great difference. Bost had been your pupil. Horst, no. But he was, as it were, your disciple, since he had pondered deeply over your writings. Lanzmann wasn't a former pupil either.

SARTRE: But from the point of view of age he could have been.

DE BEAUVOIR: Have you anything to say about your relations with them all?

SARTRE: Politics has played a part . . .

DE BEAUVOIR: Generally speaking, there has been a strong identity of political views between us all.

SARTRE: Except that now I am much closer to the Maoists, and it can't be said that Pouillon or Bost are Maos.

DE BEAUVOIR: But to come back to the group, what is it that links you to them? Is it a long story?

SARTRE: There's a genuine friendship, one that does not take the shape of violent emotion but that does mean I can rely on them, as they can rely on me. We have genuine feelings for one another. Since the departure of Pingaud and Pontalis I feel that the group is pretty homogeneous.

DE BEAUVOIR: Yes, very homogeneous. Of course there are arguments about this or that; and generally speaking, when a decision has to be made there may be a slight hesitation—shall I vote? shall I abstain? But there are disagreements of the kind that there might be between you and me. It's not at all fundamental. So there's a shared past and a very close political basis.

SARTRE: The fact is that I am much attached to them.

DE BEAUVOIR: There is a cultural identity . . .

SARTRE: We have fun together too . . .

DE BEAUVOIR: And there are philosophical affinities also. Horst and Pouillon are extremely well acquainted with your thought, and there is really an identity not only of political but also of cultural and philosophical views. Anyhow, you do like being at the *Temps modernes* Wednesday meetings, don't you?

SARTRE: Yes, I like seeing them again; it's very pleasant. I'm not always there, however.

DE BEAUVOIR: Broadly speaking, it amounts to a warmer connection than you've had with men in your life as a whole. Which doesn't mean that politically you may not be nearer to some others. But with the Maoists there's the question of age, which makes a great difference.

SARTRE: Yes, but I always like the young better than the old. In this case it's not a question of liking them better, but when I talk to a leading Mao who's not yet thirty, I'm more at my ease than I am with a fellow of fifty or sixty. Anyhow, we know how I met the Maos and we'll talk about them again later.

DE BEAUVOIR: At this point I'm talking on the plane of friendship, the plane of emotional relations with men.

SARTRE: Most of the Maos have no friendship for me nor have I for them. We do the work together, we meet to write things, we make decisions together. There's one I feel a real friendship for and that's Victor, who comes to see me once or twice a week. We discuss the current political situation, we decide on what is to be done, and above all I listen while he tells me what he's been doing. He was the head of the G.P., but the Maoist party in France has almost vanished, and now Victor is alone. He talks things over with me—you saw the little book we wrote together with Gavi.

DE BEAUVOIR: But you see him alone as well, just the two of you.

SARTRE: I see him once or twice a week. I like him, I'm very fond of him. I know he's not to everybody's taste, but I think he's intelligent. My relations with him are as much cultural as political, since he possesses a genuine culture and one that happens to connect with mine. Then again I'm in agreement with him on a certain number of political points of view that I'll talk about later. And it's pleasant, having these relations with a man of twenty-nine.

DE BEAUVOIR: Now that brings us to the question I'd like to ask you. Why do you favor the young? There are people who loathe them. Koestler was one who did, and Merleau-Ponty wasn't so very fond of them, either. Why is it that you, on the other hand, have what might be called a prejudice in favor of the young? Why do you like being with them?

SARTRE: Because on hundreds of points their thought and their life are not completely formed. A discussion with them is like a discussion between two people who have each a rather vague opinion and who try to bring their points of view nearer to one another. With old people it's completely different. They have a clear-cut opinion; I have another. It is known, it is taken into account, and when we talk things over, we set aside those aspects on which we disagree without any hope of reconciling them.

DE BEAUVOIR: Horst is very intelligent, Horst is very close to you politically. Yet you much prefer having a tête-à-tête with Victor than with Horst. Why?

SARTRE: Horst has a very intelligent system of thought that he forms for himself, and having done so he comes and talks to me. But what I like is for people not to have fixed, decided opinions. When I talk to people who are less formed than I am on some given point, who are less cultivated or who have reflected less, I can help them. On the other hand there are points on which they know more—there's one thing that it's obvious Victor knows better than I do, and that's the struggle within a party and the leadership of a party. All that is pretty well outside my range, but there are other points of view on which I can give him my considered opinion, and then when he's analyzed it and made it a part of his conception of the party, he accepts it. For example, in the dialogues with Victor and Gavi I produced some ideas, particularly that of the free militant, the idea of what discussion between free men really means. That is, something other than the Communist militant for whom that kind of freedom does not exist.

DE BEAUVOIR: In other words you feel more effective, more useful, when you're talking to young people whose minds are still quite open than when you're talking to adults who are already formed, even if their ideas are close to your own? Because it gives you a feeling of rejuvenation when you are with the young?

SARTRE: No. I don't feel old. I don't feel different from what I was at thirty-five.

DE BEAUVOIR: That's interesting. It's something we must come back to, your feeling of age.

SARTRE: I've never felt old. And since physically I don't look like the stock old man—I don't have a white beard, I don't have a white moustache; I have no beard or moustache at all—I therefore still see myself as I was at thirty-five.

DE BEAUVOIR: So talking to the young doesn't make you feel younger. That's unlike me, because I do feel my age and talking to young women does rejuvenate me. The other day you told me that you thought you had not gone far enough in the analysis of your relations with men. What would you like to add on the subject?

SARTRE: In the first place I should say that many of them—not those who are at present my best friends—have confided in me. That is, they saw me as someone to whom what is more or less secret in each of us was to be entrusted; and it was horribly boring. I submitted; I had to, because that way I could influence them, being the one who knew their secret, but I didn't like it.

DE BEAUVOIR: But where? Who? Be a little more specific. Did you receive confidences at the Ecole Normale?

SARTRE: Yes, but there it was different—they put their cards on the table and so did I. But I was thinking of the comrade I had in Alsace during the war, a soldier who confided in me. The relations between him and me were like that—they were confidential.

DE BEAUVOIR: What were his confidences about? His wife? His life?

SARTRE: That's it. He had no wife, but he did have a woman. He talked about her. The emotional bond created by his looking upon me as the person who knew about his life and with whom he talked about things that I was to remember afterward seemed to me unbearable.

DE BEAUVOIR: Why? People have often confided in me in the course of my life, and on the whole I've found it amusing.

SARTRE: Because it shifts the relationship; it is no longer the same. You are caught; you have to give advice. The other relies on you, refers to you, has a kind of respect for the person who receives his confidences. In the end I was becoming what I don't want to be, the master with his disciples, and I didn't like being confided in. I didn't seek out confidences. I didn't refuse them when they were made, but I didn't seek them.

DE BEAUVOIR: Former pupils who confided in you and asked you for advice—yes, indeed, that's happened quite often.

SARTRE: And others too. I've received a great many confidences.

DE BEAUVOIR: In other words, the role of "master," to whom people come for advice and to confide in, bored you into the ground?

SARTRE: And it didn't appear to me fair.

DE BEAUVOIR: Why? Because when it happened you felt old? And you didn't want to be? Or because it didn't put you on equal footing with them?

SARTRE: It didn't put me on an equal footing, and after all no one can give advice to anyone. All right, if it's you in relation to me or me in relation to you, then of course advice can be given. I could give advice to Bost or Victor, because of the intimacy that is between us. But in principle you can't because you lack various factors—factors that the other man lacks too, by the way. He says things, and through the things he says you have to try to make out what his real position is; and the advice should coincide with that position.

DE BEAUVOIR: Very true. Usually it's that advice he's trying to get himself given. Not always, but usually. So that's one of the things that hampered your relations with other men, is it?

SARTRE: Certainly.

DE BEAUVOIR: Whereas if women confided in you, it didn't worry you?

SARTRE: It didn't worry me at all. On the contrary, in that case I wanted to be confided in.

DE BEAUVOIR: Was that out of machismo? Was it because a woman is naturally the weaker vessel and must confide in a man?

SARTRE: I don't know if it's machismo, because I thought that on the contrary most men didn't listen to what women said.

DE BEAUVOIR: I think that refusing men's confidences with such distaste and accepting women's is a certain form of machismo.

SARTRE: I didn't refuse men's; I just didn't like them. And then again the relations were different. We'll talk about that again later.

DE BEAUVOIR: Very well: men's confidences displeased you, and not only confidences but all close personal connections I think. Although when Giacometti told very personal stories . . . they weren't confidences.

SARTRE: I see no harm in being told personal stories, far from it. When Giacometti told how he went to the brothel looking for the rather slatternly, rather ugly woman for various reasons it was very entertaining.

DE BEAUVOIR: Go on telling me about your relations with men. We've established your refusal of confidences.

SARTRE: On the other hand, although I think and say that relations should be those of equality, I did encourage a kind of way of addressing me as though I were the knowing one, and that clearly was not fair.

DE BEAUVOIR: How do you mean?

SARTRE: There was a point at which people said, shall I do this? shall I do that? And I gave advice.

DE BEAUVOIR: You're saying two things that contradict one another. You're saying that you loathed giving advice and that you liked being asked for it, aren't you?

SARTRE: No, but I did like giving the little push that in fact turned me into an adviser. It's not contradictory. That's how they were, relations with the Other—a curious mixture. Fundamentally, I've always been in relation with the Other, but it has been an abstract relation. I live beneath the consciousness of the Other, who watches me. And that consciousness could just as well be God, if you like, as Bost. It is a being other than myself, a being that is formed as I am formed and that sees me. I think of it like that.

DE BEAUVOIR: And what bearing has this on your relations with men?

SARTRE: They are all manifestations of that consciousness.

DE BEAUVOIR: You mean witnesses, judges?

SARTRE: Judges to some extent. But very benevolent judges.

DE BEAUVOIR: You say benevolent judges, yet you have had enemies, people who were against you.

SARTRE: But that doesn't count. When people are on good terms with me, I see that kind of wider consciousness that watches me reflected through them.

DE BEAUVOIR: And does that trouble you, or do you like having these witnesses?

SARTRE: On the whole I like it. Because if it troubled me I'd want to be alone, and that kind of solitude is absurd.

DE BEAUVOIR: You say that you have always been rather distant, rather indifferent in your relations with men. Yet you've never been a misanthrope, a recluse. You've always lived very much in the society of others; you've been very sociable except during the times you're writing. But you've never liked fashionable sociability!

SARTRE: No.

DE BEAUVOIR: Just after the war you used to go to Gallimard's cocktail parties, which were amusing; but in fact you've never been fashionable.

SARTRE: I've dined out grandly three times in my life. I ate in restaurants and I lived in cafés, and just three times I dined with fairly well-known people who invited me.

DE BEAUVOIR: We've talked about your relations with the young. Have you had any with people older than yourself? What effect did it have on you?

SARTRE: None whatsoever. Yes, I had contacts—very few I may say —with older men. Paulhan, Gide, and Jouhandeau, whom I saw very little and who no doubt does not even remember it.

DE BEAUVOIR: You scarcely met him.

SARTRE: No, but it's all evidence. These relations with people older than myself did exist. I adopted a somewhat self-effacing attitude and I listened to them; they spoke to me as they saw fit. But these were relations of strict politeness and they didn't correspond to anything much. I didn't look upon these men as wiser than myself just because they were older. They were exactly like me, and they told me what they had to tell and I did the same for them. For example, I remember Gide talking to me about a Dutchman in '46, a Dutchman who had come to ask him for an address. . . . He was a married man who found that he had homosexual inclinations and he came to ask for an address. I remember it now. Gide was sitting there. He told me about all this, and you would have said he took me for a pederast in spite of the mistake I had made in speaking of advice, whereas it was a question of something else.

DE BEAUVOIR: You said to him, "Did he come to ask you for advice?" and Gide replied, "No! For addresses." Could it not also be said that in a way the adult male is something like "your bad smell," as Genet would say?

SARTRE: Yes, perhaps. I don't like them. I don't like them at all, and I don't like being called one. Indeed, since I belong to old age I'm not an adult anymore, and although I'm still male, I'm only very faintly so.

DE BEAUVOIR: Yes, be specific about this. It's interesting.

SARTRE: I find the adult male deeply disgusting. What I really like is a young man, insofar as a young man is not entirely different from a young woman. It's not that I'm a pederast, but the fact is that at present young men and young women are not so very different in their clothes, their way of talking, and their way of behaving. Indeed, they've never been so very different as far as I'm concerned.

DE BEAUVOIR: When you have really personal relations, friendships, the adult male doesn't appear as such—he's Genet, he's Giacometti, or someone else. But if you come across man in general . . .

SARTRE: He is the adult male.

DE BEAUVOIR: And that's what you don't want to be.

SARTRE: Yes. That's certain.

DE BEAUVOIR: Why not? Even the term I use makes you give a little smile of disgust.

SARTRE: Because it distinguishes between the sexes in an odious, comic fashion. The male is the one with a little tube between his legs —that's how I see him—and therefore there ought to be the adult female in contrast with him. And male and female is a somewhat primitive sexuality—generally speaking, there are things over and above that. In itself that's a matter of some importance.

DE BEAUVOIR: I think there's also the word adult.

SARTRE: There's the word adult which implies that you've finished your education, that you've reached the kind of calling that is suitable for an adult, that you have your own views, that you've formed the opinions that you will retain all your life—it's part of your honor to retain them.

DE BEAUVOIR: Yes, indeed, to form, to shut in, to limit, and so on. Besides, there's something else that goes in the same direction. With regard to men and women, to mankind in general, you have an ambivalent attitude that is the opposite of mine. Perhaps that's why I find it so curious, by the way. That is, you are very free and open when someone comes to talk to you—at the Coupole, let's say, when someone comes to ask you something. For my part, I'm disagreeable. I always feel inclined to send them packing. But as for you, you're very welcoming. You readily make appointments and you readily give your time, you're generous, you're open, and yet when you have to ask the way in the street it's frightful. If I say to you, "I'm going to ask someone. We're lost in Naples and I'm going to ask where such-and-such a street is," you don't like it at all. You grow dogged. Why this welcoming attitude on the one hand, and at the same time that other attitude of almost hate-filled refusal?

SARTRE: In the first case it's people who come to ask me for something, who come to expound a point of view, or who want some of my time. But where information is concerned, it is they who give it to me and I who listen. It is the complete opposite of the first case. I am the one who is asking someone else where a street is . . .

DE BEAUVOIR: After all, asking someone for the name of a street or for a trifling service is putting oneself on the plane of reciprocity. It is recognizing him as your equal, as anyone at all, like yourself; so it is not begging like a beggar. Why do you have this attitude of reserve, of refusal, when it's no more than asking the way?

SARTRE: It obviously means addressing oneself to the other's subjectivity, and my action is determined by his reply. If he tells me I must turn left, I turn left; if he tells me I must turn right, I turn right. And it is the contact with the other's subjectivity that I like to reduce to the minimum.

DE BEAUVOIR: What he replies will have little of the subjective about it. He will reply almost like a map.

SARTRE: Never mind! He'll say to himself, "Why, here's a fellow who is asking me this." He'll say, "I don't remember exactly where it is, but still . . ." You discover a man's subjective psychology when you ask him a question. You have a subjective relation with him.

DE BEAUVOIR: You mean you put yourself in a dependent state?

SARTRE: Yes, for one thing. And what is more important, I don't much care for another's subjectivity. Except in the case of certain clearly defined persons whom I'm fond of, because then it has a meaning.

DE BEAUVOIR: Yet even so, when you say you are no matter who, as good as no matter who, it implies that you experience your relations with men in a kind of translucidity or transparence, so that if you are asked for a service you provide it, and if it is necessary for you to ask, then you ask. What's more, there are people who do manage things like that.

SARTRE: Absolutely, and they are right! That's how things ought to be. Formerly with me it was shyness, and then it became a habit. But now I'm no longer like that at all.

DE BEAUVOIR: Nevertheless, there is still a kind of stiffening at the idea that anyone might do you the slightest service—the waiter going twice to bring you something, for example, although that's his job. There's a kind of rigor that looks like a remnant of your old hatred for mankind.

SARTRE: It's quite true. Although I'm neither clever nor handy, I always prefer to manage by myself rather than ask anyone for anything. I don't like being helped. I find the idea of help quite unbearable.

DE BEAUVOIR: What kind of help?

SARTRE: Any kind at all. I mean help from people I'm scarcely acquainted with. I've not asked for much help in my life.

DE BEAUVOIR: No, but the other day I lost my money, for example: I didn't have time to change any, and quite naturally I told the hotel manager about it. He lent me two hundred thousand lire. I'm sure that if I had said to you, "I'm going to borrow two hundred thousand lire from the hotel manager"—we being old customers and they not giving a damn, since we would certainly repay them the next day—you would have said, "Ah no. I wouldn't like that at all."

SARTRE: No, I wouldn't have gone as far as that. Perhaps I might have done so ten or fifteen years ago, but not now. Indeed, I would have advised you to borrow.

DE BEAUVOIR: Even so I'd like you to give some explanation of the stiffness you have with people in general. It's perfectly understandable that one wouldn't want to be asking for help all the time or to be clinging to others, but why such a degree of reluctance? Is it perhaps connected with your childhood?

SARTRE: Yes. There was too much asking other people to do things. It used to be said, "They can certainly be useful; you only have to ask and they'll do it." My feeling was rather that asking a favor irritated people. I certainly have the impression of annoying the person if I ask for information. I remember a character you said was like me . . .

DE BEAUVOIR: Michaux's M. Plume.

SARTRE: M. Plume is perpetually irritated and harassed by other people. There is certainly something of that in me.

DE BEAUVOIR: Yes. That was just why you reminded me of M. Plume —your way of suffocating although no one prevents you from opening a window. Michaux's M. Plume was exactly like that.

SARTRE: I used to think people were hostile.

DE BEAUVOIR: Hostile to whom?

SARTRE: To me if I were to ask for anything.

DE BEAUVOIR: Hostile, therefore, to people in general?

SARTRE: As to the others, I don't know, since they had their own way of asking.

DE BEAUVOIR: Why hostile to you? To you as an anonymous passerby?

SARTRE: Because it's linked to an image of myself; I thought people did not find me physically agreeable. Perhaps it was there that the feeling of being ugly took refuge—a feeling that I did not worry about much, although it existed.

DE BEAUVOIR: You're not so ugly that you would make a pregnant woman run away if you asked her the way to the Rue de Rome . . .

SARTRE: No, I never thought I was. But it's reasonable to think that if you're ugly, then asking the way to the Rue de Rome means inflicting a disagreeable presence on the person you ask.

DE BEAUVOIR: It must be a childhood thing. Because we mustn't exaggerate—you're not uglier than the majority of men.

SARTRE: Yes I am, since I have a squint.

DE BEAUVOIR: They aren't so very handsome.

SARTRE: No, men aren't handsome, in general.

DE BEAUVOIR: But really, for such a trifling thing as that . . .

SARTRE: Yet it must count. There must have been a connection between others and me when I was young, in which the others were the essential and I the secondary element.

DE BEAUVOIR: It's always like that when you're very young. Unless you adopt an attitude of complete aggression toward things.

SARTRE: Which wasn't the case with me. No, I didn't like going into a classroom as a new boy; I didn't like it, and I didn't like the boys who were there. Later we came to know one another and we got along, but at first I saw them as hostile.

DE BEAUVOIR: That is, you had the sensation of an a priori hostility when you first entered a group? Did you also feel that when you went to your military service? At Saint Cyr, I mean, because afterward there were very few of you.

SARTRE: Yes, certainly.

DE BEAUVOIR: Not when you joined the Ecole Normale, because there you already knew . . .

SARTRE: No. I did know some, but on the whole there was hostility. Ordinarily, the person who looks at me as we pass in the street is hostile.

DE BEAUVOIR: These are very important factors for the explanation of a general attitude. I remember when I had had my bicycle accident and looked really hideous, going into a shop, talking to the shopkeeper, and saying to myself, "My God, what a frightful handicap it must be, to feel ugly!" It's so pleasant to feel that one is an attractive young woman. I didn't think I was particularly beautiful—I was about thirty—it was an a priori relation, almost a relation of charm. I'd gone to buy a loaf, and I thought my presence pleased people. I said to myself, "My God, how being disfigured for life must change relations—it must make a very subtle change, very difficult to describe."

SARTRE: Yes. Only I must admit that then you were uglier than I am at ordinary times.

DE BEAUVOIR: Naturally, but that's not what I meant. Besides, now I am old I certainly don't experience relations with people in the same way as I did when I was thirty.

SARTRE: Of course. I myself have never felt that I was agreeable to look at.

DE BEAUVOIR: I meant to speak of a way of being at ease in relation to others.

SARTRE: That's exactly what I haven't known.

DE BEAUVOIR: There are certainly many reasons other than a lack of beauty for your not having known it, since in the first place you weren't ugly.

SARTRE: Yes I was, but it shouldn't have worried me much.

DE BEAUVOIR: These are certainly complexes from childhood and adolescence. When that girl said, "Ugly fool," it must have marked you deeply.

SARTRE: Yes, and then again it's connected with my mother's remarriage and my life at La Rochelle.

DE BEAUVOIR: Once again I say it's odd, this contrast between your stiffness and a welcoming attitude, a kindness, a warmth as soon as . . .

SARTRE: As soon as anyone turns to me to ask for something, it vanishes.

DE BEAUVOIR: Yes, because at that moment you are acknowledged. We're talking in the present today, but it's not the present that is interesting. It was when you were forty, when you were fifty that this

289

contrast was so striking. You have retained something of it, but on the whole it's left behind. These are attitudes that have to be described because they struck me when you were much younger.

DE BEAUVOIR: Let's talk about your relations with women. What would you like to say about them?

SARTRE: They were the object of a great deal of show and fuss, of play-acting and of charm on my part, either in dreams or in reality, from childhood. As early as six or seven I already had fiancées, as people used to say. At Vichy I had four or five, and at Arcachon I was very fond of a little girl who was a consumptive and who died the next year. I was six—it was the time when I was photographed in a little painted wooden boat with a spade—and I showed off to this little girl who was so charming but who died. I used to sit next to her wheel-chair. She remained lying down all the time, being tubercular.

DE BEAUVOIR: Did it grieve you when she died? Did it impress you?

SARTRE: I don't remember. What I do remember is that I had written her poems, and on this occasion I sent some to my grandfather in letters to him. They were utterly impossible poems.

DE BEAUVOIR: The poems of a child.

SARTRE: Of a six-year-old child with no sense of rhythm. In short, I wrote poems. In addition to that there were girls all over the place with whom I had little contact but an idea of amorous relations nevertheless.

DE BEAUVOIR: And what gave you that particular idea? Did it come from your reading?

SARTRE: Undoubtedly. Yet I've one memory—though it's no doubt a memory shared with many boys—of when I was five. My parents and grandparents had left me with a little girl in Switzerland, on the shores of the lake. And I stayed in the bedroom with her. We looked at the lake out of the window and we played doctor. I was the doctor, she was the patient, and I gave her an enema. She pulled down her little drawers and all the rest followed. I even had an instrument—I think it must have been a nozzle I used for giving myself clysters—and I gave her one. That's a sexual memory dating from when I was five.

DE BEAUVOIR: Did the little girl like it? Did it amuse her?

SARTRE: In any case she let me do it. And I think it did amuse her. Then up until about nine I had relations in which I acted the part of the great talker, the seducer. I didn't know how seduction took place, but I'd read in books that one could be a good seducer. I thought you did it by talking about the stars, by putting your arm round a girl's waist or shoulders and using enchanted words to tell her about the beauty of the world. And then in Paris I had a puppet show made up of several little characters that fitted over one's hand. I used to carry it to the Luxembourg Gardens, slip my hand into the characters, settle myself behind a chair, and contrive a stage on which I made my characters act. My audience was female—little girls of the neighborhood who came there in the afternoons. Naturally, I cast my choice on this one or on that. This didn't last even until I was nine. More like seven or eight. After that—and did it arise from the fact that I became really ugly and therefore no longer interesting?—in any case toward the age of eight, and then for some years, I had no contacts with the little girls in the streets or gardens at all. Besides at that period, toward ten or twelve, it grows more dubious to the parents. It causes little scenes, little fusses. Perhaps that was the reason. Then again there were young women around my mother and grandmother, young women of my mother's age who were often pupils of my grandfather or his friends, and I had a certain amount of contact with them.

DE BEAUVOIR: You mean you found women of your mother's age attractive? Some of them at least?

SARTRE: Yes. Only I couldn't imagine playing the fiancé's part with women who were twenty years older. They used to caress me. It was above all with women that my first feelings of sensuality developed.

DE BEAUVOIR: With grown women rather than with little girls?

SARTRE: Yes. I was fond of the little girls. They were the real playmates spontaneously chosen, but there wasn't much sensuality between us. They weren't formed, whereas women's forms, their breasts and buttocks, interested me when I was very young. They used to fondle me, and I loved that. I recall one young woman who has left me two contradictory memories. She was a fine upstanding girl of eighteen and therefore much too old for my little games of husband and wife, yet between us there was a husband and wife relation. Perhaps she played the game out of kindness and amiability. I thought her beautiful and I was quite smitten. I was seven at that time and she was eighteen. It was in Alsace.

DE BEAUVOIR: And what about when you were a little older, when you were ten or twelve?

SARTRE: Nothing happened. Until the age of eleven I was at the Lycée

Henri IV. I saw only my mother's friends and very few little girls. And then when I was eleven I left for La Rochelle. My stepfather's circle of friends and his attitude toward life made it impossible for me to have any contacts with little girls. He thought that at my age I ought to have relations with boys. My friends should be the boys who were at the lycée with me. My parents only knew the prefect, the mayor, and some engineers—people like that—and it so happened that none of them had young daughters. So at La Rochelle I was totally lost, and all I had was some vague feeling for two or three of my mother's friends, but that didn't amount to much. I certainly did have a fairly sexual feeling for my mother. When I was thirteen or fourteen I had mastoid trouble and I was operated on. I stayed three weeks in a nursing-home room and my mother had a bed set up beside me, a bed at right angles to mine. When I was going to sleep in the evening she undressed, and she probably showed herself almost naked. I stayed awake with my eyes half closed so as to see her undressed through my eyelids. By the way, my schoolfellows must have found her to their taste, because from time to time when they listed the feminine objects or the women they liked, they would include my mother.

At La Rochelle I did have one experience with little Lisette Joirisse, a ship chandler's pretty young daughter. She used to walk along the La Rochelle quay, the inner quay, and I thought her very beautiful. She knew she was beautiful because lots of boys ran after her. I told my friends I should like to meet Lisette Joirisse and they said it was easy. Then one day they told me that all I had to do was to go up to her on the promenade. And indeed there she was, surrounded by several boys who were talking to her. I was with some friends on the other side of the promenade. I couldn't figure out what to do. She had been told, and she saw that she could get nothing amusing out of me if she stayed with the others. So she set off on her bicycle along the alleys and I followed. Nothing came of it, but the next day, when I was moving toward her, she turned in my direction and there, in front of my friends, she said, "Old fool, with his spectacles and his big hat." These words plunged me into anger and despair. I saw her two or three times after that. Once a friend who didn't want me to be first in Greek composition said she would be waiting for me at eleven o'clock. The Greek exam ran from eight to twelve, so I would have to turn in my paper at a quarter to eleven. This I did, and my marks were deplorable. Of course there was no one waiting for me at the appointed place. And then another time I saw her on the pier, jumping down from it onto the sand. I stood stupidly beside her, but I did not know how to talk to her and I said nothing. She saw I was there but she went on playing, wondering whether I was going to say something foolish or not.

DE BEAUVOIR: Did you never exchange any words with her? No walk, no conversation, no games?

SARTRE: Nothing at any time.

DE BEAUVOIR: You never had any relations with her?

SARTRE: None whatsoever.

DE BEAUVOIR: Were there any other girls at La Rochelle you paid attention to?

SARTRE: Two friends and I courted the daughter of a woman who was an usher in a movie theater. We had made her acquaintance and she was much more interested in Pelletier and Boutiller, who were quite good-looking boys, than in me, but still she did meet us all three. It didn't go far. We talked to her, we saw her home, and that was all. I talked to her like the two others. We went to the movies, and as her mother worked there she came and sat next to us and talked too. As far as I remember she was very beautiful, but nothing came of it. I was probably not a highly gifted seducer. I think those were the only two feminine episodes that existed for me up until the age of fifteen, when I left La Rochelle to go to the Lycée Henri IV in Paris. My grandfather insisted that I should work for my *bachot*** there. I could just as well have passed it at La Rochelle, but he thought the change might do me good. And indeed, my first years as a boarder in Paris made an immense change and I had the prize for general excellence, which there was no likelihood of my winning at La Rochelle.

DE BEAUVOIR: Let's go back to women. How were things in Paris?

SARTRE: In Paris I became aware of a vague homosexual inclination. I ventured to take boys' trousers off in the dormitories.

DE BEAUVOIR: It was a very slight inclination.

SARTRE: But it was there. Was it that year I took some remote cousin of Nizan's to the Louvre? She wasn't very pretty, and I don't think she found me very charming.

DE BEAUVOIR: But you had a program in your mind. A young man was to have affairs with women—that was a well-established fact.

---

* *Bachot = baccalauréat*, the certificate of graduation, as well as the university entrance examination. It was formerly in two parts. (trans.)

SARTRE: Yes, certainly. And then later, as a writer, I was to have amorous relations with scores of women, together with passions, etcetera. I learned that from the books devoted to the great writers.

DE BEAUVOIR: And did your friends—Nizan, for example—have the same program, and did they follow it?

SARTRE: Exactly the same program. They followed it only approximately, because they were very young.

DE BEAUVOIR: And not very rich. But still they did have the idea.

SARTRE: They were in love with Mme Chadel, for example, the mother of one of the boys at school whom we often used to make fun of. I don't think I had any important affairs in the first form.

DE BEAUVOIR: And after?

SARTRE: Nor in philo either.

DE BEAUVOIR: And when did you go to bed with a woman for the first time?

SARTRE: The following year. I was at the Lycée Louis le Grand. I'd passed the second *bachot* at Henri IV. There was an excellent khâgne there with Alain as teacher of philosophy, and I don't know why they took me away. They shoved me into Louis le Grand, where there was a solemn, boring khâgne in which I remained and from which I went to the Ecole Normale. It's complicated. To begin with there was a woman from Thiviers, a physician's wife. One day, I never knew why, she came to see me at the lycée. I said I was a boarder and she said that was a pity, but didn't I go out on Thursday and Sundays? I said yes and she made a rendezvous with me for two o'clock the next Thursday afternoon in an apartment belonging to a woman she was friends with. I accepted, not quite understanding. I did understand that she wanted to have physical relations with me, but I couldn't really see why, since I didn't feel that she thought me attractive.

DE BEAUVOIR: But when you knew her at Thiviers earlier, hadn't there been anything between you?

SARTRE: Nothing.

DE BEAUVOIR: Had you known her long?

SARTRE: No. Her coming to the lycée surprised me very much indeed. I can't tell you what was going on in her mind. I kept the appointment and she gave me to understand that we could go to bed together.

DE BEAUVOIR: How old was she?

SARTRE: Thirty. And I was eighteen. I did it with no great enthusiasm because she wasn't very pretty. That is, she wasn't bad—I had managed quite well, and she seemed pleased.

DE BEAUVOIR: Did she come back?

SARTRE: No.

DE BEAUVOIR: So perhaps she wasn't as pleased as all that. She didn't make another rendezvous with you?

SARTRE: No, she was leaving the next day. In other words she came to find me at the lycée in order to be made love to. And then she went back home.

DE BEAUVOIR: You never heard from her again?

SARTRE: Perhaps she didn't know where I was. I've never understood this business at all. I tell it just as it happened. It was that year or the next that I took to meeting friends from Henri IV in the Luxembourg when I went out on Thursdays. They used to meet girls, girls from the Saint Michel neighborhood and especially the daughter of the Lycée Henri IV concierge. We met them, we went out with them—I was a boarder—we fondled them a little, and then almost all of them would make a rendezvous in a room and we would make love with them. I personally went to bed with a girl I remember as being pretty; she must have been eighteen. She went to bed easily.

DE BEAUVOIR: Did you have an affair with her, or was that too only the one time?

SARTRE: The one time; but it was the same with the others. She was very kind to me both after and before, so she hadn't been disappointed; she hadn't been looking for something I didn't give her. She was pleased with things as they were.

DE BEAUVOIR: Why was it that for both you and your friends things didn't continue, last longer?

SARTRE: Because we had a sort of contempt for these girls.

DE BEAUVOIR: Why?

SARTRE: We felt that a girl shouldn't give herself like that.

DE BEAUVOIR: Oh, I see! Because you had a sexual morality! That's pretty amusing, when you come to think of it!

SARTRE: We compared the daughters of our mothers' friends with the girls we just picked up, and the daughters of the bourgeois were of course virgins. Although you might vaguely flirt with them, it never went much further than a kiss on the lips, if indeed it reached that point. Whereas with the others, if things worked out you could go to bed with them.

DE BEAUVOIR: And like the worthy little bourgeois you all were, you disapproved of that?

SARTRE: Yes. We didn't exactly disapprove of it, but . . .

DE BEAUVOIR: You were happy to take advantage of it and at the same time you had the idea, "You don't marry your mistress." Marriage was very far away from you but still, according to you, a girl oughtn't to do that. It was rather you—I mean you and your friends—who held back. You didn't want liaisons with these girls, did you?

SARTRE: There was something of that, yes.

DE BEAUVOIR: When did you lose the stupid notion that girls who went to bed freely and easily were more or less whores?

SARTRE: Oh, very soon; as soon as I had lain with a few women I no longer took it like that. It was only at that period, when I was still at the lycée.

DE BEAUVOIR: Still very deeply marked by a bourgeois upbringing.

SARTRE: Absolutely. As soon as I went to the Ecole Normale it was over.

DE BEAUVOIR: These were purely sexual little capers. Were there any others before the first big affair?

SARTRE: No.

DE BEAUVOIR: I know all about the relations with Camille, with your fiancée, and with a few Sorbonne girls. And then there was our affair, which was rather different.

SARTRE: Yes.

DE BEAUVOIR: But to understand your other relations with women we must not lose sight of it. We'll talk about it another time. What I'm going to ask you—seeing that at once, as soon as we met, you told me that you were polygamous and that you had no intention of confining yourself to a single woman, a single affair: this was understood and in fact you did have affairs—what I'd like to know is this. What was it that you found particularly attractive in the women in these affairs?

SARTRE: Anything at all!

DE BEAUVOIR: How do you mean?

SARTRE: As I saw it you possessed the qualities, the most important qualities that I could ask of women. That therefore set the other women free—they could be merely pretty, for example. What happened is that since you represented far more than I wanted to give to women, the others had less and so they committed less of themselves. In general, that is, because there were some who committed themselves a good deal. But on the whole things weren't like that.

DE BEAUVOIR: Still, your reply "anything at all" is very strange. It's as though the moment a woman happened to be within your reach, you were perfectly ready to have an affair with her.

SARTRE: My God . . .

DE BEAUVOIR: It's not the case, for women have sometimes flung themselves at your head and you have brushed them off. There have been quite a lot of women you have met and with whom you have not had affairs.

SARTRE: I dreamed a certain number of dreams, love dreams, that provided me with a kind of model. She was a blonde, and I've sometimes come across women in my life who were like her. But never in important affairs. Nevertheless, this figure is still there in my mind. She was a pretty blonde; she was dressed in little girl's clothes; I was a little older, and we were playing with a hoop by the Luxembourg pond.

DE BEAUVOIR: Is that a true story, or is it a story you dreamed?

SARTRE: No, it's . . . it's what I dreamed.

DE BEAUVOIR: Ah, I see! In short you dreamed about childhood loves.

SARTRE: No, these childhood loves stood for love itself. There I was, bare-legged and she in a little girl's frock, but it all represented events of the age I was at that time, that is, twenty. Do you understand? At twenty I was dreaming symbolically, playing hoops with a little girl.

DE BEAUVOIR: A little girl, and you yourself were a little boy.

SARTRE: In fact we were both of us older, and the game with the hoop represented sexual relations, probably because I saw the hoop and the stick as typical symbols. What's more, I felt that that was what they were as I was dreaming about them. It was a dream I had when I was about twenty. And in this dream there was no priority. The man was in no way superior to the woman; there was no machismo. Recently I've been thinking that men are without any doubt very deeply macho, but that doesn't mean that they wish to possess power. They think themselves superior to woman, but they mingle that with the notion of equality between men and women. It's very odd.

DE BEAUVOIR: That depends on what men you are talking about.

SARTRE: Well, many men. Most of the men we know. This doesn't mean that their conclusion may not be macho; but in conversation, in ordinary life, they make use of egalitarian formulas. They may say macho things without realizing it, and their egalitarian definition of the relation between the sexes doesn't amount to much in practice. Yet even so machismo is not something that men like to boast of, at least not those that we know. Yet obviously one ought to look at other circles, other milieus.

DE BEAUVOIR: But to come back to you, what was it that chiefly attracted you in women, and to what degree were you yourself egalitarian? To what degree did you play a certain role—let's say imperialist or protective—with regard to them?

SARTRE: I think I was always very protective and therefore imperialist. What's more, you've often blamed me for it, not with regard to you, but with regard to women I knew apart from you. It was not always like that, however, because my relations with the most outstanding of them were egalitarian and they would not have tolerated anything of another nature. But let's go back to what I looked for in women. I think it was above all an atmosphere of feeling, of sentiment. Not of sexuality properly so-called, but of feeling, with a sexual background.

DE BEAUVOIR: You had an affair in Berlin, for example. With someone you called the Moon Woman. What did you like about her?

SARTRE: I wonder.

DE BEAUVOIR: She wasn't very pretty, or very intelligent.

SARTRE: No.

DE BEAUVOIR: Wasn't it her rather lost aspect?

SARTRE: There was the lost side, and there was that of . . . that of a village way of talking, a village jargon, quite close to mine. She didn't exactly have our Montparnasse way of talking, but she did have that of the part round the Latin Quarter. That gave me the impression of a system of thought which, though basically less developed than ours, was nevertheless of the same nature. I was completely wrong, but that was the idea I had in my mind. It was rather a special case. Yes, I think that generally speaking I must have been macho, because I was brought up in a family of machos. My grandfather was macho.

DE BEAUVOIR: Civilization was macho.

SARTRE: Yet in my relations with these women it was not machismo that predominated. Obviously each had a part to play and mine was the more active and reasonable one; the woman's role was on the emotional plane. It's a very usual state of affairs, but I did not look upon that emotional side as inferior to the practice and exercise of reason. It was a question of different dispositions. That did not mean that women were not as capable of exercising reason as men, or that a woman could not be an engineer or a philosopher. It simply meant that most of the time a woman had emotional and sometimes sexual values; and it was that aggregate which I drew toward myself because I felt that having a connection with a woman like that was to some extent taking possessions of her affectivity. Trying to make her feel it for me, feel it deeply, meant possessing that affectivity—it was a quality that I was giving myself.

DE BEAUVOIR: In other words, you asked women to love you.

SARTRE: Yes. They had to love me for that sensibility to become something that belonged to me. When a woman gave herself to me I saw that sensibility on her face, in her expression; and seeing it on her face was like taking possession of it. Sometimes in my notes, sometimes in my books, I have stated—and I think it still—that sensibility and intelligence are not separated, that sensibility produces intelligence, or rather that it is also intelligence, and that in the end the rational man, taken up with theoretical problems, is an abstraction. I thought that one possessed a sensibility and that the task of childhood and adolescence was to cause this sensibility to become abstract, comprehensive, and enquiring, so that it should gradually turn into a man's reason, an intelligence working upon problems of an experimental nature.

DE BEAUVOIR: You mean that in women this sensibility was not diverted in favor of reason.

SARTRE: Yes, sometimes it was, when they were *agrégées* or engineers, and so on. They were perfectly capable of doing the same things as men; but a certain tendency, arising to begin with from their upbringing and then from their feelings, put affectivity first. And since for the most part they did not rise very high, because of the material and social relations of the kind of woman who is formed and maintained by society, they retained their sensibility unimpaired. This sensibility included an understanding of others. What about my relations with women from the intellectual point of view, then? I told them things that I thought. I was often misunderstood but at the same time I was understood by a sensibility that enriched my idea.

DE BEAUVOIR: Could you give examples? What kind of enrichment did it bring you?

SARTRE: An enrichment in specific, concrete cases. Emotional interpretations of what I was saying on an intellectual plane.

DE BEAUVOIR: Still, upon the whole you looked upon yourself as more intelligent than any of the women you had relations with.

SARTRE: More intelligent, yes. But I looked upon intelligence as a certain development of sensibility, and I thought they had not reached my level because social circumstances had not allowed it. I thought that fundamentally the prime relation between their sensibility and mine was the same.

DE BEAUVOIR: Still, you did say you were more or less the dominant partner with women.

SARTRE: Yes, because mine was not a single point of view. The domination came from my childhood. My grandfather dominated my grandmother. My stepfather dominated my mother.

DE BEAUVOIR: Yes.

SARTRE: And I retained that as a kind of abstract structure . . .

DE BEAUVOIR: And then in all the books, all the stories of famous men that influenced you so, it was always the man who was the hero.

SARTRE: Obviously. That was the reason why Tolstoy's case interested me. It was one of those cases which were notorious. There the man abused his power. At all events, there one had a type, a pattern. But in the end I was already coming to think that it was caused by upbringing. What I thought later, when I was, say, thirty-five or forty, was that intelligence and affectivity represent a stage in the individual's development. One is not intelligent and sensible—endowed with sensibility—at the age of five or six. One is emotionally sensible and intellectually sensible. But that doesn't go far. And then the sensibility may remain quite strong and the intelligence gradually develop, or the sensibility may overcome the intelligence, or the intelligence develop entirely by itself while the sensibility remains unimproved. The sensibility it is that has begotten the intelligence, but even so it stays down there, rough and unpolished. So that this domination, which was a pattern, a social symbol, was absolutely unjustified for me, though I was trying to set it up. I did not think that because I was more intelligent I ought to prevail and be the dominant partner. But it was so in practice, because I had a tendency that way and because it was I who sought out the women who had relations with me. And therefore for me to guide them. Basically what interested me was retempering my intelligence in another's sensibility.

DE BEAUVOIR: You took over the women's specific characteristics . . .

SARTRE: I took over the women's specific characteristics as they appeared to me at that particular time.

DE BEAUVOIR: And as they often were, by the way. Were you ever attracted by an ugly woman?

SARTRE: Truly and wholly ugly, no, never.

DE BEAUVOIR: It could even be said that all the women you were fond of were either distinctly pretty or at least very attractive and full of charm.

SARTRE: Yes, in our relations I liked a woman to be pretty because it was a way of developing my sensibility. These were irrational values

—beauty, charm, and so on. Or rational if you like, since you can provide an interpretation, a rational explanation. But when you love a person's charm you love something that is irrational, even though ideas and concepts do explain charm at a more intense degree.

DE BEAUVOIR: Were there not women you found attractive for reasons other than strictly feminine qualities—strength of character, something intellectual and mental, rather than something wholly to do with charm and femininity? There are two I'm thinking about, one with whom you did not have an affair but whom we liked very much —whom you liked very much—Christina. And the other is the woman you mentioned just now.

SARTRE: Yes, I valued Christina's strength of character. I couldn't have understood Christina if she had not had the character she did in fact possess. At the same time it rather took me aback. But it was a secondary quality. The prime quality was her, her body—not her body as a sexual object, but her body and her face as summing up that unknowable, unanalyzable affectivity that was the basis of my relations with women.

DE BEAUVOIR: In your relations with women wasn't there also something of a Pygmalion side?

SARTRE: That depends on what you mean by a Pygmalion side.

DE BEAUVOIR: Shaping a woman to some extent, showing her things, bringing her on, teaching her things.

SARTRE: Undoubtedly there was something of that. It therefore implied a provisional superiority. It was a stage, and afterward she evolved either with others or by herself. I made her reach a certain stage. And at that point sexual relations in the strict sense were an acknowledgment of this stage and of its being left behind. There was surely a great deal of that.

DE BEAUVOIR: And what did you find interesting about the Pygmalion role?

SARTRE: It ought to be the part everybody plays with regard to those they can help to develop.

DE BEAUVOIR: Yes, that's very true. But still it attracted you in a way that wasn't quite so intellectual and dialectical as you now seem to be saying. For you it was something much more to do with your feelings. It was a real pleasure.

SARTRE: Yes. If a week later I came across things I had understood and found that she had gone further, it pleased me.

DE BEAUVOIR: It wasn't like that with all your women.

SARTRE: No.

DE BEAUVOIR: There were some who were totally unamenable to any kind of molding at all.

SARTRE: Absolutely. . . . Sexual relations with women were called for because at a given point such relations are implicit in the generally accepted scheme. But I didn't attach a great deal of importance to them. And strictly speaking they didn't interest me as much as caresses. In other words I was more a masturbator of women than a copulator. And then again that is connected with me and the way in which I regarded women. That is, I think many men are more advanced than I am in the manner they perceive women. In one way they are more backward and in another more advanced, because they start from the sexual point of view, and the sexual point of view is "going to bed with."

DE BEAUVOIR: And do you call that advanced or backward?

SARTRE: Advanced. Advanced because of the consequences it has. For me, the essential and affective relation involved my embracing, caressing, and kissing a body all over. But the sexual act—it existed too, and I performed it, indeed I performed it often; but with a certain indifference.

DE BEAUVOIR: It's usually in connection with women that this sexual indifference is spoken of, but it's a certain relation with your body. . . . I'd like to try to understand why you've always had this sexual coldness, while at the same time you have liked women enormously. It was never just crude desire that set you on . . .

SARTRE: Never.

DE BEAUVOIR: It was rather the "romantic." For you, women have always been the "romantic" in Stendhal's sense of the word.

SARTRE: Yes. No doing without the romantic. It could almost be said that as man has contrived to lose part of his sensibility in order to develop his intelligence, so he has been led to call for the other's, for the woman's, sensibility—that is, to possess sensitive, percipient women so that his might become a woman's sensibility.

DE BEAUVOIR: In other words you felt an incompleteness in yourself.

SARTRE: Yes. I thought that a normal life implied a continual relation with women. A man was defined by what he did, by what he was, and by what he was by means of the woman who was with him, all at the same time.

DE BEAUVOIR: You could have contacts with women of a kind you could not have with men, because these intellectual conversations had an affective basis.

SARTRE: A basis of feeling.

DE BEAUVOIR: Something romantic. I've noticed—besides, it's very widely accepted and it even makes up part of mythology, yet at the same time it's true—that in almost every journey we've made or that you've made, there's been a woman who turned out to be the incarnation of the country for you.

SARTRE: Yes.

DE BEAUVOIR: After all, there was M. in America, Christina in Brazil, and others.

SARTRE: It's partly because although they may not thrust a woman into your arms they do set her down at your side to explain the beauty of the country to you.

DE BEAUVOIR: That's not enough. In Russia they give you a man to start with, and quite obviously it didn't create bonds of friendship with him.

SARTRE: I began by objecting to him right away. But indeed traveling, and women as I travel, have been very important to me.

DE BEAUVOIR: It's not only a sexual business. Very often the women are the best incarnation of the country one visits. When they are of superior quality they are more interesting than the men.

SARTRE: Because they possess sensibility.

DE BEAUVOIR: And they are also rather marginal with regard to society, yet nevertheless they know it well. If they are intelligent they have a much more interesting view than that of the men who are inside it. There is also the objective fact that the women you liked were truly likeable women. They really were so, and I can bear witness to that because I too liked them on another plane.

SARTRE: Yes. So when a woman represents a whole country, that makes a great many things to like. They are always richer when they live rather marginally, rather on the fringe of the country. Christina represented the Hungry Triangle. And rebelling against a country does not at all mean that one does not represent it. One represents it and then one rebels.

DE BEAUVOIR: Think aloud for a while about all this.

SARTRE: Now, when I try to remember all the women I've had, I always remember them dressed, never naked. Although nearly always I've taken great pleasure in seeing them naked. No, I see them dressed, as though nakedness were a special, very intimate relation, but . . . you have to have passed certain stages to get there.

DE BEAUVOIR: As though the person were more real . . .

SARTRE: When she's dressed, yes. Not more real but more a social being, more approachable—as though one only reached nakedness by great numbers of both physical and mental undressings. In that I'm like many other lovers of women. At all events, I lived with them in an affair, in a particular world. What prevented me from living in the real world with them was you.

DE BEAUVOIR: How do you mean?

SARTRE: The real world, that was what I lived in with you.

DE BEAUVOIR: Yes, I understand. You lived in various worlds inside this one.

SARTRE: That's what caused the inferiority of those relations, as well as the people's characters of course and all the objective aspects. It was blocked from the start.

DE BEAUVOIR: Because there were our own relations. Another question. Have you been jealous, in what circumstances, and how? What did jealousy amount to for you?

SARTRE: Basically I didn't much care whether there was another man in an affair with any given woman. The essential was that I should come first. But the idea of a triangle in which there was me and another better-established man—that was a situation I couldn't bear.

DE BEAUVOIR: Did the situation ever arise?

SARTRE: Who can tell?

DE BEAUVOIR: But have you felt it? There was a perfectly obvious case of jealousy with Olga. It was when she began liking Zuorro. Yet your relations with Olga weren't at all possessive. They were neither sexual nor possessive, yet even so it was that which started things and which finally caused the break—you wanted to be first in her heart. But although the Moon Woman had a husband, you didn't give a damn.

SARTRE: Not a damn. Because at least in her perception he was truly inferior. I think my machismo lay more in a certain way of looking upon the world of women as something inferior, but not the women I actually knew.

DE BEAUVOIR: Your Pygmalion side shows that you've never wanted to reduce, keep, or hold a woman to a state that seemed to you inferior on any plane at all.

SARTRE: No.

DE BEAUVOIR: On the contrary, you've always wanted to bring them on, to make them read and discuss things.

SARTRE: Basing myself on the notion that they ought to reach the same pitch as a very intelligent man—that there was no intellectual or mental difference between men and women.

DE BEAUVOIR: And that in any case, if they were at an inferior level, that did not give them personally any inferiority. That I know. You've never looked upon any woman as inferior.

SARTRE: Never.

DE BEAUVOIR: How did your affairs usually come to an end? Was it you who broke them off, or they, or was it circumstances?

SARTRE: Sometimes the one, sometimes the other, and sometimes circumstances.

DE BEAUVOIR: Were you ever given a bad time, upset, harassed by any of these women?

SARTRE: Harassed, yes. When Evelyne* didn't write for quite a while because she was having scores of complicated affairs.

DE BEAUVOIR: Or when M. wanted to come and settle in Paris and became exacting. And there's the infernal nuisance of women who ask more than one can give—you've known that often enough, and usually it's ended in a break. And there are those who don't give enough.

SARTRE: Yes.

DE BEAUVOIR: That usually happens to you at the beginning. You were given a bad time by Olga.

SARTRE: By Olga, yes.

DE BEAUVOIR: Evelyne gave you trouble to begin with.

SARTRE: Yes.

DE BEAUVOIR: The time when I saw you most harassed, or given a bad time, in the sense I was using, was first because of Olga and then because of Evelyne. And then most harassed in the other sense of the word, being asked for too much—that was obviously M.

SARTRE: Yes, I was dreadfully harassed by M.

DE BEAUVOIR: That was perhaps one of the only occasions on which you made a sudden break.

SARTRE: Yes. In one day.

DE BEAUVOIR: You said to her "All right, it's over. It can't work because it's a continual escalation."

SARTRE: Yes. It's strange, because I was very much attached to her, and it stopped just like that.

DE BEAUVOIR: You were immensely attached to her. Furthermore, she was the only woman who frightened me. She frightened me because she was hostile. You were immensely attached to Evelyne too. But Evelyne and I were on friendly terms. I was really fond of her and it

---

* Evelyne was Lanzmann's sister, and her stage name was Evelyne Rey. She acted in several of Sartre's plays.

was not the same kind of thing at all. She would have liked to have things you did not grant her; she would have liked to see you less secretly. But that wasn't at all against me.

SARTRE: Oh no, not at all. When I think back over my life it seems to me that women have brought me a great deal. I shouldn't have reached the point I have reached without women—you in the first place.

DE BEAUVOIR: Don't let's talk about me.

SARTRE: Very well. Then about others who have shown me various countries. M. did after all give me America. She gave me a great deal. The roads I traveled in America make a web around her.

DE BEAUVOIR: Generally speaking, the women you picked were intelligent, and some, like L. and Christina and Evelyne, even very intelligent.

SARTRE: Yes, generally speaking, they were intelligent. It's not that I wanted them intelligent, but right away something showed in addition to sensibility, something that was intelligence. And then I could talk to women for hours and hours.

DE BEAUVOIR: Yes.

SARTRE: With men I was quite ready to stop talking once what had to be said on politics or something of that kind had been said. It seems to me that two hours of a man's company in a day, and without seeing him the next day, is quite enough. Whereas with a woman it can go on all day long and then start again tomorrow.

DE BEAUVOIR: Yes, because it's based on that intimacy, of that near-possession of her being by means of the feeling she has for you. Have you sometimes been rebuffed by women? Were there women you would have liked to have certain relations with—women you have not had?

SARTRE: Yes, like everything else.

DE BEAUVOIR: There was Olga.

SARTRE: Ah, yes.

DE BEAUVOIR: But that was such a very confused situation! Have there been other women whom you've liked, whom you've more or less courted, and with whom there were no—I won't say sexual, but even well-established emotional relations?

SARTRE: Not very many.

DE BEAUVOIR: And in the course of your life you've also had relations that weren't emotional or at least not romantic—relations of plain friendship. At any rate with Mme Morel.

SARTRE: Mme Morel, yes.

DE BEAUVOIR: There was certainly something about the fact of her being a woman that gave your relations a quality that your friendship for Guille did not possess.

SARTRE: Certainly.

DE BEAUVOIR: Perhaps the question is rather stupid, but which did you like better, Guille or Mme Morel?

SARTRE: It was different. To begin with, Mme Morel was the mother of a private pupil. She had entrusted her son to me so that I should teach him things, and her relations with me were those of a private pupil's mother. Even though later on these relations became more and more intimate, she had begun by having those of a private pupil's mother with me. Certainly she had the same with Guille, but it was different. Because now I was the one who tutored the private pupil. He had left the sphere of Guille, who had tutored him in the years before.

DE BEAUVOIR: Guille had far stronger emotional relations with Mme Morel than you ever had. But whose company did you prefer, his or Mme Morel's? Once you had become friends she was no longer a private pupil's mother, was she?

SARTRE: I never asked myself that question.

DE BEAUVOIR: Still, I think you did get on better with Guille. You were very fond of Mme Morel because she was charming, but I believe you were too far apart on too many planes.

SARTRE: I think so too. Exactly. Although there may have been times when I should rather have seen Mme Morel than Guille, I never did ask myself the question in that particular way. I couldn't really see the kind of relation I might have with Mme Morel. The romantic side was cut off, since there was Guille, and then I felt that she was rather too old. The friendship-with-a-woman side I didn't care for. In fact, I've almost never had any.

DE BEAUVOIR: You almost never spent as long as two hours alone with Mme Morel, did you?

SARTRE: Oh yes, it happened, but not that often.

DE BEAUVOIR: On the whole, when I was there, your relations were more those of a group of three or four.

SARTRE: In any case I think she was the only woman friend I had.

DE BEAUVOIR: I believe she was, yes.

.   .   .

DE BEAUVOIR: Last time we talked about your relations with women, and that led you to touch upon sexuality, and now sexuality brings us to dealing with your relations with your body in a more general manner. . . . What have you to say about your relations with your body? In the first place did the fact of being small and of having often been told that you were ugly count in your relations with your body?

SARTRE: Of course it counted, and a great deal. But it counted as so many abstract truths uttered by the Other, which therefore retained the abstract character of truths enunciated by the teacher in a mathematics lesson. But this did not amount to a revelation for me. The notion of "small," for example. Of course I knew I was small; people told me so, I was called "little one," and from the beginning I could clearly see the difference between my mother's or my grandfather's size and mine. But that did not really give me a concrete intuition of the fact of being small. Since I had eyes like everybody else, I saw the difference of perspective that meant that I was smaller than a grown-up and that I saw things in a manner unlike that of the grown-ups. I knew that grown-ups were tall, and that my friends were more or less tall in relation to me. I saw all that, but I saw it as something of wordless experience, undefined by my own words. The truth is that I saw myself as big as anybody else. It's very hard to explain. But the differences that I did perceive—and I would look up to see a face or speak louder to answer someone taller than myself, the difference in loudness being considerable—belonged only to a system of motion, of grouping, of direction; they did not belong to a qualification applying to me or to my interlocutor. In fact I saw myself as big as he was. I might perfectly well be in his arms, small. But at that point the relation was one of tenderness. When I was six and my grandfather took me in his arms, that was not a relation that proved I was smaller than he. That was a notion I lacked, or one that remained abstract, but that I did not grasp in the perceptional life of every day. And things went on like that. When I was brought into contact with boys of my own age, what I thought important, by way of defining them in relation to myself, was my age. They were the same age as I was, so they were not big, big in the sense of a "grown-up" person. Physical dimensions did not qualify the adult well. It was instead a matter of air, clothes, smell, responsibility, a way of speaking; it was more spiritual than physical. And accordingly I stayed like that, as it were, suppressing my dimensions. If I were asked whether I was big or little, I replied, "little," but that was not my being's exact significance. This was something that I found out later, slowly and imperfectly.

DE BEAUVOIR: But in your relations with women, for example—when you were together with a woman—didn't it worry you if she was much taller than you?

SARTRE: It rarely happened. It did worry me a little in general, yes. I thought other people looked upon me as a figure of fun, being the lover of such a tall girl, or of a girl taller than myself. But sensually I liked it very much.

DE BEAUVOIR: And what about the ugliness?

SARTRE: It was women who made me conscious of my ugliness. I had been told I was ugly from the age of ten, but I did not see it in the mirror. I had two ways of looking at myself in the glass. One that might be called universal—looking at myself as an aggregate of signs if I wanted to know whether I should have my hair cut, whether I should wash my face, change my tie, and so on. These were combinations of signs. In that face I could see whether my hair was too long, whether I was dirty, but in effect I did not grasp my individuality. There was one thing that was always there, and that was the squinting eye. The eye, the eye remained; and it was that which I saw first. And that led me on to the other way of representing myself, of seeing myself, in the glass, and that was as a marsh. If I moved on from abstract signs to the concrete, I saw my face in this other way— the concrete was a kind of marsh. I saw features that did not possess much meaning and that did not combine to form a clear-cut human face. This was partly because of my squinting eye and partly because of the wrinkles, which came early. In short, I had a kind of landscape there, seen from the air. With stretches of land that did not make much sense other than that of being fields, and then from time to time the fields vanished, the ground rose, there were no more crops, and it was hills or mountains. It was a sort of confused, overturned earth, the substrate of what amounts to a man's face, a face that my naked eye could see in my neighbor's, but that I could not see in the mirror when I looked at myself in it. I think that this was partly because I perceived it as something made by me, and because I saw the muscles contracting in order to make it, and the play of the features. Whereas in others I saw the play of features merely as lineaments, wrinkles, surfaces that changed little, and not at all as muscles that contracted. There were these two unlinked physiognomies, neither being the continuation of the other. The universal, which provided me with a face, but only a face such as might be seen in a newspaper, with four strokes for features; and then the particular, which was something short of a face, being coarse, agricultural flesh requiring the work of perception to organize it into one. Those were my two ways of seeing myself. When I saw the agricultural flesh I was deeply grieved at not being able to see the face that others saw. And naturally, when I saw only the general features, they did not represent my face. What I lacked—and I think everyone lacks it to some degree —was the passage from one to the other, the junction that would in actual fact have been the face.

DE BEAUVOIR: You had begun telling me that it was through women you learned you were ugly.

SARTRE: It wasn't through women; it was through anyone at all who told me so. When I heard it from my companions at the age of ten, when they thought it was rather funny, it hadn't the slightest importance. But obviously, when women said it, and when one of them said it in an absolute fashion . . .

DE BEAUVOIR: The one you were talking about the other day, who said, "that old fool."

SARTRE: Yes, "old fool."

DE BEAUVOIR: But apart from that, did many women tell you that you were ugly?

SARTRE: Camille used to tell me so clearly and constantly.

DE BEAUVOIR: But almost turning it into an instrument of charm, since she told you that you had had a Mirabeau effect on her when she met you at a funeral. It had seemed to her a powerful ugliness.

SARTRE: Yes, the ugly side must have played a part at the beginning.

DE BEAUVOIR: After all, this ugliness hasn't prevented you from being successful with women.

SARTRE: Because later on I learned that there's little connection.

DE BEAUVOIR: Besides it's a commonplace that a man can very well be ugly and have a great deal of charm; people speak of great seducers who were ugly, and you must have known that. The Duke of Richelieu and so on.

SARTRE: Yes, yes, of course.

DE BEAUVOIR: So it didn't make you bashful at all?

SARTRE: No.

DE BEAUVOIR: You told me that you liked going out only with women who had at least a minimum of charm and that if possible you preferred them to be pretty.

SARTRE: Yes, because an ugly man and an ugly woman—the result is really rather too . . . rather too conspicuous. So I wanted a kind of balance, with myself representing ugliness and the woman representing, if not beauty, then at least charm or prettiness.

DE BEAUVOIR: In the course of your life have you on the whole been on good terms with your body, have you got along well with it or not? And in what way or to what degree?

SARTRE: Not very well, in the main. You are speaking of the subjective perception of the body, are you not?

DE BEAUVOIR: Yes, that's it.

SARTRE: I've known many friends who have spoken about the joy of feeling physically well. Physically, on skis, swimming, and so on. None of that has ever had much existence for me. When I skied I was mainly afraid of falling. That was the feeling of this body of mine. Balance represented a constant threat. And when I swam I was afraid of fatigue.

DE BEAUVOIR: I thought you were fond of swimming.

SARTRE: I did like swimming, but liking doesn't mean having an agreeable bodily feeling. Swimming is not particularly agreeable. There were countless things that I liked that were not my body—the sun on the waves, the currents, the waves themselves, the temperature, the wetness. I liked all that. I liked the water; but the body itself was rather the subject of feelings that might on the whole be called less agreeable or even disagreeable. And broadly speaking, when I walked—with you, for example—what I felt was tiredness. First came prefatigue, an unpleasant feeling of something that was going to descend upon you, and then fatigue itself.

DE BEAUVOIR: Yes, we've talked about that. For myself I found tiredness a rather pleasant condition, as long as it didn't go on too long, and as long as I could always stop, take off my rucksack, and sit down. Whereas you found it disagreeable.

SARTRE: Yes.

DE BEAUVOIR: Besides, your tiredness often showed in the form of blisters or little raw places, or else you had pimples or boils; there were many things in your body that didn't work very well and this certainly arose from the fact that you weren't on good terms with it. And yet your heath was excellent.

SARTRE: I did have good health, and I think that according to the rules I ought to have felt in tune with my body. Yet even now I can't say that the inward feeling, the "coenesthetic" feeling as it used to be

called, is agreeable. It's not very disagreeable; but it's not agreeable.
I don't feel well in myself.

DE BEAUVOIR: Is that one of the reasons why you've always loathed
what you called "letting go"? I mean relaxing on the grass, for example, or on the sand. On the contrary, indeed, I remember when we
were at Martigues with Bost and you sat awkwardly on blocks of stone
with sharp edges. You've always been uncomfortable in your body.

SARTRE: Yes, but this is more complex, and it will lead us to Pardaillan.

DE BEAUVOIR: To go back to the first question, to the not very agreeable coenesthesia, what do you attribute it to? Do you see any reasons
in your childhood? Is it perhaps a mental refusal to let yourself go? Is
it a sort of contradiction—that's why I spoke of letting go—possibly
connected with the fact that you've always very much disliked any
letting go as you saw it in your mother or in others?

SARTRE: Yes, I think so. I think there was an idea of what one ought
to be, and this idea did not include any letting go. And more broadly,
I think that for me my body was essentially something in action. And
everything that had to do with withdrawal or with coenesthesia—
none of it was to count; it was to be thrust away, outside my consciousness. What counted was the act I performed—the act of walking
or of taking hold of an object. I think that when I was a child I very
early conceived my body as a center of action, neglecting the aspects
of sensation and passivity. This passivity existed, of course, and all I
was doing was repressing it a little. But in doing so I emphasized
what was objective, real, an action performed by me—putting sand
in a bucket and making a castle or a house with it. But in any case
what counted was the action. And it was always by activity that I was
aware of certain elements of my body. My hands, for example: it was
always as hands in action that I was conscious of them. Clearly one
must always see things more or less in that way, a hand being something that lives; but it can also be perceived as something that undergoes, that suffers—suffers the roughness of a cloth or the hardness of
an object. But for me that was entirely secondary, and above all I
wanted to act.

DE BEAUVOIR: You spoke of Pardaillan. What did you mean?

SARTRE: What I meant exactly was this. There are imaginary bodies
that envelop one's own body in one's perception of it. My imaginary
body was that of a military captain, indeed, of a Pardaillan, that is, a
cloak-and-dagger hero. And I know when I acquired it, or at least
when I developed it. It was when I was little and when I played at

being Pardaillan while my mother was playing the piano. I've spoken about it in *The Words.*

DE BEAUVOIR: Yes.

SARTRE: Since it was a matter of killing columns of enemies who were throwing themselves upon me, I felt like a powerful warrior. And that's a feeling I've always retained; it was a kind of compensation for my shortness. But as I said I was aware of my shortness only in an abstract manner. So that in the first place this compensation was abstract too. Later it became that character who was Michel Strogoff or Pardaillan and all those people who in the end were me. In imagination, but also in reality, inasmuch as I attributed greater value to the activity of my hands, greater strength, greater power to my body. If I pushed against a stone, my act was more violent and the stone heavier in the imaginary world than it was in reality.

DE BEAUVOIR: Yet this consciousness of a powerful body is somewhat in contradiction to what you said just now—that you were afraid of fatigue right away, whether it was walking, swimming, or riding a bicycle. If you felt that you were a kind of giant and colossus you ought to have embarked upon physical exercises with an immense confidence.

SARTRE: I did have a certain amount of confidence. But here these were realities: fatigue, the whole terrestrial element, the link with the earth, with the ground, with the difficulties which at that point make you feel your body on a secondary plane, feel it weary, exhausted, and so on. I obviously gave all this a far greater importance. It was the harshness of the real. The world was much harsher for me than it was for you. Do you see what I mean?

DE BEAUVOIR: No, I'm not very clear about the connection between this imaginary body, which was thoroughly fit and capable of all sorts of exploits, and your physical timidity, since you say you were afraid of growing tired even when you swam.

SARTRE: I wasn't afraid of growing tired. I did grow tired. I flung myself into swimming so that there should be an action that I felt and that I liked. Then began the prefatigue, which was the fatigue of a body which is growing tired because it is in action. And I denied the fatigue, as it were, or thrust it away from me. And then when it grew stronger, I rejected the negation.

DE BEAUVOIR: Then what connection do you see between all that you've just told me and the reflections on your sexuality that we outlined the other day?

SARTRE: First it must be said that a full sexuality implies a double

313

relation. In a sexual act—taking it very generally; I am not speaking of the strictly sexual act but of everything that surrounds it—each takes and is taken. For example, each embraces the one by whom the embracer is at the same time embraced.

DE BEAUVOIR: Yes.

SARTRE: Consequently, each has the impression of taking—the impression of what I just now called action, the good giant's action—and the impression of being taken. In the movement that you make to caress a shoulder, for example, a naked shoulder, you perform an act. For me what counted and what always has counted is the active side, that is to say the position of my hand and of course the feeling of the flesh, but the feeling insofar as I brought it into being. The sensation I brought into being by passing my hand over the armpit, the arm, the thigh. It was my action that counted, together with what the action perceived, that is, the exterior, objective aspect of the opposing body. One ought to say that the dominant aspect was the caressing hand's active tenderness, but reciprocity was the thing I felt least—the fact that the other person might also have pleasure in feeling my body. For example, when I was in another's arms, body against body, belly against belly, chest against chest, I was aware of freely seizing the other's flesh, but not the other seizing my body.

DE BEAUVOIR: You were never aware of yourself as a passive object.

SARTRE: Never. And never as the object of caresses either. So necessarily that in itself changed the relations between the two persons. There was a gap between what the other could take and give in relation to me, since that gap existed in me. So as I was reasonably well equipped sexually my erection was quick and easy, and I often made love, but without very great pleasure. Just a little pleasure at the end, but pretty feeble. I preferred being in contact with the whole body, caressing the body—being busy with my hands and my legs, touching the other—to the act of love strictly so called. The act seemed to me required and that was why, in my relations with women, things had to end that way. . . . But this came from other people's ideas, from what was read in books, from what one was told. It wasn't my personal desire. I should have been quite happy naked in bed with a naked woman, caressing and kissing her, but without going as far as the sexual act.

DE BEAUVOIR: And what do you put this kind of frigidity down to? I think, by the way, that it happens much more often than men say, they being very reticent on the subject. They don't like talking about it—it embarrasses them. But that apart, I think each particular case has its reasons. Is this too linked with the absence of letting go, with a sort of bodily contraction? Because there are some men who when they are very young go almost to the point of fainting in their orgasm, who are really knocked sideways and bewildered by it.

SARTRE: No, as far as I'm concerned I've never been threatened with the loss of consciousness during the orgasm, or in any other love play.

DE BEAUVOIR: What do you attribute that to?

SARTRE: To the very fact that the subjective and passive aspect of the orgasm in the act of love vanished before the objective and active aspect that makes up the act of coition.

DE BEAUVOIR: So the question must be more general. To what do you attribute (perhaps by going back to your childhood—I don't know) this kind of refusal of all bodily passivity, of all delight in your own body, going as far as the rejection of what is strictly called sexual pleasure?

SARTRE: I don't know that it can be called a refusal.

DE BEAUVOIR: I don't say that it's at the level of your mind. It's somatic, it's in your body itself. But why? You'll say that in this case perhaps it's connected with things you don't know about.

SARTRE: Yes, I think it is that I don't know.

DE BEAUVOIR: It might be linked with questions of weaning, questions wholly to do with childhood.

SARTRE: That's possible.

DE BEAUVOIR: But don't you see anything that can account for it in your conscious life as a child?

SARTRE: Nothing.

DE BEAUVOIR: Yet you've sometimes told me that the refusal of letting go was linked with . . .

SARTRE: Oh yes! Even when I was very young I loathed letting go. There was something immediate about it from the very beginning. I found my mother's letting go very disagreeable. Although it was rare enough with her, poor dear!

DE BEAUVOIR: You emphasized that tendency in the character of Mme Darbida in "The Room."

SARTRE: Yes, that's right.

DE BEAUVOIR: You didn't like it at all.

SARTRE: No, absolutely not.

DE BEAUVOIR: Was it connected with a feeling of contingency, of the body?

SARTRE: Yes, it was contingency.

DE BEAUVOIR: A contingency from which one could free oneself only by activity.

SARTRE: And in the end for me activity was the fact of being human. A man or a woman is an active being. Man therefore always tends toward the future, whereas surrender, abandon, letting go is present, or tends toward the past. And because of this contradiction I preferred activity, that is, the future, to the past.

DE BEAUVOIR: May that not be connected on the one hand with your horror of stickiness or sliminess, and on the other with your very strong notions of breaking free?

SARTRE: Certainly. Sliminess and stickiness is contingency. It's all the subjective of the present moment. Whereas breaking free is toward the future. You must remember that boat. At Utrecht in the Netherlands I went to see a psychologist . . .

DE BEAUVOIR: I remember. He showed you various pictures—a boat that was going very fast, a man walking slowly, a train running along —and he asked you which in your opinion was the best symbol of speed. You picked the boat because it was breaking free from the water.

SARTRE: The water represented contingency. The boat was hard, well built, solid.

DE BEAUVOIR: And there was the idea of breaking free. I think in your case it's connected with your refusal of all the values that can be called vital, which were of very little interest for you. The values of Nature, Fecundity—all that. It has very little interest for you.

SARTRE: Very little.

DE BEAUVOIR: You've never liked animals.

SARTRE: Oh, but I have, to some extent. Dogs and cats.

DE BEAUVOIR: Not much.

SARTRE: Animals. As I see it they are a philosophical problem. Basically.

DE BEAUVOIR: And what about the time when you boxed with your pupils?

SARTRE: That was activity. I found boxing entirely accessible and agreeable, because I had seen matches and I looked upon the boxer as one engaged in total activity.

DE BEAUVOIR: There was a period when you went in for gymnastics. Well anyway for physical training.

SARTRE: I did it to get thin. I didn't find it very amusing. I'd do it for twenty minutes or half an hour every morning. But it bored me stiff.

DE BEAUVOIR: So you did take a certain amount of care of your shape, then.

SARTRE: Yes. Most of my life I've tried to lose weight so as to give the impression of a thin little man instead of a fat little man. Besides, fatness was something I thought of as surrender and contingency.

DE BEAUVOIR: But did you go so far as to follow diets in order to lose weight?

SARTRE: No. Now and then, when I was told "You mustn't eat that," I wouldn't eat it for a while. Then after a time I'd go back to it, because I have very particular tastes—tastes that are completely at variance with what I've just said.

DE BEAUVOIR: For example?

SARTRE: Fresh sausages, dry sausages, cervelat.

DE BEAUVOIR: All kinds of *charcuterie*.

SARTRE: I've eaten vast quantities of them in the course of my life.

DE BEAUVOIR: And does your Alsatian origin explain this?

SARTRE: It obviously comes from that background; but does this explain it? That's another matter.

DE BEAUVOIR: Was eating an activity you enjoyed?

SARTRE: Oh yes, very much! Besides I've eaten comparatively large quantities. Rich things, usually . . . against my imaginary Pardaillan-body, since it was rich things that made me put on weight. And that was very far from the hero Pardaillan, indeed directly opposed to him, since he was to eat only sparingly.

DE BEAUVOIR: And what about drinking? You've quite liked drinking, too.

SARTRE: I've liked drinking very much, but all that's too complicated. It has no connection with the body. Well, yes, it has a connection, but not much. I don't see it like that. Clearly it's not for the sake of ideas that I drink, for the beauty of the ideas that will emerge from it. But still it is for the sake of a certain kind of imagination.

DE BEAUVOIR: How do you mean?

SARTRE: In a certain fashion one's subjectivity grows inventive. It invents nonsense, but at the moment of its invention the nonsense gives pleasure.

DE BEAUVOIR: It must be said that you've never been a solitary drinker.

SARTRE: Never.

DE BEAUVOIR: You liked drinking among friends, with people . . .

SARTRE: With you . . .

DE BEAUVOIR: Yes, but sometimes you liked drinking more than I could bear, because I thought it made you stupid and dull. There was a stage, on the other hand, when you were very funny, very poetic and very funny, and that was wonderfully amusing, particularly during our parties or just after the war, when it was also a release from repression.

SARTRE: Yes, it was a release. We were horribly bored during the Occupation.

DE BEAUVOIR: Drinking among friends, with Camus for example— that was very amusing. You also used to say that there was a pleasure in alcohol because there was a kind of risk.

SARTRE: Yes.

DE BEAUVOIR: There was a slight risk of destruction.

SARTRE: But that point was soon passed. As soon as you were a little over the mark you began to be destroyed and the risk became a reality. I liked the destruction in itself. I liked having confused, vaguely questioning ideas that then fell apart.

DE BEAUVOIR: You never took drugs. You never took hashish or opium or anything like that. There were just your experiment with mescalin, but that was for psychological studies. Yet there was a time when, having a great deal of work to do, you abused stimulants.

SARTRE: I abused them massively for twenty years.

DE BEAUVOIR: Above all during the years of *Dialectical Reason*. There was Orthédrine, then other things, and Corydrane.

SARTRE: Yes.

DE BEAUVOIR: And what was the nature of your connection with these extremely virulent medicines?

SARTRE: What's odd about it is that I refused the connection when it was a question of writing literature. Taking stimulants was reserved for philosophy. That's why the *Critique of Dialectical Reason* is not a masterpiece of planning, composition, and clarity.

DE BEAUVOIR: Why this difference between the two?

SARTRE: It seemed to me that in a novel the way one chose the words and set them down next to one another, and the way one turned a phrase, in short the style, and then the manner in which one analyzed the feelings required that one should be absolutely normal. But why did I feel that one had to be the opposite in philosophy?

DE BEAUVOIR: Wasn't it because in the second case you thought more quickly than you wrote?

SARTRE: I imagine so.

DE BEAUVOIR: And then there was no choosing of words. I remember you used to write at a gallop. But was it necessary, or was there a kind of depraved pleasure in feeling that you were going beyond your strength? Which, I may add, ended in a pretty serious crisis in '58.

SARTRE: There was something of a depraved pleasure. There was also the possibility of things turning lethal, but there was no telling when. I went very far. I used to take not one tablet of Corydrane but ten each time.

DE BEAUVOIR: I know that you even reached the point of having no skin left on your tongue, and that at one point you became half deaf.

SARTRE: A whole tube of Orthédrine only lasted me a day.

DE BEAUVOIR: Yes, it was quite frightening. There was one idea you had, and that was the idea of full employment, that every minute had to be useful and that your body should go to the limit of its strength, including that part of the body which is the brain.

SARTRE: I thought that in my head—not separated, not analyzed, but in a shape that would become rational—that in my head I possessed all the ideas I was to put down on paper. It was only a question of separating them and of writing them on the paper, insofar as they called for numbers of different sections. Whereas in my head, without analysis, they made up a whole. So to put it briefly, in philosophy writing consisted of analyzing my ideas; and a tube of Corydrane meant "these ideas will be analyzed in the next two days."

DE BEAUVOIR: You have had illnesses in your life, haven't you?

SARTRE: Yes, there was my eye when I was a child. Mastoid trouble, much later. In '45 I had mumps.

DE BEAUVOIR: You've had quite bad flu sometimes; an intestinal flu once that kept you in bed for a month. You've had very, very bad toothaches. I'd like you to talk about your relation with sickness, fatigue, and pain. You were rather exceptional about all those things. There are some people who take great care of themselves, others who don't. There are some who take notice of the slightest symptom, others who pay no attention. Then there are those who complain when they are ill.

SARTRE: I don't know. You are the only one who can say what I was like in that respect . . .

DE BEAUVOIR: The first thing that struck me was your virtual negation of pain. When you had nephritis at Rouen you were still young. You were twenty-five or twenty-six. You took the doctors thoroughly aback when you said you had not really suffered. In fact you had had so much pain that it made you vomit. But you had the idea that suffering was always an absence of suffering, that there was always a kind of void and that it never could be fully realized.

SARTRE: Yes.

DE BEAUVOIR: So you took suffering with a kind of stoicism. And even with surprise at its not being something worse.

SARTRE: Yes, but I've never had anything worse than average pains.

DE BEAUVOIR: You've had some terrible toothaches. I remember once when Cau was your secretary and he telephoned me saying, "He's going to scream, he's going to scream." You were sitting in front of your desk and you were suffering abominably. And then at last you went to the dentist. I also remember an appalling toothache in Italy which you claimed you could deal with by yoga. You said, "All you have to do is to isolate it. Then, although the pain is there, it is only pain and it does not spread through the rest of your body."

SARTRE: Yes, indeed. I had the idea that one could almost suppress pain by assimilating it to subjectivity. Basically, the subjective relation of myself to myself cannot have been very pleasant, since I supposed that its character of pain to pain could be done away with by assimilating it to pure subjectivity.

DE BEAUVOIR: What you mean is that you cannot much like your physical presence for the very reason that you assimilate it to pain. And when you were ill, were you resigned, or impatient, or fundamentally pleased to relax a little, because you were ill and you were staying in bed? Or were you, on the other hand, irritated at being made to stay in bed?

SARTRE: Something of all that. It depended on the stage of the sickness.

DE BEAUVOIR: Have you sometimes felt a kind of pleasure in being ill?

SARTRE: Yes, certainly. When I'd worked too hard it provided me with a rest. I didn't work any more when I was ill, and I couldn't see myself as pure activity. On the contrary, I saw myself as . . . pure contingency.

DE BEAUVOIR: So illness gave you an alibi, a justification.

SARTRE: Yes. A justification. It gave me a reason for no longer being myself. It had come from the outside and turned me into a contingent viscosity, which pleased me. And I remained active only insofar as I tried—as I very often did, even when the illness was really at its height—to write a little or to think things out that I would keep to be written later. Things that were always very bad, I may add.

DE BEAUVOIR: I remember when you had mumps you tried to keep a vague sort of diary. But there were times when you gave up entirely.

SARTRE: Yes.

DE BEAUVOIR: In short, sickness was the only occasion on which you would agree to a sort of letting go. . . . You've never been much of a one for the comforts of life. You never read in bed, for example. That's something I adore, both in the evening when I go to bed and in the morning. Or in any case, even if I don't get into bed, I love lying on my divan to read.

SARTRE: Never. I always sit at my desk.

DE BEAUVOIR: You don't even sit in your armchair when you read.

SARTRE: Not usually.

DE BEAUVOIR: Now you are sitting in an armchair to talk to me. But when you read you sit on a hard chair with a severe, straight back.

SARTRE: Yes. I look upon being in this armchair as a kind of indulgence. I never sat in the one at 222 Boulevard Raspail. There were seats and armchairs that I never used. They were for visitors.

DE BEAUVOIR: You take up an almost moral attitude over it. I'd like you to give a somewhat fuller explantion of the way in which your image of your body formed and to what extent it became superimposed upon your perception of it.

SARTRE: The origin of the image? There's one precise fact. When I was about seven or eight I fooled around while my mother was playing the piano, and at that particular time I acted the part of an imaginary knight fighting imaginary dreams. This imaginary character was at the same time myself; I was playing a part, but that part had become mine by right. This character must be at the origin of my representation of myself, of my imaginary body. If I go a little further back, to the time when I was beginning to read, I used to dream as I lay in bed, and before going to sleep I pictured a character who saved girls from blazing houses. He was an adult—I've always had an adult imaginary body—and pretty well built, since he climbed up into the blazing houses and saved the girls by carrying them on his back. So from the very beginning, even before being able to read, but basing myself on stories I had been told, I put myself into the role of the stalwart hero whose aim is the rescuing of a girl or a child, a character superior to others, taking care of the young and the helpless. Where did I get it from? I don't know. I think many people have that kind of dream when they are young. But that it should have lasted all my life, that's what is more . . .

DE BEAUVOIR: So it has lasted all your life? Once you reached adolescence you lost that kind of romantic daydreaming. How much of this imaginary body remained? And what happened later, when you were grown up?

SARTRE: Well, in the first place, there remained a certain passion for physical training. As soon as I went to the Ecole Normale we haunted the gymnasiums in order to box. I still remember a fee-charging gymnasium that gave boxing lessons. We very often used to go and look at it and ask the prices, but it was always too expensive for us.

DE BEAUVOIR: But how is the wish to box linked to an imaginary body?

SARTRE: I thought that by boxing I should recover an imaginary strength I didn't possess, that I'd lost. I should develop this strength by becoming an amateur boxer and that would be a return into my true body, which was the imaginary one. In the end this did happen somewhat later, when I taught at Le Havre and boxed with the pupils. Of course it was rather imaginary—I was not a real boxer. During the contest there was a genuine action in which the imaginary no longer played a part, but before it, when I was training with a jump rope, and afterward, when Bonnafé talked to me about our style of fighting, I became the imaginary character once again.

DE BEAUVOIR: In actual fact, did you often have the upper hand or not?

SARTRE: There was never really either winner or loser. We used to box for two rounds and then stop. They were mainly encounters that led to no result. We took each other on without taking much notice of weight or size. I remember pitting myself against Bost, who was five foot nine inches whereas I was five foot three. He was middle or perhaps light weight whereas I was a feather weight.

DE BEAUVOIR: And in life, apart from boxing, did you feel stronger than other people? I mean when you were thirty or forty.

SARTRE: I was reasonable and took myself for what I was, but the image of someone who could fight anyone at all and beat him was one that often came to me.

DE BEAUVOIR: And how long did you retain it?

SARTRE: I don't know, but I do remember having resorted to it twice.

The first time was at the Laon Lycée about 1937 or 1938. I was in the common room; a teacher of about my own age saw fit to find fault with me for not having attended the honor roll meeting; but I don't know how I reached the point of hitting him. We scuffled for a good quarter of an hour, going round and round the room until a third teacher appeared, when we stopped.

DE BEAUVOIR: That was the first occasion. When was the other?

SARTRE: The other was when I was a prisoner. There were some boxers, professional trainers, and by way of amusement they organized matches on Sundays. They arranged a private fight between a very pleasant young printer and me. There were two rounds. In the first I clearly had the upper hand, but in the second I was overcome with fatigue because it was years since I had boxed and I had the worst of it. The result was a draw. Which I found disappointing, because Pardaillan did not have drawn matches.

DE BEAUVOIR: That was about '41. How long did this image of Pardaillan last?

SARTRE: It gradually passed into writing. My heroes have always been big men—Mathieu, and before him, Roquentin. Roquentin fights a Corsican at the end and overcomes him. Of course these weren't Pardaillans; they were physically normal people. But even so they were big, whereas I am small. They represented me, they were myself, and during that time I was tall and strong. I didn't worry about knowing whether psychologically these things could go together.

DE BEAUVOIR: That was literature. But to come back to my question, at what point in your life did the image vanish? It might have lasted until you were eighty, mightn't it? At present, do you no longer feel that you are big?

SARTRE: No, but I don't feel that I'm small either. What has remained is an equality of size, one might say. I am not a little man among medium-sized and big men; I am the others' equivalent. At the *Temps modernes* meetings, for example, I don't have the impression of being small when I meet middling or tall fellows. I have the feeling that we are all equal. Pouillon is no taller than I am. I see him as my equal, as far as height goes.

DE BEAUVOIR: And does your age make part of your image? Was it so in former times and is it so now?

SARTRE: It did make part of it when I was young. I remember that when I was on duty, guarding a sentry box during my military service, I knew I was young. I don't know why, but that particular night I had a very strong impression of being young, of being twenty-three (I was doing my military service very late because there had been provisional exemptions). I know I had an impression of joy, of pleasure, in feeling my youth. Obviously it's different now, but I don't feel old. I don't feel older than I did at that age. There's one thing I've always thought—I spoke about it to some extent in *Nausea*—and that is the idea that you don't have experience, that you don't grow older. The slow accumulation of events and experiences that gradually create a character is one of the myths of the late nineteenth century and of empiricism. I don't think it really exists. I don't have a life, an experience, behind me that I can turn into maxims, formulae, ways of living. So since I don't believe that I possess experience, I am the same at close on seventy as I was at thirty, as long as my body functions.

DE BEAUVOIR: But after all your body doesn't function as well as it did at thirty, does it?

SARTRE: It functions less well.

DE BEAUVOIR: For example, you find it rather hard to walk.

SARTRE: Yes, and rather hard to see too.

DE BEAUVOIR: You have to take medicines.

SARTRE: Yes, but I've adapted myself quickly. For example, I can scarcely see anymore but that doesn't worry me—I manage. I no longer see your face very clearly, and indeed, at present I can't see at all, but that doesn't make me unhappy. In other circumstances I see what things represent and how far they are from me, and that's enough for me to be able to find my way. In my present state I don't feel bad, and knowing that my condition is not normal doesn't grieve me all that much.

DE BEAUVOIR: All this could happen to someone young, you know. I think it's a characteristic of certain brave, optimistic people who take life as it comes. In the same way that you don't feel small in relation to Pouillon, do you not feel old either?

SARTRE: No, to tell the truth, I don't. I feel on exactly the same level as the young; they know some things I don't know, but then I know some things unknown to them. Of course I don't look upon myself as still being thirty, and I'm more or less settled into my fifties. In other words the man who goes downstairs at home, who walks along the street, seeing people and greeting them, is a person of fifty. In fact I rejuvenate myself by twenty years.

DE BEAUVOIR: You told me that when the doctor said you were young the other day it pleased you.

SARTRE: Yes, when people say that it always gives me pleasure. They don't say it so very often, by the way. But this time he was very distinctly surprised by my performance. It was his surprise that pleased me, even more than the words he said afterward. Then there's another thing that gives me pleasure, and that is not having white hair. It's not that my hair is any particular color, but . . .

DE BEAUVOIR: Your side whiskers are white, and when you don't shave thoroughly your stubble is white too. But since you are sensitive about what ages you, you ought to take more care and shave quite closely. Your hair in fact is gray; it's not white.

SARTRE: It's odd. According to what I've just told you I should indeed take care of my person. I should shave better, for instance; and I don't do so. The imaginary character needs a real support, and the support should be as young as possible. There's a contradiction here.

DE BEAUVOIR: Yes, the imaginary character is no doubt slim and lively, whereas the real character has something of a belly. Yet you don't do much to make yourself thin.

SARTRE: No. Now and then I do try to slim down for four or five months . . .

DE BEAUVOIR: To be sure you do take a little care, a very little care. You are not much too fat, but even so, if your fastidiousness matched your imagination you would obviously be thinner.

SARTRE: Yes, indeed.

DE BEAUVOIR: Is the imaginary still enough for you, and does it turn your interest away from your real body?

SARTRE: Yes: I think that the imaginary is still there on occasion. It's no longer Pardaillan, but something remains—a physically attractive personality. You must start with the idea that you don't see your own body, that you see very little of it—the hands, the feet, not the face. Besides, my imaginary character didn't possess three dimensions either. He had hands and eyes and that's all. His legs were much longer than mine, of course, and his hands much stronger; but it was indeed his hands that I saw and that I transfigured, as it were. Now none of that exists any more. I don't think I'm strong, nor that I'm big.

DE BEAUVOIR: The other day you said you had been on pretty bad terms with your actual body. To what extent did your connection with the imaginary body compensate for this difficulty? Or to what extent did it remain completely foreign?

SARTRE: It remained foreign. The physical aspect that caused me to find coenesthetic feelings disagreeable was still there. But I must make

325

things clear. That was the substance of my body, yet it was transcended by something that corresponded to my image; this was not my image, but it corresponded to it. I saw myself as above all active, and it is that in particular which explains my sexual relations with women. I was active, and it was an activity that brought me to the sexual act properly so called. I had no more than a moderate desire for it, but this was the activity that one had to display in a couple, and I think that was one of the reasons for a certain effacement of my feeling of equality with women. Whereas in fact I do think that men and women are equal. But the physical position of lovemaking and the activity that I exerted in it—one that is certainly not necessary but that agreed with my own somewhat misdirected sensibility—was the male activity.

DE BEAUVOIR: Why do you say misdirected?

SARTRE: Because I do not think that the perfect physical sensation at the moment of the act of love should be that of activity. It should be more complex. It is activity and also sensibility; each of the pair should be experiencing both passivity and activity. I must be passive, since the other is caressing me; I must be active, insofar as I am caressing her.

DE BEAUVOIR: Yes, I entirely agree. In your case it was only the active side that was developed. That led you to self-control, but at the same time to a certain coldness.

SARTRE: Almost to a slight touch of sadism. Since in the end the other person was yielded up and I was not. I was not? I was, but what was yielded was nothing to me, since at that very moment I was the active principle.

DE BEAUVOIR: You mean that insofar as you are pure activity and the other is pure passivity, there is something virtually sadistic about it?

SARTRE: Yes. Since activity opposed to passivity is also that which represents sadism.

DE BEAUVOIR: Because the other is reduced to the state of an object, whereas the normal would be a true reciprocity.

SARTRE: Just so.

DE BEAUVOIR: Can you explain this refusal of passivity? This refusal known and experienced in your body?

SARTRE: Insofar as I think, as I work with my pen, and as I write, I have not really refused passivity. I have been influenced by people; I have thought that they understood things that I did not—there is an element of passivity in my work.

DE BEAUVOIR: Yes, but I'm talking about the physical plane. Were you too much coddled, coaxed, kissed, by your mother and your grandfather, and did you react against that?

SARTRE: It's possible. I spoke of it in *The Words*. Yes, there was something of that nature. I felt that I was something other than a pretty little petted boy. He did not correspond at all to what I wanted to be. Grown-ups were not pretty, except for my grandfather, who was handsome. M. Simoneau, for example, was really very ugly, and so were others. I supposed that in the future I should be rather like them. So there was a very ugly man who was me and then an adorable little boy who was also me, but a me of whom I was less proud, with whom I was less pleased.

DE BEAUVOIR: Wasn't your activity a reaction against the unfair lot of ugliness?

SARTRE: I don't think so, because I was not really aware of my ugliness until I was twelve, at the time of the episode with the girl who said to me, "Old fool, with his big hat." That did make me aware of my ugliness. Before, no.

DE BEAUVOIR: But did you have that purely active attitude before? Didn't you let yourself go more?

SARTRE: Like all children I surrendered myself to my mother's caresses, but I was already active. Don't forget that I put on my puppet shows in order to attract little girls. That was an imaginary activity, but it was an activity.

DE BEAUVOIR: Yes, but all children are more or less active. It's possible to be active without entirely repressing one's passivity.

SARTRE: On that point I'm quite unable to give you an answer. It's too far in the past.

DE BEAUVOIR: Or did not the years at La Rochelle, the apprenticeship to violence, and your mother's remarriage lead you to an extreme attitude? Were you not deprived of caresses at some given moment? There are several hypotheses. Did the caresses sicken you because they were excessive and because they reduced you to the condition of an adorable object? Or was there not a sudden deprivation toward the age of twelve? There must have been much less in the way of effusions.

SARTRE: There were effusions, but there was also an inclination to slap me because I didn't work hard enough.

DE BEAUVOIR: That gave you a great firmness with regard to pain, since pain seemed to you almost like the normal coenesthesis as well as a refusal to let yourself go that strikes all the people who know you

—you work sitting on very hard chairs, and so on. Have you always been like that?

SARTRE: Yes, always. I've always supposed that activity implied the absence of surrender. And the absence of surrender is the absence of coenesthesis, but also, to a certain extent, the absence of the imaginary. In a way the imaginary hero justifies surrender, since in his world he refuses it entirely. In the real world one can therefore let oneself go. Yet, at the same time, since I had invented this hero, I thought he should not be allowed to let himself drift, and I behaved as he did.

DE BEAUVOIR: There's one characteristic that has struck many people —me to begin with. In your way of holding yourself, and in your movements, there has always been something very quick, very lively, very enterprising; even in the way you walk, for example, slightly rolling your shoulders and swinging your arms. When you were fifty or fifty-five it even became a nervous tic. For instance, Sylvie once recognized us when we were in a restaurant in Rome. She was at the window of a hotel opposite, she couldn't see us, but she did see feet moving about and fidgeting to such a degree that she said to herself, "That's Sartre without a doubt." Your feet were very restless. In the same way your elbows were so busy that they wore out the arms of my chairs with their perpetual movement. That was when you were between fifty and fifty-five.

SARTRE: I was rather overwrought for ten years or so. It's over now.

DE BEAUVOIR: It came from an excess of Corydrane, I think. You used to take quantities of stimulants . . . and what's more they brought on a crisis.

SARTRE: But do you see, my trusting in Corydrane was to some extent the pursuit of the imaginary. While I was working, after taking ten Corydranes that morning, my state was one of complete bodily surrender. I perceived myself through the motion of my pen, my forming images and ideas. I was the same active being as Pardaillan, neglecting . . .

DE BEAUVOIR: The real body, which was in the act of destroying itself and against which you have always had an almost aggressive attitude. You did not really think that you were destroying yourself, but on various occasions you did do yourself a great deal of harm. Since you have an excellent constitution you recovered extraordinarily well, but you damaged yourself on several occasions. There was a time when for an outside observer you had a perfectly balanced, quick, efficient body.

You were clumsy, but that's different, and it was a real pleasure to see you walking along the street, for instance—it was quick, it was positive, it was cheerful. Although inside yourself you were ill at ease, your body gave an impression of gaiety.

SARTRE: Because it was active.

DE BEAUVOIR: Because you were always cheerful. You have always had a cheerful temper. It could be seen in your movements and in the way you walked. You were lively, you were blithe. There was a time when you were rather battered, and then you became extremely nervous and high-strung, even to the point of wearing out the carpet in my flat, so that I had to add an extra piece to hide the threadbare patches you had made with your feet.

SARTRE: Yes, I did have some extremely nervous gestures, but you mustn't forget that that Corydrane gave me the impression of a total adhesion of myself to myself. Coenesthesis almost vanished; and there were the ideas I shaped in my mind at the very moment I was writing them, and there was the writing itself, all this going on at the same time.

DE BEAUVOIR: Yes, but I'm not talking about the Corydrane alone; I'm talking about the whole setup. Even on the days when you didn't take any, it had created a condition which was no longer the balanced state of your forties and fifties. This time of great nervous tension ranged from your fifty-fifth to your sixty-fifth year, and after that it changed because you were given drugs, sedatives, to lower your blood pressure. You have a much calmer body now. There's something we haven't talked about, and that is sleep. What is your relation with sleep?

SARTRE: It's perfect. Until I was thirty I slept without needing any drugs at all. I laid my head on the pillow and slept until the next morning.

DE BEAUVOIR: Yet you did have some odd little ways when I first met you.

SARTRE: Yes, I used to bandage my eyes and put *boules Quiès** in my ears. But it was a good sound sleep. And then after the war I took pills. In any case they were necessary to counteract the stimulants I used to swallow from eight or nine in the morning in order to write. For a long while I took Belladénal. I'd take four or five in the evening, and whenever my blood pressure was too high.

---

* Wax ear-plugs much used in France. (trans.)

DE BEAUVOIR: In 1958 your blood pressure was so high that you were on the verge of a stroke; but you didn't have one.

SARTRE: That's right. So at that point I was given sleeping pills. I was no longer taking Corydrane, of course, but I did take sleeping pills. There were various kinds, but I often came back to Belladénal. I still take things to make me sleep, but much less than before. I only take one pill of Mogadon, the sort I use now, whereas before I would take four or five.

DE BEAUVOIR: And indeed, I don't know whether now it may not be a mere habit.

SARTRE: But if I take nothing I don't feel so well.

DE BEAUVOIR: Because you imagine you won't sleep soundly. It's psychological, all that. I believe you'd sleep just as well; but what does it matter? So you sleep really soundly without any trouble.

SARTRE: But once I've swallowed a pill, I go to sleep at half past twelve and I wake up at eight or nine. In short, I have no difficulty about sleeping.

DE BEAUVOIR: Do you ever dream?

SARTRE: No. I used to do so, and even now when I wake there is a positive swarming in my head, but one that has neither shape nor name. Since I was about thirty I have completely lost the power of remembering my dreams.

DE BEAUVOIR: In fact, I believe you've never told me one in the whole course of our life. Like everybody else, you dream. But I think that you lose your dreams on waking and that you have the impression of not having dreamed at all.

SARTRE: I still remember some dreams, nightmares about madness, that I had a few days after my family took a servant of theirs to a psychiatric hospital. She imagined that she was falling into holes. Suddenly she would see holes in the street before her and she would fall into them, and she would cry and have nervous attacks. So my relations had her examined by a doctor who signed the certificate to take her to the hospital. I had been strongly against this solution, but this was my family and I could do nothing but give my opinion. Yet deep down in myself I retained a kind of uneasiness and I remember having dreamed that very night. I can still more or less see the dream I had.

DE BEAUVOIR: About when did that happen?

SARTRE: It was in Paris, before the war, when I was living with my people.

DE BEAUVOIR: So it's a very old memory. Do you still remember any other dreams?

SARTRE: No, but I know I had a great many.

DE BEAUVOIR: Bringing them back to mind didn't interest you?

SARTRE: I have done so. I wrote about dreams in *The Psychology of the Imagination*, at the time I was having them, you know. Yet after all sleep is something that doesn't exist. Or which exists as something devoid of fuss or trouble. I know, when I leave you in the evening and I climb up the stairs to bed, that I am not going to a battlefield but to a total annihilation . . . My digestive organs work very well, too.

DE BEAUVOIR: Yes, you've never been seasick.

SARTRE: Never, and I've made a good many voyages by ship.

DE BEAUVOIR: You've never vomited, even when you were drunk. The drink affected your head or your movements, but never your liver or your digestion.

SARTRE: I did vomit once. It was the day before a prize-giving. To begin with I had gone to have dinner on the beach with some pupils and then I finished the evening in a brothel, where, by the way, I drank nothing.

DE BEAUVOIR: You did so on another occasion too. It was in Japan, when you had eaten raw fish. At the moment of eating you stood it very, very well, but once you were back in your room you were sick. There was nothing wrong with your stomach; it was one of those psychological things.

SARTRE: I couldn't understand what was happening to me.

DE BEAUVOIR: On the whole you are firmly in control of yourself, highly organized, cerebral, very much aware of what is going on. Yet there have been occasions when your body has reacted almost without your knowing it, as it did in that case, for instance. Throughout the whole dinner you had been very polite, smiling as you ate dishes that sickened me. We went back to the hotel, you thought you had a high temperature, you went off to be sick, and at that point you understood that it was just nausea, but a nausea that was a psychosomatic reaction to the effort of self-control you had made all through the banquet.

DE BEAUVOIR: We are going to talk about a theme we have scarcely mentioned, and that is your attitude toward food. Can you find anything to say on the subject?

SARTRE: Essentially, that there are not many things I like to eat.

There are some things I won't eat, such as tomatoes, for example, which I've scarcely ever eaten in the course of my life. It's not that I find tomatoes too disagreeable or that their taste disgusts me. But I don't much like them, so I made a decision not to eat them, and generally speaking, the people I know respect my wishes.

DE BEAUVOIR: Do you know where a distaste of that kind comes from?

SARTRE: I should be able to, because I think that all food is a symbol. On the one hand it's food, and in that sense it's not symbolic—it nourishes, it's edible. But its taste and outward appearance evoke images and symbolize an object. An object that varies according to the food but that is symbolized by the food itself. In *Being and Nothingness* I tried to analyze certain tastes, or at any rate certain symbolic aspects of things.

DE BEAUVOIR: Apart from tomatoes, what food do you dislike most?

SARTRE: Crustaceans, oysters, shellfish.

DE BEAUVOIR: What is it that you find so disgusting about shellfish and crustaceans?

SARTRE: I think—with the crustaceans in any case—that it's their resemblance to insects and their connection with them. Insects live in air and not in water, but they have that same degree of life and doubtful consciousness that I find so irksome, and above all, in our everyday existence, they have a look of being entirely absent—almost entirely absent—from our world, which sets them totally apart. When I eat a crustacean I am eating something that belongs to another world. That white flesh is not made for us; it is stolen from another universe.

DE BEAUVOIR: When you eat vegetables you are stealing them from another universe too . . .

SARTRE: I don't much care for vegetables.

DE BEAUVOIR: There's one great difference, and that is that vegetables have no consciousness. What's unpleasant about insects, it seems, is that although they belong to another world, at the same time they are endowed with consciousness.

SARTRE: In all likelihood vegetables have none. The cooking of a vegetable is the transformation of a given object without consciousness into another object equally devoid of consciousness. And it is the taking over of the thing by the human world. If it is cooked, a vegetable stops being a vegetable and becomes a thick soup or a cooked salad. Rawness sets it farther apart from us.

DE BEAUVOIR: But shellfish don't have that insect look one sees in crustaceans. So why don't you like them?

SARTRE: It's food deep down inside an object, and you have to pry it out. It's mainly this notion of prying out that disgusts me. The fact that the creature's flesh is so snugly inside its shell that you have to use tools to get it out instead of cutting it off. That's something that makes it seem allied to minerals. It's really a mineral offering, the mineral being the shell and the offering the scrap of meat inside it.

DE BEAUVOIR: Isn't there something in the very nature of that flesh that disgusts you? Isn't there a connection with what you think about mucus and viscidity and that elementary form of life that causes you to shrink from it?

SARTRE: Certainly. The origin of my dislike for shellfish certainly lies there. It's an almost vegetative form of existence. It's organice life in the act of coming into being; or life that is organic only in that rather repulsive aspect of lymphatic flesh, strange color, and a gaping hole in its substance. The shellfish provides us with all that.

DE BEAUVOIR: Are there other things that you find repugnant?

SARTRE: There's one that I don't understand, as I've said, and that is tomatoes. Though not eating them is rather a rule that I've made for myself than a real disgust. Whenever I do happen to eat them, either out of politeness or by chance, I don't find them as unpleasant as all that. I don't like that slight acidity they give the food.

DE BEAUVOIR: Among the things you don't dislike, are there any you practically never eat?

SARTRE: Fruit. Because if I want to eat something sweet I'd rather have something man-made, a cake or a tart. In that case the appearance, the putting together and even the taste have been thought out by man and made on purpose. Whereas the taste of fruit is a matter of chance. It's on a tree—it's lying on the ground, in the grass. It's not there for me; it doesn't come from me. It's I who have decided to make a food of it. A cake, on the other hand, has a regular shape, like that of a chocolate or coffee éclair for example. It is made by pastry cooks in ovens and so on. It is therefore an entirely human object.

DE BEAUVOIR: In other words, fruit is too natural.

SARTRE: Yes. Food must be the result of work performed by men. Bread is like that. I've always thought that bread was a relation with other men.

DE BEAUVOIR: Do you like meat?

SARTRE: No. I ate it for a long while, but I eat less now. I don't much care for it. There was a time when I liked a fine rump steak, a chateaubriand, a leg of mutton, but I've more or less given it up because it made me too conscious of eating part of an animal.

DE BEAUVOIR: What do you like then?

SARTRE: Certain things among the various kinds of meat and vegetables. Eggs too. I used to be very fond of *charcuterie,* but I like it less now. It seemed to me that there man was using meat to make something entirely new—an *andouillette,** for example, an *andouille,* a sausage. All these existed only through the agency of man. The blood has been taken out in a certain manner, then treated in a certain manner. The cooking was carried out in a clearly defined fashion discovered by men. The sausage was given a shape that I found tempting, with little bits of string at either end.

DE BEAUVOIR: In other words you like *charcuterie* because the flesh is less immediately evident than it is in red meat?

SARTRE: As far as I'm concerned it's no longer meat at all. Red meat, even when it's cooked, is still meat. It has the same consistency. There is blood that oozes, it's cut up in the same way, and there's the same quantity—more than one can eat. A sausage or an *andouille* is not like that. The sausage, with its white flecks and round pink flesh, is quite another thing.

DE BEAUVOIR: In short you are resolutely on the side of the cooked and against the raw?

SARTRE: Absolutely. I can obviously eat almonds or walnuts, although they hurt my tongue. Pineapples too, because a pineapple looks like something cooked. I was acquainted with tinned pineapple, but when I ate it raw for the first time in South America, I had the feeling that what I saw was a large cooked object.

DE BEAUVOIR: Have you anything else to add on the subject of food?

SARTRE: No, not much.

DE BEAUVOIR: What have you to tell me about your relations with money?

SARTRE: I think that the essential fact—I've spoken of it in *The Words,* but it must be said again—is that I lived in other people's houses until late in my youth. I always lived on money that was given to me but that did not belong to me. The money my grandfather gave us, the money with which he maintained my mother and me—my mother explained to me that it was not mine. Then she married again, and

---

* An *andouillette* is a sausage made of chitterlings; and the *andouille,* of course, is a larger version. (trans.)

my stepfather's money was even less mine than my grandfather's. She used to give me some, but she made me feel that it wasn't mine—that it was given to me by my stepfather. And that lasted until I went to the Ecole Normale. Money coming from my mother or my stepfather diminished because I received some from the Ecole Normale and then I had private pupils, so it was there that I earned my first money. But until I was nineteen money came to me from outside, and since I was not very fond of my stepfather I felt it more deeply than if it had come from someone else. It's not that we didn't live very well, you know. As the head of a shipyard at La Rochelle my stepfather made a considerable amount of money and we therefore lived very well. Besides, I needed little; I was at the lycée and they gave me small daily sums. But still I certainly felt that I was penniless, I felt that money given by others kept me, and at this point, I having none, money assumed a somewhat ideal value for me. I was given money that I exchanged for a cake or a seat at the cinema, but this was an exchange that did not depend on me. The money was like a sort of permit to acquire an object which was given to me by my stepfather; it didn't go much further. It was as though he had said to me, "With this money you may buy yourself a madeleine or a bar of chocolate." And that meant, I am giving you this bar of chocolate. The real value of money was something I did not grasp. Besides, I was rather hostile to this money, not because I wanted less of it, but because I would have liked to do without the permission. I would have liked to have money of my own. That was why, when I was about twelve and at La Rochelle, I began taking it out of my mother's handbag.

DE BEAUVOIR: You took the money because you found being given it irksome.

SARTRE: That's right.

DE BEAUVOIR: What effect did it have on you when you earned your first money?

SARTRE: It was at the Ecole Normale. I didn't thoroughly understand what earning money meant there, either. It was money we were given at the school, a small monthly sum that we spent on cups of coffee in bars not far from the Ecole Normale. It wasn't enough to maintain us because we loathed the school's food, which was vile, and we spent a great deal of it on meals. So there was another custom at the school, that of giving lessons to pupils in the first form or philo, sometimes in the second or third. Most of them were incapable of keeping up in class and we were to enable them to do so.

DE BEAUVOIR: In that case, it was no longer like the money you received at the school. Did you then establish a relation between a certain work and a certain profit?

SARTRE: Yes. I was perfectly aware that this money was given to me for my work with my pupils, yet I did not see the relation between this money and this work very clearly. I was very conscientious. Usually I coached in philosophy, but sometimes I undertook more special tasks—I even taught music. What I felt was that I was doing an easy little job, one that meant that at the end of the month I should receive a sum that would allow me to live another month without lunching or dining at the school.

DE BEAUVOIR: Did you suffer from lack of money during those periods?

SARTRE: Yes, of course, but not to an important degree. I made a fair amount with my private pupils. The lessons were paid for according to a rate laid down by the school. The pupils of the Ecole Normale had settled it in conjunction with the vice-principal, and the fees were fixed.

DE BEAUVOIR: Yet it seems to me that there were occasions when you were short of money—when you wanted to make journeys to Toulouse to see Camille.

SARTRE: Yes, like all the pupils at the Ecole Normale I had very little money. I remember once I borrowed the price of a return ticket to Toulouse and a few drinks from all my schoolfellows, almost penny by penny. I set off with my pockets loaded with coins. Yes, we lived rather shabbily. There were months when we had no money and no private pupils; then we used to borrow and pay back later.

DE BEAUVOIR: Did you have any financial ambitions? Did you have a kind of schematic notion of the money you might have later?

SARTRE: No, not at all. I never thought about the money I'd have later. Never. When I thought of being a writer I did think of producing remarkable books, but I didn't think of their bringing me in this sum or that. In a certain way money did not exist for me. I received it and then spent it. As long as I had any I spent it freely, because it was almost like pieces of paper that I had been given and that I was returning to a common fund. I used to help my schoolfellows at the Ecole Normale. I gave away quite a lot of money.

DE BEAUVOIR: I know. When I first met you at the Ecole Normale you had the reputation of being extremely generous. And in particular it was said that when you took a girl out you did it very handsomely.

Even when you went out with your friends it was said you went to good restaurants—in short, that you spent all the money you possessed.

SARTRE: That indeed was what I used to do, but it didn't seem to me an act of generosity. One just made use of these strange objects they gave us and then one had something in their stead. And of course one extended the purchasing power of these objects to one's nearby companions. I gave my money freely because I did not have the impression of earning it, and to me it represented nothing more than tokens. Obviously it was necessary to have many of these tokens to have many objects, but one could manage.

DE BEAUVOIR: Did you accept other people's money?

SARTRE: No, but only because the occasion didn't arise.

DE BEAUVOIR: You mean you wouldn't have blamed those who did?

SARTRE: No. Because money seemed to me something outside life. I thought life wasn't formed by money; yet everything I did, I did thanks to money. If I went to the theater or the movies or if I had a vacation it was always by using money. I saved money, thinking that there were things I should like to have and that I should like to do; but I never realized that this was because I had acquired a certain amount by giving private lessons.

DE BEAUVOIR: Underlying this indifference, wasn't there the certain knowledge that you were a state employee and that your future was assured? Modestly assured, no doubt, but very solidly. Were you ever worried about your material future?

SARTRE: No, never. I never even wondered about it. Which was one way of being even easier in one's mind, you might say. As I saw it, there was the money that the pupils brought me day by day and that I spent on things that pleased me. Then later I would have the money the state would give for my teaching and I would spend it in the same way. I did not see life as being maintained by a certain monthly sum that was to be spent according to certain circumstances on clothes, rent, and so on. I didn't see things in that way. I did see that it was necessary to have money and that a profession was something that brought money in. My life would be that of the teachers I had known, and then obviously there would be the books, which would no doubt bring me something extra.

DE BEAUVOIR: But in a way nobody wants money for its own sake; one always wants it for what one can buy with it. Was there never a conflict between your dreams for the future, your wish to travel—for you often dreamed of traveling—and your knowledge that you would not have enough money to make these journeys and live the adventurous lives you longed for?

SARTRE: The adventurous lives, they were more abstract. But the traveling, yes. I know that before the war Holland seemed to me very expensive. I thought we would not be able to travel to Holland for a long time.

DE BEAUVOIR: I'm talking about the Ecole Normale when you were very young.

SARTRE: No, things did not appear in that light to me then. My needs were modest—a glass of beer or wine in a café; two or three movies a week.

DE BEAUVOIR: And did you never say to yourself for example, "Why, I shall never have enough money to go to America"?

SARTRE: I thought it would be difficult for me to go to America. But that was far away in the future, and it wasn't what I wanted to do then.

DE BEAUVOIR: And what did you think about other people's money? I mean when you saw very rich people and when you saw very poor ones, did you react? Did that have a reality for you?

SARTRE: I saw plenty of very rich people. Some of the other boys' parents were rich. But I knew that there were very poor people, and I looked upon that as a social infamy which called for political work to do away with pauperism. As you see, my ideas were pretty vague, but even so . . .

DE BEAUVOIR: But you weren't aware of the fact that money might represent something immensely important for a street sweeper or a domestic servant?

SARTRE: Yes I was, though, and the proof is that I gave money to people like that. Yet there was a contradiction. These sums, which were nothing to me, were a great deal to them. I didn't try to understand. I saw that that was how things were. In other words I had a very abstract consciousness of money. It was a coin or a note that allowed me to acquire objects that I liked, but I did not live on it. That's what you have to try to understand. I lived at the Ecole Normale. There I had my bed, which I did not pay for. I could lunch and dine there without paying a penny. So that my living, in the simplest, most material meaning of the word, was provided for me by something that was neither my family nor people who knew me but the state. All the rest, everything that was my living as I saw it, that is, cafés, restaurants, movies, and so on, I provided for myself, and I provided it for myself by means of a kind of pseudowork, since the hours I spent with my private pupils seemed to me a game. Usually I was there with a very stupid boy who vaguely listened to what I said for an hour, and then I left. I no longer even had the impression that it was teaching. It seemed to me like a kind of prattle that would bring me in, say, twenty francs.

DE BEAUVOIR: And later, when you began as a teacher?

SARTRE: Well, between times something had happened. My grandmother died and I inherited what was quite a considerable sum for the boy that I was.

DE BEAUVOIR: I believe it was eighty thousand francs of those days, which would make nearly a million now.*

SARTRE: So I spent the money without thinking. With you, for example—we traveled.

DE BEAUVOIR: Yes, our traveling was often largely paid for by that legacy.

SARTRE: And money was not a reality for me at that time either, do you see? A reality that a child in a poor family grasps so clearly. He knows what a two-franc piece means. I can't say that I knew. Money came into my hands, money that bought me various objects. Sometimes I ran out and then I either could not get more objects or I borrowed. I could not tell how I would manage to pay it back, but I did know that I could do so because next year I would have some private pupils.

DE BEAUVOIR: Yes, when we first met it sometimes happened that you lived rather beyond your means; you then borrowed from Mme Morel.

SARTRE: Yes.

DE BEAUVOIR: You had the comfort of knowing that Mme Morel was rich; she was the only one of your friends who was really rich. You didn't borrow from her often, but still it was possible. That too was a kind of security. I remember ends of the month that were rather difficult because our budgets were not balanced. I used to pawn a brooch I had inherited from I don't know whom, or else we borrowed from Colette Audry, who would pawn her typewriter. During the last days of the month we were very often short of money. But it didn't bother us.

SARTRE: After all, we had our two salaries. We used to put them into

* Old francs. In the 1950s a new or heavy franc worth 100 old francs was introduced, but many people still use the former way of counting, particularly where millions are concerned. (trans.)

a common fund and that amounted to somewhat more than the pay of an unmarried teacher or a married one whose wife did not work. We were paid very little, because we were in the lowest category.

DE BEAUVOIR: But we had enough to live on, particularly the way we lived.

SARTRE: When I was at Le Havre, my first post, I lived on very little.

DE BEAUVOIR: And did you then have rather more of a feeling that you were earning your money than when you gave lessons to private pupils?

SARTRE: Basically, I've never had the feeling that I earned my money at all. I worked. That was the natural course of life. And then every month I was given some money.

DE BEAUVOIR: But still there were certain obligations and restraints. For example, you were compelled to live at Le Havre and then after that you were compelled to live at Laon. You couldn't live in Paris, as you would have liked.

SARTRE: Yes, but my post had been chosen because of its nearness to Paris. It was only a slight constraint—I could take the train. I really liked taking the Le Havre to Paris train. I used to read the early detective stories that everybody was talking about in France, and the paper *Marianne*. It was a pleasant run, and I used to meet you at Rouen.

DE BEAUVOIR: Has the immediate lack of money in hand sometimes affected you unpleasantly? I know for example that you found borrowing much more disagreeable than I did. We once had a great quarrel. There was a hotel where we often stayed in Paris, and you were to ask Aron to lunch the next day but you had no money. For yourself you wouldn't have given a damn. You would have said, "All right, I shan't have lunch." But there it was—you had to invite Aron. I said, "There's a very simple answer; ask the hotel keeper to lend you some money just for twenty-four hours." And we really quarreled, because I said, "What does it matter? He's a nasty type, what of it? Let him at least be useful." And you said, "No, I don't want him to think that he's done me a favor."

SARTRE: That's right. I didn't want him to do me a favor.

DE BEAUVOIR: I know we wrangled about it and I said to you, "It's a good thing you're a state employee. You couldn't be anything else, because your attitude toward money is very diffident and apprehensive." You were very generous—that's not the question—but the moment you thought you were going to be short, that there was danger of not having money, then you became very anxious and nervous.

SARTRE: That's true. I have often worried about money. How could I get enough to do some given thing in three months time? I would think about ways of acquiring it, but there was what you might call a kind of gap between the money I acquired and the things I bought with it. I did not see that on the one hand this money was made for buying and that on the other it was obtained by work. Intellectually, I knew that kind of thing of course, but what I'm speaking about now is feeling. I did not feel that I was living according to the ordinary condition, the common lot—earning money and spending it on useful products.

DE BEAUVOIR: What about later on?

SARTRE: No, I never realized it. This is because mine is a profession that fluctuates—sometimes it is very well paid, but it is not at all productive, except in a wholly different and cultural way. So I looked upon the cultural thing that I taught or that I created in the form of a book as my own product, without relation to money. If people bought my books, so much the better. But I could perfectly well imagine my books not selling, at least for a very long time. I remember when I first thought of being a writer I never expected to be translated in my lifetime. For quite a while, before I understood what writing was, I expected to be an author with few readers. An author for small libraries, someone like Mallarmé, and so I should not gain much by what I wrote.

DE BEAUVOIR: There's one thing that you pointed out in an interview and that must confuse your relation as a writer to money—the fact that to some extent the earnings and the work provided are in inverse proportion. The *Critique of Dialectical Reason* called for an enormous amount of work and brought you in very little, whereas sometimes a play you'd written very quickly—*Kean* for example—all at once came to be acted a great many times, and made a great deal of money for you.

SARTRE: Yes, that's true.

DE BEAUVOIR: It's a thing you've often emphasized. The proportion is almost inverse.

SARTRE: Not entirely; but still, yes, it is like that. And that's certainly not taught me what money really is.

DE BEAUVOIR: There's something else that also comes from outside circumstances. For example, you suddenly hear that one of your plays is going to be acted in some country or other, that it's going to be acted for a long while, and that it will earn you a good deal of money, or else that there's a scenario being written, based on one of your works.

SARTRE: It amounts to this. For a very long time, for almost the whole of my life, I haven't known what money really was. What's more, there were some strange contradictions in my attitude. While I had it, I spent money without counting. But on the other hand I always wanted to have much more than I could spend. When I went away for a vacation, for example, I took far more than was needed to go to, let's say, Cagnes, where we had two rooms in a hotel where we were known. When the time came for paying the bill I would pull a great wad of notes out of my pocket. I know it looked ridiculous, and at the same time it made the woman who ran the hotel indignant.

DE BEAUVOIR: Yes, you had what I'd call a peasant's relation to money. That is, you never had a checkbook; you carried it all on you, in liquid cash, and in the form of notes that you kept in your pockets. In fact, to pay a thousand-franc bill you would bring out a roll of a hundred thousand or thereabouts. You spent without counting, but you were always afraid, and perhaps these last years you have been even more afraid, of not being able to spend without counting—afraid of being forced to count. Not really of being short, but of being forced to count.

SARTRE: At present I think I have enough money to live on for five years and then it's finished. And in fact things are all right like that. I have about five million—I mean old millions, which makes fifty thousand francs of today. I shall have to find some way of living.

DE BEAUVOIR: But what particularly worries you about this lack of security is that you hate the notion that you may be forced to count.

SARTRE: Yes, because I've earned a great deal of money.

DE BEAUVOIR: You've given enormous amounts away.

SARTRE: I have given away quite a lot. Besides, I support other people. At this moment I'm supporting about six or seven.

DE BEAUVOIR: Yes.

SARTRE: Entirely. So obviously that ties me. I mustn't lose money, because that would mean sums I could no longer give. . . . It's that aspect that worries me.

DE BEAUVOIR: Even when you were younger and freer with regard to others, there was always that fear of not having enough to be able to do without counting. It was something very near a contradiction. On the one hand your great disinterestedness with regard to money and your great generosity, and on the other a kind of—I won't say an overeagerness for money, because you never tried to profit by others —but a kind of dread. And that's so even now. If I say, "You must buy some shoes," you reply, "I've nothing to buy shoes with." With regard to yourself, one could almost speak of avarice. Although you are extremely generous to others, where you yourself are concerned your reaction is always, "Oh certainly not; I no longer have enough money." Another question to do with money, and one that is connected with those I asked you about your relations with other people —why do you give such big tips? Because your tips are not only truly generous, but sometimes you give so much that it's almost absurd.

SARTRE: I don't know. I've always given big tips, and that's the reason I don't know. I could provide you with explanations of the present state of affairs but I know that when I was twenty I gave big tips. Smaller than now, of course, since I had less money, but even so they made my companions laugh at me. So it's an old habit.

DE BEAUVOIR: Was it also in order to put a certain distance between you and other people?

SARTRE: There were various reasons. It might be both to keep the waiters at a distance and at the same time help improve their living. It's one way of giving. I didn't think that everybody behaved as I did, but I should have liked them to do so and I should have liked café waiters, for example, to have enough to live on. At that time I was on very bad terms with café waiters . . .

DE BEAUVOIR: That's why I would look upon it perhaps as an act of generosity but also as keeping your distance.

SARTRE: Maybe.

DE BEAUVOIR: It has both aspects, to some extent. However you look at it, these people have done you a service, even if it is no more than placing a glass on your table. The other day you said you detested having people do you a service even if they were paid for doing so. They therefore had to be overpaid, paid again, so that in the end you shouldn't feel that it was you who . . .

SARTRE: Who was in their debt. There was certainly something of that in it. I know I was amazed and embarrassed in Spain when tips were forbidden. I knew it was right; I was entirely in agreement. But then again I felt that the waiter had done me a service and that I was beholden to him. When I gave him money it created a certain relation with him—a relation that I no longer enjoyed. It had been taken away from me. He was a free man who did me a service and who was paid not by a tip given to him but by the price of the drink.

DE BEAUVOIR: Yes, the service was included.

SARTRE: Something more genuine had been reached. I felt it, but still I disliked not being able to give something over and above. In cafés where I often go this generosity does not create a distance. They think, here's that fool who gives too much in the way of tips, but they like serving me.

DE BEAUVOIR: Yes, of course. But insofar as you have stated that you wanted to be—indeed that you are—just an ordinary person, giving exaggerated tips is a way of distinguishing yourself from this ordinary person, isn't it? Doesn't that bother you?

SARTRE: No, because I have the feeling that that's how life should be. I'm being absurd, because in fact life shouldn't be like that at all.

DE BEAUVOIR: When you give a taxi driver an exaggerated tip, you know very well that you won't see him again.

SARTRE: Yet our relations are still genuine. I mean that's how I see those relations between the taxi driver and myself for the space of that moment. He is delighted because he has received a good tip, and he has a moment of fellow feeling for me, because I showed mine for him by giving him money. There is certainly a desire to set up a kind of economic law according to which equality will be brought into being by the fact that the richer people give more, just like that, in the course of the day.

DE BEAUVOIR: You say you support many people. But on the whole these are principally women or sometimes the young. Don't you find that embarrassing for the people you support? Would you have agreed to be supported yourself, when you were twenty?

SARTRE: No. I say no, and I think it, but for me money was something so remote from what is earned and what is given, so much more abstract, that the idea that I might have agreed to be supported for a few years does not shock me.

DE BEAUVOIR: Still, you know, being kept for a few years, it all depends. . . . If you really need it to carry on with your work. . . . No one has ever blamed Van Gogh for having been more or less supported by his brother. Because he painted, because he really had reasons for accepting. And if it's in order to do something positive— if it's a student, for example, who has his studies paid for, I'm entirely in agreement. But the people who settle down in that kind of life. . . . If need be I can imagine that you or I might have accepted if someone had said, "All right, I'll treat you to five years of schooling." You do your five years and there you are. You mustn't spoil your whole future for a question of vanity or fear of what others will say. But don't you find that it warps your relations with those people? Giving them money, for life, without any reciprocity?

SARTRE: I often tell myself that I don't. I don't, because that's how they are. They need money. And since that is so, it would be false delicacy to see them and feel friendship for them without giving them a penny when they have no way of getting money—perhaps through their own fault, but that doesn't matter. They'd starve with their mouths wide open if I didn't give them some. It appears to me in fact that friendship implies more than is ordinarily supposed. There's one thing I haven't pointed out, which is that the very modest conception of money I had when I was twenty-five, twenty, thirty, up until the war, was wholly contradicted by the rest of my life after the war. I have had a great deal of money. The money we have been talking about was primarily that of before the war; since then I've had a great deal.

DE BEAUVOIR: And what effect did that have on you, possessing great sums of money?

SARTRE: It was odd. Here again it did not concern me. The work concerned me, but the price paid for it did not. I wrote something about that in *Life Situations*—the way there is little relation between a book, the time you work to produce a book, and the money. I don't mean just the time counted in hours, but the atmosphere you plunge yourself into. You think about it all the time, just as much when you've finished writing and you're going to see friends as when you are writing the words down. You think about a book all the time. It is a thing sufficient in itself, and when it is finished you publish it; that goes without saying. But I didn't publish in order to make money. I published in order to know what people thought of my efforts and my work. And sometimes in addition to that I received a large sum of money at the end of the year. This astonished me. The two things didn't seem to me connected. In the same way, when I am sent money from abroad, it's no longer the book that is bringing it in. The book was written by a Frenchman, in French. That being so, I can understand that if it's read by five thousand or a hundred thousand people it will bring in different amounts, but the fact that two years later money should come to me from Rome, London, or Tokyo, for a translation—and I'm not even sure that it's a good translation—

is something I really cannot comprehend. The fact of my receiving money at that point is strange. In a certain sense one is no longer looked upon as a writer but as a cake of soap.

DE BEAUVOIR: As a piece of merchandise, yes. But what I meant was this. When you really had a lot of money, after the war, didn't it give you a guilty conscience? I know it gave me one. When I bought my first rather expensive dress I said, "This is my first concession . . ."

SARTRE: Ah! I remember.

DE BEAUVOIR: I used to think we ought to face up to this money question and administer the sums in a philanthropic manner; in short, to plan something. And at the same time I thoroughly realized that we were neither of us suited for this kind of planning, especially not you.

SARTRE: Certainly not. Besides planning was made difficult by the fact that we didn't receive the same amounts each year. The year a book came out we might receive a great deal. The next year, if there were only a few articles, we didn't have much. But the year before that we'd made enough to live for two years.

DE BEAUVOIR: Yet from time to time you did have little dreams. For example, you would say, "Yes, we ought to put such and such an amount aside every year for students who are in need."

SARTRE: Yes.

DE BEAUVOIR: "We ought to devote a given sum to this or that." Now in fact you have helped people a great deal, but you've done so rather by chance, at haphazard.

SARTRE: Yes, as the occasion arose.

DE BEAUVOIR: According to the occasion, and according to what people asked for.

SARTRE: I think if we'd set up a fund for students, we should have had this fund to maintain on the one hand, and on the other the same requests and the same obligations toward people we met who asked us for money. . . . So it wouldn't have changed things much, apart from making our position untenable.

DE BEAUVOIR: Go on.

SARTRE: In fact, then, during this second part of my life, from '45 until the present year, I have had a great deal of money. I've given away quite a lot, but I have not spent an immense amount on myself. Wouldn't you say that basically it has gone to others?

DE BEAUVOIR: Yes, absolutely. The only luxury that we've had for ourselves personally . . .

SARTRE: Has been traveling.

DE BEAUVOIR: And even so, that doesn't amount to a great deal. A great number of journeys were given to us as presents—Cuba, Bahia . . .

SARTRE: Egypt . . .

DE BEAUVOIR: Japan. These were trips on which we did not spend money. What we spent most on was our holidays in Rome, for example.

SARTRE: Yes.

DE BEAUVOIR: And then again we don't live extravagantly. We live very pleasantly, we go to a good hotel and to good restaurants, but after all we don't live in great luxury. In Paris we don't spend much on living. There's one thing you've never done with your money— you've never speculated.

SARTRE: Never. And you shouldn't even use the word speculated. I've never even *invested* any money.

DE BEAUVOIR: Never.

SARTRE: What I get I spend in the following two or three months, or the very next month.

DE BEAUVOIR: Sometimes you've had quite large sums lying around at Gallimard's for a year or two.

SARTRE: Because I couldn't spend them.

DE BEAUVOIR: That's right. Because you couldn't spend them right away. But you've never used them to produce an income.

SARTRE: Never.

DE BEAUVOIR: For buying shares, making deals.

SARTRE: Never.

DE BEAUVOIR: For you money has never been a means of making money.

SARTRE: That would have seemed to me squalid. Yet it's the way some people live, those who can.

DE BEAUVOIR: At this point we ought to go deeper into the reasons why it seems to you squalid, as it does to me too—I follow the same way of life. Behaving in this way we escape the feeling of being capitalists, although in spite of everything we do draw profit from others, since it is the people who buy and read our books or who go to the theater who support us.

SARTRE: Absolutely. They read the latest books as they come out; consequently, they read ours when they come out. Because we don't have the public that we would really like.

DE BEAUVOIR: Yes, of course.

SARTRE: I would like a wider public, distinctly less bourgeois, less rich, a public of proletarians and those on the lowest edge of the lower middle class. The public I do have is in the strict sense of the term a bourgeois public. There's a difficulty here that has often troubled me deeply.

DE BEAUVOIR: All the people who are at all acquainted with your philosophy know the part that the notion of freedom plays in your work. But I'd like you to tell me in a more personal way how you worked out this idea of freedom in your own mind and how you came to give it the importance it possesses.

SARTRE: Since my childhood, I have always felt free. The idea of freedom evolved in me. It lost those vague and contradictory aspects that it has in all people when they take it for granted to begin with, and it grew more complex. It became explicit. But I shall die as I have lived, with a deep feeling of liberty. When I was a child I was free in the sense that it can be said that all those who speak of their ego, of their "I"—*I* want this; *I* am like that—are free or feel that they are free. That does not mean they are really free, but they believe in their freedom. The ego becomes a real object—it's I, it's you—and at the same time a source of freedom. It is this contradiction that one feels from the beginning and that represents a truth. The ego is at the same time that mode of conscious life in which each moment opens out under its own impulse. But one also observes the continual return of the same inclinations in similar circumstances, and one can describe one's ego. Later I tried to account for this in my philosophy by making the ego a quasi-object that in certain circumstances accompanies our representations.

DE BEAUVOIR: You said that in *The Transcendence of the Ego,* didn't you?

SARTRE: Yes. As I see it this very contradiction itself is the prime source of freedom. What chiefly interested me was not so much my quasi-object ego, upon which my reflections were of no great importance, but rather the atmosphere of creation of oneself by oneself that is met with at the level of what is called experience, lived-through experience. At every moment there is on the one hand a consciousness of the objects belonging to the room or the town in which one happens to be, and on the other the manner in which these objects are seen and appreciated—a manner that is not given together with the object but that comes from oneself, though without being predetermined. It is given instantaneously; its nature is frail—it appears and it can disappear. It is at this level that we see the self-assertion of freedom, which is the very state of this consciousness and the way in which it is aware of itself, being given by nothing. It is not determined by the preceding moment—it no doubt refers back to it, but does so quite freely. From the beginning it was this particular consciousness that seemed to me to be freedom. I was living with my grandfather, and I thought it obvious that since I was free, he was too. But I could not understand the nature of his freedom very well, since it was chiefly expressed in the form of maxims, puns, and poems; and that did not seem to me to interpret freedom properly.

DE BEAUVOIR: Do you mean that you had this feeling of liberty from childhood?

SARTRE: Yes. I have always felt free by reason of the very nature of what a conscious state amounts to.

DE BEAUVOIR: Did the way you were brought up help to give you this impression of freedom?

SARTRE: This notion of freedom is to be found in everyone but it is given a differing degree of importance according to the way in which one has been brought up. As far as I am concerned—and I spoke about this in *The Words*—I was treated like a young prince that the Schweitzer family had begotten, a treasure that had not yet been clearly defined but that exceeded all its outward manifestations. I felt myself free insofar as I was a young prince, free compared with all the people I knew at that point. I had a feeling of superiority owing to my freedom, a feeling I've lost since because I am of the opinion that all men are free. But at that juncture it was vague. *I was* my freedom, and I had the impression that others did not feel it as I did.

DE BEAUVOIR: But didn't you also have a very strong feeling of dependence? What you did, the places where you went for holidays, and so on were chosen for you. Everything was chosen by others, after all.

SARTRE: Yes, but I didn't think it of much importance. I took it for granted. I obeyed just as I sat on a chair, or breathed, or went to sleep. My freedom found its expression in choices of no great consequence—one kind of food in preference to another during a meal, for example. Either walking along or going into a shop was enough for me. I thought the proof of my freedom resided in this. At that point it was above all a state, a feeling, the actual state of consciousness

349

from which at one moment or another would arise a decision—whether to buy an object or to ask my mother for one. My family and the duties they imposed upon me represented the laws of the world, and you are free in relation to these laws if you know how to manage it.

DE BEAUVOIR: Did you never feel oppressed? Didn't you feel that a free will was setting itself against yours?

SARTRE: I did feel that later. It was something I discovered at La Rochelle when I was confronted with provincial schoolboys who were evilly disposed toward a Parisian. They were big boys whereas I was small, and they combined to persecute me. But I never felt it until the end of the fifth form, that is to say until I was about eleven. The others were there to help me, get me out of trouble, advise me. I wasn't crossed. Perhaps I was once or twice, and that threw me into frightful tempers that had something metaphysical about them. But most of the time I was petted. I did not feel oppression when I was little. On the contrary, I was aware of an intelligent care designed to help me develop. And it was only when I met boys of my own age that I began to understand the hostility that forms part of men's relations with one another.

DE BEAUVOIR: Did you retain that feeling of freedom when you suffered this persecution?

SARTRE: Yes. But it became more of an inward feeling. For a while I tried to deal with the persecution by fighting, but the results were unpredictable—or rather they were only too predictable, though I could not do the predicting. Or I tried by inveigling the others into various schemes. But obviously I was perpetually aware of obstacles. Yet between the other boys and me there was also friendship. Persecution was not their only way of behaving toward me; they would also talk to me, be my friend, go for walks with me. I belonged in the group of my schoolmates and from that point of view I felt free. What tormented me more was that at this period I began falling out with my mother, my stepfather's presence certainly being the underlying cause. There was something I lacked, something connected not only with her but also with the idea of freedom. During the years before this I had played a privileged part in my mother's life and now it had been taken away from me, since there was this man who lived with her and who had the chief role. Before, I was a prince in relation to my mother; now I was only a prince of the second rank.

DE BEAUVOIR: After all these experiences—schoolmates, stepfather, and then your coming to Paris—how did your feeling of freedom evolve?

SARTRE: As I've said, I felt free during this period, but I didn't say to myself, "I'm free." It was a feeling that didn't exactly have a name, or rather that had various names. It was in Paris, in my second year at the Lycée Henri IV, that is to say in philo, that I learned the word freedom, or at least its philosophical meaning. It was then that I grew passionate about freedom and became its great defender. Nizan, at about the same time, was attracted by materialism, and later this induced him to join the Communist party. The year after I was in hypo-khâgne at Louis le Grand. I was a day boarder, and during recreation we used to walk up and down a balcony arguing about freedom and historical materialism. We were on opposite sides, he basing himself on rational, concrete arguments, and I defending a certain conception of man, a man I described without bringing forward any arguments. It must be said that we achieved nothing. We argued; neither won. The talk remained fruitless. One day Nizan, who had joined the materialist cause, gave me a proof of his freedom. He carried out an act which I, not knowing the details, could not connect with the past—I could not find its links with the past. He stayed away from the lycée from Friday until Monday afternoon. When he came back I asked him where he had been. He replied that he had gone to have himself circumcised. I was quite taken aback. Nizan was a Catholic, the son of a very Catholic mother, and I could not understand his reasons. I asked him and he told me that it was cleaner, but he gave no further explanation. The event seemed to me to have no cause. He had decided to have himself circumcised—a stupid decision since there was nothing to be said in its favor. He had been to see a doctor; the doctor had circumcised him; and he had stayed two or three days in a hotel with a bandage around the end of his penis.

DE BEAUVOIR: At that time did you put freedom and the gratuitous act on the same footing, as it were?

SARTRE: To a great extent. Yet the gratuitous act, as it is defined and described in Gide's *The Counterfeiters,* did not tempt me. When I read that book I did not find liberty in my sense of the word. But Nizan's circumcision was certainly a gratuitous act as I saw it, though it was obviously due to motives that he had hidden from me.

DE BEAUVOIR: Basically, your conception of freedom was that of the Stoic—that which does not depend on us has no importance and that which does depend on us is freedom. One is therefore free in any situation, any circumstances.

SARTRE: It was certainly that; yet at the same time an act performed by me was not always a free act. Although I may have felt free throughout. . . . As I saw it, freedom and consciousness were the same. Seeing and being free were the same. Because it wasn't given— by experiencing it, I created its reality. But not all my acts were free.

DE BEAUVOIR: Wasn't there the danger that this might have caused you to adopt extremely reactionary attitudes? If everyone is free, that's fine, there's no longer any need to do anything for anyone and each man has only to make his own life. Consequently, one can confine oneself to one's own inner life. How does it come about that this result did not occur?

SARTRE: It never did. The difficulties my idea met with later, in my relations with people, with things, and with myself led me to make it more exact and to give it another meaning. I came to understand that freedom met with obstacles, and it was then that contingency appeared to me as being opposed to freedom. And as being a kind of freedom of things, which are not strictly entailed by the preceding moment.

DE BEAUVOIR: But weren't you aware of the constraints that people undergo?

SARTRE: At a given moment, no.

DE BEAUVOIR: We talked about this when you were writing *Being and Nothingness*. You said that one could be free in any situation. When did you stop believing that?

SARTRE: Quite early. There is an artless theory of freedom: one is free, one always chooses what one does, one is free with regard to the Other, the Other is free with regard to one. This theory is to be found in the very simple philosophical books, and I kept it as a convenient way of defining my freedom; but it did not correspond to what I really meant to say. What I meant was that one is responsible for oneself even if one's acts are provoked by something external. . . . Every action includes a proportion of habit, of received ideas, of symbols; and then again there is something that comes from our remotest depths and that is related to our primary freedom.

DE BEAUVOIR: To come back to the political and social problem of freedom, how did you move on from a very individualist, very idealist theory to the idea that one ought to commit oneself to a social and political struggle?

SARTRE: I came to it much later. Don't forget that until 1937–38 I attached great importance to what I then called the "lone man." That is, fundamentally the free man, insofar as he lives apart from others because he is free and because he causes things to happen on the basis of his freedom.

DE BEAUVOIR: Yes, but even in those days that did not prevent you from being deeply interested in social problems or from violently taking sides, at least intellectually. For example, why did you violently take sides against Franco and for the Popular Front?

SARTRE: Because I thought that the free man was the one who took sides for man as he is against those who wish to replace him by an image they have made, either the image of fascist man or even that of socialist man. As I saw it, the free man set himself against these systematic representations.

DE BEAUVOIR: Your answer seems to me very idealistic. The Fascists don't only want to give man the image of fascist man. They also want to put him in prison, torture him, force him to do certain things.

SARTRE: That's obvious. But I'm talking about what I thought at that time. Torture, for example, which I think abominable, appeared to me as a consequence of the Fascists' will to compel men to be fascist men, subject to the principles arising from the fascist doctrine.

DE BEAUVOIR: Why did you find that doctrine repellant?

SARTRE: Because it denied freedom. In my opinion a man must decide for himself—in conjunction with others perhaps, but for himself. Yet in fascism he is dominated by men placed above him. I have always loathed hierarchies and in some of the present-day antihierarchical conceptions I see a sense of freedom. There cannot be any hierarchy with regard to freedom. There is nothing above freedom. I therefore decide for myself and no one can force my decisions.

DE BEAUVOIR: That also defined your relations with socialism, didn't it?

SARTRE: Yes. Socialism was a doctrine that I found fairly satisfying, but in my opinion it did not confront the real questions. For example, the question of what a man was under socialism. One had to trade the satisfaction of needs for a wholly materialist conception of human nature. It was that which worried me about socialism before the war. One had to be a materialist in order to be a consistent socialist, and I was not a materialist. I wasn't a materialist because of freedom. As long as I was unable to find a way of materializing this freedom—my task during the next thirty years of my life—there was something I found repellant in socialism because the individual was done away with in favor of the communities. They sometimes used the word liberty, but it was a group liberty, without any connection with metaphysics. I was still at that point during the war and in the Resistance. I was satisfied with myself at that period. During the evenings in the barracks, when I was a prisoner, I played the part of the storyteller, the funny man. The lights were put out at about half past eight. We stuck candles in little tins and I told stories. I was the only one sitting up and dressed while all the others lay there on their beds. I had taken on a kind of personal importance. I was the fellow who amused them, who interested them.

DE BEAUVOIR: What connection has this with freedom?

SARTRE: It was I who united the men who listened, who were interested, who laughed. It was a synthetic unit, and I was the unit that was creating the other unit, the social unit, and in this unit I committed my freedom. I saw myself creating a kind of little society on the basis of my freedom.

DE BEAUVOIR: It was the first time that you had had the feeling of a certain effectiveness of a social nature. When you tried to set up a resistance movement you called it "Socialism and Liberty." Were you therefore beginning to think that the two could be reconciled?

SARTRE: Yes. Still, I distinguished between the two concepts. I wondered whether socialism could be combined with liberty.

DE BEAUVOIR: After that you spent thirty years in defining what you meant by liberty?

SARTRE: I set myself to it very seriously in *Being and Nothingness* and in the *Critique of Dialectical Reason*.

DE BEAUVOIR: And in *Saint Genet* too. What is so striking about that book is that there's scarcely an ounce of freedom left to man anymore. You give a very great importance to the individual's upbringing and to his whole conditioning. You speak about scores of people, not only about Genet, and there's scarcely one of them who appears as a free subject.

SARTRE: Yet even so, that homosexual child, beaten, raped, and overwhelmed by young sodomites and treated rather like a toy by the toughs around him, did become the writer Jean Genet. There was a transformation here that was the work of freedom. Freedom is the metamorphosis of Jean Genet, the unhappy homosexual child, into Jean Genet, the great writer, a pederast by choice, and if not happy, then at least sure of himself. This change might very well not have taken place. Jean Genet's change came truly from the use of his freedom. It transformed the meaning of the world and gave it another value. It was indeed that freedom and nothing else that was the cause of this reversal. It was freedom choosing itself that brought the transformation about.

DE BEAUVOIR: You seem to define freedom as being a discovery of oneself that is possible at certain moments. What are the moments in your life when it appears to you that there were these free choices—or rather these discoveries?

SARTRE: I think there was one which was quite important. It was when I left La Rochelle and entered the first form at the Lycée Henri IV. There I was no longer persecuted at all. I was even given an honorary post.

DE BEAUVOIR: Yes, but it wasn't you who decided to go to Henri IV, nor no longer to be persecuted by your companions.

SARTRE: To a certain degree it was I who decided that my companions should no longer persecute me. They didn't do so because I was no longer someone who could be persecuted. I had changed myself.

DE BEAUVOIR: You had chosen a given attitude?

SARTRE: Yes. I asserted myself, and the boys I came into contact with were perfectly ready to accept the assertion because on their side they too were asserting themselves. My first form, my philo, and hypo-khâgne were very pleasant years for me. I felt completely accepted.

DE BEAUVOIR: That was one of the moments in your life when, looking back, you feel that there was a choice, that there was something free. Were there others?

SARTRE: Yes. The Ecole Normale was a very high point. It was freedom. Freedom of action was granted me by the very rules of the school. One could stay out until midnight. After midnight one climbed over the wall. We lived three or four together in a study, then two, and then finally, when Nizan left for Aden I lived in my study by myself. We lunched at the school or in a little bistro near at hand. We spent hours in another bistro where we met the local girls and young men. We went out every evening. We worked very peacefully in our studies. Twice a week I went to have lunch with my people and then I came back to the school. My relations with my family had become much gentler.

DE BEAUVOIR: Do you feel that certain choices have shaped your destiny?

SARTRE: One of the vital periods was the war.

DE BEAUVOIR: But there's one thing you don't talk about. Isn't it writing that has directed your life?

SARTRE: It has directed it since the age of eight.

DE BEAUVOIR: Yes, but wasn't there a time when you took it up again particularly? At eight, it was a child who was writing. That might have stopped.

SARTRE: It did change and it was taken up again, each time differently.

DE BEAUVOIR: But it was a fundamental choice that has always remained?

SARTRE: Yes.

DE BEAUVOIR: Let's go back to those times when perhaps you did not feel free but which seem to you to have been important choices when you look back.

SARTRE: The war. Going off to the war. I was against all war, but still that particular one had to be lived through. In myself I had built up an idea of opposition to nazism that might in case of necessity take the form of military action. That made it possible for me to communicate with my comrades at the front.

DE BEAUVOIR: In what way do you think it was important?

SARTRE: Because it was no longer a teacher's life, interspersed with a few trips abroad. I was plunged into a social situation of vast extent.

DE BEAUVOIR: It wasn't you who chose to be plunged into it. You had been called up.

SARTRE: I didn't choose it, but I had to react in one way or another. From the moment he set foot in the train, every man chose how he would live through the war. That's very important. I always wanted to assume my part in that war. My part consisted of launching balloons. It called for some mental effort to see the connection between launching a red balloon into the sky and the whole of this invisible war that surrounded us. And then there were my relations with my comrades, who on the whole were against the war for various reasons. My relations with you and with other people.

DE BEAUVOIR: You mean that you might inwardly have made another choice? A pacifist choice, for instance?

SARTRE: Yes, I was free to make any choice whatsoever.

DE BEAUVOIR: Or even a collaborationist, pro-Nazi choice.

SARTRE: No, not that, because I was against the Nazis.

DE BEAUVOIR: But pacifism might have been a temptation for you. We did talk about it. I was nearer a pacifism after Alain's pattern then you were. You had thoroughly grasped what would happen if fascism won. Your choice summed up the totality of your attitudes.

SARTRE: That choice subsequently allowed me to go further—the Resistance when I came back from being a prisoner, and then socialism. All this came from that first choice. I think it was absolutely fundamental. My comrades and I are men of the 1940 war. Those five years of war and captivity and living side by side with our conquerors were of the very first importance for me. The fact of living next to a German who had beaten us, and who was furthermore an ordinary private who knew nothing about us and who spoke no French, was an experience I underwent first as a prisoner and then as a free man in an imprisoned country. I began to have a better understanding of what resisting the authorities meant. Before the war I did not resist. I rather despised the authorities who had power over me, that is, the government, the administration. But from the moment I was a prisoner, these authorities were Nazis or in some cases Pétainists. Now you and I despised both the one and the other, and as far as possible we disobeyed the orders they gave us. For example, we weren't allowed to go into the Free Zone,* yet we crossed into it twice. We weren't allowed to go into certain parts of Paris at certain times . . .

DE BEAUVOIR: Was it from that time that you tried to reconcile the presence of an inner freedom with the requirements of freedom for everyone? Was it then that your personal freedom came into contact with that of others?

SARTRE: Yes. In the Occupied Zone we were prisoners of the Nazis. In spite of everything my freedom was much oppressed because it could not find expression in all the forms I wished. In particular, the novels that I wrote had no meaning unless the Nazis left France— they could be printed only on that condition. It was singular, now I come to think of it, the care I took in writing works that could not appear unless the Nazis vanished. As the name I picked on, "Socialism and Liberty," clearly shows, the Resistance carried with it the idea that I inclined toward socialism but that I did not know whether liberty had its place therein.

DE BEAUVOIR: You had the idea of a synthesis.

SARTRE: Yes, without a doubt. As a hope, and then at the end as a certainty; but only at the end.

---

* From 1940 until November 1942 the southern part of France, the *Zone libre*, was not occupied by the Germans. (trans.)

DE BEAUVOIR: Which were the other moments of choice that retrospectively seem to you important?

SARTRE: My relations with the Communists toward 1952–56, which were broken off at the time of the Hungarian trouble. They brought me to conceive the possibility of relations with political men who were opposed to the government but who were thoroughly established in the community.

DE BEAUVOIR: How did your passage from individual to social freedom take place?

SARTRE: I think that's important. I was working on *Being and Nothingness* at that time. It was about 1943. *Being and Nothingness* is a book about freedom. I then, like the old Stoics, believed that one was always free, even in exceedingly disagreeable circumstances that might end in death. On this point I've changed very much. I think that in fact there are situations in which one cannot be free. I explained my thoughts on the subject in *The Devil and the Good Lord* . . . Heinrich, the priest, is a man who has never been free, because he is a man of the Church and because at the same time he has a relation with the people which is absolutely unconnected with his ecclesiastical education. People and Church contradict one another. He is himself the place in which these forces come into conflict and he can never be free. He dies because he has never been able to assert himself. This change in me came toward 1942–43 or perhaps even a little later. I moved on from the Stoic idea that one is always free—a very important notion for me, since I had always felt free, never having known those extremely grave circumstances in which I could no longer feel free—to the later idea that there were circumstances in which freedom was enchained. These circumstances arose out of the freedom of others. In other words, one freedom is enchained by another freedom or by other freedoms, which is something I have always thought.

DE BEAUVOIR: Wasn't the idea of the Resistance also that there was always another possible way out in death?

SARTRE: Certainly. There was a great deal of that in it. This idea of putting an end to one's life not by suicide but by an action that may end in death and that will bear fruit insofar as one is oneself destroyed, was an idea that was present in the Resistance, and it was one that I appreciated. I looked upon dying freely as a perfect end for the human being, far more perfect than a slow end with illnesses, aging, and even senility, or in any case a weakening of the mental powers that sees liberty vanishing well before death. I preferred the idea of a total, freely conceded sacrifice, which consequently does not limit the free-dom of a being, whose freedom is his essence. And it was for this reason that I thought myself free in all circumstances. Later, in the case of Heinrich, I showed that there were many, many circumstances in which one was not free.

DE BEAUVOIR: How did you move from the idea that one was free in all circumstances to the idea that death was not a liberating issue, but on the contrary, one that did away with freedom?

SARTRE: I still retain the idea that freedom also consists of being able to die. That is, if tomorrow some threat or other menaces my freedom, death is a way of preserving it.

DE BEAUVOIR: Many people don't want to die. A factory hand work-ing on the production line does not feel free, but he's not going to liberate himself by choosing death.

SARTRE: No, he doesn't feel free. He attaches no sort of value to the freedom he still possesses. It's that confused state of mind that men have with regard to their freedom which makes things so complicated in politics.

DE BEAUVOIR: To go back to your personal problem, how did you move from the idea that your freedom was self-sufficient to the idea that for you to be free it was necessary that all others should be free too? That was the view you finally reached, wasn't it?

SARTRE: Yes. It is unacceptable, inconceivable that one man should be free if the others are not. If freedom is refused to the others it ceases to be a freedom. If men do not respect others' freedom, the freedom that for a moment showed in them is instantly destroyed.

DE BEAUVOIR: But when did you move from the one conception to the other?

SARTRE: I think it was at the same time that I moved on to a socialist polity. Not that socialism begets liberty. On the contrary, in the forms we know it refuses liberty; it bases itself upon a solidarity which itself arises from necessity. For example, the working class's class-consciousness is not a free consciousness. It is the consciousness of a class that is oppressed and outraged by the other class, the bourgeoisie. So it does not appear as being free. It appears as being produced by a hopeless situation. I reflected on liberty in a certain number of studies that I wrote down in notebooks, big notebooks that I've now lost. In these studies there were vast numbers of ethical, philosophical, and political observations. It was then that I looked at freedom with a new eye. In these studies I conceived liberty as being something that in certain circumstances might be abolished and as something that bound men to one another insofar as each, in order to be free, needed the freedom of all the rest. That was about 1945–1950.

DE BEAUVOIR: And what do you think about freedom now? About your freedom and about freedom in general?

SARTRE: As far as my freedom is concerned, I haven't changed. I think I am free. Like many others, I have been alienated on certain levels. I was oppressed at the time of the war. I was a prisoner. I was not free when I was a prisoner. Yet I lived through being a prisoner in my own way with a certain freedom. I don't know why, but I look upon myself as being very nearly responsible for everything that happens to me. Responsible in given circumstances, of course. But on the whole I see myself in everything I have done and I do not think my actions have been determined by an outside cause.

DE BEAUVOIR: That concerns your particular case, because you aren't subject to constraints. You are a privileged creature and you can do more or less what you like with your life. But when you were talking about workers on the production line, you said, "They don't feel free." Do you think that they don't *feel* free or that they *aren't* free?

SARTRE: I told you, what causes their behavior to be determined for them is the action of other men on them, which brings about restraints, duties, and pseudocontracts that muddle their minds; in short, a slavery in which freedom of thought and of action is confused. It still exists; otherwise why should they revolt? But it is hidden by collective images, by repetitive actions performed every day under constraint, by conceptions that have been learned, not thought out by themselves, and by a lack of knowledge. And sometimes freedom appears to them under names other than its own, as it did in 1968 for instance. Yet it's freedom they're after when they want to bring down, put out of action, or maybe kill the general mass of their oppressors in order to find a state in which they would be responsible for themselves and for society. I think 1968 was a time when they became aware of freedom, only to lose that awareness again afterward. But that time was important and beautiful, unreal and true. It was an action by which the technicians, the workers, the living forces of the country became aware that collective freedom was something other than the combination of all individual freedoms. That was what 1968 amounted to. And at that point I think each man grasped the nature of his own freedom and that of the group he belonged to. Moments of that kind have often happened in history. The Commune was one of them.

DE BEAUVOIR: Can you think of anything to add about your own relations with freedom?

SARTRE: Once again I say that freedom represents something that doesn't exist but that gradually creates itself, something that has always been present in me and that will leave me only when I die. And I think that all other men are like me, but that the degree of awareness and the clarity with which this freedom appears to them varies according to the circumstances, according to their origins, their development, and their knowledge. My idea of freedom has been modified by my relations with history. I was within history; whether I liked it or not I was carried along in the direction of certain social changes that were going to happen whatever my attitude toward them might be. This is what I learned at that particular time: that is to say, a healthy and sometimes horrible modesty. Then, and it is still the case, I learned that the essential part of a man's life and therefore of mine was the relation between opposing terms, as, for example, being and nothingness, being and becoming, the idea of freedom and that of the exterior world that set itself against my freedom as it were. Freedom and situation.

DE BEAUVOIR: You became aware that your freedom was in opposition to the pressure of history and of the world.

SARTRE: That's right. In order to make my freedom triumph it was necessary to act upon history and the world and bring about a different relation between man on the one hand and history and the world on the other. That was the starting point. I first experienced a kind of individual freedom before the war, or at least I believed I experienced it. That lasted quite a long time and it assumed various forms, but on the whole it was the freedom of an individual who was trying to express himself and to overcome exterior forces. During the war I experienced one thing that seemed to me the absolute contrary of freedom—the obligation to go off and fight—an obligation for which I did not clearly see the reason, although I was completely anti-Nazi. I could not really understand why it was necessary that millions of men should confront one another in a life-or-death struggle. This was the first time I grasped the contradiction of my commitment to the war, which I wanted to be a free commitment, but which nevertheless imposed something on me that I had not truly and freely desired, and imposed it even to the point of my death. Then came the freedom of the Resistance, which led me to contrast the strength of a tyrannical society with the freedom of individuals opposed to it, individuals who I thought should win because they were free and because they freely saw what it was they wanted. At the Liberation I felt that the forces they had set free were of the same nature as those of the Nazis. Not that they had the same aims or that they made use of methods such as the murder of millions of Jews and millions of Russians, but the collective strength, the obedience to orders, were of the same kind. And the arrival of the American Army in France seemed to many people, including myself, like a tyranny.

People were Gaullist. I wasn't, but I did feel something that the others felt, the necessity of a French state power, a state strength, and therefore the legitimacy of a power like de Gaulle's. I did not think that, but I did feel the force of that point of view. Then, from the moment of the Liberation, a very strong Communist party began to appear, much stronger than it had ever been in France before the war, a party that included a third of all Frenchmen. It now became necessary to take up one's stand with regard to the groups that governed us. For my part I stayed outside them, as did Merleau-Ponty, by the way, though for different reasons. I founded the review, *Les Temps modernes,* in which we were left-wing, but not Communist.

DE BEAUVOIR: Didn't you found it partly for the very purpose of taking part in the political struggle?

SARTRE: Not exactly. It was rather to show the importance on all levels of the happenings in everyday life and in the diplomatic, political, and economic aspects of collective life. It was a matter of showing that every event had different strata and that each of them constituted a meaning of the event, the same meaning, furthermore, from stratum to stratum, merely changed by whatever happened to be involved at that particular level. The chief idea was to make it plain that in a society everything possesses many facets and that each expresses, in its own manner but completely, a meaning that is the meaning of the event. This meaning is to be found in entirely different forms and more or less developed at each level of the strata that make them up in depth.

DE BEAUVOIR: But it seems to me that there is a great deal of consistency in all this. A little while back you spoke of contradiction, yet here you are leading the life of a man of letters, your writing has found its own definition—it is committed. You edit *Les Temps modernes,* which also represents the same tendency. All this seems thoroughly coherent to me. Why did you speak of contradiction just now and say that since the war your life has been lived in a certain contradiction?

SARTRE: Because in a man's life consistency is desirable, but it applies only to the thesis or the antithesis. The thesis is a sum of ideas, ways, and customs that should for preference be roughly consistent even if it does include some minor contradictions, and in the same way the antithesis should possess a certain coherence. Each of the two, thesis and antithesis, is explained by its opposition to the other. Now here I have laid out what may be called the thesis for you; all that is left is to explain the antithesis. What I observed, though still rather vaguely, during the first part of my life, was the opposition between my freedom and the world. The war and the years after the war were no more than a development of this opposition, and it was that which I meant to point out when I chose "Socialism and Liberty" as the name of our Resistance movement. The idea of an orderly community in which each develops according to his own principles, and then on the other hand the idea of freedom, that is, a free development of each and all, are ideas that then seemed to me to be opposed—even now each exists separately, apart one from the other. What I discovered after the war was that my contradiction and this world's contradiction lay in the area of freedom, in the idea of the person's full development and complete fulfilment confronted with the equally full development of the community to which he belongs, the two appearing at first to be contradictory. The full development of a citizen is not necessarily preceded by the full development of society. It is at this level that one may provide the explanation of my history, of my plain, evident history since the war and my dark, clouded history before it; that is, the idea of my liberty implies the idea of the liberty of others. I cannot feel free if others are not free. My freedom implies the freedom of others and it is not subject to limitation. But then again I know that there are institutions, a state, laws, in short, a collection of restraints that are imposed on the individual and that do not leave him free in any way to do what he wants. That's where I see a contradiction, for a social world has to possess certain forms and my freedom has to be entire. This was also evident during the Occupation. Resistance implied very strict and important norms, such as secret work or special and dangerous missions, whose underlying meaning was the building of another society that was to be free. It followed that the ideal of the individual's freedom was the free society for which he was fighting.

DE BEAUVOIR: At what times did you experience this contradiction most intensely? And how did you resolve it in each situation?

SARTRE: Necessarily, they were no more than provisional solutions. First there was the R.D.R., the *Rassemblement Démocratique Révolution-*

naire, with Rousset and people like Altmann, the editor of *Libéra-tion* . . .

DE BEAUVOIR: The *Libération* of those days . . .

SARTRE: The *Libération* of those days, which was a Radical-Socialist paper, then more or less pro-Communist, then Communist, and then more or less pro-Communist again. The movement wanted to be separate from the Communist party, but revolutionary, trying to bring about socialism by means of revolution. Those are very high-sounding words, and they can mean nothing. In the first place, the question reform/revolution arises immediately. What revolution is concerned? A revolution that just wants to set reforms in motion and support them? In that case it's something to set oneself against—it's the reformist socialism of before the war. Or was it really a revolution-ary movement? It seems to me that although there were a few people of that tendency, the measures that the R.D.R. took were much more reformist than revolutionary, particularly because Rousset, a former Trotskyist, had absolutely nothing of the revolutionary about him, apart from his big mouth. And as far as I was concerned, it was a question of being drawn into the R.D.R. rather than joining it reso-lutely and of my own accord. Once I was in they wanted to give me an important place, and I fell in with their wishes; but there was a considerable degree of opposition between Rousset and me. I saw that Rousset was turning toward reformism, that he wanted to get funds for the R.D.R. by begging from the American workers' unions. This seemed to me absolutely mad, for it meant making a French group financially dependent on the great American organizations, which are so different from ours and from the left-wing policy that we put forward. I was against this tendency of Rousset's.

The contradiction broke out after Rousset had been to America, where he had collected a little money. He, and even more Altmann, organized a kind of congress in France for people who might take an interest in the R.D.R., and he invited the Americans.

DE BEAUVOIR: But you've already spoken about that. What interests me is seeing that what you looked upon as a solution for a while was in fact unsound.

SARTRE: No, because very soon the movement showed that it was not revolutionary but reformist and that the chosen form was not a pos-sible one. At that juncture it was just not possible to set up a different revolutionary force side by side with the Communist party. There was a contradiction between a freedom that set itself against the Communist party and a revolution, that is, a mass movement, insofar as that revolution refused the idea of freedom. Subsequently, after a great many hesitations, there was another period of contradiction—the period of Operation Ridgway. Ridgway came to Paris. There was a Communist demonstration against him, a violent demonstration, and a few hours later Duclos, who was going by in a car with two pigeons on the seat, was arrested on the pretext that they were carrier pigeons. It was a grotesque accusation and it had the result of making me write an article in defense of the Communists, an article that was published in several installments in *Les Temps modernes* and that brought about a change in the party's attitude toward me.

DE BEAUVOIR: What induced you to write this article?

SARTRE: Oddly enough it was Henri Guillemin. His book on Napoleon III's taking power, *Le Coup du 2 décembre*, in which he gave extracts from newspapers, private diaries, and books by writers favorable to Napoleon III's coming to power, decided me to look upon Duclos's arrest as very serious.

DE BEAUVOIR: So you made the decision to support the Communist party, though without joining it of course.

SARTRE: I wrote *The Communists and Peace* without having any communication with the party and being hostile to it on the whole, in order to say that Duclos's arrest was shameful. Then gradually the articles changed into a kind of semipanegyric and then even an actual panegyric of the Communist party against the then current French formations. The result was that the party sent me Claude Roy and another man—Claude Roy representing the element that could speak to non-Communist intellectuals—to ask me whether I wouldn't join with those of the intellectuals who were protesting against the arrest of Henri Martin. I agreed. I attended the meetings of these intellectuals. I suggested the writing of a book calling for the release of Henri Martin, a book made up of various articles for which I would provide a sort of commentary. I did so; the book was called *L'affaire Henry Martin* and it was published. Unfortunately, because of technical difficulties, it came out a couple of weeks after Henri Martin had been released, but it is a fact that he was released at that particular time.

DE BEAUVOIR: Then you went to the Peace Congress.

SARTRE: At that time the Communist party's attitude toward me had changed and so had mine toward it; we had become allies. The rest of the left wing no longer existed. The Socialists were on the side of the Right, they fought against the Communist party, battering it as hard as they could, and it seemed to me that the only surviving Left would be one attached to the Communists. In spite of great mental reservations, *Les Temps modernes* allied itself to the Communists in order to carry on a policy favorable to the party.

DE BEAUVOIR: In what way did that represent a solution of your contradictions?

SARTRE: Fundamentally it was not a solution. They never lasted long, but several times in the course of my life there have been short periods in which I have dropped freedom in favor of a group idea.

DE BEAUVOIR: At that time did you think that the Communist party was something like a stage in the direction of socialism?

SARTRE: Yes, I did. I did not think our aims were the same, but going along with them was easy enough.

DE BEAUVOIR: And until when did that last?

SARTRE: It lasted from '52 to '56 . . .

DE BEAUVOIR: It was in '54 that you went to the USSR. You were still on good terms with them at that time.

SARTRE: Yes, but what I saw in the USSR did not fill me with enthusiasm. Of course they just showed me what could be shown, and I had a great many reservations.

DE BEAUVOIR: Yet you wrote a very laudatory piece in *Libération*.

SARTRE: It was Cau who wrote it.

DE BEAUVOIR: It must be admitted that you were exhausted.

SARTRE: I gave him a certain number of leading points and then I went off for a holiday with you.

DE BEAUVOIR: Yes, to get some rest. Then there was Helsinki, which was another Peace Congress. Where I went with you. That was in 1955.

SARTRE: Yes, and we met some Algerians who told us about the situation in Algeria.

DE BEAUVOIR: Yes, indeed. And then there was 1956, which was the time of your break with the Communist party.

SARTRE: A break that has never really been healed. It was healed to a certain extent from '62 on, when I went back to the USSR.

DE BEAUVOIR: We went back together in '62, twice in fact; and then in '63, '64 and '65.

SARTRE: Yet I wasn't on such very good terms with the Communists.

DE BEAUVOIR: But we had friends there among those who were deeply opposed to Stalinism. Then there was another commitment that was important to you—against the war in Algeria. You did a lot of pretty

important things during that war. Then after '68 there were your
relations with the Maos. How did you come to reconcile your desire
for individual freedom with a collective action that implied discipline
and orders?

SARTRE: Whenever I committed myself in one way or another to
politics and carried out an action, I never abandoned the idea of
freedom. On the contrary, every time I acted I felt free. I've never
belonged to a party. I may have felt sympathetic toward some party
for a while—at present I have a fellow feeling for the Maoist tendency,
which is now beginning to disperse in France but which nevertheless
is not dead—and more lasting sympathies. I have therefore been in
touch with various groups, but without belonging to them. They
asked me to do things. I was free to say yes or no, and I always felt
free whether I agreed or refused. Take my attitude during the Algerian
war, for example. That was the time at which I separated myself from
the Communist party because the party and we did not want exactly
the same thing. The party did envisage the independence of Algeria
but only as one possibility among others, whereas we agreed with the
F.L.N. in calling for that independence in the immediate future. We
and the Communists came together again to some extent in order to
try to set up an anti-O.A.S. group. It didn't lead to much, I may
add, because the Communists intended to spoil our efforts. I've always
looked upon colonialism as an action of pure theft, the brutal conquest
of a country and the absolutely intolerable exploitation of one country
by another; I thought that all the colonial states would have to get rid
of their colonies sooner or later. In the Algerian war I was completely
in agreement with the Algerians against the French government, the
government, I say emphatically, although many Frenchmen were in
favor of keeping a French Algeria. There were continual struggles
with certain Frenchmen, and the tightening of friendships and bonds
between others who were in favor of the liberation of Algeria. I went
even further. With Jeanson I was in touch with the F.L.N. and I
wrote for their secret paper—I speak of these things merely to show
how freedom was involved in this business. It was certainly original
freedom that made me at sixteen look upon colonialism as an antihu-
man brutality, as an action that destroyed men for the sake of material
interests. The freedom that made me a man made colonialism something abject. In making me a man it destroyed other men and for that
reason setting myself up as a man meant being opposed to colonialism.
What I thought when I was about sixteen may have grown stronger

and deeper but I always thought it even until after the Algerian war and I think it still. I was in Brazil in 1960. Friends in Paris telephoned me in Rio, telling me when Jeanson, his friends, and the women who had worked with him were to be tried and asking me to write a testimony that would be read to the court, since I could not get back by the date they gave me. I obviously could not dictate this testimony. The telephone was very bad, I could not hear them well nor could they hear me. I confined myself to repeating the few essential points upon which I wanted the testimony to bear; my friends knew them in any case, and I knew that they would make a good job of it. I let them write the testimony, and when I came to read it I found it perfectly correct.

DE BEAUVOIR: You also wrote a great many articles before '60.

SARTRE: Of course I did! I wrote articles against the war in Algeria and against the torture that was going on.

DE BEAUVOIR: Where did you publish them?

SARTRE: In *Les Temps modernes,* in *L'Express,* and also in Jeanson's little paper *Vérité pour,* which was more or less clandestine.

DE BEAUVOIR: Were there other things?

SARTRE: In Brazil the Algerian representative asked to meet me. I went to see him and we talked about propaganda in favor of the Algerians; we were in complete agreement. Apart from that I gave a lecture on the Algerian war in Saõ Paulo. I remember that lecture. It was a positive tidal wave, with people rushing in, mostly students. They burst open the doors and filled the hall from one side to the other. I explained my conception of the war in Algeria, which was also that of the F.L.N. A Frenchman tried to answer me, which called for a certain amount of courage, because the audience as a whole was on the side of the Algerians. He was booed and he had the greatest difficulty in speaking. I replied to him; he disappeared and the meeting turned into a demonstration in favor of the Algerians. Throughout all this I felt perfectly free; I could have refused to give a lecture on the war in Algeria and I could have chosen a literary subject instead. But I wanted to describe the exact and immediate facts that were putting freedom in danger. Within myself I was free as I gave this lecture, and at the same time its subject was the freedom of the Algerian people. At this level I find that the connection between freedom, my freedom, freedom as an end in itself, and the exercise of freedom against anything that might interfere with it, that is, the action of other men, is evident once more. It was therefore a question of presenting the freedom of the Algerian people as a supreme and absolute end, and the war as an attempt to prevent men from liberating themselves.

DE BEAUVOIR: Since you are citing facts, there is one you've forgotten, a fact that made it reasonable that you should have been asked for your testimony, and that's the *Manifeste des 121*. It was very important. We were threatened with prison when we should return to France for having signed that manifesto. Jeanson's trial largely turned on it.

SARTRE: Yes, and at that time people who were in favor of the Algerian war held marches in the Champs Elysées and there were cries of "Death to Sartre!" The French government wanted to prosecute me for having signed the manifesto like the hundred and twenty other signatories. That too was a minor detail, and in that case too I was free. I never belonged to any pro-Algerian organization, but I was in sympathy with all of them and was welcomed in all of them. What I've been trying to show is how that little action of no great importance and the whole of what I did to make the Algerian cause popular in Brazil arose from my freedom. I've been trying to show that I was not conditioned by anyone, that I acted by myself in relation to my own theories, my own political beliefs, and that I committed myself completely. After that we went to Cuba and came home by way of Spain. When we crossed the frontier there was a certain amount of argument with the customs men, who let us through in the end but not without having told Paris of our return. Some of our friends would have liked us to come back by plane so that if there were an arrest it would be carried out in front of everybody, but we thought that provocation was useless and that it would be better to go quietly back to Paris, officially but discreetly. Friends came to meet us in Barcelona —Pouillon, Lanzmann, and Bost. They took us back to Paris, where the police started taking our evidence and where it was understood that in a week we should go before the instructing magistrate. The day before we were due to go the poor magistrate fell ill, as we learned from the papers. A week later he was still ill, and that was where the joke ended. We never heard any more of our indictment as signatories of the *Manifeste des 121*. I am only mentioning one small event among hundreds of others. I wanted to point out how at a given juncture freedom made me discover the true relation of the Algerians to the French or of the French to the Algerians—an oppression. I was necessarily against this oppression, in the name of the freedom that seems to me to form the basis of every man's existence; and as a man I was required to act every time and as far as I could in favor of freedom. The means I made use of depended on necessary causes and connections that no longer had anything to do with free assertion. Yet when I used them they were shot through and through with freedom—they were necessary for asserting liberty in the world.

DE BEAUVOIR: Was it also the love of freedom that made you try to do something with the writers and intellectuals of the Eastern countries? I mean weren't your journeys to the USSR between '62 and '66 intended to try to help the liberal intellectuals become liberalized?

SARTRE: Liberal is an ignoble word.

DE BEAUVOIR: Still, that's the name they used themselves. Wasn't that the reason?

SARTRE: Yes. I wanted to see whether by talking it might be possible to make some small change in their view of the world, of the forces confronting one another and of what was to be done. But above all I went to Russia to meet people who thought as I did—intellectuals who had already carried out this work themselves. Two or three of them.

DE BEAUVOIR: You stopped going to the USSR in '66 when there were the Daniel and Siniavsky trials. You thought the cause of what were called the liberal intellectuals was more or less lost. But there was one fact that was still more important in making up your mind and that was the invasion of Czechoslovakia.

SARTRE: Yes. There had already been the invasion of Hungary.

DE BEAUVOIR: Which had made you break with the Communists. You had, after all, to some extent resumed relations with the USSR toward '62, as we have just said. But this break was definitive. How did you express your attitude at the time of Czechoslovakia?

SARTRE: The intervention in Czechoslovakia seemed to me particularly revolting because it clearly showed the attitude of the USSR toward the socialist countries of what was called the Soviet glacis. It was a matter of preventing the régimes from changing, if necessary by armed force. I was invited by my Czechoslovak friends during a rather strange period that soon came to an end. As the Soviet troops were there, the Czechoslovaks organized an intellectual resistance, particularly in Prague. They were staging two plays of mine at the same time, *The Flies* and *Dirty Hands,* with obvious anti-Soviet intentions. I was present at both. I spoke to the audience about the Soviet aggression without disguising my feelings; I also spoke on television, though in rather more moderate terms. In short they used me to help them in the struggle against the enemy, who was present but who was not to be seen. I stayed there a few days and I met and talked to various Czech and Slovak intellectuals. They were all deeply disgusted by this attack and they were determined to resist. When I left I was not cheerful, to be sure, but I was convinced that the business would not be settled easily, and that the Czechoslovak people had begun a struggle against their Soviet oppressors that would undoubtedly continue. Shortly after this I wrote an article on the subject, a preface to a book of Liehm's.

DE BEAUVOIR: Yes, a book in which he had collected the testimonies . . .

SARTRE: Testimonies of the majority of well-known Czechoslovak intellectuals, all of them against the intervention.

DE BEAUVOIR: And after Czechoslovakia, what was your political activity? Had you any connection with the events of May '68?

SARTRE: Yes, but late. We had paid some attention to the university problems in *Les Temps modernes.* In particular, we had spoken about the lectures, the professorial lectures. There had been some articles by Kravetz; and then like everyone else in France we were caught unawares by the events of May '68. At that time the young did not think too badly of me.

DE BEAUVOIR: You made a statement on Radio Luxembourg in favor of the students, and it was even handed about in the Latin Quarter in the form of leaflets.

SARTRE: So it was. And I spoke in the great hall of the Sorbonne one day in May '68; I was asked to go, and I spoke to a crowded hall. The Sorbonne was in a strange state, occupied by the students. It was a curious sight. And then I also spoke at the Cité Universitaire. So I did have a certain contact with May '68. Afterward it was vaguer. I remember being called upon to speak at the Sorbonne by some student friends who were arguing about one particular point: should they have a demonstration the next day or not? It had nothing to do with me and I could only speak on a general plane. A piece of paper was put on the table for me saying, "Keep it short, Sartre." That meant they did not particularly want to hear what I had to say to them, and that in fact I had nothing to say to them, not having been a student for a great while and not being a teacher either. There was nothing that qualified me to speak. I did speak a little, nevertheless. They clapped quite heartily when I went up to the rostrum, less when I came down, because what I said was not what they had expected. They expected people who would say, "There must be a demonstration for this reason or that, and these are the conditions in which it must be carried out, etcetera." I did play a part later. In '70, when the two successive editors of *La Cause du peuple*, Le Bris and Le Dantec, were both put in prison, the Maoists, whom I didn't know and who only the day before were attacking me in *La Cause du peuple*, asked me to edit the paper.

DE BEAUVOIR: It was the *Gauche prolétarienne* at that particular time.

SARTRE: Yes, a Maoist party led by the man who called himself Pierre Victor. There again it was a free act. Nothing obliged me to agree, seeing that the Maos had not been particularly kind to me. But one morning a Mao—I no longer remember who—came to talk to me, and I said that I would edit the paper from that day on. I had agreed to be a kind of figurehead, since I had no very clear idea of their tendency and their principles. I did not intend to edit and they themselves did not ask me to do so. I only thought of giving them my name and, if the occasion arose, of acting with them in order to give them a little peace and to prevent them from being suppressed as a paper and as a group. What made things rather more complicated was the fact that a little while after this there was the trial of Le Bris and Le Dantec, which I attended to give evidence as the third editor of *La Cause du peuple* and to express my solidarity with them. That day a decision of the Ministry of the Interior suppressed the *Gauche prolétarienne*. The party was forbidden. At the same time Le Bris and Le Dantec were given quite heavy prison sentences. Shortly after, Geismar was himself prosecuted; he hid but in the end he was found and brought to trial. I went to give evidence for him too. I was not troubled myself, I was not arrested; it was thought that I was not really the editor of *La Cause du peuple*, which was true in one sense, since I had no connection with what was written in it. But everyone knew that I was the editor so as to prevent the arrest of the other editors. I was not arrested because they thought it would make too much noise. *La Cause du peuple* thus led a strange life, official in one way, since it was published and I was its editor, yet at the same time, forbidden. When people were found selling *La Cause du peuple* they were arrested and given a few weeks in prison. Very few issues were seized at the printers, because we sent large quantities off in trucks the day before, and they were distributed in the provinces and in Paris. We distributed some in the Avenue du Général Leclerc and then on the Boulevard Poissonière, two separate ventures. I was put into a police van and then kept under surveillance. These actions brought about closer relations with the Maos who worked on the paper. They began to want to talk to me. We had meetings at which Victor, Geismar, and others discussed various positions with me or various attitudes, and in the end, although during this first period I did not really become the editor, I began to be aware of the value of the *Gauche prolétarienne*. In it I began to discover a kind of militant freedom, a freedom that influenced me on the social and the political level. In this freedom I saw the possibility of conceiving of militants who were free in their militant activities, which at first sight may seem a contradiction. And which is certainly not the case with a militant Communist. Although I never joined the *Gauche prolétarienne* —which in any case was broken up, as I've said, but which continued to exist under another form—I gradually came nearer to some of the Maos' positions. My discussions, often alone with Victor, grew closer and closer; I saw how important the *Gauche prolétarienne* might be for me; I began talking with the editorial staff about the issues of *La Cause du peuple* and the articles, and finally I edited one or two issues myself, bringing together various contributors. The leaders were not against it; they wanted to see what the result would be. Obviously I adopted the general trend of the Maoist ideas, but only insofar as they . . . charmed me. So I produced two issues of this kind and then I more or less withdrew, though I still kept my name on the front page, and finally *La Cause du peuple* disappeared. But not the Maoist spirit, which still exists and of which I look upon myself as one of the representatives, although the name Mao no longer means anything much. Victor, Gavi, and I expressed something of our ideas in the book we published, *On a raison de se révolter* (To Rebel is Justified). So that was what my political passage in the *Gauche prolétarienne* from '70 to '73 was like.

DE BEAUVOIR: But what about later? Was there another paper?

SARTRE: *Libération!* It seemed natural that I should be the editor of *Libération,* which was not a Maoist paper but which had been launched by Maos and some other representatives of left-wing groups. I was asked to do so because I had been editor of *La Cause du peuple.* I agreed because I thought it might mean real progress to have a genuinely left-wing, an extreme left-wing paper in which to say quite unambiguously what we thought about every event as it occurred. Here again I was rather a figurehead of an editor. To begin with, the editor's role was not clearly defined. And then quite simply I am sick and that prevented me from playing a real part in *Libération.* At present I'm no longer editor because I had to resign on account of illness, but I'm one of the new editorial committee that decides on the paper's broad lines. As you know, I'm still very tired; I can neither read nor write —can write still, after a fashion, but not read what I've written. Yet one way or another I do manage to make my opinions known. Here again freedom has always been the essence, the reason for my choices. And the new *Libération* was restructured this summer; the new form was studied by Gavi, Victor, me, and a few others, and this time the new *Libération,* which is going to appear in a few days, may make a thoroughly good start.

DE BEAUVOIR: In these conversations you seem immensely eager to talk about your relations with politics. You spoke about them in your conversations with Victor and Gavi and you're still anxious to speak about them now with me. Why? Since you're first and foremost a writer and a philosopher.

SARTRE: Because political life represents something I haven't been able to avoid, something into which I've been plunged. I haven't been a politician, but I've had political reactions to a great many political events, so that the state of a politician in the broad sense, that is of a man moved by politics, steeped in politics, is something that does characterize me. For some time the Maos looked upon my friendship with Victor only as a political relation, for example.

DE BEAUVOIR: The Maos' point of view is not a universal and everlasting point of view. Posterity will not think of you as a politician but essentially as a writer, a philosopher, who also had certain political attitudes, like almost all intellectuals. Why do you attribute this special importance to the political dimension of your life?

SARTRE: At twenty I was apolitical—which is perhaps only another kind of political attitude—and I am ending as a Socialist-Communist, envisaging a certain political destiny for mankind. It seems to me that this represents a life, passing from an apolitical to a political attitude properly so-called. It has taken up a great deal of my lifetime. There was the R.D.N., my relations with the Communists, my relations with the Maos and all that. It makes a whole.

DE BEAUVOIR: Would you like to go back to your political biography, then?

SARTRE: There must be an explanation of what it means to be apolitical, where it comes from, why I was apolitical when I first met you, and then how it happens that political ideas gather and tighten around one so that in the end they cause themselves to be taken up in one way or another. That seems to me essential.

DE BEAUVOIR: Well then, let's talk about it.

SARTRE: When I was a child politics was something that concerned everybody. Every man was to perform certain duties, such as voting, for example, and the result of everyone voting was that the country was a republic and not the Second Empire or a monarchy.

DE BEAUVOIR: You mean there was a political atmosphere in the home where you lived with your grandparents?

SARTRE: Yes; my grandfather adopted the principles of the Third Republic. I think he voted for the Center; he didn't say much about the people he voted for. He thought one should keep that to oneself. Which was comic in that household made up of his wife, who didn't give a damn, of his daughter, who knew nothing whatsoever about it, and me, who was too small to ask. But still, he preferred to keep his distance. That was the secrecy of the man who votes; it was the political power he wields in voting. But he did tell us that he would vote for Poincaré.

DE BEAUVOIR: So people talked about politics when you were small?

SARTRE: Oh, very little. Just a very little.

DE BEAUVOIR: I believe there were also questions of nationalism that were of importance, weren't there?

SARTRE: Yes. Alsace—the war.

DE BEAUVOIR: So in your childhood you had a civic dimension.

SARTRE: Yes, Alsace was the important point with my grandfather. Alsace had been taken by the Germans. So I had the political idea that is to be found in textbooks, and it stayed that way until the war. During the war there were the brave little Frenchmen, the heroic *poilus,* who fought aginst the wicked Germans; it was a simple kind of patriotism taught in the schools and I believed in it completely. I even wrote an adventure story at that time, just when I was entering the sixth form in Paris, a tale in which the hero was a soldier who took the crown prince prisoner. He was stronger than the crown prince and he beat him in the front of a crowd of soldiers who laughed with delight.

DE BEAUVOIR: So you felt you were a citizen. Well, at least there was a civic dimension. What's more, you acted in the patriotic plays written by your grandfather.

SARTRE: Yes.

DE BEAUVOIR: In which you said "Farewell, farewell, our dear Alsace," or words to that effect.

SARTRE: Just so. During the holidays, with acquaintances we met at hotels. It was owing to the war, and before the war it was owing to my family's bourgeois, republican atmosphere. And very quickly I came by the notion that that was how a man's life should develop—to begin with one was not political, then toward fifty one did become political, like Zola, for instance, who went in for politics at the time of the Dreyfus affair.

DE BEAUVOIR: But where did you get that notion from?

SARTRE: It came from the fact that I identified myself with the life of writers. A writer's life was shown as having a youth, a middle part which was the production of his works, and a later part in which he engaged in politics in his capacity as a writer and in which he intervened in the country's affairs.

DE BEAUVOIR: But that's not the biography of all writers. There are plenty who never went in for politics. Why did that kind of biography strike you? Why did it seem to you more exemplary than that of, say, Stendhal, who was never politically active in that sense but whom you were nevertheless very fond of?

SARTRE: Still, he was politically active in another way.

DE BEAUVOIR: But not at all in the fashion you were talking about. Why did biographies of this kind impress you particularly?

SARTRE: The writers I was told about had almost all gone in for politics.

DE BEAUVOIR: Yes, but things never influence us except as we are able to be influenced by them, so if you were very much struck by biographies of this kind and if you identified your own with them, it must be because there was something in you that made you look upon them as exemplary.

SARTRE: Yes, I knew that politics could be a matter of writing too. It wasn't effected merely by elections and wars, it was also written. There were pieces that were satires or discussions of a specific political fact; for me, politics was like a side issue of literature. And I thought that I too should undertake it toward the end of my days, when I was less capable of producing literature. In any case, I saw my life—it was above all my life that I saw, not so much my works; I didn't think about my works a great deal—I saw my life like that, ending in politics. Gide too. In his last period he went to the USSR, he went to Tchad; he had a great many contacts with postwar politics.

DE BEAUVOIR: Yes, but you've just said something very odd. You said, "It seemed to me like a side issue." Did you think it was something a writer could still do when he had almost nothing left to say? Or did you, on the contrary, think that it was a kind of apotheosis which earned him a very much wider audience and which allowed him to pass from the written word to action?

SARTRE: He was old; he was not well suited to action. He could give the young advice and devote himself to some particular concern. The Dreyfus affair, for example, or Victor Hugo, exiling himself on his island and condemning the Second Empire. To tell the truth there was something of both. At the same time I looked upon politics as a side issue of the writer's tasks. It could not be a work that had the worth of a great poem or a novel. But it belonged to him. The written side of politics must belong to the writer. And then again since it belonged to the aging writer it was also his apotheosis. It was something less than what he had done before yet at the same time it was his apotheosis.

DE BEAUVOIR: Both decline and apotheosis.

SARTRE: Both decline and apotheosis. I lived with those ideas quite a long time—until I was middle-aged.

DE BEAUVOIR: We were still at your childhood. When you came to Paris, when you were at the École Normale and when you were friends with Nizan and others who were I think fairly committed politically. . . . Were you yourself committed, even to the very slightest degree, and what did you think of those who were?

SARTRE: No, I wasn't. In one way they amused me. Because I thought it was a game quite outside their work, which was the Ecole Normale. On the other hand I admired them because I myself was not capable of countering their arguments or defining their aims. But none of that interested me. Socialism, for instance, which attracted many of my comrades at the Ecole Normale, did not affect me at all.

DE BEAUVOIR: Aron, for instance.

SARTRE: To begin with, Aron was a Socialist. He didn't stay one long. All these people were much taken up with what was called socialism, that is, a certain form of society. I wasn't against it, but I wasn't for it either. Nor was I for capitalism, but then I wasn't exactly opposed to it. In the end I thought one always had more or less the same relations with society. It was a collection of institutions with statesmen who made them change a little; but with regard to all these institutions one had to manage for oneself as best one could. It never occurred to me that I might act on them. To do so, I should really have had to go into politics and join a party, and then that party would have had to win in the elections. I never even considered it.

DE BEAUVOIR: When I first knew you you had what you called an aesthetic of opposition. You thought it was just as well that a very great part of the world should be detestable, that there should be a bourgeoisie, that there should be . . . in short, a world to loathe.

SARTRE: Yes.

DE BEAUVOIR: And that the part the writer had to play was in fact to observe this world, denouncing it and hating it, but not so much wanting to change it. If it had changed, if it had been a world one could have enjoyed, one could no longer have loathed it in the same way. In your case there was an almost aesthetic attitude. Yet you did have convictions about society as it was.

SARTRE: I remember one of the first reactions I ever had was when I was about fifteen, which had to do with the colonies. I looked upon them as an infamous seizure on the part of the state. They implied wars, unjust wars; they implied the conquest of a country, the settling of the conquerors, and the enslavement of the inhabitants of that country. And I looked upon the action as totally discreditable.

DE BEAUVOIR: Why? It wasn't your circle that gave you those notions.

SARTRE: Certainly not. Perhaps I came to them to some extent by reading. At La Rochelle when I was fourteen the boys weren't at all interested in those things.

DE BEAUVOIR: Well then? There was a whole mythology about the civilizing role of the white man. You were a person for whom culture mattered a great deal. So might you not have fallen for all those myths?

SARTRE: But I didn't.

DE BEAUVOIR: Why not? Try to find out why not.

SARTRE: When we were in the first form, in hypo-khâgne, and in khâgne there was a legendary character, Félicien Challaye, the philosophy teacher, who was against the colonies. He talked to the boys and convinced them. And I was told about this character right away, at first by Nizan, who was naturally anticolonialist, though not very strongly. It was national questions that he was concerned with.

DE BEAUVOIR: It's interesting to see that even when you were very young you had absolutely no feeling of the superiority of one race, one culture, one civilization over another.

SARTRE: Absolutely not.

DE BEAUVOIR: But this is important. How does it come about that your formation and the sense of belonging to the élite you were brought up with did not rub off on you, at least to some degree?

SARTRE: It really was the idea of equality that came first with me. I thought that people were my equals. I think I had it from my grandfather, who stated it categorically. For him, democracy was all people being equal. And like a spontaneous perception, I had a vision of the injustice of treating a fellow as less important than myself when in fact he was an equal. That I remember, and from the age of fourteen, in my own mind, I always took Algeria as an example. And that was still with me when I thought about Algeria much later, when France was at war with that country.

DE BEAUVOIR: That was your first strongly marked political reaction. That's important. And the exploitation of the workers, did you feel that fairly young?

SARTRE: It's hard to say. I no longer remember very clearly. My stepfather was the head of a shipyard at La Rochelle. He had a large number of workmen under him. I can't remember now how I looked upon them—certainly to some extent through my stepfather's eyes. He treated them as minors—I mean as people under twenty.

DE BEAUVOIR: Yes, as so many children.

SARTRE: Later, he was very much hurt by communism, which amounted to a repudiation of his whole life. I was never in favor of a socialist society before the '39 war.

DE BEAUVOIR: No.

SARTRE: I still remember that during the phony war I wrote in my notebook that society should not be socialist.

DE BEAUVOIR: You thought that you would find living in it unbearable.

SARTRE: Yes. From the descriptions of the USSR we possessed I thought I couldn't live in that country.

DE BEAUVOIR: Yet you weren't at your ease in this bourgeois society either, were you?

SARTRE: No. So I invented mythical societies—good societies in which one ought to live. It was unreality which became the general direction of my political thinking, and I was in something of that state when I came to politics.

DE BEAUVOIR: Let's stay at the time when you were not yet there. You did have reactions against class division. I clearly remember that one of the things that irritated that lady and Guille when we were traveling about Spain together was that at Ronda, for instance, you would say in a disgusted tone, "Those are all aristocrats' houses." And you were furious. It angered you.

SARTRE: It's very mysterious. I was certainly very much against the life proletarians were made to lead; I thought it distressing and I was certainly on their side. Yet in spite of everything I had a kind of mistrust that undoubtedly came from the fact that I was the stepson of the head of a shipyard.

DE BEAUVOIR: You mean when you were very young?

SARTRE: Yes, when I was fourteen.

DE BEAUVOIR: I remember when we were in London you were immensely interested in questions to do with unemployment. You wanted to go and see the districts where the unemployed lived, whereas I was in favor of looking at museums. You had much more of a social dimension.

SARTRE: Yes.

DE BEAUVOIR: In khâgne, in hypo-khâgne, and at the Ecole Normale you had comrades who possessed political convictions; all those you were friends with were more or less left wing. You've spoken about some of Alain's pupils who were more or less left wing, who were radicals, in the sense the word might possess in those days. Nizan was left wing; so were your other friends.

SARTRE: All left wing. They were either Socialists or Communists. It was much more daring to be a Communist at that time.

DE BEAUVOIR: But there was also quite a strong Holy-Joe right-wing tendency at the Ecole Normale. And you were very hostile to that. I think it was at the same time a distinct attitude with regard to mores.

SARTRE: Yes, as far as mores are concerned I was markedly left wing. I was markedly anti-Christian, for instance. As you know, when I was twelve I decided that God did not exist and I've never changed. That led me to reconsider the idea of what a religion was. The lycée teaching about religions—the religions of the ancient world, Catholicism, and Protestantism—led me to look upon religion as a collection of precepts, commandments, and morals that varied from one country to another and that had no relation to God. God did not exist. Consequently, I was not religious, I was not a believer, and all the believers' optimistic tendencies disgusted me. I thought they were deceiving themselves.

DE BEAUVOIR: In principle you were in favor of the broadest freedom of conduct.

SARTRE: Yes.

DE BEAUVOIR: And of speech?

SARTRE: And of speech.

DE BEAUVOIR: Could not the genral body of your metaphysical or religious convictions and of your ideas on conduct or ethics be defined as a kind of left-wing individualism?

SARTRE: That's right. The individual mattered much more to me then than in later times. Besides, I was living in a world of individualism. My grandfather was an individualist and I had acquired individualistic ways. Nizan was an individualist . . .

DE BEAUVOIR: Yes, Nizan, although he was a member. . . . At what period did he become a member of the Communist party?

SARTRE: He joined twice. In khâgne, and then after that he came back more or less to the Right. And he joined the Communist party again in his second year at the Ecole Normale.

DE BEAUVOIR: He didn't try to put pressure on you to follow him?

SARTRE: No, not at all.

DE BEAUVOIR: And your other comrades, the Socialists for instance, didn't they try to indoctrinate you either?

SARTRE: No. If I asked them, they would explain what they were doing and what they felt, and I could join them or not as I chose. On the whole they looked upon me as someone who might move toward socialism one day or another, but it wasn't for them to force me.

DE BEAUVOIR: When did you first read Marx?

SARTRE: In my third year at the Ecole Normale. The third and fourth years.

DE BEAUVOIR: What effect did it have on you?

SARTRE: The effect of a socialist doctrine that seemed to me well thought out. As I told you, I thought I understood it and in fact I understood nothing. I did not see the meaning it possessed at the very time I was reading it. I understood the words, I understood the ideas, but what I did not understand was that it could be applied to the world of today or that the notion of surplus value could have a meaning for the present.

DE BEAUVOIR: And it didn't strike you?

SARTRE: No. It wasn't the first socialist system that I'd had occasion to read . . .

DE BEAUVOIR: No, but the others were utopian. In this case there was an analysis of the reality.

SARTRE: Yes, but I lacked a criterion to distinguish between utopia and what was not utopia.

DE BEAUVOIR: So it didn't have a striking effect on you? For my part,

381

I did not understand Marx at all well, but even so that notion of surplus value gave me a shock when I was eighteen or nineteen. Since I'd seen that there were the rich and the poor and the exploited, I did have some inklings of injustice and exploitation, but they were only vague. In Marx I saw how they had been made into a system. It impressed me deeply.

SARTRE: As far as I was concerned, I understood, but I did not feel. I thought that it was important and that the texts I was reading were interesting. But there was no shock, because there were too many things to read at that particular time.

DE BEAUVOIR: You mean there were too many philosophical shocks of every kind?

SARTRE: Yes.

DE BEAUVOIR: What are your earliest recollections of taking part in politics, of . . .

SARTRE: It's very vague. The way I spent my life from a political point of view up until '39 is very vague.

DE BEAUVOIR: But still, did you have political emotions of some kind?

SARTRE: Yes, from Doumergue's time on.

DE BEAUVOIR: The first time we went to Italy you had a very disagreeable political feeling. And when you went to Berlin what was important for you was to study philosophy, but you were nevertheless very much aware of the presence of the S.A. in the streets.

SARTRE: Yes, I was anti-Nazi, and I loathed the Fascists. In Siena I remember seeing Fascists marching, a group of Fascists with an important man at their head, a bloated great fellow in a black shirt, and he filled me with disgust.

DE BEAUVOIR: After that there was the war in Spain, which affected you.

SARTRE: Which affected us—it affected you too. There was Gérassi's enlisting, and that also connected us with it.

DE BEAUVOIR: That was one of the first breaks with Mme Morel and Guille. We thought it was fine that Gérassi, as a republican Spaniard, should go off and fight, even if he didn't know much about fighting. Guille and that lady said, "He ought to have thought of his wife and child." That was a right-wing reaction. They were for the republic, of course, but only insofar as the republic was a liberal democracy, very repressive with regard to the workers. When it began to go a little further, they didn't like it at all. But we were furious that Blum did not give arms to Spain when Italy and Germany were giving them in great quantities, particularly Italy. We were interventionists.

SARTRE: Yes.

DE BEAUVOIR: Then there was the Popular Front.

SARTRE: Yes, the Popular Front. We were in a strange sort of a position during those years. We had the feeling not exactly of collaborating with the political formation that made up the Popular Front but of going along beside it.

DE BEAUVOIR: Explain rather more clearly.

SARTRE: There was the Popular Front and then there were the people who were more or less attached to it. We didn't belong to them. We were very pleased that the Popular Front had succeeded. Our feelings linked us to these groups, but we did nothing for them. On the whole we were spectators.

DE BEAUVOIR: There was one thing that separated us from Guille and that lady. When the workers began to strike, Guille said, "No, that's going to hamper Blum's actions." He could accept Blum as long as Blum maintained order and did not allow the workers too much freedom in making decisions. Whereas for our part we were very extreme, very radical, very much "power to the soviets." We were delighted with the taking over of the factories by the workers and with the workers' councils. In theory we were as extreme as it is possible to be.

SARTRE: Yes, we were extremists, but we did nothing. . . . Others, like Colette Audry, devoted themselves to left-wing politics. They didn't do much, because nobody could do much, but they were active and we were not.

DE BEAUVOIR: In those days you were nobody. Your name had no weight, you belonged to no party and you didn't want to belong as a private person, and you had not yet published *Nausea*. So you were nobody. Besides, the claims of the committed intellectuals made us laugh. Still, you did follow the course of events with great interest. Your conversations with Guille, Aron, Colette Audry were often political, and you were not at all the sort of man who is shut up in an ivory tower and for whom all this doesn't matter.

SARTRE: Absolutely not. It mattered enormously; it was everyday life; it was what was happening to me.

DE BEAUVOIR: How did you react to the great threat of war in '38 and then to Munich?

SARTRE: I was in favor of the Czechoslovaks resisting and therefore

383

against the abandonment of that country by the powers allied to it. But for all that, after Munich I did feel a kind of relief at the fact that war was further off. Yet we were pessimistic, you and I, and we thought war was coming soon.

DE BEAUVOIR: I was much more relieved than you, much more cowardly. I was much more afraid of a war, and we often had discussions in which I took up Alain's pacifist arguments. I told you that a shepherd in the Landes didn't give a damn for Hitler, and you replied that it wasn't true, that he would give a damn, and that he too would feel that it mattered to him if Hitler won. You said you didn't want Nizan's eyes to be scooped out with a teaspoon or you yourself to be forced to burn your manuscripts. You were violently in favor of war, perhaps not just at the moment of Munich itself, but in any case during the next year. You thought it wasn't possible to let Hitler win, that it just wasn't possible to fold one's arms and let him win. What was it that prevented you from falling into that pacifism that many of Alain's pupils fell into and which I was somewhat inclined to accept—a fall, of course, into irresponsibility?

SARTRE: I think it was because I had no distinct political ideas. One commits a political act if one refuses or if one accepts a declaration of war—if one is among those who decide to fight or those who decide to resist and not fight; one has a clear line of conduct. I had no clear line. I had been deeply hostile to Hitler ever since he came to power; his attitude toward the Jews seemed to me intolerable. I could not bring myself to think that he would continue to be the head of a neighboring state indefinitely. So from the moment the Danzig business broke out or even earlier, toward March of that same year, I was against Hitler. After Munich I felt relief like everybody else, without realizing that it was a relief that implied a policy of perpetually acceding to what Hitler did. Relief was an attitude to reject. I did not retain it long. There was self-contradiction in having it at all. I was at least partly against Munich, yet I was relieved that Munich had taken place. The war withdrew for a while. Then in the course of the year Poland became the center of Hitler's plans. Besides, according to what has been learned since and to what we are learning now from J. Fest's book on Hitler, Hitler was not fully determined to make war; he did not know exactly when he should do so. And when he carried out his action in Poland, he was convinced that he would keep England, and consequently France, out of the war. As for us, we were convinced that the Polish crisis and Hitler's attempt at annexation had to be resisted, otherwise all was up.

DE BEAUVOIR: Resisted in the name of what? Was it in the name of morality? Was it an injustice? . . .

SARTRE: In the name of a vague political conception that I had, which was not socialist but republican. My grandfather would have protested as I did. He would have protested because it was a rape, an aggression.

DE BEAUVOIR: Was it a truly moral attitude or a more political one that glimpsed what the state of the world would be if Hitler reigned?

SARTRE: It was that. Hitler's power was increasing every day, and if he were allowed to go on he would finally become the master of the world. Of Europe, in any event. And that was something that could not be borne. And it was simple things that made me rise up against him. It was my feeling of liberty, the feeling that all Frenchmen had —a certain political freedom. Although at that time I'd never voted. (You mustn't forget that I did not vote. I did not vote before the end of the war.) And at this point we prized our republic because it was thought that what the vote gave was men's freedom.

DE BEAUVOIR: Why did you value it, since you didn't vote?

SARTRE: I was eager that others should vote. I thought I might vote if the occasion seemed to me important. There was no prohibition. It just didn't interest me. And the Assemblies that governed between the two wars seemed to me grotesque.

DE BEAUVOIR: Yet you wanted these Assemblies to go on existing?

SARTRE: At that time I thought they had to go on. I had nothing against the Constitution. It so happened that the political world I beheld was grotesque.

DE BEAUVOIR: A grotesque world, a class world. A world in which the rulers defended the privileged class.

SARTRE: I didn't think that that was an absolutely inevitable consequence of the fact that there were elections and assemblies. I thought it was possible to conceive elections that really corresponded to the people. As you know, I didn't reflect upon class war. I didn't understand class war until the time of the actual war, and after it.

DE BEAUVOIR: You did understand something of it, since when there was the Popular Front we were very happy at its being the workers' victory, and we gave money for the strikers.

SARTRE: Yes. But I didn't see it as a movement that set two classes against one another, the bourgeois and the proletariat, and that necessarily, historically set them against one another.

DE BEAUVOIR: It's rather much to say you were unaware of class war.

SARTRE: I came from a bourgeois environment and therefore I had not so much as heard of class war. My mother, and even my grandfather, did not know what it was. Consequently I looked upon my neighbor, whether he was a proletarian or a bourgeois, as a man like me. I did not at all anticipate those distinctions that subsequently appeared to me so important.

DE BEAUVOIR: Yet upon the whole you had a horror of the bourgeoisie, didn't you?

SARTRE: I didn't have a horror of the bourgeoisie as a class. The people who thought of themselves as bourgeois in 1920 or 1930 did not think of themselves as a class. They thought of themselves as an elite, and I had a horror of the bourgeois elite and of bourgeois morality. But I didn't see them as a class, a possessing class that oppressed the people. I saw them as people who, through certain qualities, had attained a kind of reality as an elite and who dominated the others. We lacked the idea of class: so did you, by the way.

DE BEAUVOIR: I don't think that's quite fair. We knew perfectly well that the Spanish war was a class struggle, for instance.

SARTRE: Yes, we knew that. We were acquainted with the words. Nizan, being a Communist, used to speak of classes. But one might say that we had not assimilated it as a concept. I began to be concerned with class war during and after our war.

DE BEAUVOIR: Yet when we read Jaurès' *Histoire de la Révolution française* . . .

SARTRE: That was later. It was in '37, '38.

DE BEAUVOIR: At that time we certainly understood the Revolution in terms of class war.

SARTRE: Yes, but at that point there was no proletariat. The Revolution was the triumph of the bourgeoisie. It was different. That's why it is taught with such pomp in the schools.

DE BEAUVOIR: The reason I speak of the *Histoire* written by Jaurès is that he strongly emphasizes the bourgeois aspect, which does not fully radicalize matters and which leaves what were called the people out of the bourgeois victory. I think you are exaggerating and simplifying a little. Still, you did know about class war.

SARTRE: I did know about it, but it was a notion I did not use. I didn't interpret a historical event as an opposition between classes.

DE BEAUVOIR: Yet when we were reading Lissagaray's *Histoire de la Commune* we knew very well that it was a question of a class struggle.

SARTRE: We knew, but it was an interpretation that seemed valid in certain cases and invalid in others. We should certainly not have brought history down to a struggle between classes. You didn't think that Greco-Roman history or the *ancien régime* were to be explained by classes being at war with one another.

DE BEAUVOIR: We still don't know how far class war alone should be seen in historical events. The Israeli-Arab war, for instance, is something quite different.

SARTRE: I was just about to say the same thing. Class war appeared to us to be of the essence after '45—during the war and after '45. We looked upon it as one of the essential causes of historical facts; but other causes also existed.

DE BEAUVOIR: How did you move on from a certain conception of class war which you did not use, though you were acquainted with it, to a conception that for you has become an essential explanation of the world?

SARTRE: Everything changed from the war on. When I was in contact with other men who were linked to me because they were in the same regiment, when I saw how they looked on the world and what might happen in either of two hypotheses, that in which Hitler won and that in which he was beaten, then I—who like all other Frenchmen had set off for a three-month, a six-month war—I began to reflect upon what it meant to be historical, to be part of a piece of history that was continually being decided by collective occurrences. That made me become aware of what history meant to each of us. Each one of us was history. It was certainly the phony war, that is to say, the confrontation of two armies that scarcely moved, which opened my eyes.

DE BEAUVOIR: I can't see how that gave you the meaning of class war.

SARTRE: I didn't say class war. History.

DE BEAUVOIR: Yes, of course. History.

SARTRE: The fact is that from '39 on I no longer belonged to myself. Up until then I thought I was leading the life of a totally free individual. I chose my own clothes, I chose what I ate, I wrote things. In my opinion I was therefore a free man within a society; I had not the slightest notion that this life was entirely conditioned by the presence of Hitler and his armies threatening us. Later I did come to understand it, and in my novel (the first volume of *Roads to Freedom* and a little of the second) I tried to express it to some extent. So there I was, in military clothes that fitted me badly, surrounded by other men who wore the same clothes as myself. We were connected by a bond that was neither of family nor friendship but that was nevertheless very important. We had parts to play, and these parts were given to us from outside. I launched balloons and watched them with binoculars.

I had been taught this at a time when I never thought I should make use of it, during my military service. And there I was, engaged in this occupation, among other men I did not know who were following the same pursuit, men who helped me to do so and whom I helped, and we watched my balloons vanish in the clouds. All this was a few miles from the German army in which there were people like us busily doing the same thing; and there were other men who were preparing an attack. There one had an absolutely historical occurrence. All at once I found myself part of a mass of men in which I had been given an exact and stupid part to play, a part I was playing against opposite other men, dressed as I was in military clothes, whose part was to thwart what we were doing and finally to attack.

The second and most important event that made me aware of things was defeat and being captured. After a certain time my companions and I were driven back to other positions. We arrived at a town in a truck and stopped there, sleeping in people's houses. We had to deal with Alsatians whose attitudes varied greatly. I remember one peasant who was for the other side and who argued against us, maintaining his pro-German theories. We slept there and later we left, but we did not know whether we should manage to escape the German army. We stayed in that place three or four days. The Germans came nearer. One evening we heard guns firing on a village that was about six miles away. We could see it fairly well along the flat road, and we knew that the Germans would arrive in the course of the next day. And there again from a historical point of view I was deeply impressed by occurrences that were trifling in themselves and that wouldn't appear in any textbook or any history of the war. One little village was being shelled; another, which was going to be taken in its turn, was waiting. There were people trapped there, waiting for the Germans to deal with them. I went to bed. We had been abandoned by our officers, who had walked off into a forest with a white flag in front of them and who like us were taken prisoner but at a different time. We, the privates and sergeants, stayed together; we went to sleep and the next morning we heard voices, shots, cries. I dressed quickly; I knew that it meant I was going to be taken prisoner. I went out—I'd slept in a peasant's house on the square—I went out and I remember the strange feeling I had of a film, the feeling that I was acting in a scene in a film and that it was not true. There was a gun firing at the church, where there were no doubt some men who had arrived the day before and who were holding out. They were certainly not people belonging to us, because we had no notion of resisting—in any case we did not possess the means of doing so. Under the Germans' rifles I crossed the square to go from where I was to where they were. They hurried me along and put me into an immense troop of young men who were moving off toward Germany. I gave an account of that in *Troubled Sleep,* but I attributed it to Brunet. We marched, and we didn't know what they were going to do with us. There were some who hoped they would set us free in a week or two. It was actually June 21, my birthday and also the day of the armistice. We were taken prisoner a few hours before the armistice. We were marched to a gendarmerie barracks, and there again I learned what historical truth really was. I learned that I was someone who lived in a nation exposed to various dangers, and that this someone was himself exposed to these dangers. There was a kind of unity among the men who were there—an idea of defeat, an idea of being a prisoner, which seemed at that particular time much more important than anything else. All I had learned and written during the years before seemed to me no longer valid nor even as having any content. One was obliged to be there, and eat when they gave us anything to eat—which was very seldom, I may add. There were days when we did not eat at all, because feeding so many prisoners had not been foreseen. In this barracks we slept on the floor.

DE BEAUVOIR: At Baccarat, wasn't it?

SARTRE: Yes. On the floor of the various rooms. I was in the garret with a whole lot of friends, and we slept on the floor. Like many of my companions, I was a little out of my wits with hunger for two or three days. We were in a strange emotional state because we had nothing to eat and there we were, lying on the ground. There were periods of strong emotion and periods of calm. It all depended. The Germans didn't pay any attention to us; they had just parked us there. But then one fine day they gave us some bread and we began to feel better. Then finally we got into a train and went to Germany. That was a blow, because we had still been vaguely hopeful. I thought we would stay there, in France until one day, when the Germans had settled down, they would let us out and send us home. Which was not at all what they intended to do, since we went to a prison camp above Treves. On the other side of the camp there was a road, and on the other side of the road a German barracks. Many of us worked in the German barracks. I stayed there as a prisoner without doing anything. I did nothing. I saw prisoners; I made friends with some priests and with a journalist.

DE BEAUVOIR: We talked about that the other day. But what I'd like to know is how far did all this reveal class war to you? I quite agree that you discovered a historical dimension in war.

SARTRE: Wait.

DE BEAUVOIR: All right.

SARTRE: I stayed in Germany until March. And there, in a strange way but in one that marked me, I became acquainted with a society, a society that had classes and sets, with certain people belonging in some groups, others in different ones; a society of defeated men who were fed by an army that held them prisoner. Yet society was there in its entirety. There were no officers; we were ordinary privates. I was a second-class soldier, and I learned to obey spiteful orders and to understand what a hostile army amounted to. Like everybody else I had contacts with the Germans, either to obey them or sometimes to listen to their stupid boastful conversation. I stayed there until the time I was passed as a civilian and liberated. I was taken to Drancy by train and put into one of the Gardes Mobiles barracks, which were enormous, like so many skyscrapers. There were three or four of them and they were filled with prisoners of war. I was set free two weeks later.

DE BEAUVOIR: By then you'd already written me letters in which you said, "I shall take up politics." What did that mean at the time you wrote those words?

SARTRE: It meant that I had discovered a social world, as it were, and that at least from one point of view I was shaped by society—shaped in my culture and also in some of my needs and my way of living. I had been reshaped, one might say, by the prison camp. We lived in a crowd, perpetually touching one another, and I remember writing that the first time I was free in Paris I was astonished to see people sitting so far apart in a café. It seemed to me space wasted. So I came back to France with the idea that other Frenchmen did not realize all this—that some of them, those who came back from the front and were liberated, realized it, but there was no one to make them decide to resist. That's what seemed to me the first thing to do on coming back to Paris—to create a resistance group; to try, step by step, to win over the majority to resistance and thus bring into being a violent movement that would expel the Germans. I was not wholly persuaded that they would be expelled, but I thought there was an eighty percent chance—I was always optimistic—that it would happen. There remained twenty chances out of the hundred that they might be victorious. Even in that event I thought it was still necessary to resist, because in the end they would get tired of it one way or another. Like Rome, which conquered countries but at the same time destroyed itself in doing so.

DE BEAUVOIR: But you didn't envisage just any kind of resistance, did you? Your movement was called "Socialism and Liberty." What was the relation between the socialist and resister sides within yourself? You had got in touch with right-wing resisters. You had also made contact, or caused contacts to be made, with left-wing resisters. Where did you place the connection between resistance and socialism in your mind?

SARTRE: Fascism put itself forward primarily as anti-Communism. It followed that one of the forms of resistance was to be Communist, or at least Socialist. That is, to take a position absolutely opposed to that of National Socialism. The best way of opposing the Nazis was to emphasize the desire for a Socialist society. We therefore created this movement, of which I, and you too, could almost be looked upon as the founders.

DE BEAUVOIR: Talk about your relations with Communism during the Resistance. The Germano-Soviet pact and Nizan's reaction affected you deeply.

SARTRE: Nizan left the Communist party. During the war, before I was taken prisoner and before he was killed, he wrote me a letter in which he said he was no longer a Communist and he was thinking about it all. He had decided upon a period of reflection before adopting a distinct political attitude once more. For us, as for most people, the Germano-Soviet pact was an absolutely stupefying event.

DE BEAUVOIR: Why did you create a personal movement? Why did you not work with the Communists right away?

SARTRE: I did offer to do so. I caused the proposal to be made by friends who were in close contact with the Communist party. The reply was, "Sartre was sent back by the Germans to carry out Nazi propaganda among the French under the pretense of resistance. We would not work with Sartre for anything on earth."

DE BEAUVOIR: Why was there this hostility on the part of the Communists?

SARTRE: I don't know. They didn't want to ally themselves with people who hadn't been with them before the war. . . . They knew very well that I was not a traitor as they said, but they didn't know whether I would go along with them. Two years later they knew it very well.

DE BEAUVOIR: So you came back. The Communists didn't want to go along with you, and you founded a movement.

SARTRE: We founded "Socialism and Liberty." I had chosen that title because I thought that a socialism or a liberty might exist. At that point I had become a Socialist. I had become one partly because on the one hand our prisoner's life was, to put it briefly, a kind of socialism—a dismal kind, but it was a collective life, a community. No money: food handed out and duties imposed by a conqueror. Ours was therefore a communal life, and it could be supposed that a life which was not that of a prisoner but which remained communal might be a happy one. Yet even so, I did not envisage a socialism of that sort, with everybody eating at the same table, etcetera, and I'm sure you didn't either.

DE BEAUVOIR: Certainly not.

SARTRE: Besides, you weren't very keen on the idea of socialism.

DE BEAUVOIR: I don't know. There was an aspect of equality in poverty that I liked very much during the Occupation. And I thought that a genuine socialism which had positive, constructive reasons would really be a very good thing. But let's stay with your own personal progress. So you had come back with the idea that socialism was tolerable.

SARTRE: Yes. But I wasn't yet thoroughly convinced. I remember I worked out a positive constitution for after the war.

DE BEAUVOIR: Who asked you to write this constitution?

SARTRE: I don't remember now. I think it was when de Gaulle was in Algiers.

DE BEAUVOIR: The fact remains that you were asked to work out a draft constitution.

SARTRE: That's right. There were two copies of it, one of which was sent to de Gaulle. The other, which was lost, I don't know where, has been found again by Kanapa.

DE BEAUVOIR: Kanapa was one of your former pupils. Was he already a Communist?

SARTRE: Yes, of course. So in writing this draft of a constitution there was a way of getting myself used to socialism and of doing some work on that idea so that it would become something consistent and so that I should understand its meaning.

DE BEAUVOIR: Have you any recollection of what was in it and how it was directed?

SARTRE: There was a long section on the Jews.

DE BEAUVOIR: That I remember, because we discussed it; and you were in the right of it, by the way. I thought the Jews ought to be looked upon as having the same rights as all citizens, but neither more nor less. You wanted very exact rights to be granted to them—the right to speak their language, to have their religion, to have their culture, and so on.

SARTRE: Yes. That came to me from the days before the war. When I wrote *Nausea* I knew a Jew called Mendel, whom we've often spoke about since. I wanted to make the Jews citizens like the Christians, and he convinced me of the specific nature of the Jewish fact and of the necessity for giving Jews particular rights. To go back to my conversion to socialism, it was certainly one of the elements that made me accept the Communists' proposal—a surprising proposal, but one that was connected with the party's evolution. They did so by means of a Communist I'd known when I was a prisoner at Treves, Billet.

DE BEAUVOIR: Oh yes, I remember. I met him.

SARTRE: He was a Communist. He was setting up an organization of resisters associated with the Communists and he suggested that I join it. For a year I had no longer been doing anything whatsoever. Our group had fallen to pieces.

DE BEAUVOIR: So having turned their backs on you and having refused to work with you, spreading the rumor that you were a stool pigeon, the Communists finally made up their minds to cooperate with you. How did it happen?

SARTRE: I don't know. One day I met a man who'd been a prisoner with me and he said, "Why don't you carry out resistance with us? Why don't you join the group in our organization that looks after art and literature?" I was very much surprised; I said I asked nothing better, and so an appointment was made and a few days later I was a member of the C.N.E., the Comité National des Ecrivains. The C.N.E. included various people—there were Claude Morgan, Leiris, Camus, Debû-Bridel, and many others.

DE BEAUVOIR: And what did you do?

SARTRE: I joined this committee. Obviously something had happened, a change . . .

DE BEAUVOIR: In any case there weren't only Communists in it, since you speak of Leiris.

SARTRE: No. Leiris or Debû-Bridel were absolutely not Communists. But I think there had been a change in the orientation of the Communist party as far as recruitment was concerned. They must have said, We must show ourselves as being more open. Anyhow, in '43 I became a member of the C.N.E. and I worked with them on documents, clandestine publications, particularly *Les Lettres françaises*, in which I published an article against Drieu La Rochelle. Later, at the time of the Liberation, we were given the mission of guarding the Comédie Française, arms in hand, that is, with one pistol that was common to us all, the actors and ourselves. We therefore settled down in the Comédie Française, sometimes one set of us, sometimes another; and at one point I acted the part of the director of the Comédie Française. I was in the director's office for one night and I lay on the floor pretty uncomfortably. And the next day I refused Barrault admittance. I said he was not to be let in. And then on the day of the Liberation there was fighting in the streets, and there were little battles at the Comédie Française. We put up a barricade, and I still remember seeing the man in charge of a troop of captive German soldiers in the Rue de la Comédie Française, leading them to the Cour des Comptes. I also had to sleep with Salacrou for one night. We slept in the same room. In short, there was a certain amount of activity.

DE BEAUVOIR: And after the war, what was your political attitude?

SARTRE: After the war, as soon as de Gaulle arrived, the first official issues of *Les Lettres françaises* came out and in the first number I remember having published an article on the Occupation and the fighting record of the Resistance.

DE BEAUVOIR: You began contributing to *Les Lettres françaises*?

SARTRE: Yes. Anyhow, I wrote that article. I don't remember whether I wrote any others. From the beginning, from the moment the Communists made their appearance as an official party, things didn't work anymore. It was obvious that the Communists were not pleased with the fact that I had become a well-known writer. It happened suddenly. People coming back from England or America looked upon me as a well-known writer. Besides I too had come back from America—I'd been sent there by *Combat*. The Americans had asked for French journalists.

DE BEAUVOIR: Yes, by *Le Figaro* and by *Combat*.

SARTRE: So I came back and there I found myself confronted by the Communist party's *Les Lettres françaises* and by some of the writers of *Les Lettres françaises* . . .

DE BEAUVOIR: And of *Action* too.

SARTRE: And of *Action*, yes. *Action* was a pro-Communist weekly which at one time had been edited by Ponge and Hervé. And I contributed to *Action* too.

394

DE BEAUVOIR: You weren't just a well-known writer. You had also founded a review in '45, one which was supported by many people and intellectuals, and which was not Communist. For the left-wing writers you therefore represented a possibility other than communism. How did you feel with regard to them?

SARTRE: Well, I didn't envisage communism in the form they did, that is, in the Soviet form, but I did think that the fate of mankind lay in the application of a certain kind of communism.

DE BEAUVOIR: But did you think that there could have been a dialogue? They were furious at your having put forward what amounted to a spare ideology, as they called it, and they borrowed all the right-wing insults to use against you. How did you react to that?

SARTRE: There are several ways of looking at it. There's the personal point of view of my relations with the Communists. I thought they behaved disgustingly toward me and I fought against them. And I only changed later.

DE BEAUVOIR: Yes, in '52.

SARTRE: And so I was fairly hostile to the Communists as individuals. They hadn't the slightest kind feeling toward me. They had orders to obey, but no feelings of any sort. Except perhaps in the case of Claude Roy, who may have felt a vague liking for me.

DE BEAUVOIR: What I'd like to know is how important these political feuds were to you, and as far as the R.D.N. is concerned, to what extent you were wholly committed and to what extent you remained somewhat skeptical.

SARTRE: I was skeptical. I was not wholly committed.

DE BEAUVOIR: And what effect did it have on you, when the Communists slung mud at you on the subject of *Dirty Hands*?

SARTRE: Oh, it seemed natural to me. They were against the R.D.R. and that was their way of attacking.

DE BEAUVOIR: So it seemed natural to you, not because of what the play said but because of the political attitude they had to adopt toward you whatever happened?

SARTRE: That's right. I found it rather unpleasant, mainly because among them there were some people we were fond of, such as Marguerite Duras, who was a Communist at that period and who wrote a treacherous article, in *Les Lettres françaises,* I think. You remember?

DE BEAUVOIR: I remember that generally speaking all the Communists were against you. So how did you place yourself politically? Because although you did not have much confidence in the R.D.R., on the other hand you had not the slightest wish to ally yourself with the Communist party and be a sympathizer at any cost. That wouldn't have been like you. On the other hand, if people kick my bottom, I am quite happy to put up with it.

SARTRE: Well, I had no political position. At that time, toward '50, we saw things in terms of the threat of war. The Soviets disliked me, and if they invaded Europe, as it was supposed they would, I did not want to leave. I wanted to stay in France. That being so, I had no notion of who would be on my side.

DE BEAUVOIR: How much did this aspect of your life count for you? Your writing was still the main thing, after all.

SARTRE: Yes, it was my writing that mattered.

DE BEAUVOIR: Did you think from the time you began writing committed literature, from the time you found out that naming and revealing meant changing the world—did you think that in the end your personal action as a writer would have weight? Would have a future?

SARTRE: Yes, I did think so.

DE BEAUVOIR: Furthermore, I believe you were right.

SARTRE: I thought so. I've always thought so.

DE BEAUVOIR: Then why were you eager to be attached to a political movement, such as the R.D.R.?

SARTRE: I wasn't eager. But when it was suggested to me I thought I ought to accept. I hoped the R.D.R. would be a movement linked with communism but one that would stand for something rather like Nenni's socialism in Italy.

DE BEAUVOIR: The French Communists wanted no part of it. The Italian Communists were much easier to get on with; they could agree to an alliance with Nenni's Socialist party, that is to say with a left-wing Socialist party.

SARTRE: Yes.

DE BEAUVOIR: So that was the idea, then. But in France it wasn't possible. Another thing. When you had the Soviet administrative code of labor legislation in your possession, the code according to which people can be interned by a simple administrative decision, you published it.

SARTRE: Yes.

DE BEAUVOIR: And what did you think at that particular moment? When you knew that the camps really existed and that there were considerable numbers of people deported?

SARTRE: I thought it was an unacceptable régime.

DE BEAUVOIR: Yes. You wrote an article on the subject with Merleau-Ponty.

SARTRE: It was Merleau-Ponty who wrote it.

DE BEAUVOIR: And both of you put your names to it. You said that a country in which there were so many people deported and shot could not be called a socialist country. In short, from the time of your break with the R.D.R. you lived in a great political solitude, did you not?

SARTRE: A total solitude.

DE BEAUVOIR: Let's say you were no longer politically active.

SARTRE: The long and the short of it is that I was no longer politically active until . . . '68.

DE BEAUVOIR: Wait a moment. In '52 you came nearer to the Communists. Do you remember the period between the break with the R.D.R. and this reconciliation?

SARTRE: I was writing books, and that took all my time.

DE BEAUVOIR: But didn't it mean a certain lack, a certain emptiness, no longer being attached to any political organization?

SARTRE: No. I was not yet really a political being; I didn't look upon it as essential. I wrote that politics was a human dimension. But in fact it was scarcely one of mine. In reality it was, but I didn't know it. I began to realize this from the time I became allied to the Communists four years later. During those earlier years I had a kind of political aestheticism. For a long while America had been a country of dreams for me, from the days of Nick Carter and Buffalo Bill. Then it was a country I should have liked to live in, a country that in some of its aspects had charmed me and repelled me in others. In short it was not a country I should have liked to see destroyed in a war with the USSR. And as for the USSR, which still put itself forward as the country of socialism, I thought its destruction would be terrible too. So I looked upon a Russo-American war as a double catastrophe. And I remained in this state of mind for a considerable while, without much idea of what I ought to do. If there was a war, I ought not to leave, of course, I ought to stay in France. I thought I should carry out resistance for a certain socialism and not for the Americans; so I ought to be a hidden resister.

DE BEAUVOIR: Let's move on to the war in Indochina.

SARTRE: We were the first to condemn the Indochinese war, in *Les Temps modernes*. We were friends with a number of Vietnamese, above all, one whom I knew well—Van Chi. He used to bring us intelligence.

DE BEAUVOIR: He wasn't a philosopher but a politician.

SARTRE: But he was a teacher as well.

DE BEAUVOIR: Now and then he would ask us to lunch at a Vietnamese restaurant. But apart from the articles in *Les Temps modernes* we had hardly any way of being active.

SARTRE: Just so. We did bring out a special issue of *Les Temps modernes* on Indochina and Van Chi helped us by bringing Indochinese documents.

DE BEAUVOIR: Yes. That war was an important dimension in our general political life.

SARTRE: In short we had the same position as the Communists.

DE BEAUVOIR: On that particular plane, yes, we were very close.

DE BEAUVOIR: In yesterday's conversation you told me that there was one thing you had not sufficiently emphasized, and that was the connection you had always wanted to establish between socialism and freedom.

SARTRE: Yes. For many people socialism represents a greater freedom; an economic freedom in the first place and then a cultural freedom, a freedom of action, experienced every day, a freedom in the great choices. They want to see themselves as free, not conditioned by a society but shaping themselves according to their own options. But socialism as it is shown us by the Marxists, for example, does not include this notion. Marx had it, and when he looked forward to the distant period of communism he imagined that society would be made up of free men. The freedom he envisaged was not exactly that which I envisage, yet even so the two resemble one another. But in France the Marxists no longer give the notion of freedom any place whatsoever. What matters to them is the kind of society they are going to build; but in the structures of this society the people are inserted like so many machines. This socialism does acknowledge certain values, such as justice, for instance, that is, a kind of equality between what a person gives and what he receives. But the idea that beyond socialism a free man may exist—when I say *beyond* I do not mean at a later period but going beyond the rules of socialism at every moment— that is an idea the Russians have never possessed. It does not appear that the socialism of the USSR—if it can still be called a socialism— includes the permission given to the individual to develop in the way he chooses. That's what I wanted to say when I gave the meager little group that we formed in '40 and '41 the name of "Socialism and Liberty." Although it was very hard to realize on the basis of socialism, it was that bond, that connection of socialism and freedom, which represented my political tendency. It was my political tendency then and I've never changed it. Even now at the present time it was socialism and liberty that I tried to defend in our conversations with Gavi and Victor.

DE BEAUVOIR: Yes, but that's the present. To go back to what we were talking about yesterday, it was that wish to link socialism and freedom that caused you to swing between the Communist party, the formation of the R.D.R., solitude, a return to the Communist party, and so on. We mustn't go back over the entire chronicle of your political life up until '62, because I've written it, partly under your dictation, in *Force of Circumstance*. But what I should like to know is what you think of the road you've traveled, let's say until the end of the Algerian war.

SARTRE: Well, I think that I followed my line, that it was difficult, that it was hard, that I often found myself in a minority, often alone, but it was certainly what I had always wanted—socialism and liberty. I'd believed in freedom for a long while, and I'd already written of it in *Being and Nothingness*. I feel that I have lived free, from my childhood until the present, although of course I have followed the general current. But I have lived free, and now here I am at last with the same idea in which socialism and freedom are still bound up together.

DE BEAUVOIR: You've always dreamed of this harmony; you've never come across it. Did you sometimes have the illusion of meeting it? In Cuba, perhaps?

SARTRE: Cuba, yes. There were various opposing tendencies, but at that point, when I was there, Castro possessed no real cultural principles. He did not want to impose a given culture. Later on he changed.

DE BEAUVOIR: That was in '60, shortly after his coming to power.

SARTRE: He did not even want socialism to be spoken of at that time. He asked me not to mention socialism when I wrote articles about him in France.

DE BEAUVOIR: In fact one spoke of Castroism.

SARTRE: To tell the truth, it was a revolution that was not yet accomplished. I remember I always asked them, "If you are confronted with a reign of terror, what will you do?"

DE BEAUVOIR: And indeed they certainly had a kind of terror later on.

399

SARTRE: They already had a hint of its coming. They wondered what they should do, but either they didn't answer me, or they said there wouldn't be a terror.

DE BEAUVOIR: To return to my question, can you tell me what you remember having felt and thought? What effect does it have on you now, this road you have traveled? Do you think you made many mistakes? Do you think that you couldn't have done anything but what you did do? That you have always acted well? In short, how do you look upon it all?

SARTRE: I've made quantities of mistakes, of that there is no doubt. But not mistakes of principle—mistaken methods, mistakes in the opinions expressed about some given fact. But in general I am still in agreement with my past—wholly in agreement with my past. I think it had to lead me to the point I have reached, and from this point I look back on my past with a benevolent eye.

DE BEAUVOIR: What are the mistakes you think you have committed?

SARTRE: Not having joined in violently and wholeheartedly with certain people when I was of the right age to do so.

DE BEAUVOIR: You mean before the war?

SARTRE: Before and after.

DE BEAUVOIR: Who could you have committed yourself to?

SARTRE: There was after all a Marxist left wing that was not Communist.

DE BEAUVOIR: You did all you could to come close to them.

SARTRE: Perhaps not all. To the left of the Communists there were groups that challenged the official communism and that were sometimes right on a great many points. I did nothing to get to know them. I let everything that was to the left of the Communist party drop until '66.

I thought that politics was a matter in which one dealt with the Socialists and the Communists, period. And like all the people around me I was still impressed by the old Popular Front of before the '39 war. Later on I found those I really should have allied myself with— the young left wingers.

DE BEAUVOIR: Still, there were occasions on which you made decisions. What were the choices you congratulate yourself upon when you look back? I imagine you're not displeased with your attitude during the Algerian war, for example?

SARTRE: No. I think that was the right attitude to adopt.

DE BEAUVOIR: In that instance you outflanked the Communists in your desire to struggle for Algerian independence. You went much further than they did.

SARTRE: Yes. They wanted the possibility of independence, and I, together with the Algerians, wanted independence in the strict sense. I don't understand that prudence of the Communists, I may add.

DE BEAUVOIR: There were still more serious things on the part of the Communists. They voted the full powers.*

SARTRE: Yes, but I don't understand the Communists' attitude. That clearly shows, as I've often said, that they don't want revolution.

DE BEAUVOIR: Of course. At the time we thought that as they wanted to have a large and powerful party, and therefore one that pleased the French, they had to be nationalist. They didn't want people to be able to say they were ready to sell off the colonies cheap.

SARTRE: But being nationalist doesn't mean being colonialist.

DE BEAUVOIR: At that time . . .

SARTRE: Being a nationalist means having strong bonds with the country in which you're born and in which you live. It doesn't mean that you accept a given policy of that country—a colonial policy, for example.

DE BEAUVOIR: But don't you think their attitude was demagogic? They didn't want anyone to be able to say they were anti-French.

SARTRE: Yes, that's certain.

DE BEAUVOIR: We sometimes collaborated with them during the Algerian war. I remember a number of demonstrations we held together. And then at the end, when it was a question of fighting the O.A.S., we created a kind of league in which there were Communists. It was then that you said, "One can't do anything with them; one can't do anything without them." What is your recollection of these attempts at a joint effort?

SARTRE: There was a time when it didn't go badly . . .

DE BEAUVOIR: But you never had friendly relations with them, did you?

SARTRE: Never.

DE BEAUVOIR: After *The Victors,* Ehrenburg told you that it was shameful to speak of resisters as you had done. After *Dirty Hands* he was one of those who said you had sold your soul for a mess of pottage. And then suddenly there you were with Ehrenburg, all smiles. At

* Full powers granted to Guy Mollet, the Socialist prime minister, to deal with the Algerian rising. (trans.)

Helsinki in '55 I saw you with Ehrenburg and you were all smiles. Until he died we were on very good terms with him. How did that come about? Didn't it disturb you to think he had . . .

SARTRE: It didn't worry me; he was the one who made advances. He received me in Moscow when I was there for the second time with great cordiality, and I went to the dacha where he lived with his wife and sisters. When I went to see him—we may have seen one another before at a meeting, but only to shake hands—when of my own accord I went to visit him I was glad to see Ehrenburg. Something had eased between him and me, and I had the feeling that we'd always been on good terms. Besides, I was really fond of Ehrenburg.

DE BEAUVOIR: But on the whole the way the Communist party made use of you—for the book on Henri Martin, for instance—without your being able to have really human, personal, friendly, trustful relations with them; didn't you find that disagreeable?

SARTRE: Yes, it was extremely disagreeable. The relations were indeed impossible, and that was why I cut myself off from them entirely; and I was quite right to do so. What was striking among the Maos I knew, on the other hand, was that they treated people like human beings.

DE BEAUVOIR: And why, having yourself denounced the existence of labor camps in *Les Temps modernes,* did you write *The Ghost of Stalin,* in which you said that the USSR was socialism made flesh and therefore bloody and full of faults, but that nevertheless it was socialism?

SARTRE: There I was mistaken. It was no longer socialism. Socialism vanished after the seizing of power by the soviets: at that juncture it had a chance of developing, but gradually with Stalin, and even already in Lenin's last years, it changed.

DE BEAUVOIR: You no longer thought the Communist party was revolutionary, but even so you did think it was the Communists who defended the interests of the proletariat. I believe that's what counted for you.

SARTRE: Yes, certainly. But since then I've seen that the strikes, the union policy, the C.G.T., and the policy of workers connected with the party showed enormous numbers of mistakes—mistakes that have often been shown up.

I'd like to explain my opinion of the Communists I've met, under the circumstances in which I met them. They had, as it were, masks covering their faces. They smiled, they talked, they replied to the questions I asked them, but in fact it was not they who were replying. "They" vanished and became characters whose principles one knew and who gave the answer *L'Humanité* would have given in the name of these principles.

DE BEAUVOIR: Like a programmed computer?

SARTRE: There was never any solidarity between them and me, except the immediate solidarity of having to resolve a particular problem together.

DE BEAUVOIR: Yet you stayed with them?

SARTRE: Because there was nobody with whom I could have other political relations. In fact they did have a personal life; there were moments when they took off their masks to some degree; but that was only when they were together, among themselves. Their relations with people from outside did not include that kind of brotherhood.

DE BEAUVOIR: Wasn't there a time when you came close to some of them who took up positions more or less like yours after Budapest, and who were then expelled from the party or who moved away from it?

SARTRE: In about '57 there were Vigier, Victor Leduc, and a certain number of others who tried to carry out not something different from the party but another way of orienting it. And indeed they did work in the same direction as I at the "Fac"; and their attitude toward the Algerian war was the same as mine.

DE BEAUVOIR: Vercors said in a rather amusing way that he felt he was something of a large ornamental china vase for the Communist party: did you have that impression?

SARTRE: Not exactly. It was not quite the same period as Vercors.

DE BEAUVOIR: And then Vercors was more docile than you. He was more of a china pot.

SARTRE: I used to see him at meetings where he would speak, expressing an opinion that was usually that of the party. Then he would sit down and say no more. But they made me work actively and in public. It would be a question of some action we had decided upon together, an action about which a public meeting was then organized, one in which each had a pretty well fixed part to play and in which I was to speak. All this is perfectly natural, and that's not what I blame the Communists for. What I do blame them for is the rejection of all subjectivity, the absence of any man-to-man contact.

DE BEAUVOIR: Do you think you wasted your time, trying to work with the Communists?

SARTRE: No, it wasn't time wasted. It taught me what a Communist was. Later, when I allied myself with the Maos, who were by no means friendly with the Communists, I found that I was perfectly at ease with them, because they had the same ideas as mine about relations with the Communist party.

DE BEAUVOIR: If you hadn't made all these attempts as working with the Communists, if you'd kept more time for writing and philosophy, and if you'd stayed in the distant background with regard to politics, would that have changed anything in your present relations with the Maos?

SARTRE: Yes. Because it was through politics that I came to the Maos. It was through my reflections on '68 and the obligation of committing myself that I came to be engaged on the Maos' side; but this necessarily implied the engagements at the time of the Occupation and of the Liberation—it was not an apolitical man who was allying himself with them, and they understood that. No, I don't think I would have been with the Maos at my age if I had not been engaged in politics before. I would just have gone on not being engaged in politics. When you are active in a movement there are necessarily comings and goings; there is a great deal of time wasted. But what is time wasted? There is time wasted, and then there is time in which you gain a knowledge of people and learn to keep them at a distance, or on the contrary you find that something works well between them and you.

DE BEAUVOIR: What are your political prospects at present?

SARTRE: I'm an old man. I'm sixty-nine and I don't think that anything I might undertake now could see an end.

DE BEAUVOIR: How do you mean?

SARTRE: Why, I shall disappear before any movement of which I might be a member could take on a clear shape and reach a given aim. Yet although I shall not be there for the defeats, I shall always be there for the beginnings, which is better. For the moment I am at the beginnings and I shall not see anything broader, anything more powerful—there are many, many people who don't want to join the Communist party but who nevertheless do want to be active.

DE BEAUVOIR: Isn't there a hope that the Communist party may be rejuvenated, may change? Or do you think that's quite out of the question?

SARTRE: In any case it would be extraordinarily hard. All the adults, almost all the adults already have the mask, already have the computer in their brains. If the young are different, perhaps things will go better, but I can't see it.

DE BEAUVOIR: It remains to be seen whether the young will provide the Communist party with new blood or whether, on the contrary, theirs will freeze.

SARTRE: There you are.

DE BEAUVOIR: Today I'd like to talk about an important theme—your relations with time. I'm by no means sure how to phrase the questions, and I think it would be better if you yourself were to speak about what seems to you important in your relations with time.

SARTRE: That's very difficult, because there is objective time and subjective time. There's the time when I'm waiting for a train that leaves at 8:55, and then there's the time at home when I'm working. It's very difficult. I'll try to speak of both, but without any real philosophical basis.

I think that until I was about eight or nine my time was little divided. There was one great subjective time with exterior objects that every now and then came to divide it—truly objective objects. Toward ten—and, as you will see, for a long while—there was a very exact division of my time. Each year was cut into nine months of work at the lycée and three months of vacation.

DE BEAUVOIR: Is that what you could call objective division?

SARTRE: Objective *and* experienced subjectively. It was objective in the first place—the nine months of lycée were programs that were imposed upon me. I lived the three months of holidays subjectively. Going into school in the morning with my pen was not the same thing as waking up somewhere in the country with the sun over my head. This brought about alterations in what I expected of that kind of time. During the first nine months I expected monotony—exercises that were marked, exams in which I might be first or last, the general body of work that was set and that I did at home in the family drawing room. Then for three months I expected the wonderful, that is to say something that would not belong to the same order as the routine of school, something that would appear in the country or abroad in the places where I passed my holidays, something that would have nothing in common with the daily round of the first nine months but that would represent a foreign reality, appearing to me and eluding me at the same time, and very beautiful. That's the idea I had of the holidays —the country or the seashore, and within this time, when I was in contact with the country and the sea, things appeared that were indeed wonderful: it was the very being of the sea or the countryside. A ship seen far away on the water might be a wonderful object; a little stream in the woods might also be wonderful. It was another kind of reality, one which I've never defined more clearly than that, but which made a strong contrast with the rest of the world. There was the reality of everyday life in which nothing could surprise, and there was the reality of the holidays in which, on the contrary, some things could surprise and enrich you. That was how I experienced time until I reached the Ecole Normale, and even when I was there. After that I did my military service. I'd had a postponement, and I did my service when I was twenty-four, in meteorology. I was in a little house in the neighborhood of Tours. There I made notes on the humidity and the weather; I learned something about radio; I knew the Morse code and I received meteorological information from various places. Sometimes I went out at night to check the temperature, the humidity measurement, and so on, with instruments assembled in a hut near the house. In short, I led a very ordered life, and at that time the division into three months of vacation and nine of work no longer existed. When my military service was over I became a teacher and once again I recovered the rhythm of nine months—three months, no longer as a pupil but as a teacher, which in a way comes to the same thing. For nine months I prepared lessons and gave them. I had my private life, which was considerable since I only taught for fifteen or sixteen hours a week, with as much for preparation, the whole coming to thirty-two or thirty-three hours a week. I spent hours and hours on literary work. And then there were the days that I spent at Rouen with you; and we both used to go to Paris to spend a couple of days when we had no lessons to give. I had a very regular life and subjective time played a very great part in it. At Le Havre, what I mostly did was to think, feel, and develop philosophical thoughts; or I worked on *Nausea*. In Paris and at Rouen, there were things to do, meetings, friends to see. Le Havre represented a subjectivity—not solely, of course, but to a very large extent. The future was its essential dimension. My subjective time was turned toward the future. I lived in work and I was working in order to bring a work into existence. The work was obviously a future work. I worked on *Nausea* until the end of my years at Le Havre, and that constituted a bond as lasting, as steady, and in a way as objective as the time at the lycée during which I taught philosophy or as my relations with my friends or with you.

During the vacations I left France. We used to wander about, you and I, all over the place, in Spain, Italy, Greece, and that too was a time set apart. I could not imagine seeing Spain or Greece except in those particular months. And the wonderful reappeared, since I was going off to see something I had never seen before—a Greek peasant, a Greek landscape, the Acropolis for the first time. It was indeed the wonder of the holidays that stood out so sharply against the nine months of the lycée where I was always teaching the same thing. These three months, perpetually fresh and never comparable from one year to the next, were the time of discovery.

This lasted until the war. During the war and up until my return from the prison camp the earlier division of my time was entirely gone. Everything was always the same, at least as far as my occupations were concerned. A soldier does the same things in summer and in winter. I was a meteorologist and I led a meteorologist's existence. After that I was in a stalag, where the days went by, one much the same as the other. Then I got away and came back to France, and at that point I recovered the same divisions that I had had before—nine months at the Lycée Pasteur in Paris and three months of vacation— vacations usually in the Free Zone, which represented abroad and even more than abroad, since one had to be smuggled over the demarcation line. At the end of the war, when the Germans had gone, I withdrew from the lycée. I took a leave of absence that finally turned into a retirement. I became a writer and nothing else, living only on what my books brought in. Yet the year was still divided into nine months and three months, and it has stayed like that all my life. Even now I take three months of holidays. I always go to the same places, and therefore the wonderful has narrower limits and is less unexpected. I go to Rome during my vacation, but during that time life is much more supple, much freer. I talk to you about anything and everything, and we go for walks together. So it is a different kind of time in a way, but one that does not bring important new experiences, since I know Italy fairly well and I never see anything that I have not seen before. But the division of time remains. I go back to Paris in October as if I were still teaching, and I leave in July as though the term were over. It could be said that the nine-months–three-months rhythm has lasted from the age of eight to my present seventy. It has been the typical division of my years. The real time of my literary work is those nine months in Paris. I usually go on working during the three months of vacation, but I work less and the world spreads out around me without any set timetable. During the nine months there is a set timetable; it depends on the book I am writing. During vacation I am much more in contact with the place where I happen to be. It is there that subjective time is recovered. I am subjectively affected by Paris, which I love and where I have always spent more time than anywhere else. Or again by the time in Brazil or Japan, which is a different kind of time, one that comes to me from people and one in which I often go for excursions and see things that those who live there tell me must be seen. It's a strange, confused time, with now and then some remarkable experiences. Those three months are the time in which I experience the world. There are different ways of grasping the minutes that go by during the holidays. During the year the days tend to run into one another. They are separated by the nights, when I sleep, but in fact they run on, the nights merely representing a pause for rest. And in my memory the days of the nine months glide slowly together and end up by making no more than one. By the next year the nine months have become a single day. That is how my time has always been divided, and in this it is not like the time of a working man with twenty days of holiday—if he has so much—for whom the rest of the year is entirely made up of days of the same work.

DE BEAUVOIR: Still, your life—at least since the war—has not been quite as methodical and regular as you say. There have been times when you have not spent your nine months in Paris. One year you spent four months in America, and the year after that you went back to America at times that were not vacations. When you went to Cuba, it was in February. In 1950 we also traveled in Algeria and then in black Africa, about April. And that year we didn't have a long vacation in the summer months. The rhythm is rather more supple, rather more fanciful than you say. Besides, we also go away for the Easter holidays.

SARTRE: That's true. But it always remains within the framework of nine months–three months. Unforeseen things happen during the nine months, but I still keep the nine-months–three-months division. And even if I do take a trip during the working year, it hasn't quite the same meaning as a summer journey.

DE BEAUVOIR: You say that in your memory the nine months boil down to a single day. Yet your life in Paris is quite varied. And it's programmed too.

SARTRE: It's programmed day by day and every day has the same program. I get up about half past eight; at half past nine I'm at work and I go on working until half past one—half past twelve on the days when someone comes to see me. Then I go and have lunch, usually at the Coupole. I finish lunch about three, and from three o'clock to five I see friends. From five till nine I work at home. At least that's how it was until these last years when I became blind—or in any case I see very little and am no longer able to read or write. Even now I often sit in my chair at my desk without writing much. Making notes sometimes, which I can't reread, but you read them to me. At nine o'clock I go and have dinner with you or someone else—generally with you. For some time now we have been having dinner at your apartment. We used to go to a restaurant, but now we dine off a slice of pâté or something like that at your place and we spend the evening talking or listening to music. At midnight I go to bed. That's how the days are made up. Yet they do vary a little. I may see more of you one day and less during those that follow.

DE BEAUVOIR: You don't always lunch with the same person or spend the evening with the same person, but it is very much a fixed program —on Monday, one person, on Tuesday another, on Wednesday, a third, and so on. So the program for the week is more or less unchanging. That's important, because it means that in addition to your nine-months–three-months division you also have a highly detailed program for the life of each day and of each week. It's a very regular existence. Why is it programmed like this?

SARTRE: I don't know. But you mustn't forget that this timetable is above all a form; its content depends only on me. If, for example, I have three hours to work in the afternoon, it's not the same work every day.

DE BEAUVOIR: Of course not. As far as appointments are concerned, there are people who would like to see you and who want to know when they can do so. And it would be too complicated if you had to make an appointment every time. People could no longer entirely rely on you. I think you've rather let yourself be taken over by the practico-inert aspect of your relations with others, which means that you'll never change the times of the people you have to see. Everybody is rather like that, yet even so, my relations with people are much suppler. In your case it's particularly hampering.

SARTRE: Yes, but the constraining element in this hampering is the hour set for the meetings. What happens at the meetings is variable.

DE BEAUVOIR: That's true. Sometimes we spend the evening talking, sometimes I read to you, and sometimes we listen to music.

SARTRE: There are people with whom I go through very repetitive hours.

DE BEAUVOIR: Let's go back to subjective time. Has time ever seemed to you too short or too long?

SARTRE: Most of the time too long, but also too short on occasion.

DE BEAUVOIR: Does that mean you're often bored?

SARTRE: It's not exactly that, but I do think that things might be tightened up. People's lives might contain fewer repetitions. But that doesn't bore me. I can be amused by hearing the same people say the same thing twice. No, it's not boredom. But the fact is that time is usually too long. Now and then too short, as it is when there's not enough time allowed for one to prepare and carry out the action one wishes to perform. There's not enough, either because of the people who are against the action or because of the difficulties one meets. Then again, when I'm having an agreeable time and it has to come to an end at ten o'clock because I must work, the time has been too short. The time is never exactly what it ought to be, that is, the time that suits a given thing exactly, without excess and without loss.

DE BEAUVOIR: At one point you often used to speak of a "race against the clock." When you had very heavy work in hand, like the Flaubert or before that the *Critique of Dialectical Reason*. You had the feeling that you lacked time to finish them and that you had to fight against the clock in an almost neurotic fashion. It was that which explained the Corydrane, by the way.

SARTRE: Far less in the case of the Flaubert. Very much so for the *Critique of Dialectical Reason*. And in the end I never did finish the book. I kept a long piece that hasn't been published and that wasn't finished, a piece that might represent another volume. Furthermore, one of the characteristics of my relation with time is the number of works that I haven't finished: my novel, *Being and Nothingness*, the *Critique of Dialectical Reason*, the Flaubert, etcetera. It's not a disaster that they are unfinished, because people who are interested in those things could finish them or produce similar works. But it is a fact that with me there's usually been a kind of panic or a change that made me suddenly decide—a disagreeable decision—to stop there and not to finish the book I was working on. It's odd, because I used to have a perfectly calm and classic image of myself; I saw my books rather as I saw those my grandfather wrote—books for reading. You began at the beginning and you finished at the end. They were rigorous. When I was about ten I thought that all the books I wrote would have a beginning and an end, that they would be severely written, and that they would include everything there was to be said. And now at seventy, looking back at what lies behind me, I observe that there are a good many works that have not been finished.

DE BEAUVOIR: Isn't that because your projects stretch out over an enormous future? While you are living through this future other things importune you, gain your interest, and take up your attention, so that you then abandon the former plan.

SARTRE: I think that's it. There's no doubt that my novel stopped because the last volume, which was about the Resistance in Paris during the war, no longer squared with political life in France under the Fourth Republic. I could not at the same time live politically in 1950 and try, by an effort of imagination, to recover the life we led in 1942–43. There I was faced with a difficulty that a historian might have been able to deal with but that a novelist could not.

DE BEAUVOIR: I think it's roughly the same thing for the other unfinished works. The project stretched forward over too great a length of time, and when you planned it you did not consider that other specific importunities would arise, finally winning the day because they were situated in the present.

SARTRE: The *Critique of Dialectical Reason* and *The Family Idiot* dealt in part with the present day; *The Family Idiot* at the beginning and the *Critique of Dialectical Reason* at the end. Those sections did them some harm.

DE BEAUVOIR: You said time was never quite right, that it was always too short or too long. But still, aren't there periods when you're relaxed, when you just stroll about or contemplate, periods when there's no tension in your relations with time?

SARTRE: There are plenty of those moments; they happen every day. I am tense when I'm sitting at my desk writing. It's a time of tension and I find it hard to overcome. I feel that by the end of three hours I shan't have done the work I wanted to do. And then there are the hours that I'll call those of private life, although in fact they are as communal, as social as the rest. When I'm with you it may happen that we have set things to do, and then time grows tense again. But on an evening like yesterday nothing hurried us and time just wafted by.

DE BEAUVOIR: Yes. One mustn't give the impression that you are as tense with regard to time as you are with regard to your body. You don't accept the surrender of your body, but giving yourself up to time, to duration, is something you're good at, even better than I am, I should say. When we were traveling I was always intensely eager to see everything and hurry everywhere, whereas you far preferred being quiet and contemplative and taking your time. The fact that you smoked a pipe was perhaps also a way of filling your time without overfilling it.

SARTRE: To smoke a pipe you have to be settled in a specific place, at a café table, for instance, and then you have to stare at the world around you as you smoke. A pipe is an immobilizing element. Since I've taken to smoking cigarettes things are different. It's quite certain that during the holidays I had a stronger wish to "take my time" than during the nine months of the school year. Even during those nine months there were hours of private life when I liked to take my time. I used to gaze at things and talk about what I saw, the objects around me, the men who passed by.

DE BEAUVOIR: I think that although you've worked even harder than I have in the course of your life, you've always been more able to sit and do nothing.

SARTRE: Yes, and that's the case even now. Yesterday morning I sat for three hours in this armchair, from which I didn't see much, since I can scarcely make things out anymore. I didn't listen to music because there was the strike, and I sat there, reflecting, dreaming, without going far back into the past, because I'm not very fond of my past. Not that I find it drearier than others, but it belongs to the past. The past exists for me insofar as when I am asked what I was doing in 1924 I can say that I was at the Ecole Normale. But it doesn't exist insofar as scenes from my youth, my childhood, my middle years could reappear but do not do so. You're not like that.

DE BEAUVOIR: No, not at all. Do you never inwardly recount some journey you've made?

SARTRE: Never. I do have fleeting recollections. For example I have a memory of Cordes, of little beds of larkspur along the walls in the streets leading up. I don't know why, but a street in Cordes may come into my mind again.

DE BEAUVOIR: Do things call up memories for you when you are living in the present? Is the present surrounded by the past?

SARTRE: No, it's always new. That was why I maintained in *Nausea* that experience of life doesn't exist.

DE BEAUVOIR: That's not quite what I'm thinking of. I'm thinking of those superimpositions of the past on the present which happen—in any case they very often happen with me—and which give the present a particularly poetic dimension. A snowy landscape will remind me of another snowy landscape in which I skied with you, and that makes the landscape all the more precious to me. The smell of mown grass will instantly bring the meadows of the Limousin to my mind.

SARTRE: Yes, of course. Smells can recall other smells; but the snowy landscape that evokes a skiing scene—a whole made up of things that happened at another period in the same kind of landscape—no. My past life comes back to me only in a contemplative form, not at all as though it were dwelling in present recollections. Of course I do have recollections; I have them continually. But they are there as moments that are losing themselves in the present and not as exact things that might refer me back to the past. They belong to the past, but to a past that flows into the present.

DE BEAUVOIR: For example, when you look at Rome in the morning from your terrace, it's the Rome you've seen countless times, but you grasp it in the immediate present.

SARTRE: Yes, always. I don't attach my past to the present. No doubt it does the attaching on its own.

DE BEAUVOIR: Yes, because as you've explained, the world's objects are made up of all the values one has endowed them with; but that's not directly given like something situated in time.

SARTRE: I had another kind of time when I was young. It was the duration of my life from fifteen until my death. But in the days when notions of fame and genius interested me, until I was between thirty and forty, I used to divide time into an indefinite period of real life and then another infinitely longer period which was the time after my death during which my works would influence people.

DE BEAUVOIR: Real time nevertheless finished with death?

SARTRE: Yes, but in one sense it did not finish. Life did not come to an end. One died in the midst of a whole mass of plans that one did not carry out. But after death I survived in the form of my books; in my books I was found again. It was immortal life. The real life, in which one no longer needs to possess a body and a consciousness but in which one gives out facts and meanings that vary according to the outside world.

DE BEAUVOIR: Were you aware of the various stages of your life?

SARTRE: Yes and no. I did not grasp them clearly. As soon as I had written ten lines when I was fourteen, for instance, I had the feeling that it was the work of a genius. In fact they were sentences devoid of importance, but I thought them inspired. At the same time it was a way of seeing myself as an adult. When I wrote I saw myself as an adult, though of my own age. I had no notion, for example, that at sixteen I was writing mere drafts. Every time I thought I was writing something that was the final version and that would please my readers.

DE BEAUVOIR: Did you ever have the idea of apprenticeship?

SARTRE: That came later. But to begin with, no. I went through my apprenticeship in the novel itself. *Nausea* was a real apprenticeship. I had to learn how to tell a tale and to give ideas flesh in a narrative. It was as much an apprenticeship as any other.

DE BEAUVOIR: There's one idea that has been very important to you —that of progress.

SARTRE: Certainly. I thought my first books would be inferior to those that came after. I thought my main work would be completed by the time I was about fifty and that then I should die. Obviously, this idea of progress came to me from the lessons in which progress was taught, and from my grandfather who believed in it.

DE BEAUVOIR: And from your choice of the future too. You think that tomorrow will be better than today. How do you reconcile this notion of progress that you've always had with your denial of experience?

SARTRE: I thought that for me progress was concerned with form. It was a question of learning how to write better, how to acquire a style and to put books together according to a certain program. But it wasn't a progress in knowledge.

DE BEAUVOIR: Yet it seems to me that in philosophy the idea of progress implies an increasing wealth of knowledge and a deeper and deeper degree of reflection.

SARTRE: Yes, but I did not really think of it like that.

DE BEAUVOIR: You did not think it was the past that made you richer. Did you think that there was a form which was going to be more strongly asserted, and that it was the movement toward the future itself that had a validity?

SARTRE: Basically I believed in Comte's words: "Progress is the bringing out of a hidden order." That seemed to me true.

DE BEAUVOIR: It was a very optimistic outlook, compared with the attitude of all the many people who, like Fitzgerald for example, think that life is a process of disintegration—that the whole of life is a downfall, a defeat.

SARTRE: I used to think that too. I thought it at various times in my life. Things that had been begun and that ought to have been successfully carried out came to a halt. One therefore ended in failure.

DE BEAUVOIR: The idea of failure is not the same as that of disintegration, of decomposition.

SARTRE: That I never thought. I always thought that life was progress up until death—that it must be progress.

DE BEAUVOIR: What do you think about it now?

SARTRE: The same thing. Progress does stop at some point before death because one is weary, because one is near senility, or because one has private worries. But by rights it should go on for a long time. Fifty's better than thirty-five. Of course, the progress may be interrupted; one may suddenly turn one's back on the road one had begun to follow.

DE BEAUVOIR: And then again, there are works that can't be looked upon as being either an advance or a retreat because they are a whole. It can't be said that *Nausea* is less good than *The Words*. On the other hand one can say that the *Critique of Dialectical Reason* represents progress in comparison with *Being and Nothingness,* as does the Flaubert, to a certain extent, in comparison with the *Critique,* because on certain points it goes further. There one can speak of progress. But for what are called works of art it's impossible, because if a work is carried out, it's carried out.

SARTRE: Even so, there is, for example, an enormous progress between what Van Gogh painted in Holland and his last pictures.

DE BEAUVOIR: It very often happens that painters' last works are by far their best, because there is a mastery of the craft, which is much more complex than it is in writing.

SARTRE: As I see it, the moment itself is already progress. It is the present and it flows on toward the future, leaving behind it the poor, disdained, despised, denied past. For this reason I've always readily admitted misdeeds or mistakes, since they were committed by someone else.

DE BEAUVOIR: You've always been steadfast in your life, both in your work and in your affections; but at the same time you don't possess any deep solidarity with your past. Yet it's certainly the twenty-year-old Sartre one still sees today.

SARTRE: Having a solidarity with one's past or not having it is a secondary matter. The work to be done remains the same. In a certain fashion the past enriches the present and is also transformed by it. But that's never been one of my problems.

DE BEAUVOIR: I'd like to know this. What have been your relations with your age according to your various ages?

SARTRE: I never had any. At any age.

DE BEAUVOIR: No? When you were a child you certainly felt that you were a child, didn't you?

SARTRE: Yes, but from the time I was thirteen or fourteen my family avoided making me feel that I was a child. I began thinking I was a young man, because there are particular hardships for a young man.

DE BEAUVOIR: What do you mean by hardships?

SARTRE: You're not completely free; you're dependent on your family. I met with opposition, and there were clashes. I began to be completely free when I was at the Ecole Normale. From then on, yes, I could certainly say, "I'm twenty, I'm twenty-five," and that corresponded to certain very exact powers that come with age; but I did not feel the age in itself.

DE BEAUVOIR: Didn't you feel a certain connection with an immensely open future?

SARTRE: Yes, I felt that I was committed to a business I did not understand very well, but for me that did not represent an age. It meant that I had to go to work, that I had to do something.

DE BEAUVOIR: I mean everything was still in front of you at that time.

SARTRE: Yes, but I didn't think of that as an age. It was like the beginning of a book that is going to take two or three years to write, a book of which we are writing the first line. It was an activity that would last quite a while or even forever. The idea of getting old, of having worn arteries, bad eyes, etcetera, all the troubles you have when you grow old, never occurred to me at all.

DE BEAUVOIR: Of course not. But didn't you feel positively young? Didn't you go about with friends of the same age as yourself? Didn't you have any contacts with people of forty or fifty who belonged to a category different from your own?

SARTRE: Yes, but I didn't think I should ever become one of them.

DE BEAUVOIR: So you didn't feel "I'm young"?

SARTRE: No. That's one of the things I've felt least. Naturally, that doesn't mean that I didn't feel it at all. It was blurred, you might say. I did have a faint impression of being young, but it was blurred. I've never felt very young.

DE BEAUVOIR: And has there been a time when you've felt that you were a given age?

SARTRE: No, not exactly. These last years . . .

DE BEAUVOIR: No, before these last years. Wasn't there a time when you felt that you were reaching the age of an adult?

SARTRE: No.

DE BEAUVOIR: Yet as I remember it you did. You had that kind of neurosis, with the crayfish following you about and so on, and it was to some extent because you saw yourself as being settled into adult life. In any case that's what I said in my memoirs, and you didn't contradict it. You were twenty-six or twenty-seven and you were beginning to have the feeling that your life was over.

SARTRE: Yes, but that wasn't a question of age. I felt young

DE BEAUVOIR: And so you were, in a certain fashion.

SARTRE: Furthermore, that's what made the contrast between the life I was leading and the one that was waiting for me, the life of a teacher established in life. And writing rather floated above it all. But it can't be said that at that point I had the feeling of my age, or that I associated it with a great many things—connections, profession, friendship—which would have made a living reality of it. No, that went over my head.

DE BEAUVOIR: But still, when you were in contact with Bost, Palle, and Olga, didn't you feel that you were in the presence of people distinctly younger than yourself?

SARTRE: Yes, to some extent. Not with Olga. That was the relation with women, which is different. But with Bost and Palle, yes. Yet there was something in the intimacy between Bost, Palle, and me that went beyond age; they were comrades as well. They'll tell you so themselves; they never felt my age.

DE BEAUVOIR: Yes, as you said yourself, age is something that cannot be realized. One can never realize one's age oneself—it is not present to us. But doesn't the fact of being thirty or forty or fifty or sixty give different relations with the future, with the past, and many, many other things? Doesn't it make a difference?

SARTRE: So long as there was a future, one's age remained the same. There was a future at thirty; there was a future at fifty. It was perhaps rather more shriveled at fifty than at thirty. That wasn't for me to judge. But after sixty-five or sixty-six there's no longer any future. Of course there is the immediate future, the five coming years, but I'd said pretty well all I had to say, and broadly speaking I knew that I wouldn't write much more and that ten years later it would all be over. I remembered my grandfather's old age, which was sad. When he was eighty-five he was finished; he went on living but why he lived was not obvious. There were times when I thought I wanted no part of an old age like that; and there were others when I thought one should be unassuming, live out the allotted time, and disappear when one was told.

DE BEAUVOIR: But though you may not have had experience, you do have memories, don't you?

SARTRE: Very, very few, as you know. Now, as I'm talking to you, I do recall a certain number and I expand them; but that's because we are working over the past.

DE BEAUVOIR: In short, you've never had the full command of your memories?

SARTRE: No. I do bring memories to mind when the past is spoken of, but they have already become a little commonplace and are about three-quarters reconstituted. When I'm by myself, the direction of my thoughts is not toward reminiscence.

DE BEAUVOIR: Still, you do possess a certain store. If I talk to you about Brazil or Havana, for example, your perception of them is not the same as if you had never been to Brazil or Havana.

SARTRE: Yes, but it's things of the present day that may lead me to think of my connection with Brazil or Havana.

DE BEAUVOIR: You mean you've spent your life from thirteen until today without ever having different relations with the future or with the present. Has it always been exactly the same with the past?

SARTRE: Yes.

DE BEAUVOIR: I don't believe it's possible.

SARTRE: Not exactly. Nevertheless, in general, that's how it is.

DE BEAUVOIR: It's completely abnormal. What do you attribute it to? People usually realize that they're twenty and they are more or less pleased about it; others realize that they're fifty. There are times when people are aware of being a certain age. Myself, for instance—it's perfectly obvious that I've been various ages. How do you explain that this doesn't apply to you?

SARTRE: I don't know. But I do know that that's how it is. I feel like a young man, surrounded by the possibilities that are offered to a young man. Clearly, I loathe thinking that my powers have diminished and that I am not what I was at thirty.

DE BEAUVOIR: After a certain age everyone is forced to think that and loathes thinking it.

SARTRE: For example, I find the fact of being sixty-nine—which I mentally transcribe as seventy—disagreeable. For the first time I now and then think about my age—I'm seventy: that is, I'm finished. Yet this is accompanied by things that certainly come from my bodily state and therefore from my age but which I do not connect with age —with the fact that I see badly and that I no longer write. I can no longer write, or read, because I don't see. All these things are connected with age . . .

DE BEAUVOIR: You feel them more as a man of fifty who has had an accident might feel them than as a man of seventy whose age has unpleasant repercussions in his body, don't you?

SARTRE: Much more.

DE BEAUVOIR: So at present you do feel you are a given age?

SARTRE: At times. I thought about it yesterday, and last week too, or a couple of weeks ago. Clearly, it's a factual reality that I thin!· about now and then. Yet even so, on the whole I go on feeling young.

DE BEAUVOIR: Timeless, as it were?

SARTRE: Yes; or young. Perhaps it would be better to say that I am young in my head. Maybe I was aware of my youth; in any case I've kept it.

DE BEAUVOIR: How then do you explain the fact—the curious fact, after all—that upon the whole you've never been a particular age? Is it because you always lived intensely in the present, a present reaching out toward the future, toward action?

SARTRE: Yes. I've probably not had much spare time for looking back to those moments of the past that are valued for themselves, for their aesthetic or emotional worth. I haven't had much time for that.

DE BEAUVOIR: Or is it because of a total absence of narcissism? You have in fact almost no relations with yourself, almost none with your image.

SARTRE: Certainly my recollections of the past aren't connected with my image. But wait, I've just recaptured a memory that has remained very sharp and clear—that of the day I took mescalin. I was coming back by train; you were sitting next to me, and there was an ape that leaned out of the window. I can see that very clearly. I see you and I see the ape leaning against the window, head down.

DE BEAUVOIR: *The Words* proves that you do have memories, and when we talked about it here, the memories came. But what I meant is that on the whole your consciousness is directed toward the outside world and not toward your state, your position in the world; not toward an image of yourself.

SARTRE: Just so.

DE BEAUVOIR: Perhaps it's that which makes you remain younger than others.

SARTRE: Subjectively, of course. I go through the same periods as others and I comply with them. I'm the same or not the same, but within foreseeable limits; and then I think differently, I think as though I were not changing.

DE BEAUVOIR: Isn't that also linked with your utter indifference to death? There's a passage in *The Words* where you say that you were very afraid of death as a child. But after that time it seems to me that you have never worried about it at all. You never thought, Now I'm forty . . .

SARTRE: Never. For the last ten years I have thought about it, but objectively, and without its upsetting me in any way. I was thinking about it again two or three days ago—I've reached the age at which human life comes to an end nowadays. I believe that for the French seventy is . . .

DE BEAUVOIR: No, a privileged Frenchman like you may live to eighty or eighty-five. But still that does make a rather limited space; I feel it myself. One no longer dares to say, "In twenty years I'll do this—in twenty years I'll go there." But in your case, do you not mind coming up against this limit? This kind of wall?

SARTRE: Gradually an age takes shape, an age that is itself shaped by that limit. Apart from that, when I'm well, I still feel as I did thirty years ago. But I do know that in fifteen years I'll be eighty-five. If I'm still alive.

DE BEAUVOIR: But that's a knowledge that comes from outside. You've explained that fifty times. The ego is not in the consciousness, and the consciousness is therefore always perpetually present, fresh, unchanged. But what about your relations with others? Don't they make you feel that you are a certain age?

SARTRE: As I see them, they don't age much either. Look at the *Temps modernes* fellows—I'm thinking of Bost or Pouillon, just as they've always been.

DE BEAUVOIR: You don't see them growing old?

SARTRE: No, I see young men to whom I teach philosophy or to whom I have taught philosophy.

DE BEAUVOIR: And what about your relations with the young? With Victor, for instance. One of the things that moves you is that you can teach him certain things, that you can help him. So it is then a question of experience, at least of something that is linked to the very few gains of old age.

SARTRE: Yes, we must look into what that means. At present it's rather a question of envisaging things, not with the experience, but with the age I have. Yes, I'm fond of seeing Victor, but after a minute our conversation is that of one person to another, not that of a young man who has come to see an old one. We argue; we have two points of view about some political or other reality that crops up. At that point he is as old as I am.

DE BEAUVOIR: Yes, I understand that. There are other things to say about relations with time that may perhaps explain this absence of a feeling of age. To begin with that way you've always had of preferring the present to the past. I mean if you drink whiskey you'll say, "Ha, this is a wonderful whiskey; it's better than yesterday's." On the whole, you always prefer the present.

SARTRE: The present is concrete and real. Yesterday is not so sharp and clear, and I'm not yet thinking of tomorrow. For me there is a preference for the present over the past. There are people who are like the past better because they attribute an aesthetic or a cultural value to it. I don't. In moving into the past the present dies. It loses its value of dawning life. It still belongs to life; I can refer back to it; but it no longer possesses that quality that is given to every moment insofar as I am living it and which it loses when I am living it no more.

DE BEAUVOIR: No doubt that's why you've never found it very hard to break with your friends.

SARTRE: Yes. I began a new life without them.

DE BEAUVOIR: Is that because as soon as a thing belongs to the past it is really abolished for you?

SARTRE: Yes. And as for the friends who are still left to me, still living, they have to have a fresh present immediacy so as not to be continually harking back to the same one. I mustn't see them as they were yesterday or the day before, with the same worries, the same ideas, the same ways of speaking. There has to be a change.

DE BEAUVOIR: According to these definitions of your relation with time it could be thought that you were a very changeable man who easily drops his past and throws himself into new adventures, whereas it's not that at all. You're a very steadfast being. We've lived together forty-five years and you have friendships, like that with Bost, that have lasted a very, very long time. And you have long-standing friendships with other members of the *Temps modernes* team as well. How do you explain this mixture of constancy, of fidelity, and of living in the present?

SARTRE: Living in the present is made up of these very constancies. Living in the present doesn't mean running after God knows what new object or God knows what new person. It means living with people and at the same time giving them a kind of present dimension which in fact they possess. You, for example. I've never thought of you in the past, I've always thought of you in the present; so I contrive to link this present with the former pasts.

DE BEAUVOIR: And is it the same in your relation with work? Do you still think the last book you wrote was the best? Or have you a certain affection for earlier works?

SARTRE: I do have affection for earlier works. *Nausea,* for instance. I used to think of my work as dated. There were some books that were understood at a given time, not before and not after, because of the circumstances.

DE BEAUVOIR: But intellectually do you have the impression of going further, the impression of progress? Or do certain works seem to you so definitive, so final that in a way you yourself could not go beyond them?

SARTRE: I have a feeling of progress. You won't make me say that *The Words* is better than *Nausea,* but still, in spite of everything, going forward did mean producing something of greater value, since I benefited from the earlier works.

DE BEAUVOIR: In any case, should we not distinguish—and this brings us back to speaking of your works—between the literary and the philosophical books? Because although you can't be made to say that *The Words* is better than *Nausea,* you're quite ready to state—and it's obvious—that the *Critique of Dialectical Reason* is better than *Being and Nothingness.*

SARTRE: I think that's true, but I shouldn't say so very willingly because in a way my earlier books are marked by the gratification I had when I was writing them. It's very hard for me really to think of the *Critique of Dialectical Reason* as superior to *Being and Nothingness.*

DE BEAUVOIR: Do you mean it goes no further?

SARTRE: No, it does go further.

DE BEAUVOIR: It solves more problems; it gives a more exact description of society. Only it wouldn't have been possible without *Being and Nothingness;* and I think that too is a fact.

SARTRE: In philosophy and in my private life I have always defined the present—it's the full moment—in relation to the future, and I have made it contain the qualities of the future. Whereas in the triad, present, future, past, the past has always been deprived of real action upon the present. Yet I know that in a way the past is more important than the future; it brings us something.

DE BEAUVOIR: You've often said that it defines the situation that one outstrips. The present is a resumption of the past toward a future. But it is the movement in the direction of the future that has interested you—personally, at any rate—more than the resumption of the past.

SARTRE: If you consider the very meaning of my life, which is to write, it consists of setting off from a present which becomes a past in which I did not write, to reach a present in which I am writing and in which a book is being formed that will be finished in the future. The moment of writing is a moment that includes the future and the present, the present determined in relation to the future. You write a chapter of a novel; you write chapter twelve which comes after chapter eleven and which comes before chapter fourteen; time therefore appears as a call from the future to the present.

DE BEAUVOIR: But haven't there been, and aren't there now, moments in your life when the present is experienced really for its own sake? As a kind of contemplation, of enjoyment, and not only as a project, or activity, or work?

SARTRE: Yes, and there still are. There are such moments here in the morning,* for instance, when I wake up before you're there and I go and sit in the armchair on the terrace and gaze at the sky.

DE BEAUVOIR: Have there been many times like that in your life?

SARTRE: A good many. I've looked upon them as being superior to the others, as more worthwhile.

DE BEAUVOIR: Because you've been a very active man and you've worked a great deal, yet in spite of that there have been moments of surrender, of sinking into that immediate present?

SARTRE: Yes. There have been a great many moments like that.

DE BEAUVOIR: And with just what in the way of content?

SARTRE: An agreeable content.

DE BEAUVOIR: Yes, but I mean what is it that puts you into that kind of immediate state?

SARTRE: No matter what. A lovely morning sky, and I go to look at things in that particular light. There is a time of perfect contentment —the things are there under this sky that I am looking at. I am that alone, someone who is looking at the morning sky.

DE BEAUVOIR: And does music—you're very fond of music—give you something of the same state at times?

SARTRE: Yes, as long as it is not I who am playing. At a concert or when I am listening to a record I sometimes have feelings of that kind. They might be called connections with happiness. It's not exactly happiness itself since these are moments that are going to disappear, but they are the elements that make up happiness.

DE BEAUVOIR: You live in the future as far as the future is activity,

* In Rome.

but do you also experience it as a kind of joyful anticipation? When you were setting off for your journey in America, for instance?

SARTRE: Yes, I imagined myself there in America.

DE BEAUVOIR: You thought about it very much indeed. For quite a long while you made the necessary preparations, but in your imagination you were already there in America. Do times like that often come to you? Are there things you've wanted very much, that you've imagined, waited for, and longed for with all your might?

SARTRE: Certainly.

DE BEAUVOIR: And if there is a confrontation between that dreamed-of, imagined future and the present, are you conscious of what might be called disappointment? Or on the contrary, does the reality give you more than you had imagined?

SARTRE: It gives me more and something else. Usually more, because it's a present in which every object contains infinite parts; everything can be found in a new present, and therefore more than you can imagine. What I could imagine were directions, qualities, limits, but not real objects, and the reality was something other than that which was expected because in spite of everything the truth cannot be imagined. Nick Carter's New York was not the one I discovered when I got there.

DE BEAUVOIR: You're not one of those people who are continually disappointed by the sight of what they'd been expecting?

SARTRE: I was not disappointed in New York; no, on the contrary. I know that what I imagine will not be what I shall see. It's there that a disappointment might be conceived. And perhaps there have been some small ones; but they vanish.

DE BEAUVOIR: Wasn't your tale "Le Soleil de minuit" (The Midnight Sun) in one way the story of a disappointment?

SARTRE: Yes, the little girl had imagined the midnight sun as having a magical form and when she was confronted with the real object she was disappointed.

DE BEAUVOIR: But that's very rarely happened to you in the course of your life?

SARTRE: In any case the tale showed this disappointment to be mistaken. By means of the little girl's disappointment I meant to make it apparent that the white night was a beautiful thing.

DE BEAUVOIR: Have you had regrets in your life? Have you said to yourself, "Ah, I ought to have done this—I let that go by—I've wasted my time here?"

SARTRE: Not a great many. When it's urgent, yes—when it's a decision that commits part of my life and which is therefore urgent—a decision that has to be made the next day. A decision's not a simple thing. If I have a decision of this kind to make in all its details, why then I may have regrets.

DE BEAUVOIR: Once the decision is made?

SARTRE: Yes, because I haven't foreseen everything.

DE BEAUVOIR: Do you mean that if you're forced to decide too quickly, you sometimes make a bad decision?

SARTRE: No, not a bad decision, but an imperfect one.

DE BEAUVOIR: Can you give an example of this happening to you?

SARTRE: I've no exact example to give you.

DE BEAUVOIR: In the few cases of making a decision in one's life—and one doesn't make so very many—I've had the feeling you've been pleased: the decision to go to Germany, to go to Le Havre as early as the first term, not to accept a khâgne at Lyons as your family wished, but to take a post at Laon. You've been pleased with all these decisions, haven't you?

SARTRE: I've been pleased with them all.

DE BEAUVOIR: As far as I know, whenever you had regrets it was because the world had refused you something. You regretted not going to Japan, for instance.

SARTRE: I didn't regret it much. There are people who would have regretted it much more than I did. But generally speaking, I haven't had many regrets in my life. I have had some; there are books that I began to write and never finished and never published.

DE BEAUVOIR: Yes, but the regret can't be very strong, since as it happened you didn't write them because you preferred doing something else.

DE BEAUVOIR: I'd like to ask you in a very general way how you see your life as a whole.

SARTRE: I've always looked upon every man's life as something adjoining and surrounding him. Generally, I see not only my life but all lives roughly in this way—a threadlike beginning that slowly broadens with the acquisition of knowledge and the earliest experiences, adventures, and a whole range of feelings. Then from a certain age that varies according to the person, partly because of himself, partly because of his body, and partly because of circumstances, life moves toward its close, death being the final closing as birth was the opening. But as I see it this time of closure is accompanied by a continual broadening toward the universal. A man of fifty or sixty who is traveling toward death, is at the same time learning and also experiencing a certain number of relations with others and with society, relations that grow wider and wider. He learns the social dimension; he learns to reflect upon others' lives and upon his own. He grows richer, while beneath all this he is dying. A certain form moves toward its completion, and at the same time the individual acquires knowledge or patterns of thought that are universal, that go in the direction of universality. He acts either in favor of a certain society and for its preservation, or in favor of the creation of another society. And this society will perhaps only appear after his death. In any event its development will take place after his death. In the same way most of the undertakings that concern him in the last part of his life will be successful if they are carried on after his death—if, for instance, he can leave his children the shop he has built up—but will come to nothing if they end before it—for example, if he is ruined and can leave them nothing. In other words there is a future that lies beyond death and that almost turns death into an accident in the individual's life, a life that goes on without him. For many people this is not true. The old men in poorhouses who have been laborers or who have followed very humble trades have no future left anymore. They live in the present and their life moves toward death with no future other than that of the moment immediately following the present.

DE BEAUVOIR: I believe your description is one that certainly applies to you, to a certain number of privileged people, and particularly to intellectuals when they retain an interest in life. But I believe that even apart from the poorhouses, the vast majority of old people are cut off from their work and from the world as a whole once they have reached retirement. Old age is very rarely the kind of broadening that you speak of. But since it's you that we're talking about, what you've just said is still very interesting. I'd like you to tell me in more detail just how far you personally have the feeling that life continues to be a broadening process for you. From that point of view, where would you place the high point of your life? I mean the point at which you had the greatest number of contacts with the world, with people, and with knowledge.

SARTRE: The greatest number of relations that are real and that do not end in a future in which I shall no longer exist—I think it was between forty-five and sixty.

DE BEAUVOIR: You think that until you were sixty your life continually broadened and grew richer?

SARTRE: Roughly that. It was then that I wrote philosophical works. But my life always had a future that was not dependent on my death. There was that notion of immortality, which I believed in for a long while and then believed in no more. In any event, for a writer there is still the idea that he will go on being read when he no longer exists. And that's his future. One goes on being read—how long? Fifty years, a hundred years, five hundred years? It depends on the writers. In any case I can rely on fifty years. It doesn't matter if I'm read little or much, but in fifty years there will still be my books, just as André Gide's books still exit for the young—exist less and less, by the way —that is, fifty years after his death or even more.

DE BEAUVOIR: You think that since you were sixty there's been a broadening together with a shrinking, don't you? How do you see these two movements in detail?

SARTRE: Let's take the shrinking. I'd no longer be interested in writing a novel that described another life I might have led. Mathieu and Antoine Roquentin had lives different from mine but close to it, explaining what I looked upon as the deepest in my own. I could no longer write that. I often think of writing a short story and then I never do it. So there are elements in my profession itself that are suppressed, lopped off, amputated—a whole romantic side of life, with hopes that are vain but that increase in value because they are vain. That entire aspect, relations with the future, relations with hope, relations with a real life in a real society answering my wishes —all that is over. And then there's the whole of the universal—the meaning of my life in the twentieth century—I try to get that clear in my mind. It takes me away from the twentieth century. It's in the twenty-first that one will be able to judge the lives belonging to the twentieth and give them their place. I'm certainly wrong in my picture of all this, but in spite of everything, I do try to project my vision of myself into the twenty-first century. There's that and a thousand other things—a knowledge of economics and the social sciences has come into my life. At the same time they have changed it to a certain extent (and may therefore perish with it), but they are also laws that act upon all lives, which, from this point of view, represent the universal. These laws will change with the twenty-first and twenty-second centuries. But they will allow an understanding of us. All this is a universal that I feel, that I partly grasp, and that I imagine either in the future or from my present onward. This corpus of knowledge is constant. It's in my head because I'm here, in the twentieth century; but it's also in my head because it exists—these are laws that have to be discovered as one discovers a rock in the darkness, by running into it.

DE BEAUVOIR: Do you mean that you've been learning since you were sixty?

SARTRE: Since I was one.

DE BEAUVOIR: Fine. But I was asking what you meant by broadening since the age of sixty.

SARTRE: I go on acquiring, of course. And the knowledge I acquire is in books, but it is also in my head because I develop it and try to link it with other aspects of knowledge that I possess. This knowledge is universal. It not only applies to an infinity of cases but also goes beyond time; it has a future; it will be found again in other circumstances in the next century. And for that very reason it gives me its future, as it were. In any case it gives it to me in a formal manner. The knowledge that I possess and that characterizes me is also future and will characterize me in the future. Thus I am and thus shall I be, even though I have lost my consciousness.

DE BEAUVOIR: Could you speak about this knowledge in more detail?

SARTRE: That would be difficult, because it is a question of knowledge of every kind. For example, the last little work I wrote in collaboration with Victor and Gavi was about that alone. We speak of the present, but also of the future, of the revolutionary future and of the conditions that will form it. This future is my object and at the same time it is myself.

DE BEAUVOIR: In other words, you feel that you have a broader, more valid vision of understanding the world, a broader, more valid idea of it than you have had up until now?

SARTRE: Yes, but it mustn't be said to start at sixty. It starts at any time and it broadens continually.

DE BEAUVOIR: Then the shrinking world would be that of certain projects, such as that of no longer writing novels, for instance.

SARTRE: Yes, or of no longer making long journeys because they tire me. That's the shrinking caused by old age properly so called and by the diseases that strike everyone. And this slow progress toward death can only be shown as a stipple beneath the corpus of universal knowledge that creates a future for me beyond death. I should therefore describe my life toward the end as a series of straight parallel lines.

These would be my knowledge, my actions, and my loyalties. All this would represent a world in which the future is present and in which it characterizes me as much as the present. And beneath it I should trace a dotted line showing what happens moment by moment and which has little future apart from my death—this real life of each moment, with the illnesses that may damage my inner organs, the mental blanks that I have had all my life but that may now grow still worse, etcetera. This is my death, but I draw it with a dotted line. And over it I set this knowledge and these actions that imply the future.

DE BEAUVOIR: I understand what you mean. But now let us look at your life from another angle. I'd like you to look at it as I tried to look at mine when I wrote the beginning of *All Said and Done*. In your life what has there been in the way of luck, opportunities, chance, moments of freedom or obstacles to that freedom? And to begin with—always supposing, which I believe to be the case, that you are pleased with your life as a whole, with what you've done and with having been what you are—what could you point out as the chances that have made you what you are?

SARTRE: It seems to me there is no question but that my greatest stroke of luck was being born into a teaching family, that is, a family of intellectuals of a certain kind who had a certain conception of work, of vacations, of daily life, who could give me a good start for writing. It's obvious that as soon as I could look around me I regarded my family's condition, and therefore my own, not as one social state among others but as *the* social state. Living meant living in society, and living in society meant living as my grandparents or my mother lived. It follows that my having begun by living with a grandfather who worked chiefly among books and who had pupils, as I've said in *The Words*, counted a great deal. And the fact that I had no father certainly counted a great deal too. If I'd had a father he would have followed a much more obvious, much more demanding profession. When I was born my grandfather had retired, or almost retired. He had a school of his own. He gave German lectures at the Hautes Etudes Sociales.* So he did have a profession, but the profession was remote. I saw his pupils at the parties given at the Institut and at my grandparents' house at Meudon. In short, all I knew of his working

---

* The Institut des Hautes Etudes Sociales, a school of very high standing, close to the Sorbonne. (trans.)

life was his periods of rest, and of his working relations with his pupils only the times when he invited them to dinner.

DE BEAUVOIR: How important was it for you, the fact of knowing nothing about a profession necessary for the earning of one's living?

SARTRE: Immensely important, because it did away with the relation between the work done and the money received for doing it. I did not see the connection between this life of parties and of my grandfather's relations with his pupils—which looked like those of fellowship and friendliness—and the money he received at the end of the month. And since then I've never very clearly seen the relation between what I did and what I earned, even when I was a teacher. And I've never very clearly seen the relation between the books I wrote and the money my publisher gave me at the end of each year.

DE BEAUVOIR: Since we are talking about freedom, choices, and so on, was this choice of the teaching profession a free one or was it imposed by the family?

SARTRE: That's rather complex. I think my grandfather took it for granted that I would become a teacher. His eldest son had not done so—he was an engineer—but his younger son had, and he was a teacher still. So that my grandfather thought it natural that I, whom he thought so gifted, would be a teacher like him. But still, if I had had a very clear vocation for another career—as an engineer trained at the Polytechnique, for example, or a naval engineer—he would have let me follow it. But I drifted into teaching because I looked upon that class of intellectual workers as the spring and origin of the novelists and writers I wanted to belong to. I thought that the teachers' profession gave a considerable amount of knowledge about human life, and that a considerable amount of knowledge was required to write a book. I saw a connection between the teacher of literature, who forms a style for himself by being a teacher and by correcting his pupils' style, and this same teacher making use of the style he has thus formed in order to write a book that may ensure his immortality.

DE BEAUVOIR: So there was a concordance between your own wishes and the family circumstances that encouraged you to become a teacher?

SARTRE: Yes, if it can be called a concordance, agreement, since one can be a dung collector and a writer. There is only a secondary connection between the fact of being a teacher and that of writing. But still I did choose that particular concordance. That is, I saw the world through my grandfather's career and through my own desire to write. The two are linked, since it was my grandfather who said to me, "You will be a writer." He was lying, by the way, since he did not give a damn about the writing. He just wanted me to be a teacher. But I took him very seriously, and consequently my teacher-grandfather, superior to all other teachers of course, told me this as though he had been a writer himself.

DE BEAUVOIR: So teaching might be looked upon as a kind of free election, but one that agreed with what had been wished for you. In your childhood or youth do you see any times when this freedom was more solitary, isolated? Did you feel that you had entirely personal initiatives at any time during this whole first part of your life?

SARTRE: It's hard to say.

DE BEAUVOIR: In the fact of writing, for instance.

SARTRE: Writing was perhaps not wholly personal when I was eight and when, as I've said in *The Words*, I chiefly copied and recast pieces that had already been written. Yet there was something that came from me. I wanted to be the person who wrote those books. After the fifth form I left for La Rochelle with my mother and stepfather, and at La Rochelle there was nothing that warranted my choice of writing anymore. In Paris I had had schoolmates who had made the same choice as myself, but at La Rochelle there was not a single one who wanted to become a writer.

DE BEAUVOIR: But for all that you wrote there?

SARTRE: I wrote, having no public for my works other than the schoolmates to whom I read a few pages and who were totally unimpressed.

DE BEAUVOIR: And you weren't encouraged at home either?

SARTRE: Absolutely not.

DE BEAUVOIR: In a word, for you writing was a kind of apprenticeship to loneliness and freedom.

SARTRE: I went on writing when I was in the fourth form; much less, and perhaps not at all, in the third and second. I thought of the writer as an unhappy creature who was neither read nor acknowledged by his fellows. It was after his death that fame came to him. As I wrote, I was aware of my schoolmates' actual or potential hostility. In those days, then, I saw the writer as a poor devil, unfortunate and damned. I was going in for romanticism.

DE BEAUVOIR: When all is said and done, you look upon death with great serenity.

SARTRE: Even so, the approach of death does look like a series of deprivations. For instance, I was a heavy drinker, as you know, and one of the pleasures of my life, even when I was worried for objective reasons, was to end the evening by drinking a great deal. That's vanished. It's vanished because the doctors have forbidden me to drink. I doubt the doctors' knowledge, I may add; but I submit. So there are these deprivations, which are like things being taken away before the moment everything is taken from me, which will be death. And then there is this dispersal, which is the advent of old age. Instead of still having a perfectly clear idea of a synthesis of myself which should make one single man, it's all dispersed in a mass of activities, of trifling things. The synthesis is begun, but it will never be finished. I feel all this, therefore I am in a less comfortable state than I was ten years ago. But death, as a serious matter that comes at a given moment and which I expect, does not frighten me. It seems to me natural. Natural as opposed to my life as a whole, which has been cultural. It is after all the return to nature and the assertion that I was a part of nature. And then the fact remains that what I remember of my life, even with this new point of view and even with the erroneous notion about immortality that I entertained for many years, seems to me valid. It's a kind of a premortal point of view; not quite the dying point of view but a point of view of before death. I don't regret anything I've done. Even my greatest faults are bound to me and commit me. I've often come to an end of them by other reversals.

DE BEAUVOIR: It's another subject, but I should be interested to know what you look upon as your greatest faults.

SARTRE: Oh, for the moment nothing in particular, really. But I think there have been some.

DE BEAUVOIR: Mistakes, in any case. That's certain.

SARTRE: Mistakes, yes. In short, I think this is a life that is coming to pieces. So one never has a life that comes to an end as it began, in a single point that is the last. Instead of that it . . .

DE BEAUVOIR: It wears away.

SARTRE: It disperses, it wears away. So setting aside this period of wearing away—which I don't grieve over, since it's the common lot —I think I've had a period, from the age of thirty to sixty-five, in which I kept a hold on myself and in which I was not very different at the beginning from what I became. A period in which there was indeed a continuity during which I used my freedom properly to do what I intended; in which I was able to be of use and to help spread certain ideas; and in which I did what I wanted—that is, I wrote, which has been the essence of my life. I've succeeded in what I longed for from the age of seven or eight. To what extent have I succeeded? I've no idea; but I have written what I wanted to write, books that have had an influence and that have been read. So when I die I shall not die as many people do, saying, "Oh, if I had my life to live over again I should live it in another way; I have failed; I have made a mess of it." No. I accept myself entirely, and I feel that I am exactly what I wanted to be. And certainly, if I look back to the past, to my childhood or my youth, I see that I asked for less than I have accomplished. I had a different conception of fame. I imagined it for a small audience, a select few, and in fact I have reached almost everybody. So when I die I shall die content. Displeased at dying that particular day rather than ten years later, but content. And up until the present, death has never weighed upon my life and probably it never will. It is on those words that I should like to end this chapter.

DE BEAUVOIR: Yes, but there is still one question that I should like to ask you. Has the idea of the survival of the soul, of a spiritual principle in us, a survival such as the Christians think of, for example —has that ever crossed your mind?

SARTRE: I think it has, but rather as an almost natural fact. The difficulty I had, because of the very structure of the consciousness, in imagining a time when I should no longer exist. Every future that one imagines in one's consciousness refers back to consciousness. You can't imagine a moment in which there is no consciousness anymore. You can imagine a world in which the body no longer exists, but the fact of imagining implies consciousness, not only now, but also in the future. Consequently I think one of the difficulties in thinking about death is this very impossibility of getting rid of consciousness. For example, if I imagine my funeral, it is I who am imagining my funeral. I am therefore hidden at the corner of the street, watching it pass. In the same way, when I was young, when I was fifteen, I had a vague tendency to conceive this life that would always go on simply because when I imagined the future I imagined myself as being there to see it. But that never amounted to much. In fact, as an atheist, I've always thought there was nothing after death, except for the immortality that I saw as a quasi-survival.

DE BEAUVOIR: I'd like to know how your atheism began and how it evolved in your mind.

SARTRE: In *The Words* I've told how, even as early as eight or nine, I had only neighborly relations with God, not really those of subservience or of understanding. He was there, and now and then he appeared, as he did on the day when it seems I set the house on fire. He was an eye that rested on me from time to time.

DE BEAUVOIR: How do you mean, you set the house on fire?

SARTRE: I told in *The Words* how I used to get hold of boxes of matches and how I started the fire—only a modest blaze, however. In fact he used to watch me every now and then; I imagined that a gaze enfolded me. But all this was vague, without much connection with the catechism, with all the lessons about that intuition that was in itself mistaken. My parents had rented a villa a little way out of La Rochelle when I was about twelve, and in the morning I used to take the tram with the girls next door, three Brazilians called Machado who went to the girls' lycée. One day I was walking up and down outside their house for a few minutes waiting for them to get ready. I don't know where the thought came from or how it struck me, yet all at once I said to myself, "But God doesn't exist!" It's quite certain that before this I must have had new ideas about God and that I had begun solving the problem for myself. But still, as I remember very well, it was on that day and in the form of a momentary intuition, that I said to myself, "God doesn't exist." It's striking to reflect that I thought this at the age of eleven and that I never asked myself the question again until today, that is, for sixty years.

DE BEAUVOIR: Could you go back and recover the details of the mental workings that preceded this intuition?

SARTRE: Absolutely not. All the more so since I remember very well that when I was twelve I looked upon it as a manifest truth that had come to me without any foregoing thought. That was obviously untrue, but it was how I always saw it—a thought that came suddenly, an intuition that rose up and that determined my life. I think the Machado girls appeared at that moment, and the thought went back under the surface. No doubt I thought of it again the next day or the day after that, and I went on stating that God did not exist.

DE BEAUVOIR: And did this revelation have any consequences for you?

SARTRE: Not many at the time; nor were they really determinant. My behavior was linked to other principles, other wishes. Above all I wanted to have contacts with the boys at my school. And then there was also a girl I wanted to meet—she was at the girls' lycée. I was not at all attached to the Catholic religion; I didn't go to church before or after. So this had no exact relation with my life at that time. I don't remember that I was ever astonished or grieved that God did not exist. I thought it was just a story that I had been told, a story that people believed, but one that I had seen to be false. Of course, since mine was a decently, respectably believing family, I knew nothing about atheists.

DE BEAUVOIR: And didn't it worry you, being opposed to your family on such an important point, a family you respected and were fond of?

SARTRE: No, indeed. In *The Words* I tried to explain how I'd already built myself up a positive arsenal of little private thoughts which were in direct opposition to those of my family. I had but a moderate belief in what my grandfather told me were other people's thoughts and conceptions. I thought one had to discover one's own way of thinking. He told me that too, by the way, but he didn't mean it to the same degree of depth that I did.

DE BEAUVOIR: And when you grew older, when you were in Paris, did your atheism change? Was it ever shaken? Did it become stronger?

SARTRE: You might say it became stronger. Above all, I think it changed from an idealist to a materialist atheism, and that was chiefly during my conversations with Nizan. Idealist atheism is difficult to explain. But when I said, "God doesn't exist," it was as though I had got rid of an idea that was in the world and in its place I had set a spiritual void, a certain abortive idea, in the framework of my ideas as a whole. And the result was that this had little direct connection with the street, the trees, the benches people sat on. It was a great synthetic idea that vanished without directly affecting the world at all. Gradually, my conversations with Nizan and my own reflections led me to something else, to a different concept of the world, which was not something that was to vanish, putting me in touch with a Paradise where I should behold God, but which was the sole reality. The absence of God was to be read everywhere. Things were alone, and above all man was alone. Was alone like an absolute. He was a curious thing, a man. That came to me gradually. He was both a being lost in the world and consequently surrounded by it on all sides—imprisoned in the world, as it were—and at the same time he was a being who could synthesize this world and see it as his object, he being over against the world and outside. He was no longer in it; he was outside. It's this binding together of without and within that constitutes man. Do you see what I mean?

DE BEAUVOIR: Yes, perfectly.

SARTRE: And it took me some years to convince myself of that. Obviously, it is much easier to see him just as a mere within or as a mere without. The difficulty is that there are the two and that this contradicts itself—is its own profound and basic contradiction. There I would be, in Tours, for example, sitting at a café table. Not outside Tours but in Tours itself, never stirring, yet at the same time, by refusing to be an object defined solely by my being there, I could see the world as a synthesis, as the totality of the objects around me that I could see, and beyond them other objects, the horizons, as Heidegger puts it. In short, grasp the world as the sum of these horizons, a sum also made up of the objects.

DE BEAUVOIR: When you learned philosophy in philo, in hypo-khâgne, in khâgne, and so on and at the Ecole Normale up until the *agrégation,* did it have any connection with your atheism? Did it strengthen it, or at least provide it with arguments?

SARTRE: I decided to do philosophy in hypo-khâgne and in khâgne itself. And at that point I was absolutely certain of the nonexistence of God, and what I wanted was a philosophy that accounted for my object—"my" in the human sense, that is, your object too: man's object. That is to say his own particular being, in the world and outside it; and the world without God. What's more, since I hardly knew anything about the atheists' books, this seemed to me a new undertaking. In any case they've written little philosophy. All the great philosophers have been believers more or less. That means different things at different times. Spinoza's belief in God is not the same as Descartes' or Kant's. But it seemed to me that a great atheist, truly atheist philosophy was something philosophy lacked. And that it was in this direction that one should now endeavor to work.

DE BEAUVOIR: To put it briefly, you wanted to make a philosophy of man.

SARTRE: Yes, to make a philosophy of man in a material world.

DE BEAUVOIR: Did you have friends—to keep to your young days still —did you have friends who were not atheist? What were your relations with them? Did it bother you? Did it bother them?

SARTRE: Bother is not the right word. I was on very, very good terms with Laroutis, who was a delightful fellow and whom I was very fond of. But obviously it set us apart. We talked about the same things, and yet we were perfectly aware that we weren't talking in quite the same manner. Laroutis's way of having a drink was so like my way of having a drink that you could hardly tell the difference; yet it was not the same.

DE BEAUVOIR: Among these friends were there any who tried to persuade you—I don't say to convert you—but to persuade you of God's existence?

SARTRE: No, never. In any case, with those I used to see, I either didn't know whether they were atheists or Christians, or else if I did know it, they were extremely discreet, because they were at the Ecole Normale and they were intellectuals. They therefore considered that they were in touch with men who believed wrongly, who believed little, or who did not believe at all, and that it was up to each to manage for himself as best he might. They were merely to be there and do nothing, say nothing that might offend another's conscience. It meant that I was always left in peace.

DE BEAUVOIR: There was a time when you knew some Christians very intimately, and that was in the prison camp. Indeed, your best friend was a priest.

SARTRE: Yes, most of the people I mixed with there were priests. But at that time, in the prison camp, they represented the only intellectuals I knew. Not all, but in any case my friend the Jesuit, Feller, and the priest who later left holy orders and married.

DE BEAUVOIR: The Abbé Leroy?

SARTRE: The Abbé Leroy. They were intellectuals, people who thought about the same things as I did. Not always as I thought, but even so reflecting upon the same things was a bond. So I could much more easily talk to the Abbé Leroy or the Abbé Perrin or to Feller, the Jesuit, than to the peasant prisoners.

DE BEAUVOIR: Your atheism did not worry them?

SARTRE: It seems not. The Abbé Leroy told me quite spontaneously that he would not accept a place in Heaven if I were turned away. Though in fact he thought that I should not be turned away, but that I should learn to know God either in my lifetime or after my death. So he looked upon it as a frontier that would vanish. A barrier between us that would disappear.

DE BEAUVOIR: And when you wrote *Being and Nothingness* did you vindicate or try to vindicate your disbelief in God philosophically?

SARTRE: Yes, of course, it had to be vindicated. I tried to show that God would have had to be the "in-itself for itself," that is, an infinite in-itself inhabited by an infinite for-itself, and that this notion of "in-itself for itself" was in itself contradictory and could not constitute a proof of God's existence.

DE BEAUVOIR: It was, on the contrary, a proof of God's nonexistence.

SARTRE: It did provide a proof of God's nonexistence.

DE BEAUVOIR: Yes.

SARTRE: All this centered about the notion of God. In *Being and Nothingness* I set out reasons for my denial of God's existence that were not actually the real reasons. The real reasons were much more direct and childish—since I was only twelve—than theses on the impossibility of this reason or that for God's existence.

DE BEAUVOIR: Somewhere you said that atheism was a long-term task and that you had carried it through to the end, thought not without some labor. Just what did you mean by that?

SARTRE: Just that moving on from idealist atheism to materialist atheism was difficult. It implied long-drawn-out work. I've told you what I meant by idealist atheism. It's the absence of an idea, an idea that is refused, that is shut out; but in the absence of an *idea,* the idea of God. Whereas materialistic atheism is the world seen without God, and obviously it's a very long-term affair, passing from that absence of an idea to this new conception of the being—of the being that is left among things and is not set apart from them by a divine consciousness that contemplates them and causes them to exist.

DE BEAUVOIR: You mean that even if one does not believe in God there is a way of viewing the world . . .

SARTRE: Even if one does not believe in God, there are elements of the idea of God that remain in us and that cause us to see the world with some divine aspects.

DE BEAUVOIR: What, for example?

SARTRE: That varies according to the person.

DE BEAUVOIR: But for you?

SARTRE: I don't see myself as so much dust that has appeared in the world, but as a being that was expected, prefigured, called forth. In short, as a being that could, it seems, come only from a creator; and this idea of a creating hand that created me refers me back to God. Naturally, this is not a clear, exact idea that I set in motion every time I think of myself. It contradicts many of my other ideas; but it is there, floating vaguely. And when I think of myself I often think rather in this way, for want of being able to think otherwise. Because the consciousness in each man vindicates his way of being, and it is not there like a gradual formation or something built up by a series of chances, but on the contrary, like a thing, a reality that is continually present, that is not formed, that is not created, but that appears to be continually present as a complete whole. And consciousness, I may add, is consciousness of the world. So one is not quite sure whether one means consciousness or the world, and consequently one is back in reality once more.

DE BEAUVOIR: Apart from that feeling of not being here by chance, are there other fields in which there are traces of God? In the moral field, for example?

SARTRE: Yes. In the moral field I've retained one single thing to do with the existence of God, and that is Good and Evil as absolutes. The usual consequence of atheism is the suppression of Good and Evil. It's a certain relativism—for example, it's regarding morals as being variable according to the point on the earth's surface at which they are seen.

DE BEAUVOIR: Or as Dostoievski says, "If God does not exist, everything is allowed." You don't think that, do you?

SARTRE: In one way I clearly see what he means, and abstractly it's true; but in another I clearly see that killing a man is wrong. Is directly, absolutely wrong; is wrong for another man; is doubtless not wrong for an eagle or a lion, but is wrong for a man. It might be said that I look upon man's morals and moral activity as an absolute in the midst of the relative. There is the relative, which I may add is not the whole man, but which is man in the world and his problems within it. And then there is the absolute, which is the decision he takes with regard to other men in reference to these problems, which in its turn is therefore an absolute that arises in him insofar as the problems he sets himself are relative. So I look upon the absolute as a product of the relative, the opposite of the usual view. Furthermore, this is linked to those "within-without" notions I was talking about just now.

DE BEAUVOIR: Broadly speaking, how would you define what you call Good and what you call Evil?

SARTRE: Essentially, the Good is that which is useful to human freedom, that which allows it to give their full value to objects it has realized. Evil is that which is harmful to human freedom, that which holds men out as not being free and which, for example, creates the determinism of the sociologists of a certain period.

DE BEAUVOIR: So your morality is based on man and no longer has much relation to God.

SARTRE: None, at present. But it is certain that the notions of absolute Good and Evil arose from the catechism I was taught.

DE BEAUVOIR: Couldn't it be said that a morality without God is more demanding, since if you believe in God you can always be forgiven for your sins, at least in the Catholic Church, whereas if you don't believe in God a wrong done to man is absolutely irreparable?

SARTRE: Absolutely. I think that all evil is in itself irreparable, because not only has it taken place and is wrong, but it also has consequences of hatred, rebellion, and reciprocal evil, even if there is a better way out. In any case the evil is there, deep down.

DE BEAUVOIR: Wasn't there a kind of remaining whiff of the belief in God in the faith you had in literary creation, in your determination to sacrifice everything to the work of art when you were young?

SARTRE: Oh yes, I've said that—it's the last page of *The Words*. I said that the work of art seemed to me like Christian immortality, and at the same time it was the creating of something in the absolute that escaped man and that ought to be read by the eye of God. And it took its absolute, transhuman value from the fact that basically it was given to the creator. The first relation between the work of art and God was therefore given by my first conception of art. I created a work, and beyond any human audience, God looked at it. It's that which has vanished, although when one is writing one still gives a kind of transhuman value to what one puts down. The beautiful appears as what men approve of in that which is beyond the reach of mere human approval. Men's approval is a sign that the object has a transhuman value. Of course it's an illusion and it corresponds to nothing true, but one retains it when one is writing. Because if it is going to be successful, the work one is engaged upon goes beyond the present, living, existing public and is also directed at a future public. Furthermore, it carries with it the judgment of two or three generations, which is handed on, slightly modified but retained, by subsequent generations. So there is as it were a kind of view of the work that is fundamentally the view of men, somewhat multiplied, somewhat changed. When, for example, Voltaire reaches the consciousness of the twentieth century, he is a Voltaire already lit by a light that considers him as Voltaire and that we do not feel to be quite human —that we feel to be a light that comes from him and that at the same time might be as it were another consciousness shining on him. That is, something like God. It is among very cloudy, very ill-matched notions of this kind, very hard to understand, that the remaining elements of a divine idea revolve; elements that will, I think, steadily lose their strength as the world goes on.

DE BEAUVOIR: You said that it was hard, in a materialist fashion, to realize the world without God, to feel it in the objects, the things, the people. How was it difficult? And how did you manage it? Was there an evolution? If you don't mind, I will go back to the question of your passage from idealist atheism to materialist atheism. What did that call for?

SARTRE: In the first place it called for the idea that objects have no consciousness, an essential idea that people often overlook. When people speak about objects it is as though they thought they had a dim kind of consciousness. And when we live in the world, surrounded by people, we often look upon objects in that way. And it is that consciousness which must be made to disappear. One has to discover for oneself how things exist—a material, opaque existence with no connection with a consciousness that illuminates them apart from our consciousness, which in any case has no relation to any inner consciousness of theirs.

DE BEAUVOIR: Do you mean that we attribute consciousness to them because, in short, it is God's consciousness seeing them that we impute to the objects?

SARTRE: Absolutely. It's God seeing them, it's God giving them consciousness of himself. And what we do perceive on the contrary is these objects as we behold them. That is, the consciousness is in us, and for its part the object is totally devoid of consciousness. It exists on the in-itself plane. And that's a complicated matter that has to be carefully studied before saying that one is certain that an object has no consciousness. A great deal of effort is required before one reaches the summing up of a whole sector of the world's objects with no consciousness, for as I said a moment ago, the divine consciousness tends to revive in one shape or another and slip into them. And it's precisely that which must be avoided, because it is not right.

DE BEAUVOIR: You speak of the object's in-itself, but you won't say that an object possesses a kind of being that is absolutely definite, determined, and independent of human consciousness. It is an in-itself, it is not a for-itself. But surely this doesn't mean that, apart from your consciousness, it has a reality that obtrudes itself on the consciousness and that is the reality that God is said to have created?

SARTRE: That is what I mean. I think the objects I see here do indeed exist apart from me. It's not my consciousness that makes them exist. They don't exist for the sake of my consciousness and merely for that; they don't exist for the sake of the consciousness of mankind as a whole and merely for that. They exist without consciousness in the first place.

DE BEAUVOIR: They exist in relation to your consciousness and not in a kind of supreme objectivity arising from their being seen by God in a certain way.

SARTRE: They are not seen by God in a certain way because God doesn't exist. They are seen by consciousness, but the consciousnesses don't invent what they see, they perceive a real object that is outside.

DE BEAUVOIR: In short, according to you, they perceive them under various aspects that are all equally valid.

SARTRE: Yes.

DE BEAUVOIR: There's no kind of especially favored aspect that is the one that God perceives.

SARTRE: Absolutely. The object is very complicated, very complex; it offers various aspects to the people who look at it. And then there are consciousnesses other than human; there are those of animals and insects, for instance. So the objects yield themselves up in completely different ways according to the consciousnesses that apprehend them. But the object is outside these consciousnesses; it *is,* but without self-awareness; it is in itself. Although of course in-itself and for-itself are linked, not at all as is usually thought for God, but almost like two of Spinoza's attributes, the in-itself being that of which there is consciousness, the consciousness existing only as consciousness of the in-itself. No doubt it can be consciousness of the for-itself. But there is no consciousness of the for-itself except insofar as there is consciousness of the in-itself. Consequently, the in-itself for-itself perceived as the being of God is an impossibility, a mere idea of the reason, without reality. And then again there is the in-itself for-itself link of the consciousness and the thing, which is another form of the in-itself for-itself and which exists at every moment. At this particular moment I am conscious of a mass of things that are here before me, that really exist, and that I perceive in their very existence itself. I perceive the in-itself of a table or a chair or a rock.

DE BEAUVOIR: For you, atheism is one of the bases of your life, then, one of your obvious facts. So what do you think of people who say they are believers? There are some you've met whom you've valued, others no doubt whom you did not. And I think there are some who say they believe but in fact do not. But still what do you think the fact of believing represents, when one has a certain amount of culture of course? When a man like Merleau-Ponty—who's stopped, by the way—said he believed in God, or when your friends the priests, the Jesuits, said that they believed in God? On the whole what do you think the fact of stating that he believes in God represents in the way a man leads his life?

SARTRE: It seems to me a survival. I think there was a time when it was normal to believe in God—in the seventeenth century, for instance. At present, in view of the way people live, the manner in which they become aware of their consciousness and in which they see how God slips away, there is no intuition of the divine. I think that nowadays the notion of God is already dated, and I've always felt that there was something old-fashioned, outworn, in the people who as believers have talked to me about God.

DE BEAUVOIR: But why do you think they cling to this old-fashioned, out-of-date notion?

SARTRE: Why, they do so just as people often cling to other old-fashioned, out-of-date notions and other old-fashioned, out-of-date systems, because they have preserved elements from the great period of the divine synthesis of the seventeenth century, for example, that cannot find a place in another synthesis, a modern synthesis. They can't live without that already-dead synthesis coming from the earlier centuries, and when you see them they are dated, aged, and outside our epoch Although they may be excellent mathematicians or physicists. They have a vision of the world that belongs to a past age.

DE BEAUVOIR: But where do you think they get this vision of the world?

SARTRE: From their options, from themselves, from their freedom; and then from various influences. They have been influenced by people who themselves retained the seventeenth-century vision, priests, for example, or very Christian mothers, mothers being more attached to religion than men, at least in the earlier period. So these men seem to me to represent something that would not tempt a young man who still has to form himself, something that already smells of the past, of an aged past. The young men who believe in God must have links with tradition . . . different from ours.

DE BEAUVOIR: You spoke of the choice of a certain vision of the world. Do you think that their choice brings them advantages and that it's for that reason they make it?

SARTRE: It certainly brings them advantages. It's much pleasanter to believe that the world is thoroughly closed, with a synthesis made not by us but elsewhere by an all-powerful Being, and that this world is made for each of us. That all suffering is a trial allowed or desired by the Supreme Being and that one must take things as they are—that is to say undeserved sufferings that are wanted by nobody and that bring nothing to the person who undergoes them. Favors too, which are not any particular person's favors, but which in the same way represent something that is given without anyone having done the giving. In order to reestablish the old notion of a God aware of everything, seeing the relations between everything and establishing, deliberately establishing these relations as well as their consequences, one has to turn one's back on science, on the social as well as the natural sciences, and go back to a world totally opposed to the one that we have established since then. That is, one has to preserve a notion which the sciences of man and nature, without saying so and without directly intending to do so, have largely helped to dispel.

DE BEAUVOIR: On the other hand, do you see—I won't say advantages, but a certain moral and psychological enrichment for man—in being an atheist?

SARTRE: Yes, but it will take a long time. Because one has to disentangle oneself from every vestige of the principle of Good and Evil which is God, and one has to try to rethink and rebuild a world set free from all divine notions putting themselves forward as an immensity of in-itself. It's hard. Even those who think they have succeeded in becoming conscious, deliberate atheists are certainly still imbued with divine notions, elements of the divine idea, and therefore they rather miss what they are aiming at. They do introduce more and more atheism into their thinking, but it cannot be said that the world is atheist, that the human world is atheist. There are still too many people who believe.

DE BEAUVOIR: And for a given individual—let's think simply of you, for example, what is the . . . as one might say the benefit, apart from that of having thought what was true, of course—what is the benefit that the fact of not believing in God has given you?

SARTRE: It has strengthened my freedom and made it sounder. At the present time this freedom is not there so that I may give God what he asks me for; it is there for the discovery of myself and to give me what I ask of myself. That's essential. And then my relations with others are direct. They no longer are mediated by the Omnipotent. I don't need God in order to love my neighbor. It's a direct relation between men and man; I don't have to deal with the infinite at all. And then my acts have made up a life, my life, which is going to end, which is almost over, and which I judge without too many errors. This life owes nothing to God; it was what I wanted it to be and to some extent what I made it without meaning to. And when now I reflect on it, it satisfies me; and I do not need to refer to God for that. I only have to refer to what is human, that is, other men and myself. And I think that insofar as we more or less all work at building up a human race that will have its principles, its aims, and its unity without God, we are all atheists, not perhaps at every moment, but in reality at all times of our lives—at least atheists of an atheism that is expanding and becoming more and more of a reality.

DE BEAUVOIR: You think that the way for man to cure himself—to do away with his alienation—is first of all not to believe in God.

SARTRE: Absolutely.

DE BEAUVOIR: It means taking man alone as the measure and the future of mankind.

SARTRE: God is a prefabricated image of man, man multiplied by infinity; and men stand before this image, obliged to labor to satisfy it. So it is always a question of a relation with oneself, a relation that is absurd, but that is also enormous and demanding. It is that relation that must be suppressed, because it is not the true relation with oneself. The true relation with oneself is with that which we really are, and not with that self we have formed roughly in our own shape.

DE BEAUVOIR: Have you anything else to say?

SARTRE: Yes and no. Chiefly that this fact of living very close to people who do not themselves believe in God completely does away, between them and oneself, with that infinite intermediary who is God. You and I, for example, have lived without paying attention to the problem. I don't think many of our conversations have been concerned with it.

DE BEAUVOIR: No, none.

SARTRE: And yet we've lived; we feel that we've taken an interest in our world and that we've tried to see and understand it.

Index

ABOUT THE AUTHOR

Born in Paris in 1908, Simone de Beauvoir is France's most celebrated living writer. A lifelong companion of Jean-Paul Sartre and a pioneering feminist, she has written books famous throughout the world. Her works of fiction include *The Mandarins, All Men Are Mortal, The Blood of Others, When Things of the Spirit Come First* and *A Woman Destroyed.* Her nonfiction includes *The Second Sex, A Very Easy Death, Memoirs of a Dutiful Daughter, Force of Circumstance, The Prime of Life,* and *The Coming of Age.*

Simone de Beauvoir lives in Paris.

PANTHEON MODERN WRITERS SERIES

ADIEUX: *A Farewell to Sartre*
by Simone de Beauvoir, translated by Patrick O'Brian

Simone de Beauvoir's moving farewell to Jean-Paul Sartre, her lifelong companion, in two parts: an account of his last ten years and an interview with him about his life and work.
"An intimate, personal, and honest portrait of a relationship unlike any other in literary history." —Deirdre Bair

0-394-72898-X $8.95

A VERY EASY DEATH
by Simone de Beauvoir, translated by Patrick O'Brian

The profoundly moving, day-by-day account of the death of the author's mother, at once intimate and universal.
"A beautiful book, sincere and sensitive." —Pierre-Henri Simon

0-394-72899-8 $4.95

WHEN THINGS OF THE SPIRIT COME FIRST: *Five Early Tales*
by Simone de Beauvoir, translated by Patrick O'Brian

The first paperback edition of the marvelous early fiction of Simone de Beauvoir.
"An event for celebration." —*The New York Times Book Review*

0-394-72235-3 $5.95

THE BLOOD OF OTHERS
by Simone de Beauvoir, translated by Roger Senhouse and Yvonne Moyse

A brilliant existentialist novel about the French resistance.
"A novel with a remarkably sustained note of suspense and mounting excitement due to the sheer vitality and force of de Beauvoir's ideas." —*Saturday Review*

0-394-72411-9 $6.95

NAPLES '44
by Norman Lewis

A young British intelligence officer's powerful journal of his year in Allied-occupied Naples.
"An immensely gripping experience . . . a marvelous book . . . his compassion and humor are just plain terrific." —S. J. Perelman

0-394-72300-7 $7.95

PANTHEON MODERN WRITERS SERIES

BLOW-UP AND OTHER STORIES
by Julio Cortázar, translated by Paul Blackburn

A celebrated masterpiece: fifteen eerie and brilliant short stories by the great Latin American writer.
"A splendid collection." —*The New Yorker*
"Cortázar at his best." —Michael Wood
"Maddeningly unforgettable." —*Saturday Review*

0-394-72881-5 $6.95

THE WINNERS
by Julio Cortázar, translated by Elaine Kerrigan

Julio Cortázar's superb first novel about life—and death—on a South American luxury cruise.
"This formidable novel . . . introduces a dazzling writer. . . . [*The Winners*] is irresistibly readable." —*The New York Times Book Review*

0-394-72301-5 $8.95

FRIDAY
by Michel Tournier, translated by Norman Denny

A sly, enchanting retelling of the story of Robinson Crusoe, in which Friday teaches Crusoe that there are better things in life than civilization.
"A literary pleasure not to miss."—Janet Flanner
"A fascinating, unusual novel . . . a remarkably heady French wine in the old English bottle." —*The New York Times Book Review*

0-394-72880-7 $7.95

THE OGRE
by Michel Tournier, translated by Barbara Bray

The story of a gentle giant's extraordinary experiences in World War II—a gripping tale of innocence, perversion, and obsession.
"The most important novel to come out of France since Proust."—Janet Flanner
"Quite simply, a great novel." —*The New Yorker*

0-394-72407-0 $8.95

THE WALL JUMPER
by Peter Schneider, translated by Leigh Hafrey

A wry, witty novel of life in modern Berlin.
"Marvelous . . . creates, in very few words, the unreal reality of Berlin." —Salman Rushdie, *The New York Times Book Review*
"A document of our time, in which fiction has the force of an eyewitness account." —*The* [London] *Times Literary Supplement*

0-394-72882-3 $6.95